Archaeological Investigations on Guadeloupe, French West Indies

C000017269

Comprising 20 scientific contributions to the archaeology of Guadeloupe, French West Indies, this volume places the latter Caribbean island in the spotlight by presenting the results of four contemporaneous archaeological sites.

By means of these four sites, this book explores a variety of issues contemplating the transition from the Early to the Late Ceramic Age in the Lesser Antilles. Studies of pre-Columbian material culture (ceramics, lithics, faunal, shell, and human bone remains) are combined with additional microanalyses (starch and phytolith analyses, micromorphology and thin sections) to sort out the processes that triggered the cultural transition just before the end of the first millennium CE.

The multidisciplinary approach to address these Saladoid sites shows the current state of affairs on project-led archaeology in the French West Indies and should be of great value to both researchers and students of Caribbean archaeology, material cultures, zooarchaeology, environmental studies, historical ecology, and other related fields.

Martijn M. van den Bel is an archaeologist and project leader for Inrap in the Lesser Antilles and French Guiana. In addition to his work in project-led archaeology, he participates in various multidisciplinary projects as an archaeologist addressing the impact of ancient human presence in the tropical forest of French Guiana. He also conducts archival research contemplating the Colonial Encounter in the Lesser Antilles and the Coastal Guianas during the 17th century.

Archaeological Investigations on Guadeloupe, French West Indies

The Troumassoid Turning Point

Edited by Martijn M. van den Bel

Routledge
Taylor & Francis Group

LONDON AND NEW YORK

First published 2022
by Routledge
2 Park Square, Milton Park, Abingdon, Oxon OX14 4RN

and by Routledge
605 Third Avenue, New York, NY 10158

Routledge is an imprint of the Taylor & Francis Group, an informa business

British Library Cataloguing-in-Publication Data
A catalogue record for this book is available from the British Library

Library of Congress Cataloging-in-Publication Data
A catalog record for this book has been requested

ISBN: 978-1-032-02054-9 (hbk)
ISBN: 978-1-032-02058-7 (pbk)
ISBN: 978-1-003-18165-1 (ebk)

DOI: 10.4324/9781003181651

Typeset in Times New Roman
by Apex CoVantage, LLC

Contents

Figures

Plates

Tables

Contributors

Arie Boomert (Ph.D. Leiden University) was attached as an archaeologist to the Surinaams Museum (Paramaribo, Suriname), the University of the West Indies (St. Augustine, Trinidad), the University of Amsterdam, and Leiden University. He is the author of more than 80 publications, including articles in scholarly journals, papers in congress proceedings, contributions to encyclopedias and edited works, book reviews, and several monographs. His research interests encompass the archaeology, anthropology, and ethnohistory of the West Indies, Guianas, Venezuela, and Amazonia. In 2005 the International Association for Caribbean Archaeology awarded him a plaque "in recognition of years of dedicated service and commitment to the promotion and development of the Archaeology of Trinidad and Tobago." In 2011 he retired as an assistant professor and senior researcher from the Faculty of Archaeology, Leiden University. At present he is a guest researcher at the Royal Netherlands Institute of Southeast Asian and Caribbean Studies of the Royal Netherlands Academy of Arts and Sciences, Leiden, and a curatorial affiliate in the Division of Anthropology, Peabody Museum of Natural History, Yale University, New Haven, Connecticut, USA.

Jeanne Brancier is a geoarchaeologist specializing in dark earths. She obtained her Ph.D. from Paris I–Panthéon Sorbonne University in 2016. Her research has focused on the micromorphology of anthropogenic soils in French Guiana. She continued her research as a post-doctorate fellow in the interdisciplinary project LongTime (Labex CEBA, CNRS).

Cécilia Cammas is a geomorphologist and geoarchaeologist specializing in dark earths. She obtained her Ph.D. from Paris-Saclay University in 2015. Her research has focused on the micromorphology of European anthropogenic soils. She is a member of ParisAgroTech and a researcher at Inrap.

Fabrice Casagrande is a project leader for Inrap in the Lesser Antilles and French Guiana. Since 2005 he has specialized in imported European earthenware and sugar production in the Lesser Antilles.

Ruth Dickau is an archaeologist and archaeobotanist specializing in human-environmental interactions and ancient foodways. She obtained her Ph.D. from Temple University, Philadelphia, Pennsylvania, USA, in 2005. Her research has focused mainly on indigenous subsistence and the origins of food production in the Neotropics, and the resulting paleoenvironmental impacts. She currently works in CRM in Canada and conducts archaeobotanical investigations into plant use and diet of precontact indigenous and post-contact Euro-Canadian communities.

Gilles Fronteau is a full professor at Reims University and a director of the GEGENAA research unit, and a specialist in petrography applied to rock materials and ceramics. His main research focuses on the various uses of georesources as geomaterials. First specializing in limestone weathering studies (Ph.D. in 2000), he is now involved in various research programs on characterization of ceramics and macrolithic tools (notably milling stones).

Sandrine Grouard, Ph.D., HDR, is a researcher at the Musée National d'Histoire naturelle, a zooarchaeologist and archaeologist, and a specialist in the fossil vertebrates of the Caribbean and Latin America. She collaborates in different international programs of research on Antigua and Barbuda, Puerto Rico, Trinidad, Nicaragua, Brazil, Colombia, and the French Lesser Antilles. She has directed several Collective Research Programs (PCR), excavations, and Ph.D. programs in the French Lesser Antilles. Her current research examines the archaeoethnozoology of the pre-Columbian Caribbean islands (hunting, fishing, taming practices). She also focuses on the insular historic biogeography of the Lesser Antilles and its human impacts: late Pleistocene and Holocene species replacements, prehistoric and historic introductions, extinctions, and translocations.

Christophe Jorda is a geoarchaeologist specialized in littoral geomorphology and archaeopedology. His particular interests include the processes of anthropization during the Holocene and the impact of societies on their environment. He works for Inrap and is a member of the CNRS research laboratory UMR 5140 Archaeology of Mediterranean Societies. He has worked in several regions around the world, such as Algeria, Armenia, Corsica, French Guiana, and French Lesser Antilles, always considering the relations between societies and the environment.

Karlis Karklins is the former head of the Material Culture Research Section, Federal Archaeology Office, Parks Canada, Ottawa. He is also the long-standing editor of the *Beads: Journal of Society of Bead Researchers*. His principal interests include European trade beads of the post-medieval period, their production technology, compositional analysis, and use by the various cultural groups that obtained them.

Sebastiaan Knippenberg holds a Ph.D. in Caribbean Archaeology, obtained at Leiden University in 2006. He currently works at Archol BV, the contract archaeological firm affiliated with Leiden University. His main research interests relate to stone material sourcing, raw material procurement, lithic tool production and distribution, as well as the study of the underlying exchange systems and social networks within the Caribbean archipelago. His other research focus is on Dutch prehistory, particularly on Neolithic and Bronze Age settlement systems, as well as on lithic procurement, technology, and use. He has supervised numerous excavation projects in the Caribbean as well as the Netherlands.

Jaime Pagán-Jiménez holds a Ph.D. in Anthropology (National Autonomous University of Mexico, 2005) with special emphasis on archaeology and paleoethnobotany. He has more than 25 years of experience in Caribbean archaeology and has undertaken fieldwork or analyzed microbotanical materials from numerous sites on many of the islands through research collaborations with Leiden University, University College London (UK), University of Puerto Rico, University of Havana (Cuba), and Inrap and CNRS (both from France). As a research fellow at the National Institute of Cultural Heritage of Ecuador (2012–2015), he coordinated an extensive paleoethnobotanical research program spanning the whole country. More than 20 archaeological sites from the coast, the Andean Range, and Amazonia were studied, though he focused his paleoethnobotanical research in some late Pleistocene and early to mid-Holocene sites in the highlands, and in several sites ascribed to Valdivia, Chorrera, and Jambelí cultures from Isla Puná, in the Pacific Ocean. Until recently, Pagán-Jiménez was a senior researcher in paleoethnobotany and Caribbean archaeology at the Faculty of Archaeology, Leiden University. Currently, he is the research director, senior paleoethnobotanist, and senior archaeologist at Cultural Heritage & Plantscape Research based at Leiden, the Netherlands.

Thomas Romon is an archaeologist and project leader for Inrap in the Lesser Antilles. He is a member of the research unit UMR 5199 Préhistoire à l'Actuel, Culture, Environnement and Anthropologie (PACEA) of the University of Bordeaux, conducting research on pre-Columbian funerary rites in the Lesser Antilles.

Nathalie Serrand earned her Ph.D. at Paris I-Sorbonne University in 2002. She is an archaeologist and projectleader and in charge of research for Inrap in the French Antilles, and is a member of the research laboratory UMR 7209 Archaeozoology and Archaeobotany at the Museum of Natural History in Paris. As an archaeologist, she specialized in the malacological remains, society, and environmental changes of pre-Columbian sites in the Lesser Antilles.

Noémie Tomadini holds a Ph.D. thesis in Zooarchaeology at the National Museum of Natural History (Paris, France) under the supervision of Dr. Christine Lefèvre and Dr. Sandrine Grouard. Her research deals with daily life in the French West Indies during the colonial period from a zooarchaeological point of view (diet, resources management, social practices, cultural and symbolic). Since earning her master's degree in 2009, she had the opportunity to work regularly in the French West Indies in collaboration with various archaeological institutions doing fieldwork and analysis.

Martijn M. van den Bel is an archaeologist and project leader for Inrap in the Lesser Antilles and French Guiana. In 2015 he earned his Ph.D. at Leiden University, the Netherlands, focusing on the Ceramic Age of French Guiana. In addition to his work in project-led archaeology, he participates in various multidisciplinary projects as an archaeologist addressing the impact of ancient human presence in the tropical forest of French Guiana. He also conducts archival research contemplating the Colonial Encounter in the Lesser Antilles and the Coastal Guianas during the 17th century.

Jennifer Watling is an archaeologist who specializes in microbotanical analyses (phytoliths and starch grains) applied to Amazonian archaeology and landscapes. Her particular interests include plant domestication, the origins and spread of agriculture, paleoecology, human impacts on tropical ecosystems, and people-climate interactions. She has worked in several regions of Amazonia, most notably with the raised fields of French Guiana, the geoglyphs of Brazil and Bolivia, and Mid-Holocene *terra preta* sites also in Brazil, while also collaborating with projects based in Peru and Mexico.

Foreword

The archaeology of the Guadeloupe is barely known among Anglo-Saxon scholars working in the Caribbean despite the fact that much work has been done since the late 1990s. Researchers got acquainted with the Anse à la Gourde site and the Pointe des Chateaux peninsula and surrounding islets because of various English publications by André Delpuech, Corinne Hofman, and Menno Hoogland, as well as the doctoral dissertations written by Sandrine Grouard (2001) and Maaike de Waal (2006). However, much more research has been done since the beginning of the second millennium, but all this research, primarily executed by Inrap, is in French and thus virtually unknown to those with no French language skills. Although a handful of scholars might attempt to read the reports and minor publications of the regional journal called *Bilan scientifique* of Guadeloupe, the island remains a blank spot in many Anglo-Saxon publications. For example, in the *Handbook of Latin American Studies*, Guadeloupe was cited only for the already mentioned *Bilan scientifique* as "Annual review of archeological investigations on Guadeloupe and associated islands" (Keegan 2006:34); nor does *The Oxford Handbook of Caribbean Archaeology* contain a chapter on Guadeloupe with recent archaeological results (Keegan et al. 2013) or other compilations (Reid 2018). Little has changed despite good efforts by Dominique Bonnissent (2013) and Benoît Bérard (2013a); nonetheless, we hope this book represents another step to bridge this gap in Caribbean scholarship.

Archaeological heritage is important and this notion has led the French government to create the Inrap (Institut national de recherches archéologiques préventives) out of a previous national archaeological association, Afan, in 2002, and this was amended in 2003. According to law, the "disturber" is obliged to investigate the (potential) presence of archaeological remains prior to the planned disturbance, and to subsequently take measures to safeguard this heritage, either in situ or ex situ. Archaeological heritage is primarily the responsibility of the Ministry of Culture and in particular the SRA (Service regional de l'archéologie), or the local authorities. Hence, there is no nationwide policy on how to deal with the legislative obligations. For example, the context of significance assessment and subsequent selection of which sites should be surveyed or excavated is decided and regulated by sole expertise of the SRA members. They are guided by a common national archaeological agenda, established every four years by the CNRA, but the CNRA, in collaboration with the chosen members of the CTRA who evaluate the archaeological reports, eventually define the scientific reference framework for decision making and, for this matter, also represent a starting point for research design.[1]

Although an evaluation of the effectiveness of the previously described "heritage management cycle" under the 2003 amendment is certainly needed, it is strongly felt among archaeologists that development-led research and reports lag behind with respect to the interpretation and synthesis of excavation results, relative to the research themes of the national agenda or even the regional scientific framework. This raises the next question: What can we learn from all these investigations that have found their way into reports? For this purpose, the national agenda as well as Inrap provides regional themes to which one can subscribe and ask for so-called study days. For example, for this book we were accorded 20 days. This recognition is important because the results of development-led research most often dissolve in grey literature resting in archives. On the one hand, there is simply no time available for the excavation team to reflect and sit down together to write a synthesis. On the other hand, results often "disappear" in overarching themes or complementary (master) studies exploited by other researchers, mostly from the Metropole, of which the original excavating team is most often unaware.

Thus, this book presents the results of four compliance excavations conducted on four different sites, which have various elements in common. First, they are all habitation sites featuring many postholes, numerous pits, and burials. The presence of the burial site is interesting because (human) bone, but also shell and vertebrate remains, are most often absent in volcanic soils, another element these sites share. Thirdly, all sites have been damaged by recent agricultural works, notably plowing and leveling, meaning that the ancient surface and possibly middens have been eliminated. (The sites of La Pointe de Grande-Anse at Trois-Rivières and the STEP Goyave at Sainte-Claire were also occupied during colonial times by the pottery of Fidelin and the plantation site of La Grange, respectively. These occupations, however, are not presented in this book, which is dedicated to the pre-Columbian occupation.) Fourthly, all sites yielded predominantly ceramics attributed to the Troumassoid ceramic series of the Lesser Antilles, which has been confirmed by the results of the radiocarbon dating. Finally, with the exception of one site, which is situated on Grande-Terre (Belle-Plaine), all sites are located along the coastline of the windward side of Basse-Terre, commonly called Capesterre in French.[2]

With the results of these four excavations, we tried to open up the discussion on the transition from Terminal or Late Saladoid to Troumassoid in the Lesser Antilles as proposed in our subtitle: The Troumassoid Turning Point. When putting our data together and comparing it to current literature, we felt that our data did not match the generally held idea that the Troumassoid culture evolved rather slowly out of the Saladoid one. Although this may be evident for the southern Lesser Antilles where Troumassoid was defined, the northern part, as we shall demonstrate in this book, reveals important or perhaps radical innovations around 1000 CE, when Troumassoid culture had taken over Guadeloupe. These changes took place within only 100 years or the tenth century CE. We observed important changes in modes of house construction, mortuary practices, and pottery production, which may have arrived from the southern Lesser Antilles, or even further from the *Terra firma*. Although the origins are still a mystery, the archaeological record cannot ignore these differences with the previous Saladoid period. What happened remains rather mysterious, but their end is definite around 1000 CE. The famous pan-Caribbean drought may have finished off a waning culture that was simply surpassed by another. But these others were different, as witnessed by their way of house construction and burying their dead, possibly venerating their ancestors through cemeteries and petroglyph sites representing another turning point in this part of the Caribbean, as did the Saladoid arrival about 1,000 years before and the Barrancoid innovation a few hundred years later. We believe these changes were inspired by exterior influences and perhaps immigration that is not always flagrantly visible in the material record and /or is difficult to decipher. Perhaps in the future, when microscopical research becomes even more important than it is already, and without doubt, surpasses the traditional large-scale dirt excavations, we will have more concise data to understand the mechanisms of cultural continuity, migration, and change.

But first we must present the data. We start with a general description of each site, considering geographical, geological, and environmental aspects. This contextual introduction is followed by the results of archaeological research conducted at each site presented by the different contributors. All these results are then discussed and synthesized on a regional level in order to present our point of view on the Troumassoid period and the current state of archaeological research on Guadeloupe and the surrounding islands.

The book has greatly profited from comments on previous drafts by Arie Boomert (Leiden University). The authors want to thank all archaeologists in the field and in the lab for their work and their willingness to cooperate, as well as Inrap for granting us time to do so. Any mistakes and omissions remain our responsibility. We hope you enjoy this book.

Bonne lecture.
Martijn M. van den Bel

Preface

Inrap (Institut national de recherches archéologiques preventives, the French National Institute of Preventive Archaeology) was created in 2001 in application of the law on preventive archaeology. The institute ensures the detection and study of archaeological remains that are threatened by construction projects in France and its overseas territories. It reports the results of its research to the scientific community and participates in teaching, cultural diffusion, and public outreach.

Largely self-funded, Inrap is a research establishment in the public sector under the auspices of the Ministries of Culture and Communication, National Education, Higher Education and Research. In addition to its state representatives, its board of directors is composed of representatives of research organizations and local governments, as well as developers and qualified persons in the field of archaeology.

Its research activity is conducted under the aegis of a scientific committee composed of the associated ministries and members of the archaeological community: CNRS, universities, and the archaeology services of local governments.

During the different phases of archaeological research, Inrap shares the results of its work with the public. It develops diverse resources that are widely diffused via site visits, colloquia and exhibitions, publications, audiovisual documentaries, radio programs, and digital tools. Each year since 2009, under the aegis of the Ministry of Culture and Communication, Inrap organizes the French National Archaeology Days.

In the context of the its diagnostic operations and excavations, Inrap collaborates each year with more than 700 private and public partners: property developers, motorway enterprises, quarry enterprises, regional councils, departmental councils, town associations (*communautés de communes*), cities, public enterprises, public housing offices, and so forth.

With approximately 2,000 collaborators and researchers and more than 40 research centers, Inrap is present throughout metropolitan France, French Guiana, Guadeloupe, and Martinique. It is the main preventive archaeology operator in the field, in both rural and urban zones. Its national organization and the number and diversity of the competencies of its personnel make Inrap a research institute with no equivalent in Europe.

The French West Indies (Guadeloupe, Martinique, and French Guiana) are part of France and European law is also applicable in these Overseas Departments. Inrap has one office in Guadeloupe and one in French Guiana, and about 25 agents are stationed in the West Indies to conduct surveys and project-led or commercial archaeological excavations.

This type of archaeology produces many reports, which certainly merit a wider distribution than, for example, the sole archipelago of Guadeloupe, when considering that the Lesser Antilles forms an international string of different types of archaeology and research. Despite the presence of Inrap agents at the International Congress of Caribbean Archaeology, foreign students and researchers are not very familiar with the results of excavations in the French West Indies. The language barrier may partially explain this bias and therefore this book is a first attempt made by Inrap to bridge this gap.

Indeed, Inrap is working hard to emphasize the role of archaeology and to build public awareness of archaeology on a national and international level. It is the wish of our institute to share our experience, ideas, and archaeological data beyond the French West Indies and to connect with the neighboring islands in the Lesser Antilles.

As president of Inrap, I sincerely hope that this book produced by the Inrap agents of Guadeloupe will be an important contribution to the knowedge of archaeology of Guadeloupe and the Caribbean in general.

President of Inrap, Dominique Garcia

Acknowledgments

First of all, we would like to show our gratitude to the archaeologists who worked in the field for collaborating and sharing their expertise, experience, and moral support during all these years.

For *La Pointe de Grande Anse*, excavated between March and May 2008, we would like to thank Pierre Texier, Monique Ruig, Jérôme Briand, Rosemond Martias, and Jean-Jacques Faillot. The *CHU Belle-Plaine* site was excavated between October and December 2013 by Pierre-Yves Devillers, Elza Jovenet, Solène "Sue Ellen" le Padelec, Nicolas Biwer, Philippe Gilette, and André Novée-Josserand, as well as Gaby and Gendaub from the Jahsi enterprise. Special thanks goes to Jago Birk for his test for steroids. The team of *STEP Goyave*, excavated between October and November 2014, consisted of Mehdi Belarbi, Nicolas Biwer, Hélène Civalleri, Gaëlle Lavoix, Coraline Martin, Fréderic Messager, and Julien Pellissier, with special thanks to Jacques Beauchêne, Ludovic Ibba, Gérard Lafleur, and Alexandre Coulaud concerning the study of the water mill. The *Parking de Roseau* site was excavated between February and April 2015 by Mehdi Belarbi, Laurent Bernard, Joël Cornec, Fabrice Chevreuse, Hélène Civalleri, Christophe Grancha, and Solène "Sue Ellen" le Padelec. Special thanks goes to Tanguy Leblanc for the phosphor analysis. We also have to thank Christine Fouilloud for editing the final reports.

During the period between 2008 and 2015, the excavations were prepared by many Inrap agents in Bordeaux, Cayenne, and Guadeloupe, notably the agents in *Outre-mer*, especially Annette d'Alexis, Pierre Longchambon, and Rosemond Martias, as well as the various regional directors: Sylvie Jérémie, Thierry Cornec, and Aurélie Schneider. On Guadeloupe, the excavations were visited and controlled by agents of the French government, to wit Anne-Marie Fourteau, Christian Stouvenot, Dominique Bonnissent, Tristan Yvon, and Gwenola Robert. We wish to thank them for their collaboration and professional input. Sandrine Grouard and Noémi Tomadini would like to thank Gwenola Robert and Dominique Bonnissent in particular for their eagerness and goodwill to provide authorizations for the study of the vertebrate remains.

Finally, we would to thank Inrap, Aimara Foundation (French Guiana), and Archol BV (The Netherlands) for the financial support to publish this work.

Notes

1 The archaeology of the so-called Overseas Departments is described in Axe 15 of the National Chart of Archaeological Research containing subjects such as anthropization of the environment, chrono-cultural phases, site functionality, necropoles, and so on. It is noteworthy that members of the SRA also define the national agenda. Inrap also holds a proper scientific agenda that is roughly similar to

the national one. In short, the CNRA is the national committee on archaeological research that defines future research and the CTRA is the committee that verifies the execution of it.

2 *"Nous divisons encore la Guadelouppe seule en deux parties: Cabseterre, des sauvages Balaorgon qui est du costé du vent quasi caput terrae, et Basseterre, Kerabon, qui est au dessoubs du vent"* (Breton 1978:30).

1   General presentation

Martijn M. van den Bel

Guadeloupe (*Gwadloup* in Creole) is an insular region of France that is part of the Leeward Islands of the Lesser Antilles (Figures 1.1 and 1.2). This tropical archipelago consists of a series of islands: Basse-Terre, Grande-Terre, Marie-Galante, La Désirade, Les Saintes, and the Îles de la Petite Terre. The largest islands of Guadeloupe are Basse-Terre to the west and Grande-Terre to the east, which are separated by a narrow saltwater stream (Figure 1.3). Administratively, it is an Overseas Region (*Région d'outre-mer*) and represents one *département* covering approximately 1600 km² and counting about 400,000 inhabitants. Guadeloupe is an integral portion of France and, consequently, part of the European Union and the Eurozone.

Columbus visited Guadeloupe during his second voyage to the Americas, but the Spanish did not pay much attention to the Lesser Antilles. In 1635 the French took the island from the so-called Kalinago (Island Carib), the Amerindians who populated Guadeloupe and surrounding islands during the 17th century. In the second half of that century, peace was made

Figure 1.1 Map of the Antilles.
Source: www.naturalearthdata.com

DOI: 10.4324/9781003181651-1

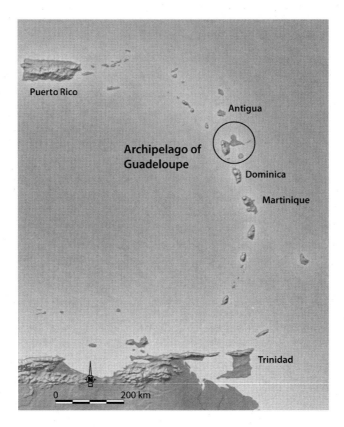

Figure 1.2 Map of the Lesser Antilles.
Source: www.naturalearthdata.com.

with the Amerindians and the French started to grow sugarcane on the island. As a result, Guadeloupe became one of the most important sugar islands of the Lesser Antilles. It was occupied by the English during the Seven Years' War, which ended with the retrocession of Guadeloupe but the loss of Canada for the French in 1763. During the French Revolution, the population declared its independence, but after a quarrelsome time, Napoleon restored slavery and governance on the island in 1802 by subjecting the rebels. The English got hold of Guadeloupe once again in 1810 for five years, and eventually slavery was abolished by the French in 1848. One century later, Guadeloupe became a department of France (971).

1.1 Short history and "state of affairs" of archaeological research on Guadeloupe

It is only recently that tangible traces of probably the first inhabitants of Guadeloupe have been found, somewhat surprisingly at the slopes of Capesterre-Belle-Eau (Stouvenot and Casa-grande 2015) and on Marie-Galante (Fouéré et al. 2015; Siegel et al. 2015).[1] The Capesterre site comprises a pre-Ceramic Archaic campsite with blade *débitage*. However, this site remains unique and the Archaic population of the Lesser Antilles is better known from sites beyond the Guadeloupean archipelago, notably those excavated by Inrap on the island of St. Martin (see Bonnissent 2008) and by the rich archive on the island of Antigua (see DeMille 2005).

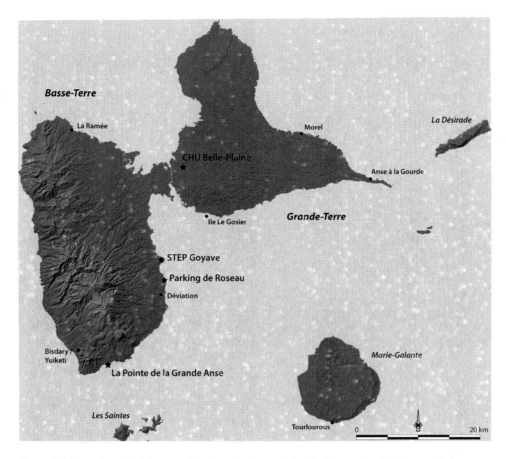

Figure 1.3 Map of the Guadeloupe archipelago with presented and other discussed Late Ceramic Age sites.
Source: www.naturalearthdata.com.

The Early Ceramic Age

The first pottery-making populations of Guadeloupe arrived around the beginning of the first millennium CE and came from the mainland of South America, but probably after they had touched upon Puerto Rico where older radiocarbon dates have been attested for them (see S. Fitzpatrick 2013) (Table 1.1). Highly recognizable ceramic fine wares have been found along the coast at the beach of Morel, on Grande-Terre along the shore, in the center of Basse-Terre and at Folle Anse, on Marie-Galante. The ongoing scientific debate allows for a unique Huecoid migration towards Puerto Rico, from where it would have spread eastward across the Lesser Antilles, colliding with a Cedrosan Saladoid migration from the mainland at the Lesser Antilles. Interestingly, the Guadeloupean sites feature a mixture of both ceramic wares, suggesting a more intimate relationship (see Hofman et al. 1999; Romon et al. 2013).

These very early Ceramic Age sites are rare on Guadeloupe and the Lesser Antilles as a whole, but certainly need more attention, as witnessed by the results of the Inrap excavation in the capital of Basse-Terre (Bonnissent and Romon 2004; Romon et al. 2006; Bonnissent 2006). Large-scale excavations conducted at the Déviation of Capesterre-Belle-Eau in the early 2000s yielded a bit more Cedrosan Saladoid ceramics. This material hinted at the presence of a Cedrosan site in the vicinity of the excavations, which revealed later (Modified and

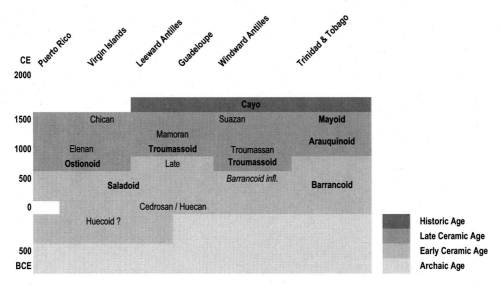

Table 1.1 Chronocultural chart of the Lesser Antilles (after Petersen et al. 2004).

Late) Saladoid wares and Troumassoid materials (Etrich et al. 2003, 2013; Mestre et al. 2001; Toledo y Mur et al. 2004). Considering the whole of Basse-Terre, we may also invoke the excavations conducted at Yuiketi and Bisdary (Gourbeyre) as well as La Ramée (Sainte-Rose) sharing Early and Late Ceramic Age assemblages (see Bonnissent 2011; Casagrande et al. 2016; Romon et al. 2006). The sites of Goyave and Roseau, both hamlets to the north of Capesterre-Belle-Eau, which are presented here, can be aligned with the excavations of the Déviation of Capesterre-Belle-Eau. Without doubt, the La Pointe de Grande Anse site can also be added to this ensemble, knowing that both occupations have been clearly identified. The CHU Belle-Plaine site is truly Troumassoid, lacking Saladoid elements (see Table 1.3). The Cedrosan Saladoid ceramics in the Windward Islands and Guadeloupe reveal Barrancoid influence after about cal 300 CE, also known as the Modified Saladoid period, which changes again in Late or Terminal Saladoid after cal 500 CE (Petersen et al. 2004). The aftermath of the Saladoid series in the latter half of the first millennium CE is marked on the one hand by climate change, regionalization, and the persistence of the Late Saladoid series into the Mamoran Troumassoid subseries in the Leeward Islands until cal 1000 ce. On the other hand, the Late Saladoid in the Windward Islands had diverged into the Troumassan Troumassoid subseries a few centuries earlier (Bonnissent 2008; Hofman 2013; Hofman et al. 2007; Versteeg and Schinkel 1992).

The Late Ceramic Age

The post-Saladoid chronology of the Leeward Islands as well as that of Guadeloupe is dominated by the excavations of Irving Rouse at Indian Creek (Antigua) conducted in the early 1970s. Concerning the Late Ceramic Age (LCA) in the Leeward Islands, the excavations at Savanne Suazey (Grenada) and Troumassée (St. Lucia) in the Windward Islands and the origins of the Troumassan and Suazan Troumassoid subseries are of lesser importance, despite the important work on Martinique by Louis Allaire (1977, 1990b).

Prior to Rouse's excavations on Antigua and his reconstruction of Caribbean chronology, archaeological research on Guadeloupe was largely embodied by Edgar Clerc and Father Maurice Barbotin. The former proposed a chronology based on his excavations on the beach of Morel, situated on the Atlantic coast to the south of Le Moule on Grande-Terre. The actual Troumassoid series were named Morel IV or "*un peuplement différent du précédent*" and placed towards the end of the first millennium CE (Clerc 1968:54, 1970:86) or called Caraïbe (Barbotin 1970:36), which is still common ground in schoolbooks and among local historians. More generally, the beautiful older (Saladoid) ceramics were thought to have been made by the (supposedly civilized) Arawaks and the later (Troumassoid/Suazoid) crude, evidently only domestic pots and pans were obviously made by the allegedly savage Caribs (see, for example, Burac 2000). It is evident that this two-step classification is obsolete and needs to be discarded.

Following Clerc, the Late Ceramic Age of Guadeloupe was studied in the 1990s by Dutch archaeologists Corinne Hofman and Menno Hoogland of Leiden University in collaboration with André Delpuech of the French Ministry of Culture. Hofman identified stylistic resemblances between the ceramics of Anse à la Gourde, on Grande-Terre, and those found at Mamora Bay, Antigua (Delpuech et al. 2001b). The latter site is situated on the southern shore of Antigua, facing Anse à la Gourde, about 60 km distant. As proposed by Irving Rouse and Birgit Faber Morse (1999), the Mamora Bay style was defined as intermediate between the Mill Reef style (Late Saladoid) and the subsequent Freeman's Bay style (Troumassoid). It was recognized as such at the site of Indian Creek, Antigua. At first, Rouse called this assemblage the Marmora Bay complex (yes, with an r), following the analysis of his student Charles Hoffman Jr.:

> Sides of the vessels characteristically curve upwards or inwards, forming the so-called cazuela shape. This shape is sometimes accentuated by adding a thick ring or fold of clay to the rim. The rings and folds take the place of the flanges that had been present in the previous complexes [Mill Reef]. Scratching to roughen the sherd surfaces becomes more common. Painting is now limited to positive, rectilinear white-on-red designs, typically in the form of chevrons, and to a red or black slip, applied areally. Lugs are simpler, cruder, and rarer; and handles are virtually non-existent. Shallow-and broad-line curvilinear incision is now diagnostic. Griddles continue to be provided with legs.
> (Rouse 1974:174–175)

Two years later, Rouse presented four radiocarbon dates, revealing a first indication for this ceramic complex, that range between 930 and 1105 CE (Rouse 1976:39). Here, he also evoked for the first time the Freeman's Bay complex, or the ceramic assemblage that succeeded his Marmora Bay complex (ibid.). However, the Freeman's Bay complex is discussed 20 years later as a different assemblage, but still comparable to the Mamora Bay style (without r, or the original eponym of this bay):

> Our comparison of the Mamora Bay and Freeman's Bay assemblages indicates a continuation of the previous trend towards simplification of the ceramics. The Freeman's Bay potters retained the red slip of the Mamora Bay period but dropped its white painting, limited themselves to plain tabular lugs, and ceased to make any but the simplest modeled and incised designs. They no longer attached legs to their griddles and, if the limited evidence is correct, stopped producing figurines, stamps, and ornaments of clay.
> (Rouse et al. 1995:449)

Freeman's Bay received several radiocarbon dates, which largely outdate the youngest date for Indian Creek. This made Rouse think that Freeman's Bay could be dated after Mamora Bay (ibid.). Interestingly, in this publication Rouse and coworkers also proposed to insert the Leeward Islands, hitherto attached traditionally to the Elenan Ostionoid subseries (cal 900–1200 CE), which after cal 1300 CE featured influences attributed to the Chican Ostionoid subseries, into the Troumassoid series of the Windward Islands and, consequently, added the Mamoran to the Troumassan and Suazan Troumassoid subseries (Rouse et al. 1995:450–451).[2]

According to the last Rousean publication concerning the "styles" or "periods" of Antigua, only a few sherd profiles were presented, but the descriptions of the morphology and decoration modes differed barely from the previous ones (see Rouse and Faber Morse 1999:41). We must add, however, that they insisted on the fact that, according to their observations, the Mamora Bay style did not feature Saladoid characteristics anymore, with the exception of strapped handles (ibid.). Consequently, Hofman proposed a Guadeloupean equivalent of the Mamoran Troumassoid subseries for the Late Ceramic Age assemblage at Anse à la Gourde, which is characterized by *"des récipients avec des formes simples, rarement décorés mais souvent couverts d'un engobe rouge. Les décors consistent en des motifs incisés larges et peu profonds. Des adornos zoomorphes embellissent les bords de ces récipients. Les platines ont pour la plupart des pieds"* (Delpuech et al. 2001b:280). Next to these excavations, a large-scale pedestrian survey was conducted by the Leiden student Maaike de Waal and colleagues on the island of La Désirade and at the eastern tip of Grande-Terre. Her works revealed a multitude of sites for this particular area of which the majority can be attributed to the Late Ceramic Age or post-Saladoid sequence of Guadeloupe (de Waal 2006, Figs. 6.7–9). The new Rousean chronology (see Rouse and Faber Morse 1999:48, Fig. 26) was eventually crystallized a few years afterwards by Petersen et al. (2004:33, Fig. 1). The definition of the Mamoran Troumassoid subseries, to which we can immediately add the Freeman's Bay complex, is thus based mainly upon the excavations realized by Rouse in the 1970s. In addition, we must also point out the contribution made through the works conducted by Leiden University and the French Ministry of Culture at Anse à la Gourde and the dissertation written by Reginald Murphy (1999), concerning Antigua during the 1990s:

> In the subsequent Mamora Bay style, Cedrosan Saladoid elements still persisted, albeit in a limited and vestigial way. Red-slipped surfaces gradually replaced the bicolour and polychrome painting. The patterns in bicoloured painting in the Mamora Bay style were now simplified. Incisions were broad-lined, with either curvilinear or parallel linear designs, and they appeared on the exterior of shallow vessels. Cedrosan style handles had completely disappeared and lugs were rare. Rims were typically folded or thickened by adding a coil of clay. The pottery was less well finished and certainly les commonly decorated than its predecessors [. . .].
>
> Incised elements tended to be deeper, narrower, more irregular and U-shaped, as characteristic of the Freeman's Bay style. Scratched surfaces were more common on Freeman's Bay pottery, which was characterized by an absence of white painting and the presence of shallow dimpled-based vessels.
>
> (Petersen et al. 2004:27)

Considering the sites presented here, we must point out the omnipresence of red coloring (paint/slip), thus without bichrome or polychrome painting, applied to bowls, basins, and platters, but also to large, shallow bowls and footed griddles. We can observe some scratching applied to the exterior, broad-line incisions (*cannelures*) applied to the exterior, forming sometimes rather complex designs, which are often encountered in combination with red slip. The Mamora Bay description may also pass for the Freeman's Bay style, but the latter has been inadequately defined. For this matter, we must also consider the final Late Ceramic Age sites from the Windward Islands, known as the Suazan Troumassoid subseries, despite the presence of Chican Ostionoid influences in the Leeward Islands.

Succeeding the troublesome Troumassan Troumassoid subseries in the Windward Islands, the chronology of the Suazan Troumassoid subseries ranges between cal 1000 and 1500 CE (Allaire 2013b). This range corresponds better to the Mamoran chronology, given that Petersen et al. (2001:28) proposed two phases for this period: one early phase between cal 1000 and 1200 CE and a later one between cal 1200 and 1500 CE. Considering Guadeloupe, the earlier phase "clearly shows affiliation between the early part of the Suazan Troumassoid and the Mamoran Troumassoid subseries from the nearby northern Lesser Antilles, suggesting mutual relations and the fusion of certain styles" (ibid.). Ceramic materials from the later phase have also been found on Guadeloupe, but a detailed description for each phase has not been presented by these same authors, who have drawn largely on the dissertations written by McKusick (1960) and Allaire (1977) for a general description of this subseries:

> Suazan Troumassoid ceramics are among the least finished and crudest Amerindian pottery in the entire West Indies, rivaling the Palmetto ware from the Bahamas. Suazan pottery is famous for its scratched, finger-indented surfaces and legged vessels and griddles. Vessels are thick and poorly made. Most were clearly utilitarian vessels, belonging to undecorated plain ware, with oval diameters reaching 40 cm, along with some finer ware having polished surfaces. The latter are often decorated with red paint, linear or zoned painting, or simple incisions of parallel lines, circles, or scrolls on the rims or walls. Flat human-head adornos with flaring pierced ears, figurines and clay pestles were typical.
> (Petersen et al. 2004:28)

When reconsidering the two last citations or definitions of these subseries, the ceramic studies of the presented sites reveal characteristics of both subseries. On the one hand, there is perhaps a slight preference for Mamoran when considering the broad-line incisions but, on the other hand, the absence of bichrome/polychrome painting or slipping is in favor of Suazan. This being said, more data and further study is certainly needed in order to better define the different Troumassoid assemblages on Guadeloupe. For this matter, a revision of the Troumassan Troumassoid and Late Cedrosan Saladoid subseries of the Windward Islands as well as one of the Elenan and Chican Ostionoid subseries of the Leeward Islands are needed to better define the end of the Saladoid and the inception of the Troumassoid series on Guadeloupe and surrounding islands.

1.2 Historic Age

As mentioned previously, the beach at Roseau is considered the landing place of Christopher Columbus' crew during his second voyage to the Americas, but many other beaches at the leeward side of Basse-Terre have also been considered as such by historians (Petitjean Roget 2015; Vauchelet 1892:94, note 1; Yacou and Adélaïde-Merlande 1993:81). However, Fortuné Chalumeau (2009) proposed a landing place at the windward side near Anse à la Barque of Basse-Terre. Whatever the case may be, one must not forget that Columbus landed first at Marie-Galante when exploring the Guadeloupean archipelago (M. de Navarrete 1922:215–216) without knowing the exact disembarking place either! During the 16th century, the

Europeans and Amerindians had much contact in exchanging goods or conducting war according to the historic documents, but few archaeological sites attest to this important period except for the Greater Antilles. In fact, it forms a problem when discussing the material culture of the so-called Caribes, as the Amerindians are referred to by the Spanish, as well as to sort out the different populations that dwelled in the Lesser Antilles who were, in the Spanish view, all enemies and cannibals (Jesse 1963; Sued Badillo 1995). For this matter, it is important to separate the Kalinago as encountered by the French in the second quarter of the 17th century and the Caribes as described by the Spanish in the 16th century, for they may not be the same people (see van den Bel 2020).

Once Columbus got hold of Hispaniola, Guadeloupe or the Lesser Antilles more generally remained *islas inútiles* for the Spanish, who frequented these islands mainly to water and refresh. By the end of the 16th century, they actually wanted to install outposts in the Leeward Islands, but many attempts failed, with the exception of St. Martin in the second quarter of the 17th century when the Europeans established themselves permanently in the Lesser Antilles (Moreau 1992). Indeed, in the second half of the 16th century the English, French, and Dutch infested the Caribbean looking for (illegal) commerce and hoping to attack any Spanish convoys. For these explorers—privateers and pirates or *vrijbuiters*—the Lesser Antilles represented a rather safe haven, away from the Spanish domination of the larger islands, in order to replenish their water, often relying on the refreshments of the indigenous population with whom they bartered.

Considering Guadeloupe, one has to wait for the year 1635 in order to have more information about its Amerindians. In this year, the French arrived at Sainte-Rose at the northern tip of Basse-Terre, but this first implantation failed rapidly due to the death of Jean du Plessis, Sieur d'Ossonville, one of the two stakeholders. The colony relocated to Vieux-Fort, at the utmost southern tip of Basse-Terre, but members had already swarmed out to Vieux Habitants and Basse-Terre at the windward side, and also to Sainte-Marie on the leeward coast, where they constructed a fortress (Figure 1.4).[3] The latter installation was probably made in collaboration with a Kalinago leader called Le Borgne who resided there (Breton 1978:105; Du Tertre 1667, Book I:148).

In 1642 Governor Jean Aubert was replaced by Charles Houël, Sieur de Petit-Pré, who, in association with his brother-in-law Jean de Boisseret d'Herblay, bought the island of Guadeloupe in 1649 from the Compagnie des Isles des Amériques, which was near bankruptcy and abandoned by the governors (see Mims 1912, Chapter 1). Relying heavily on tobacco, Houël decided to accept the installation of "Dutch Brazilians" in the mid-1650s in order to switch to the production of sugar. The latter, rich merchants, bought land from the small French colonists in different quarters of Basse-Terre. They also brought in African slave labor and lent money to other landowners in order to allow them to convert to sugar production. This Dutch commercial dominance, also present in the wider Caribbean region and supported by the French colonial governors, was eventually ended by the French Crown and Colbert, who founded the Compagnie des Indes occidentales in 1664 (see Lafleur 1993). Finally, the faith and relocation of the Guadeloupean Kalinago, who found themselves in the midst of these European struggles, was concluded by signing a "peace" document in 1660 (Bérard and Lafleur 2013).

1.3   Regional setting and site presentation

Trois-Rivières

Of the four municipalities presented here, that of Trois-Rivières is probably the best-known from an archaeological point of view because of its famous rock engravings or petroglyphs (see Dubelaar 1995; Gilbert 1990; Ruig 2001). This important rock art site certainly competes

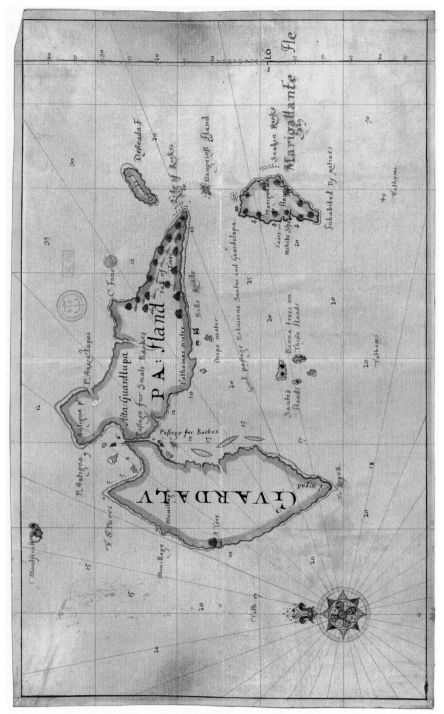

Figure 1.4 English map of Guadeloupe, anonymous, c. 1635 (Bibliothèque nationale de France, Paris, Département des cartes et plans CPL GE SH 18E PF 155 DIV 2 P 1 RES-3). With kind permission.

Source: www.bnf.fr.

with the site of Roseau Beach when considering the supposed disembarkation of Christopher Columbus' crew during his second voyage to the Americas (see Richard 2004, 2005).[4] An unusually high concentration of rock art sites is to be found on the slopes of three different rivers, which represent the heart of this village, situated at the southern tip of Basse-Terre. The center of this cluster of engraved boulders is part nowadays of the Parc archéologique des roches gravées (PARG) at Trois-Rivières, waiting for UNESCO status as of this writing.[5]

Next to interpretation of these petroglyphs, their dating remains a difficult task and many archaeologists have strived to establish a link between the petroglyphs and known archaeological complexes. In 1994 members of the Ministry of Cultural Affairs (DAC) and the University of Leiden attempted to make this connection by digging 12 one-square-meter test pits in the surrounding terrain of the PARG; they dug at Derussy and Romuald, but also at Anse Duquery and La Pointe de Grande Anse (Delpuech 2007; Delpuech et al. 1994). The latter site was detected using *Volontaire à l'aide technique* (VAT) by Pierre Bodu in January 1984. It is situated on the left bank, opposite our 2007 excavations (Figure 1.5).[6] Bodu attributed the numerous sherds to the Arawak and Carib populations of prehistory, that is, the Saladoid period and post-Saladoid sequence (Bodu 1984). The French-Dutch combination collected a grand total of 441 sherds of which a few showed red-on-white painting, some red slipping, and five D-shaped handles which, according to the authors, should be attributed to the Cedrosan Saladoid subseries (Delpuech et al. 1994).

In 1995 another test pit campaign was conducted at a site on the island of Terre-de-Bas of Les Saintes, a small archipelago opposite La Pointe de Grande Anse (Delpuech et al. 1995). This site has been attributed to the Suazan Troumassoid subseries according to the authors; however, the site also yielded a radiocarbon date of 810 ± 30 BP (GrN-20874). The

Figure 1.5 Excavating postholes at La Pointe de Grande Anse.

Photo: M. van den Bel, Inrap.

latter date is much younger than a radiocarbon measurement of the collagen of an individual buried at this same site, 1210 ± 50 BP (GrN-21562). Both dates fall within the range of radiocarbon dates obtained for La Pointe de Grande Anse. More recently, another excavation was realized for the reconstruction of the parking lot at the PARG (Romon et al. 2019). The radiocarbon dates and ceramics found during this excavation elucidate the assumption that the extensive rock art site of Trois-Rivières may be placed in the second half of the first millennium. This is considered a transitional period between the Saladoid and Troumassoid ceramic series, which, according to Henri Peititjean Roget (2010, 2011, 2015), is marked by a circum-Caribbean climatic change or drought (for Guadeloupe, see Beets et al. 2006).

La Pointe de Grande-Anse[7]

The pre-Columbian site of La Pointe de Grande Anse, on the right bank of the Granse Anse River, situated in the Municipality of Trois-Rivières, was discovered in 2006 when a mechanical survey for a future parking allotment was conducted (van den Bel 2007). The site is located at the summit of an important volcanic flow jutting into the sea, which is cut by the Grande Anse River at approximately 60 m from the Caribbean Sea, facing Les Saintes (Figure 1.3 and Table 1.1). Today, the right bank of this point features a restaurant, a discotheque, and the municipal swimming pool. The left bank has a football field and a restaurant where a few test pits were dug previously (as mentioned earlier). In colonial times, this point housed a local pottery (Fils Fidelin) and a sugarcane factory (Butel) that ended its rum production during the 1970s. The colonial presence and its activities disturbed the pre-Columbian site, leaving only sterile yellowish-brown subsoil with darker-colored features below the dark subsoil. However, during the excavations the northern and southern slopes of the point still evidenced an ancient surface, but unfortunately yielded very little material. No midden area was encountered within the perimeter of the excavation.

In all, 1784 m² has been uncovered by means of a mechanical shovel revealing more than 1,200 features ascribed to both pre-Columbian and colonial times (van den Bel et al. 2009). The features of the colonial occupation were abundant and in most cases easily distinguishable from the pre-Columbian ones. The latter were represented by postholes, circular pits, and burials, revealing at least two house locations of which one constituted a perfect house plan consisting of four central postholes surrounded by 17 smaller ones. Five burials were located in the northwestern quadrant of this dwelling, suggesting an intimate relationship with it (van den Bel and Romon 2010) (see Figure 1.5). Twenty-two radiocarbon dates revealed a persistent occupation, during primarily the Late Ceramic Age, with dates ranging from 600 to 1300 BP (Table 1.3). Relatively small amounts of artifacts were retrieved (ceramics, lithics, faunal remains), of which the pottery was attributed to the Late Cedrosan Saladoid and Mamoran Troumassoid subseries.

Les Abymes

Prior to the large-scale excavation at Belle-Plaine, this municipality was virtually devoid of (large-scale) archaeological research and archaeological sites, except for some surface finds. In 2007 the first test pits were dug by Christian Stouvenot on top of a small *morne*, situated in the Belle-Plaine area at 1.5 km distance from the 2013 excavations. He detected a midden area and attributed the ceramics to the Troumassan Troumassoid subseries (Stouvenot 2010).[8]

Table 1.2 General information per site.

Site	Number	Year	Report	Surface	RC	All features	Pits	Postholes	Burials	Ceramics	Lithics	Vertebrates	Invertebrates
La Pointe de Grande Anse	97132-0116	2007	2009	1784	22	1234	14	179	16	1505	189	3429	x
CHU Belle-Plaine	97101-0105	2013	2016	6348	10	321	34	126	2	2458	496	4004	39
STEP Goyave	97114-0046	2014	2017	3473	10	416	26	42	0	2062	261	x	72
Parking de Roseau	97107-0005	2015	2018	2523	10	422	32	143	1	6392	773	26	484

Table 1.3 Results of radiocarbon dates per site.

La Pointe de Grande Anse

N° Lab.	Material	Feature	Type	Age bp	Deviation	cal. CE 2 σ	HL
KIA-36671	Charcoal	7	Posthole	1230	30	689–884	1
KIA-36672	Charcoal	32	Posthole	1340	25	646–765	1
KIA-36673	Charcoal	1	Burial	945	35	1019–1166	1
KIA-36675	Human bone, collagen	1	Burial	915	50		1
KIA-36676	Human bone, collagen	2	Burial	565	25	1308–1423	1
KIA-36676	Human bone, apatite A	2	Burial	348	39		1
KIA-36676	Human bone, apatite B	2	Burial	431	22		1
KIA-36674	Charcoal	3	Pit	945	30	1025–1158	1
KIA-36677	Charcoal	935	Posthole	1245	30	683–870	2
KIA-36678	Charcoal	81	Posthole	1065	30	895–1023	2
KIA-36679	Charcoal	33	Burial	625	30	1291–1398	2
KIA-36681	Human bone, collagen	33	Burial	x	x	x	2
KIA-36681	Human bone, apatite A	33	Burial	620	25		2
KIA-36681	Human bone, apatite B	33	Burial	625	25		2
KIA-36680	Charcoal	351	Burial	690	30	1267–1386	2
KIA-36682	Human bone, collagen	351	Burial	650	140		2
KIA-36683	Charcoal	265	Posthole	330	25	1482–1642	2
KIA-36684	Charcoal	834	Posthole	1000	30	1084–1151	Other
KIA-36685	Human bone, collagen	571	Burial	x	x	x	Other
KIA-36685	Human bone, apatite A	571	Burial	1435	20		Other
KIA-36685	Human bone, apatite B	571	Burial	1340	20		Other
KIA-31187	Charcoal	9	Pit	1210	20	773–890	Other

CHU Belle-Plaine

N° Lab.	Material	Feature	Type	Age bp	Deviation	cal. CE 2 sigma	Zone
POZ-63014	Charcoal	73	Pit	960	40	997–1164	North
POZ-63015	Charcoal	157	Pit	900	30	1039–1210	North
POZ-63016	Charcoal	248.3	Pit	870	30	1045–1250	South
POZ-63017	Charcoal	66.1	Pit	885	30	1041–1108	North
POZ-63018	Charcoal	15.1	Pit	915	30	1030–1189	North
POZ-63019	Charcoal	216.1	Pit	875	30	1043–1241	South

(*Continued*)

Table 1.3 (Continued)

La Pointe de Grande Anse

N° Lab.	Material	Feature	Type	Age bp	Deviation	cal. CE 2 σ	HL
POZ-63020	Charcoal	218.3	Pit	930	30	1025–1165	South
POZ-63021	Charcoal	74	Pit	1030	35	898–1147	North
POZ-63022	Charcoal	140	Hearth	890	30	1041–1218	North
POZ-63024	Charcoal	160	Hearth	960	30	1020–1155	North

STEP Goyave

N° Lab.	Material	Feature	Type	Age bp	Deviation	cal. CE 2 sigma
POZ-75039	Charcoal	5	Posthole	835	30	1157–1264
POZ-75040	Charcoal	6.4	Pit	1145	35	776–979
POZ-75041	Charcoal	55.2	Pit	905	35	1035–1209
POZ-75042	Charcoal	56.1	Posthole	950	30	1024–1155
POZ-75043	Charcoal	62.1	Pit	825	30	1163–1264
POZ-75044	Charcoal	77	Posthole	1060	30	897–1024
POZ-75045	Charcoal	112	Pit	1640	35	335–536
POZ-75046	Charcoal	174.1	Pit	1170	30	771–965
POZ-75047	Charcoal	207	Pit	985	30	990–1154
POZ-75049	Charcoal	415	Posthole	1070	30	895–1021

Parking de Roseau

N° Lab.	Material	Feature	Type	Age bp	Deviation	cal. CE 2 sigma	Assemblage
POZ-84383	Charcoal	156.3	Pit	720	30	1246–1383	E
POZ-84384	Charcoal	174.4	Pit	1170	30	771–965	A
POZ-84387	Charcoal	178.4	Pit	870	30	1045–1250	A
POZ-84388	Charcoal	197.6	Pit	805	30	1170–1273	A
POZ-84389	Charcoal	222.5	Pit	875	30	1053–1241	B
POZ-84390	Charcoal	337	Pit	735	30	1223–1295	C
POZ-84391	Charcoal	365	Pit	670	30	1274–1391	D
POZ-84392	Charcoal	412.4	Pit	805	30	1170–1273	E
UBA-25514	Charcoal	403	Pit	840	42	1150–1270	T 21 Morne
UBA-25187	Bone	2	Layer	254	25	1631–1670	T 19 Beach

Since 2008 Inrap has executed various systematic mechanical surveys to the west of Les Abymes and north of the city of Pointe-à-Pitre that yielded pre-Columbian sites showing numerous features.

At Morne l'Épingle, situated at a distance of 1500 m from the excavated site, a circular pit was discovered (Romon 2010). This pit contained a handful of sherds; a fragment of charcoal taken from this pit yielded a radiocarbon date of 1145 ± 30 BP (KIA-37497). At Mamiel, situated to the northeast of Raizet Airport, a petaloid axe and one polishing stone were found on the surface of the ground (Serrand 2011; van den Bel 2012). The latter artifact may be related to the recently discovered pre-Columbian called Petit-Pérou to the east of Mamiel (Serrand 2018b). The excavations at this Troumassoid site, realized between September 2020 and April 2021, were led by Nathalie Serrand and the present author. Interestingly, this site yielded about 100 burials for an excavated area of approximately 8000 m².

Other individual finds, mainly ceramics, from the surroundings of the Belle-Plaine site have been encountered at Pont à Popo at a distance of approximately 300 m (Sellier-Ségard 2013), at Boisripeau and Dothémare (Stouvenot 2010:29).

CHU Belle-Plaine

The pre-Columbian site of CHU Abymes, at the hamlet of Belle-Plaine, situated in the Municipality of Les Abymes, was discovered in 2010 when conducting a mechanical survey for the future Centre hospitalier universitaire (CHU), the new hospital of Pointe-à-Pitre (Briand 2012). The site is located at the summit of a rather low elevation belonging to the littoral plains of western Grande-Terre to the northwest of the village of Les Abymes (Figure 1.3 and Table 1.2). Today, these plains constitute the intermediate area between the Grand-Cul-de-Sac-Marin, in the west, and the Grands-Fonds, to the east. Although located on Grande-Terre, the substratum of this plain belongs geologically to the younger volcanic island of Basse-Terre. The plain, however, is dotted with karstic "islands" belonging to Grande-Terre, stressing its status as an intermediate area. Since the early 18th century, these highly fertile plains have been used incessantly to grow sugarcane. The wavy landscape has been flattened out more recently by bulldozer activity in order to facilitate the access of vehicles to harvest the cane. This has modified the landscape drastically, and the pre-Columbian site of CHU Belle-Plaine suffered dearly by decapitation of the features and disappearance of the ancient walking surface. Fortunately, during the excavations, the northern slope still evidenced the ancient surface, but it yielded very little archaeological material; no midden area was encountered within the perimeter of the excavation.

In all, 6348 m² has been uncovered by means of a mechanical shovel revealing more than 300 features that can be ascribed entirely to the pre-Columbian era (van den Bel et al. 2016). The spatial distribution of these features showed two distinct areas with circular pits of which the northern area also yielded a house location with two burials. Next to this site, in the hinterland of the Grand-Cul-de-Sac Marin, the distribution and function of these large, mysterious pits represent a particular subject of interest of this small habitation site (see van den Bel 2017). Ten radiocarbon dates revealed a short occupation of about 200 years in the Late Ceramic Age, with dates ranging from 800 to 1000 BP (Table 1.3). Relatively small amounts of artifacts were retrieved (ceramics, lithics, faunal remains) of which the pottery was attributed to the Mamoran and Suazan Troumassoid subseries.

Goyave

The municipality of Goyave features today 74 archaeological sites of which nine date from pre-Columbian times. These sites are mainly individual finds of stone axes and a few sherds. The excavations at the STEP were a very welcome contribution to the history of this municipality.

STEP Goyave

The pre-Columbian site of STEP Goyave, at the hamlet of Sainte-Claire, situated in the Municipality of Goyave, was discovered in 2012 during a mechanical survey for the future Station d'épuration (STEP), the water treatment terminal of Goyave (Briand 2013). This site is located at the summit of a *morne*, or hilly cliff, along the Petite Rivière de Goyave to the north and the bay of Sainte-Claire to the south (Figure 1.3 and Table 1.2).

Since the late 17th century, this particular cliff housed an important plantation site of which the water mill, situated at the foot of the *morne*, was partially excavated (van den Bel et al. 2017, 2018b). The pre-Columbian remains were concentrated at the summit of the *morne* and disturbed by the colonial plantation site and afterwards by the growing of sugarcane and bananas.

In all, 3473 m² has been uncovered by means of a mechanical shovel revealing more than 400 features ascribed to both the pre-Columbian period and the colonial era (van den Bel et al. 2017). The spatial distribution of the pre-Columbian features revealed the solid main frame of a house plan consisting of eight postholes surrounded by numerous circular pits and possible burials, but due to the acidity of the volcanic sediment of this *morne*, (human) bones as well as shell materials were unrecognizable or dissolved. Ten radiocarbon dates revealed a short occupation of about 400 years during the Late Ceramic Age, with dates ranging mainly from 800 to 1200 BP (Table 1.2). Relatively small amounts of artifacts were retrieved (ceramics, lithics) of which the pottery was attributed to the Late Cedrosan Saladoid and Mamoran Troumassoid subseries.

Capesterre-Belle-Eau

The municipality of Capesterre-Belle-Eau features today approximately 82 pre-Columbian sites. This high number is mainly due to the implementation of compliance archaeology at Guadeloupe in 2001. A first major project was the Déviation routière de Capesterre-Belle-Eau (DRC), the road diversion of the village of Capesterre-Belle-Eau, which yielded numerous pre-Columbian and colonial sites of which many were subsequently excavated (see Stouvenot 2001). The DAC and the municipality of Capesterre-Belle-Eau have a rather good relationship, which favors archaeological research in their municipality. It may be noted that the leeward side of Basse-Terre is developing rapidly due to its vicinity to Pointe-à-Pitre. The majority of the pre-Columbian sites excavated during the DRC project have been attributed to the Ceramic Age and hopefully will be soon summarized by Christine Etrich. Important sites are most certainly Moulin-à-Eau 1, Allée Dumanoir, Fromager, and Rivière Grand Carbet, all excavated in the early 2000s. Only Moulin-à-Eau 2 was excavated more recently (Table 1.4). All sites can be attributed roughly to the Early Ceramic Age and pertain to the Cedrosan Saladoid subseries, whereas Fromager and Moulin-à-Eau 2 may also feature a Late Ceramic Age occupation.

Here, our interest goes first out to the site of Arrière Plage de Roseau (No. 97107-0034) as our excavations can be added to those conducted by Gérard Richard in 2001 and 2002 (Richard 2004, 2005). According to Richard, highly interesting ceramic body stamps of "Insular Caribs" were discovered at the (artificial) beach of Roseau after Hurricane Lenny in 1999. Knowing that Sainte-Marie is considered by many Guadeloupeans as the place where Columbus' crew disembarked, Richard's excavations were expected to provide additional information (Richard 2004). Situated at approximately 300 m to the north of our excavations, Richard and his team excavated a gully in the plateau that was directed towards the sea. The fill of this gully, perhaps a waste deposit, comprised four layers with ceramics attributed to post-Saladoid times, including the Troumassan and Suazan Troumassoid subseries and the Cayoid series (Boomert 2010; Le Lay 2013; Richard 2004, 2005). Three layers (I–III) have been dated by radiocarbon dating: Level I yielded a date of 865 ± 30 BP, Level II was dated 1080 ± 30 BP, and Level III yielded a date of 1370 ± 30 BP (Richard 2005:20). The fourth level was not dated, but it has to be noted that Richard did not publish all his dates and did not specify either that nearly all dates were taken from shell samples (see Table 1.3). Eventually, when ignoring the oldest and youngest dates,

Table 1.4 Overview of large-scale excavations on Guadeloupe involving pre-Columbian sites.

Site	Surface m²	Calibrated range ce	Reference
Parking de Roseau	2523	1100–1300	van den Bel et al. 2018a
STEP Goyave	3450	750–1250	van den Bel et al. 2017
Stade José Bade / Tourlourous	1273	950–1250*	Serrand et al. 2016
CHU Belle-Plaine	6348	1000–1200	van den Bel et al. 2016
La Ramée	6335	650–1000	Casagrande et al. 2016
Moulin à Eau 2	3000	650–1000	Etrich et al. 2013
Yuiketi	4000	400–900	Bonnissent 2011
La Pointe de Grande Anse	1784	650–1400	van den Bel et al. 2009
Bisdary	5000	1100–1400	Romon et al. 2006
Rivière du Grand Carbet	960	0–650	Toledo i Mur et al. 2004
Fromager	2300	650–1100	Toledo i Mur et al. 2003
Allée Dumanoir	6783	0–650	Etrich et al. 2003
Tourlourous	c. 1000	300–600	Colas et al. 2002
Anse à la Gourde	1650	1000–1300	Delpuech et al. 2001b
Moulin à Eau 1	18,000	0–650	Mestre et al. 2001

the range for this site could be dated between cal 1000 and 1200 CE, corresponding clearly to the excavations.

In October 2013, Christian Stouvenot of the SRA, the archaeological service of the Ministry of Culture, conducted a mechanized quick-scan of 13 trenches at the future parking lot of Roseau Beach (Stouvenot 2013). The SRA excavated both the plateau and the beach area of which the latter area yielded fragments of Spanish olive jars as well as fragments of Cayoid series pottery. Notably the presence of both types of ceramics at a depth of approximately 1 m in Trench 9 might suggest a possible contact between Europeans and the historic population of the Lesser Antilles, such as the Kalinago or 'Island Carib' (Allaire and Duval 1995; Boomert 1986, 2011; Hofman and Hoogland 2012).

A complementary investigation was conducted by members of Inrap in 2014 in order to better understand the stratigraphy of the Roseau beach area, but also to look for features at the plateau (Serrand et al. 2014:30). Indeed, the plateau yielded interesting pit and posthole features while important geomorphological research was conducted at the beach by Christophe Jorda who established a first detailed stratigraphy of this area (see Chapter 2). Jorda describes the latest phase of the beach as a 'laguna beach which is regularly disturbed by marine incursions'. This layer also yielded many fragments of Spanish olive jars, but, according to Fabrice Casagrande, these examples can be attributed to the first half of the 17th century (see Chapter 4). Another interesting find at the beach was the metatarsus of a horse, found in association with Cayoid pottery, with a date of 254 ± 25 BP (UB-25187) and calibrated 1630–1670 CE at 2σ (70%), highlighting the early 17th century again and the relationship between the Kalinago and the Europeans (see Tomadini and Grouard 2018).

Parking de Roseau

The pre-Columbian site of Parking de Roseau is situated to the south of the hamlet of Sainte-Marie in the Municipality of Capesterre-Belle-Eau. This site was discovered in 2013 when a mechanical test-trench survey for the future parking at the highly frequented beach of

Figure 1.6 Excavating the northern beach zone at Parking de Roseau.
Photo: M. van den Bel, Inrap.

Roseau was conducted (Stouvenot 2013), and was surveyed one year later, again mechanically (Serrand et al. 2014) (Figure 1.3 and Table 1.2). This particular beach, situated at the edge of a plateau, which is eroded by the Ravine Point to the north and Ravine Bourgeois to the south, is first of all known archaeologically for excavations realized by Gérard Richard in 2001 and 2002 to which our excavations can be connected. The excavations by Richard and those by Inrap confirmed an early European presence (*pacotilla* and olive jars) as well as one by the Kalinago (Island Carib), as testified by indigenous ceramics of the Cayoid series, dating to early colonial times.

In all, 2523 m² has been uncovered by means of a mechanical shovel revealing more than 400 features, which can be attributed mainly to the pre-Columbian era (van den Bel et al. 2018a). The spatial distribution of the features revealed three rather large house locations, each associated with circular pits and possible burials. Ten radiocarbon dates revealed a short occupation of about 200 years during the Late Ceramic Age, with dates ranging mainly from 700 to 1200 BP (Table 1.2). Large amounts of artifacts were retrieved (ceramics, lithics) of which the pottery was attributed to the Mamoran Troumassoid subseries (Figure 1.6).

Notes

1   In the early 1990s, Gérard Richard dated a shell tool from La Pointe des Pies near St. François, which is perhaps the first pre-Ceramic tool found on Guadeloupe (Richard 1994).
2   A few years before this publication, Rouse actually attributed the infamous Igneris to the Suazan Troumassoid subseries and, consequently, these historic Amerindians would have been the last producers of Mamoran Troumassoid ceramics (Rouse 1992:131–132).
3   Interestingly, Moulin-à-Eau 1 also yielded a very early colonial occupation (c. 1635–1660), probably based on the production of tobacco (Mestre et al. 2001; Roulet 2016; Rousseau 2004).
4   For an overview of the pre-Columbian cultures on Guadeloupe written in French, see the works of the former DAC conservator André Delpuech (1998, 2001, 2007, and 2016).

5   The reconnaissance and pinpointing of more engraved boulders is still ongoing with the recent survey project and PCR of Julien Monney.

6   A so-called VAT mission is mostly applied for in order to avoid enlistment in the French national army. Archaeology in the French Overseas Departments has greatly benefited from these missions by receiving many archaeologistsin the territories of which a large number are still working in the Caribbean (e.g., Thomas Romon, Benoit Bérard, and Michaël Mestre) or have left behind an important contribution (e.g., Pierre Bodu and Alain Cornette).

7   Throughout this work, the presented sites have been called La Pointe de Grande Anse, CHU Belle-Plaine, STEP Goyave, and Parking Roseau. However, in tables, titles, and subtitles either full names or acronyms are used.

8   In collaboration with Christian Stouvenot (SRA), it was decided to baptize the site of the future University Hospital (CHU) at Belle-Plaine CHU Belle-Plaine in order to avoid a second Belle-Plaine site.

2 Context

2.1 Methods and techniques

Martijn M. van den Bel

The methods and techniques used and developed in project-led archaeology in France have been applied on Guadeloupe since the 1990s. Mechanized excavating is almost imperative in order to cope with the time pressure in public works, the large surfaces to be examined, and the regional economic interest and development. This local development is firmly related to the existing infrastructure, which is extending down the line or expanding agglomerations. In fact, the geographical expansion predicts and decides where future archaeological research will be conducted. This means that we do not choose our area of research but conduct research if a construction site reveals potential artifacts, representing, obviously, a major difference from programmed, often university led archaeological research.

In this manner, the intensification of archaeological research in Guadeloupe since the foundation of Inrap in 2001 has yielded a large body of archaeological data. Next to huge amounts of typical artifact categories (ceramics, lithics, faunal remains, shell, etc.), these excavations also obtained numerous radiometric dates, much feature information, and micro- and macroanalytic data. In most cases, the quantities of artifacts that were exhumed per site surpass the total number of pottery fragments that were once used to identify a regional ceramic tradition such as, for example, the Mamoran Troumassoid subseries.

2.1.1 Survey phase

Within development-led archaeology, the archaeological work is often divided into different phases. The first is the survey phase. In this phase, the goals are (1) to detect any sites in the area to be developed, (2) to delimit the size of any site present, and (3) to provide a first characterization of the sites with regard to preservation, chronology, type, and richness of archaeological remains. When starting the survey phase, all sorts of maps and documents concerning the existing local archaeological and geological data are to be checked, including all available geotechnical and other environmental impact studies. (The last are most often supplied by the developer.) This information will get one started at possible sites or landscape markers within the project limits or in its vicinity. It will also provide data on the depths of various geomorphological deposits or layers that may contain remains of human occupation. It will finally determine the choice of the excavation strategy to be followed.

Depending on the type and extent of development, mechanical intervention in a regular grid is most often applied in compliance archaeology to detect sites. In specific cases, when

DOI: 10.4324/9781003181651-2

forest is still standing and/or the project is of vast dimensions, a pedestrian reconnaissance can first be conducted based on topographic maps and GPS field walking. When orienting the grid for archaeological trenches, digging perpendicularly to the existing geomorphological landscape is preferred in order to better understand the successive geological layers and their connection with possible human occupations. Multiple studies have shown that trenches every 20 meters in quincunx, representing an excavated surface of 5–10%, are an efficient sampling grid. However, this system must often be adapted in continuous trenches in order to check the geomorphological direction of the sediments, cut by, for instance, a future road construction. This system of diagnostic research is a tool to cover large areas quickly, in the most efficient way, to detect sites, but one must always be aware and use apparent features in the landscape for further exploration with different (traditional) techniques.[1]

In principle, all trenches must be dug until the oldest geological formations have been reached. The sterile layers are quickly attained on Grande-Terre, but may create problems at beaches and in swampy and lagoon areas (*salinas, marigots*). Basse-Terre consists of thick layers of volcanic debris that may have covered archaeological sites, but very little is known about such sites at present. In general, the sterile subsoil is often reached after 40–60 cm once the A-horizon and/or plow zone has been removed (Figure 2.1). Geological sections are recorded in both negative and positive trenches, which are all georeferenced with an infrared theodolite, if not with a precise GPS handheld device. When a site is encountered, additional trenches or extensions may be dug in order to uncover more anthropogenic features for radiocarbon sampling or to obtain a larger ceramic sample for chronocultural purposes. Meanwhile, the regular grid of trenches is often sufficient to limit the extensions of the new site, if it is not already delimited by topographical features such as creeks or a mountaintop. When excavating trenches, the archaeologist is "following" the scraping movements of the machine and must continuously test the subsoil for possible artifacts and estimate the necessity of testing deeper levels. This ability can be learned or experienced only in the field and often means the difference between a positive or negative survey. The presence of geomorphological and lithic specialists in the field (on demand of the field supervisor) can be a guiding element in detecting and recognizing less evident sites, such as lithic workshops or funerary sites.

On Guadeloupe, recent perturbation is evident: The interpretation of geological profiles, the nature and density of artifacts, and various taphonomic processes must be evaluated attentively in order to determine the general conditions of the site. On the one hand, archaeological sites may have been disturbed (partially) by recent bulldozing or agricultural activities and accordingly may not have a general scientific interest. On the other hand, however, they can have a local or even regional interest regarding a specific archaeological period. The survey and its product (i.e., the report) play a very important role in our understanding of pre-Columbian society and landscape, and the report is often the only archaeological document with respect to a particular area (often for decades to come).

2.1.2 *Excavations*

Based on the survey report as well as other existing data and the concluding (personal) opinion of the state supervisor, the supervisor decides whether a positive survey will be (partially) excavated or not. In France, this second phase in compliance archaeology is submitted to the public market, which means that other institutions and commercial companies, having a legal permit to excavate, can offer their services (i.e. the commercial amendment of 2003). The future excavation is regulated by a *cahier des charges*, written by the SRA. This official document represents a methodological framework for every site to be excavated

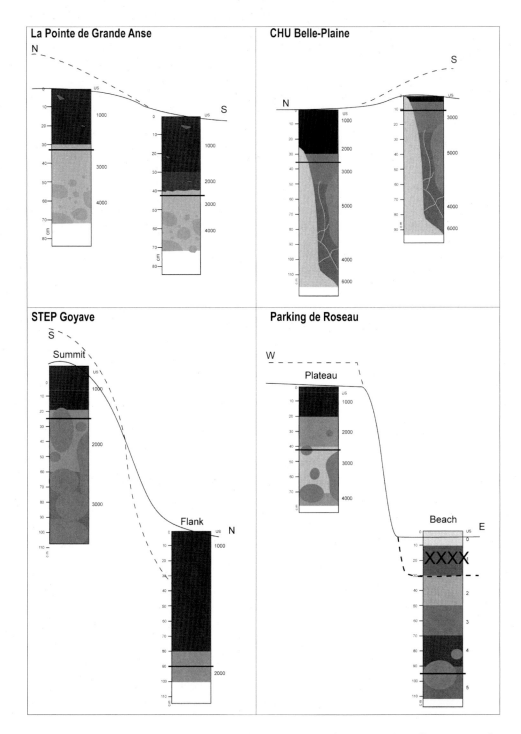

Figure 2.1 Schematic stratigraphy per site. The horizontal fat black line in each profile represents the excavation level.

(compliance or programmed), often including general and specific research questions, the use of special field techniques, the (obligatory) presence of specialists during fieldwork and during post-excavation studies, and so on. Next to these general elements, the limits of the excavation are determined by the SRA, culminating in a certain number of square meters to be excavated.

The developer is the only person who is legally allowed to choose an archaeological project as well as its future partner to conduct the excavations. The developer is the executive, whereas the archaeological partner (Inrap or any other legal party) is paid for its services. For that matter, the developer is also responsible for safety and security during the excavations as he is the Master of Works for the whole construction project. Once the necessary equipment has arrived, such as stocking containers, excavating tools, lunch cabins, and the like, and connections for running water and electricity (if possible) are made, the project can be started by the project leader. The project leader is proposed by the excavating company and nominally designated by the SRA. Any unforeseen anomalies or discoveries during fieldwork that may alter the content of the scientific program envisaged must rapidly be signaled to both parties.

From this moment on, the project leader applies the excavation techniques that are best suited to the proposed research questions, the total surface to be excavated and the budget agreed upon. As mentioned previously, most excavations in the Guadeloupean archipelago are situated in the coastal area and represent predominantly Late Ceramic Age sites. Depending on the extent of any Historic Age or later disturbances (plowing), these sites generally still have (part of) the original dark occupation layer of several decimeters that preserved the archaeological finds, either dispersed or sometimes appearing in various spatially concentrated areas or middens. Depending on the already mentioned parameters and possible disturbances, the archaeological materials in the dark layer are systematically gathered in squares by handpicking or sieving, and per arbitrary level and/or geological layer (see Harris et al. 1993), sampled or simply taken off without any collecting. The last-named case is often applied when manpower is low, a fairly large surface has to be excavated, or when the dark layer is disturbed by (recent) activities. Once the dark layer is taken off, dark features appear in the light-colored subsoil. Usually, these features are manually sectioned and excavated in order to determine their origin (anthropogenic or natural) and to gather artifacts and possible soil samples. During and after excavation, all features are recorded by photography, drawing, and georeferencing with a theodolite to obtain a spatial overview. Geological profiles and/or sections are also photoreferenced, drawn, and sometimes sampled for further soil analysis (micromorphology).

The sampling protocol for zooarchaeological analysis is systematic: features and specific layers are sampled and sieved on a fine mesh with water (1–2.7 mm screen). The sorting of the samples may be realized both in the field and in the laboratory.

During the fieldwork, the project leader takes care of the general progress of the project on a logistic and scientific level, ensuring that the excavation will be finished in time and all research questions will be answered apart from any possible additional questions that are raised during the fieldwork. This protocol is common to Neolithic, Bronze Age, and Iron Age sites in western Europe. It may be evident that Lithic and Archaic Age sites as well as Ceramic Age sites with special landscape features (ball courts, megaliths, etc.) in the West Indies follow specific protocols.

It is important to understand that these compliance excavations, as we know them today, yield information only on the part of the site that is going to be destroyed and therefore was excavated, whereas programmed excavations generally can investigate an entire site.

If programmed excavations do not excavate the whole site, they usually perform additional test pitting and/or auger campaigns around the excavation in order to test its surrounding area to assure a more secure extrapolation of the excavated data. Compliance archaeology is clearly restricted to the excavation perimeter as excavations beyond this limit are considered to be illegal and may result in legal prosecution, involving fines or even imprisonment of the project leader(!). On the other hand, local economic development increases continuously in the Guadeloupean archipelago, and will most certainly touch upon adjacent parcels for construction. In this manner, sites can be excavated completely in multiple phases that theoretically may take several years or decades. In sum, all sites presented in this work have been excavated following the procedures of compliance archaeology.

2.1.3   The post-excavation: analysis and report

The processing of artifacts (cleaning and bagging) is usually begun during the fieldwork and may provide feedback for the excavation. The studies that follow the excavation are determined by the research outline of the project. These may, however, change if the excavation has come up with unexpected results. Although the budget has also been fixed for this part of the project, it can be redistributed if unexpected material has been found or if quantities turn out to be different than originally estimated. For example, if eventually there appear to be few pottery fragments and abundant lithic remains, each study will receive a proportional part of the budget for analysis. Inrap agents realize most of the common studies (material culture, shell, animal and human bones); however, micro- and chemical analyses are most often done by external national or international research institutes or private companies. This accounts for radiometric dating, soil analysis, zooarchaeological identifications, and starch as well as phytolith identification. The analytical methods presented here will be discussed in the designated sections.

The reports of all these studies are compiled, and based on the results, a synthesis is written by the project leader, who edits the final report that is destined for the developer. The survey phase and final excavation report must be written in French and both have a legal status, since it is the outcome of both a public and a private demand. Unfortunately, these reports are not easily accessible, but recently excavation reports have been put online by Inrap at the website called Dolia (http://dolia.inrap.fr) and can be downloaded if you are member.

2.2   Radiocarbon dates

Martijn M. van den Bel

The regional chronology of Guadeloupe is actually based on 246 radiocarbon dates, using both conventional and AMS dating methods according to the SRA (information transmitted by SRA Guadeloupe 2020). Table 1.3 lists the results of all radiocarbon dates analyzed for the four sites presented here (see also Appendix 1). They have been listed per site, reporting laboratory number, dated material, feature number, and uncalibrated radiocarbon measurements in years Before Present (BP). The ^{14}C ages have been calibrated to obtain calendar years at 2σ or 95% intervals for the Northern Hemisphere using Stuiver et al. (1998) and, if not, either to Reimer et al. (2004) or Reimer et al. (2009).

The sampled materials consist of charcoal, wood, (human) bone, and carbonized residues. Analysis of charcoal in ceramic sherds has also been done, but this technique is still problematic and needs to be tested and comparted with "regular" charcoal samples. In order to

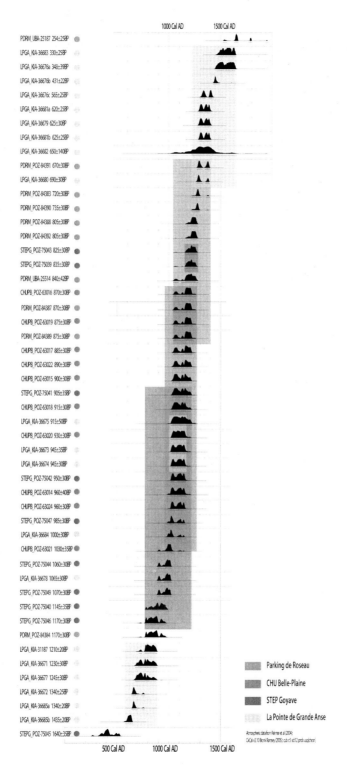

Figure 2.2 Plot of radiocarbon dates in chronological order. [OxCal v3.10 Bronk Ramsey (2005), cub r:5 sd:12 prob usp[chron] with atmospheric data from Reimer et al. (2004).]

minimize the outcome of incoherent dates, most charcoal samples were taken from restricted environments, such as postholes and pits, despite the fact that an occasional sample from an archaeological layer has been dated. Inconsistencies in the results of the radiocarbon dates will be discussed per site. Finally, the marine or riverine effect of human bone (i.e., due to the consumption of freshwater or sea fish by ancient populations) may distort the real age, but has been backed up by charcoal samples in the case of La Pointe de Grande Anse. Figure 2.2 shows all dates obtained in chronological order.

2.2.1   *La Pointe de Grande Anse*

In all, ten charcoal samples and five human bone samples were sent for radiocarbon analysis to Kiel, Germany. These samples were chosen in order to determine the contemporaneity of the burials encountered and the site's house plans to confirm a diachronic/continuous occupation of the site. Unfortunately, four out of five human bone samples did not contain sufficient collagen to obtain a date. In order to obtain dates from the burials, apatite has been extracted two times (A and B) per burial and these extraction samples have been dated. Since this is not a common procedure, the results will be discussed here in more detail.

According to Matthias Hüls (University of Kiel, Germany; pers. comm. 2020), who dated these samples, all apatite fractions, with the exception of the apatite A fraction of Burial 2 (KIA-36676), gave more than the 1 mg of carbon recommended for a precise measurement and produced sufficient ion beam, and insofar the results are reliable. The $\delta^{13}C$ values are in the normal range for apatite with a conjectural C3-diet signal. According to Kiel, the $\delta^{13}C$ value of the human bone sample (KIA-36676) is somewhat heavy for collagen from a C3 diet. If the deviation reflects a C4 component in the diet, it has no consequences for the measured ^{14}C age. If, however, it reflects a diet based on fish or shell, one has to consider a possible reservoir age and the measured age may be too old. The carbon recovered represents only 0.1% of the original bone and, although the collagen was "cleaned," the age obtained is very sensitive to even small contaminations and in this respect should be used with some caution.

The $\delta^{13}C$ value of KIA-36675 (Burial 1) is more negative than usual for collagen and suggests C3 contamination. The age, although in range with the others, should thus be interpreted with caution as well. Considering the very small sample size of KIA-36682 (second extraction), the low ion beams, and the large age difference between the two collagen extractions from one sample, the results are clearly not reliable. The quite negative $\delta^{13}C$ value of the first preparation suggests that the carbon measured in the target did not derive from the original bone collagen but is a contaminant. The $\delta^{13}C$ of the second preparation is near the collagen range and the measured age is in the range of the other samples of this series. Yet, this cannot be considered a usable age.

Nonetheless, the probability range of the calibrated dates is rather satisfying. The chronological extension of the pre-Columbian occupation represents about seven centuries, spanning from the end of the seventh to the end of the 14th century CE, knowing that the latter limit is represented by one radiocarbon date. This period of about 700 years covers the Late Saladoid and Troumassoid ceramic series, suggesting various successive occupations of this site.

However, when dating charcoal one must keep in mind the pitfall of the "old wood effect" in the Antilles, where long-life trees are used for various purposes (see Stouvenot et al. 2015). The question remains of what tree species were used by the inhabitants to construct their houses, as La Pointe de Grande Anse shows a difference between the dates of the postholes and burials. This problem has partly been solved by Christophe Tardy's identification of the tree species as locust, or courbaril, that was used for the charred wooden post F 935 in House Location 2, which was also radiocarbon dated (KIA-36677). For further discussion, see Chapter 6.

Eventually, the date obtained for posthole F 81 is more likely a better range for House Location 2, shortening also the range between this posthole and the adjacent burials. The range between the postholes and burials in this particular house location of about 600 years still surpasses the lifespan of a very old locust. The date of Burial 1, however, remains isolated when compared to the other burials, which are neatly grouped around the 13th century. It is noteworthy that the results of pit F 3 and Burial 1, situated only a few meters apart from each other, are similar. Finally, the radiocarbon result of posthole F 265 is probably anecdotal, but certainly reflects the entire chronology of the site, which is also present at the other sites discussed here (see also Chapters 3.1 and 3.2).[2]

2.2.2   CHU Belle-Plaine

Ten charcoal samples from CHU Belle-Plaine were dispatched to Poznán, Poland, for analysis. All samples were taken from features and the goal was to test the contemporaneity of the two zones with circular pits identified during the excavations: the northern zone (N=7) and the southern one (N=3), of which the former zone also featured two burials and numerous small postholes.

The results show that both zones certainly were occupied simultaneously or perhaps somewhat alternatingly, for at least 200 years. This range is believed to be confined to a calibrated date of cal 1000 to 1200 CE. In fact, the oldest date (POZ-63021), taken from pit F 74, is slightly out of the proposed range, but this feature is situated in the center of an important concentration of circular pits and might mark the beginning of the occupation at this site. This series of ten radiocarbon dates is very limited in range and may point to a short occupation. In combination with the small quantities of features and material finds, it might represent a small habitation site linked to the function of these circular pits. The range for Belle-Plaine clearly falls within the Late Ceramic Age; its pottery finds belong to the Mamoran and Suazan Troumassoid subseries of Grande-Terre. Here we must refer to the radiocarbon dates obtained for the La Pointe des Châteaux peninsula and La Désirade by De Waal (2006), showing similar ceramic materials, as well as to those obtained for Anse à la Gourde (Hofman et al. 2001).

2.2.3   STEP Goyave

In order to catch the chronology of the pre-Columbian occupation of this site, ten charcoal samples were sent to Poznán. All samples were taken from anthropogenic features (pits and postholes) in order to obtain a reliable range of the occupation and to better place in time the ceramics taken from these pits. Just like La Pointe de Grande Anse, all results together represent a large range of about five centuries, which spans a calibrated period between CE 750 and 1250 at 2σ range. Only one date (POZ-75045), taken from charcoal of pit F 112, has not been taken into account for this proposed range. This date is much older and falls out of this range; however, the old-wood effect cannot be excluded here. It can be concluded that all dates are within the range of the Late Cedrosan Saladoid and Mamoran Troumassoid ceramic subseries or the Late Ceramic Age more generally.

2.2.4   Parking de Roseau

Eight charcoal samples have been sent to Poznán for radiocarbon dating, and with the two samples from the 2014 survey (dated at Queen's University in Belfast, Ireland), a total of ten samples has been dated for the Parking of Roseau. The samples were taken from the pits and postholes in order to date a well-restricted context in time and space. The main goal was not only to get a better grip of the occupation span but also to untangle the different activity zones (A–E), as defined after the excavation, and to date the ceramic sequence. Together, the results of the radiocarbon dates suggest a chronological range roughly between 700 and 900 BP when omitting the oldest and youngest dates (POZ-84383 and UBA-21587), of which the former may recall the old-wood effect. Nonetheless, this rather homogeneous range suggests a calibrated range at 2σ between cal 1100 and 1300 CE, or a "short" period of approximately 200 years, just like CHU Belle-Plaine. This range corresponds clearly to the Late Ceramic Age or the Troumassoid ceramic series, also attested for in the adjacent excavations by Richard (2004, 2005) and more recently by Le Lay (2013) and Bochaton et al. (2021).

2.3   Geomorphology and environment

Christophe Jorda

The archipelago of Guadeloupe consists of five islands and many small islets, divided into two main geological formations (see Figure 1.3). The island of Basse-Terre and the islets of Les Saintes represent the most recent inner volcanic belt, whereas Marie-Galante, Grande-Terre, and La Désirade can be attributed to the oldest outer volcanic belt (Lasserre 1978).

The island of Basse-Terre consists of a chain of volcanoes of which Mont Soufrière is still active. Sharp ridges and important river or gully systems characterize these mountains and they consist of thick volcanic layers or flows emitted by various volcanoes. These layers have been altered or eroded in the course of time (Figure 2.3). As the geological map shows, all sites are situated on outcrops of Pliocene volcanic debris that touches the sea, except for CHU Belle-Plaine. The latter is situated at the geological intersection of Basse-Terre and Grande-Terre, giving easy access to the Grand Cul-de-Sac Marin in the north. This lagoon is connected to Basse-Terre by a natural mangrove channel called the Rivière Salée. The other three sites are on the eastern façade of the volcanic ridge of Basse-Terre. Sainte-Claire and Roseau face Marie-Galante to the southeast and the southern edge of Grande-Terre to the northeast. From La Pointe de Grande Anse, situated in the very south of Basse-Terre, there is a spectacular view of Les Saintes.

2.3.1   *La Pointe de Grande Anse*

La Pointe de Grande Anse (LPGA) concerns a volcanic flow that drops into the sea. It is cut by the Grande Anse River, being the most western gully of the Trois-Rivières drainage system (Figure 2.3a). This gully and flow divide the western part of Trois-Rivières in the Anse des Pères to the east and the much larger Grande Anse to the west. The La Pointe de Grande Anse Pliocene flow consists of volcanic debris composed of lapilli and dacitic pumice (Pϱ1). The soil of the excavated area can be described as ferralitic but well drained. The volcanic flows in the Trois-Rivières area present themselves as an undulating hillscape, which was modified during colonial times to create optimal and accessible plantations. In this way, natural depressions and elevations were flattened out, creating a smoother hillscape. These depressions reveal most of the scattered material that can be attributed to the ancient walking surfaces, whereas the higher parts do not reveal A-Horizons anymore because of voluntary leveling. The absence of large boulders at the site is another aspect of the purging of the terrain for habitation (Habitation Marre and Poterie Fidelin), but can also result from the growing of sugarcane and bananas.

a.

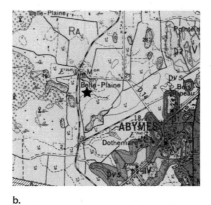

b.

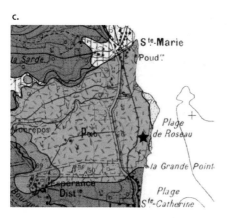

c.

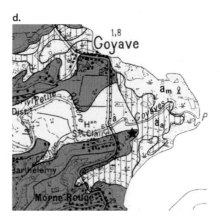

d.

Figure 2.3 Geology of the presented sites: (a) La Pointe de Grande Anse, (b) CHU Belle-Plaine, (c) STEP Goyave, and (d) Parking de Roseau (after Reynal de Saint-Michel 1966; Garrabé and Andreieff 1988).

Source: www.infoterre.brgm.fr

2.3.2   CHU Belle-Plaine

This site is situated on the littoral plain north of Les Abymes (also known as Belle-Plaine) in the western part of Grande-Terre (Figure 2.3b). This plain represents an intermediate or transition zone between the lagoon of Grand-Cul-de-Sac Marin in the west and the calcareous hillocks called Grands-Fonds in the east. This undulating plain consists of volcano-detrital matter that has been deposited between the islands. The pre-Columbian site is situated at a natural undulation or elevation of this plain at about 15 m above Mean Guadeloupe Level (NGG). To the south a gully is still visible in the landscape, which gathers much water during heavy rainfall.

To the north of the site there is a small karstic hillock, or *morne*, which, together with a few other hillocks, is part of the karstic hillscape of the Grands-Fonds. Beyond this hillock is a mangrove area that forms the source of the Belle-Plaine Creek, which today is canalized. This wetland area, called *taonaba* in the Kalinago language, leads towards the lagoon and contains many red and black halophyte mangrove (*Rhizophora*) trees. Higher up the creek, where the water is brackish (*icopoui*) or sweet (*ouloua*), one can find mahoes, pite, and reed and many different animal species (Barfleur 2002:43–46).

The large plain of Belle-Plaine has been planted with sugarcane and plowed since the first Europeans settled Pointe-à-Pitre by the end of the 17th century. At first, the original landscape was drained with ditches and with a tube-drainage system (see Briand 2012); more recently, the landscape was flattened with a bulldozer for better mechanized passage. This means that the ancient pre-Columbian surface has disappeared, at least in the higher parts of the landscape and, in most cases, the center of villages. This decapitation of the landscape can be traced in the depth of features such as pits, post molds, and burials, which most often do not surpass 20 cm in depth.

2.3.3   STEP Goyave

This site is situated upon a high *morne* that protrudes into the sea, called La Pointe de la Rivière de Goyave. This point is situated between the village of Goyave to the north and the beach of Anse de Sainte-Claire to the south. The Petite Rivière de Goyave runs along the northern flank of the same hillock and is bordered by plains and mangrove forests on its left bank; the right bank pertains to the *morne*. At much of this point a reef is present, obstructing the outflow of the river.

The northern part of Capesterre is characterized by a steep hillscape of volcanic flows, which has been eroded by rivers exposing the pre-Miocene deposits (I). The lava flows of the southern part of Basse-Terre are composed of Pliocene breccias of andesitic lava flows (qαb) (Figure 2.3c). The flows that reached the sea were eroded by the currents running from Marie-Galante. Over time this created cliffs, exposing their red color along the Capesterre coast and giving birth to hamlets such as Morne Rouge, to the south of Saint-Claire beach.

Interestingly, Father Raymond Breton (1665:431) noted in his French-Kalinago dictionary that the Kalinago called these red cliffs *ponócouboutou*, meaning "the hillock of red earth along the seaside of Capesterre." Next to the important pre-Columbian habitation site found at this *morne* (of which we do not know the total extension), it also features a sugar plantation which originated in the second half of the 17th century (Habitation Lagrange, later called Fond Val).

The excavations revealed the presence of pre-Columbian features and many colonial features, at least on the summit of the hill, including barracks of different sizes as well as a water mill constructed at its foot (see van den Bel et al. 2018b). The ancient walking surface has completely disappeared due to the early colonial occupation and subsequently by the sugarcane and banana cultivation; the sterile soils were reached rapidly during mechanical excavation (Briand 2013). Indeed, the continuous tilling and plowing of the surface must have disturbed the pre-Columbian surface. In more recent times, this mixed layer has been bulldozed away towards the flanks of the hillock. These events eventually secured the ancient water mill but did not save the pre-Columbian features.

2.3.4   Parking de Roseau

This site is at a point south of the village of Sainte-Marie and the Pont River overlooking the beach. Like Sainte-Claire, the hamlet of Roseau is part of the *mornes rouges* and features the same volcanic deposits (Figure 2.3d). The site probably covers numerous hectares, but additional surveying is necessary to detect its limits. However, rampant (illegal) construction makes it difficult to access this area.

The Parking de Roseau excavations comprised a very small part of the beach site but mainly the *morne* at about 5 m above Mean Guadeloupe Level (NGG). Today, the beach is entirely artificial and protected by numerous groins dating back to the 1960s and restored around 2016. The surroundings of Sainte-Marie were planted with sugarcane and during the 20th century with bananas. East of the national road one can also find the remnants of a railway that served to transport rum from the 19th-century Marquisat factory in Capesterre-Belle-Eau to the port of Goyave.

The embouchure of the Pont River represents a swampy area where rain and seawater stagnate because of the sandbars that block the access to it. According to local people, Roseau also features sweet water wells that rise from the rocky cliffs at various points where arrow reed, or *roseaux*, grows. Interestingly, the latter name is rather frequent as a toponym in the French Antilles and often refers to places of the earliest European settlement. One can find this expression as a place name also on Dominica and St. Lucia (Jesse 1966:55). According to Father Breton (1665:90), the reed, or *bouléoüa* in Kalinago, is used "to make the body of the arrow which carries the same name as the reed."

The beach at Parking de Roseau

At the foot of the cliffs at Parking de Roseau, the beach area was excavated by means of numerous trenches. It must be realized that we have not been able to study this area properly due to its high water level and the absence of a permanent draining system. Nonetheless, it was clear that the beach area, where previously a few 16th-century European objects had been found, represents an important stratified context to better comprehend the sequence of different phases of human occupation upon the plateau. The supposed sequence of more or less sandy layers related to the marine and lagoon environments, in combination with the marshy area of the river, might have captured objects or other information mirroring the human occupation of the plateau (see Figure 2.1). Therefore, it was necessary to study the geomorphological evolution of this part of the Capesterre littoral. In addition to our trenches, the results of previous research executed during the initial Inrap survey (Serrand et al. 2014) were added in order to propose a schematic evolution of the beach at this site during the last millennium.

In addition, this study should also be understood in a larger framework focusing on the adaptation of humans to varying sea levels, about 1 m lower one millennium ago (Anderson et al. 2010, 2014; Burney and Pigott-Burney 1994; Kemp et al. 2011; Klosowska et al. 2004). Figure 2.4 shows the actual situation of Roseau beach, with the keys situated at approximately 50 m at large. This reef probably contributed to the construction and protection of the beach, and it is believed that this feature played a significant role in the Amerindians' choice of the *morne* of Roseau as their settlement location.

The sea level rise in the Lesser Antilles since the last Postglacial (after 18,000 BP) is mostly extrapolated by research conducted in the Mexican Gulf, the southern littoral of the United States, and, to a lesser extent, by punctual research in the Antillean reefs. According to these studies, notwithstanding the complex tectonics of the region, the Holocene sea level rise (since 10,000 BP) of the Mexican Gulf and the Antilles is considered to have been similar to those conceived for other parts of the world (Anderson et al. 2010; Blum et al. 2003).

In detail, however, the Caribbean region shows a few particularities concerning the last millennia of the sea level rise because the stabilization of this level is considered to have been somewhat later than elsewhere and notably the last centuries BP (Feller et al. 1992; Milliken et al. 2008). Indeed, recent studies show a still lower marine level throughout the

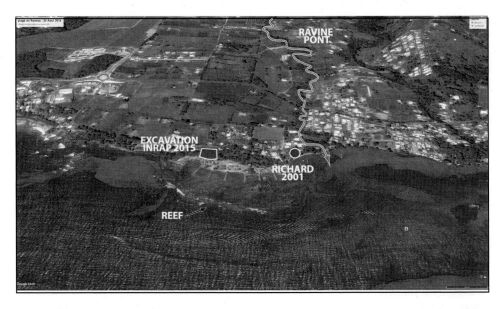

Figure 2.4 Bird's-eye view of Roseau beach.
Source: www.Géoportail.fr

first millennium CE, which is not the case in, for example, Europe, the Atlantic, the Pacific, or the Indian Ocean (outside the active tectonic zones), where a full stop of the marine sea level rise has been attested for at the beginning of the first millennium CE. Therefore, we may identify three phases during the Holocene:

(1) A first phase of a rapid sea level rising until approximately 5000 BCE of several meters attaining −4.00 to −5.00 m;
(2) A second phase of a slower sea level rise until about 3000 to 2000 BCE in which the sea reached a level of −1.50 to −2.00 m below the present level;
(3) A third and last phase of this final sea level rise slowing down in the Mexican Gulf and the Antilles.

Despite the fact that the data for this period are more abundant albeit also heterogeneous, there is general consent that a progressive and linear sea level rise is involved. However, there are two curves showing the evolution of this rise: one is based on the dating of coral and the other one on that of littoral peat. The curve that is discussed here is based on the latter material. This curve, based on vegetal matter, has a less important deviation and inspires more confidence than the other one. Based on this dataset, mean sea level during the Late Ceramic Age occupation of the Parking de Roseau site (cal 1100–1300 CE) (see Figure 2.2) must have been 50 cm lower than the actual sea level. This notion is crucial when discussing the evolution of the Roseau beach, and it is necessary to date the different beach layers of which only the Amerindian ones have been dated correctly.

During the excavations ten trenches were dug perpendicular to the cliff in order to establish a link between the volcanic substratum and the marine or marsh deposits (see Figures 1.5 and 2.5a-b). The first goal was to establish a relationship between the Amerindian

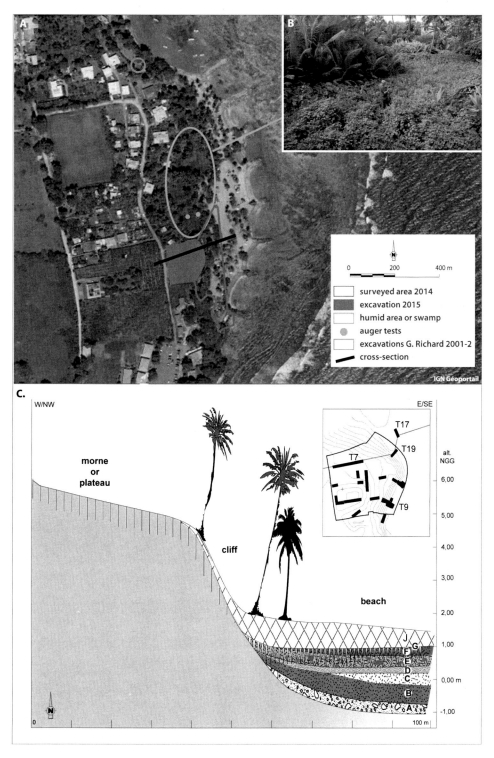

Figure 2.5 General plan of Roseau beach: (a) plan of various excavations, (b) photograph of the swamp area, and (c) schematic cross-section of Parking de Roseau with different layers (A–G). C. Jorda, Inrap.

occupation upon the plateau and the evolution of the littoral. The second goal was to distinguish one or multiple marine transgressions. Three trenches (S 5, 6, and 9) have been selected to serve as a reference sequence, which has been associated to the five trenches (TR 15–19) studied during the 2014 Inrap survey. In this manner, we were able to establish seven phases (Phases A to G) that reflect the evolution of Roseau beach (Figure 2.5c).

Lithostratigraphic description of the trenches

S 9. This trench provided an almost complete sequence of the beach development or evolution (Figure 2.6a). During the 2014 survey, TR 19 was dug approximately 10 m away from S 9, but slightly more towards the cliff, thus revealing more colluvium. However, both sequences were most certainly complementary. Simon Troelstra (Free University of Amsterdam, The Netherlands) scanned two layers (US 4 and 2) representing the base and summit of Phase C.[3] At its base, Phase A revealed very fine-layered black and red sand at about −0.50 and 0.00 m NGG; it reflects a relatively rapid sea level rise without containing any colluvium from the cliffs.

Indeed, from 0.00 to 0.30 m NGG, Phase B is composed of volcanic boulders and small angular pebbles within a grey, sandy context. It is believed that sea level stabilized as the marine sands are enriched with detritic material being deposited there because of the hustling of the volcanic substratum of the plateau. The presence and degree of the angular blocks and boulders in front of the plateau represents erosion by the sea (swash and backwash). At the summit of this deposit, at about 0.30 m NGG, a few Amerindian sherds and consumed conch shells were found (see Chapter 4).

Phase C, framed between 0.30 and 0.50 m NGG, is composed mainly of grey to yellow-colored coarse sands containing much debris of *Halimedas* (macroalgae). The macroalgae clearly testify to the presence of an emerged beach much resembling the beach at Roseau. A few sherds and some consumed shells have been found in these deposits. Troelstra's scan confirmed this interpretation, revealing a large input of volcanic sand (erosion) linked to a few faunal remains such as foraminifera (*Cibicides*), which are common in the Mexican Gulf and Caribbean, as well as an urchin spine.

The subsequent Phases D and E could not be distinguished clearly and these deposits have been grouped as one. Between 0.50 and 0.75 m NGG they reveal a grey-colored sandy ooze representing an important modification of the local environment. The role of the sea as a littoral constructing agent is diminishing in such a way that clays (more or less silty) are deposited on the beach. This phenomenon can be interpreted as an invasion of lagoon sediments suggesting the appearance of a barrier between the sea and the beach. This supposed barrier might well be the actual reef nowadays situated a few hundred meters at large, given that there are no sandbars in this part of the Guadeloupean archipelago (see Figure 2.4).

Returning to the discussion of the local mean sea level, it should be noted that, notwithstanding tectonic difficulties (subsidence or the eustatic sea level), most researchers agree that the postglacial sea level rise reached actual zero and that there is no positive sea level. However, current ideas about the subduction of the Caribbean volcanic arc with the American plates do not provide entirely sufficient answers because the recent phenomena of subsidence or resurrection of the islands situated in this important tectonically active area are poorly known (Feuillet et al. 2002; Samper et al. 2007). Therefore, we can only suppose that the sea level rise around Basse-Terre complies with the relative marine level curve of the Mexican Gulf. It is therefore plausible that sea level stabilized about 50 cm below the sandy ooze (Phases D and E). The sea had less impact on the construction of this part of the littoral, and in this way the small Pont River became the main player regarding the local morphogenesis.

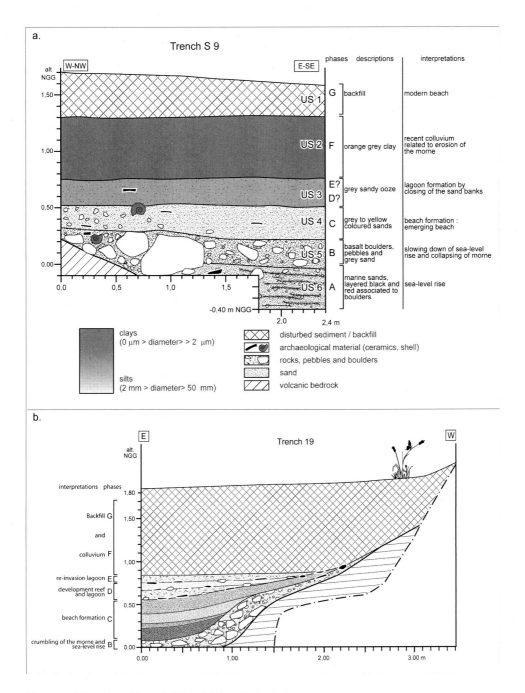

Figure 2.6 Drawing of Trench S 9 and TR 9. C. Jorda, Inrap.

Roseau beach became a salty marsh, or *salina*, enriched with clays and silts coming down from the gully and occasionally some marine sands, too, surpassing the barrier.

The subsequent Phase F, situated between 0.75 and 1.30 m NGG, consists of grey-orange clay, which represents colluvial material from the plateau a few meters higher up. Although reliable chronological elements are missing for Trench S 9, Trench TR 19 allows for a better comprehension of the entire sequence (Figure 2.5b). In fact, it was in the middle of the oozy layers of Phase D that we encountered Amerindian and European archaeological material as well as a horse bone dated to 254 ± 25 BP (UBA-25187), which calibrated range at 2σ between cal 1631 and 1670 CE (see Table 1.3).

S 5. Situated in the northern part of the excavated beach area, the sequence encountered in Trench S 5 allows for characterization of the local geoarchaeological development as we were able to identify former walking surfaces (Figure 2.7a). Phase B revealed angular boulders and small volcanic pebbles associated with sandy deposits of marine origin, which were recorded between −0.50 and −0.30 m NGG. This phase also represents cliff erosion associated with a slowing down or partially stabilized marine level. It is topped with yellow, laminated coarse sand containing *Halimeda* debris between −0.30 and −0.05 m NGG, which corresponds to a submerged beach (Phase C). At the summit of these sands, one observes a thin layer with some Amerindian ceramics associated with charcoal particles and shell-food remains, probably corresponding to a beach visited by Amerindians that may be linked to the Troumassoid occupation of the plateau.

Phase D has been well identified in this trench, as one observes a deflated layer between −0.05 and +0.50 m NGG. At its base it shows a dark grey, slightly sandy ooze that develops into silty clay at the top. One must also note here that the quantity of archaeological material increases from the bottom towards the top of this phase. The top actually shows slight pedogenetic development revealing submergence, at least seasonally, of this area. It contains some archaeological material. We believe that it reflects a rapid change from a marshy back fan to a lagoon. As attested for in Trench S 9, the stabilization of the sea level and the keys at large are probably the two reasons behind the shutting off of the Roseau beach and its subsequent isolation from marine dynamics. The top of these deposits at +0.50 m NGG reflects an uplift with regard to the sea level and explains the trigger of the pedogenetics visible in the profile. From this point onwards, it represents a beach exclusively supplied with clayey sediment and fresh water from the springs and the Pont River. During this period, the Amerindians visited or even occupied the beach area as evidenced by the artifacts at the top of this phase.

Phase E, still being a marshy environment, is made up of dark grey ooze that is heavily disturbed by crab holes (*Cardisoma guanhumi*). The presence of sea almonds and coconuts in the sediment suggests that this is an extremely recent formation. Concerning these two phases, Troelstra's observations point again in the same direction, showing a predominance of oozy marshy formations for Phase D, associated to the top of the profile (Phase E) and consisting of sand and small pebbles reflecting the closing of the lagoon and its enrichment with fine colluvial sediment. This phase is sealed again off by the backfill or embankment of Phase G, corresponding to the actual beach modifications, perhaps dating back to the 1960s.

Trench 17, excavated during the 2014 survey, yielded Phases B to G. Five samples taken from this trench were scanned by Troelstra of which four were taken from Phase C or the emergence of Roseau beach. From bottom to top, he describes rolled volcanic sand associated with freshwater foraminifera, followed by a decrease of volcanic (black) sand and an increase of marine shell sand in combination with a spectrum of species living in relatively shallow water (>30 m) as well as some ostracod debris (seed shrimp) of which the carbonated armor does not withstand acid environments. It appears as if the beach started to stabilize and that the input of material from the slopes diminished. At the summit of Phase C, Troelstra describes a calm environment with less sand but containing some *Halimeda* detritus, small gastropods, and ostracods. This assemblage can be interpreted as purely marine,

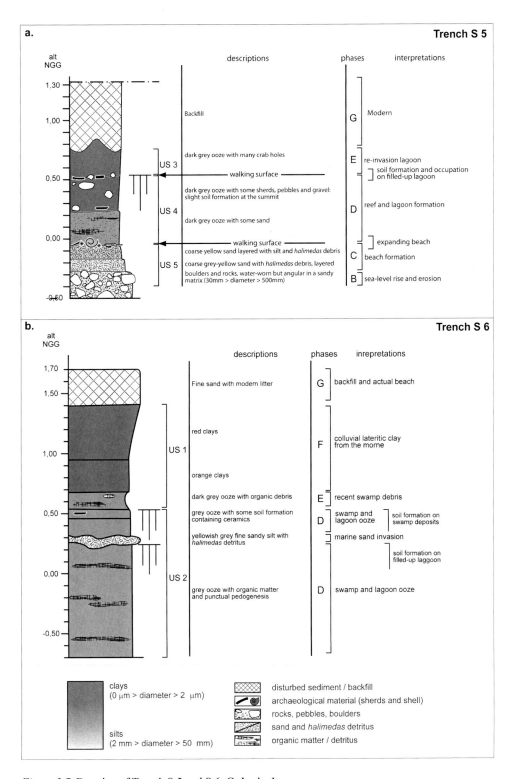

Figure 2.7 Drawing of Trench S 5 and S 6. C. Jorda, Inrap.

but the relatively calm environment suggests that it could also be associated with the ongo-ing closing of this area by the reef. The closure becomes complete in the following Phase D. Troelstra also detected *Halimeda* at the top of the profile, corresponding to Phase E, but they appear to have been found in a disturbed context. Nonetheless, this entirely corresponds to a lagoon development and the full stop of marine input.

S 6. This last trench is more problematic because we were not able to identify Phases A, B, and C (Figure 2.7b). At its base, between −0.70 and +0.25 m NGG, the trench yielded grey ooze with organic debris that can be attributed by default to Phase D. This trench was not dug directly at the foot of the cliff and, as a result, it does not feature the geological links with the cliff, cliff erosion (Phase B) and the beach bar formation (Phase C). In fact, this trench pro-vides information only about the dynamics of the Pont River embouchure to the north. How-ever, one can imagine it remains highly probable that this marshy environment at the mouth of the Pont River was cleaned through its principal discharge channel when the sea occasionally came in. Whatever the case may be, at +0.25 m NGG, when sea level had stabilized, we note the punctual invasion of marine sands to fossilize the oozy sediment, which can be associated with phenomena of strong marine activity. Above and until +0.50 m NGG, silty clays have been deposited, which affirms the continuous clogging of the marshy area, finished with the soil formation that was just described for the top of Phase D in Trench S 5.

Phase E is represented by another more recent swamp invasion, of vegetal matter such as that of the before-mentioned sea almonds. Finally, Phase F developed from +0.65 to +1.40 m NGG and concerns the reddish to orange clays reflecting the erosion of the red lateritic cliffs, or *mornes rouges*.

Synthesis

Although our stratigraphic data are coherent per phase, it is true that some aspects of our interpretation can be viewed differently and certainly need additional research in the future. First of all, the difficult terrain conditions did not facilitate the investigations. All our mechanical trenches stopped at about −0.50 m NGG for technical and security reasons, meaning that we were not able to perceive older phenomena. Secondly, we also wished to radiocarbon date each phase but unfortunately did not retrieve sufficiently qualified material due to thousands of crab holes. From a paleogeographical point of view, however, the data obtained during the 2014 survey associated to our selection of three trenches dug during the 2015 excavations permit us to propose this synthesis of the littoral development at Roseau beach. The main ingredients of this evolution are: (1) the sea level rise, (2) the role of the Pont River, and (3) the development of the marsh. Although it needs further fine-tuning, we are now able to present a cinematic overview of this development from the transgression identified as Phase A until the most recent modifications of Roseau beach (Phase G).

Phase A (Figure 2.8) represents a much smaller littoral than today. Deposits of this first phase of marine transgression have only been observed in Trench S 9. It contained laminated sands without any material deriving from the slope, suggesting a relatively rapid swell. Con-sidering its altitude (above −0.50 m NGG), it is highly probable that this transgression is posterior to the end of the first millennium CE as suggested by the sea level rise curves in the Mexican Gulf and the Antilles.

Phase B (Figure 2.8), from 0.00 m NGG onwards, corresponds to the final stabilization of the marine transgression because we are at the actual zero NGG and, historically, the sea did not rise higher than today. The angular boulders and pebbles encountered here reflect erosion of the plateau, depositing detritic material on the beach. Only the blocks and sand are left behind, but we assume that lateritic clays also came down to the beach and were taken by the sea. To the north, the humid zone is not attested for in the trenches yet; hence, we should realize that this area had been under water, whereas its associated sediment is to be found at a deeper level.

Phase C (Figure 2.8), situated between 0.00 and 0.50 m NGG, corresponds to the reinforcement of the marine dynamics and the emerging of a beach. This is confirmed by the grain size and yellow color of the sand as well as the *Halimeda* debris. The humid zone is now retracting under the influence of marine incursions and it is highly probable that a channel was to be present separating the sea from the marshy zone in the north.

Phase D (Figure 2.8) marks a major change for the Roseau beach. Dated by ceramics from 12th century CE, it yielded oozy clays spreading over the entire beach of the previous phase, suggesting the existence of a lagoon environment. This oozy sediment is the result of suspended material, deriving from springs but also originating from the Pont River. This sediment is referenced between 0.50 and 0.75 m NGG, thus above the actual sea level, and it shows some soil formation, suggesting that it was not always or punctually underwater. The absence of sand for this beach phase also suggests an absence of marine influence to be associated with reef formation at large (see Figure 2.4). In this manner, the beach was perfectly protected from the sea and stayed under the influence of the Pont River. The northern humid zone of Roseau beach was now subjected to clogging, as seen in the sections of S 5 and S 6. It is in this context that we identified the Amerindian presence at the beach that clearly postdates the Troumassoid village excavated at the plateau. It might represent the beach that was frequented by the Caribes who were sighted by Columbus' crew in 1493.

Phase E (Figure 2.8) is without doubt post-Columbian, since sea almonds were imported by the Europeans from Asia. The clogging of the back-fan continued and this is visible in the most southern trenches of the 2014 survey. Apparently, the reef still played an important role as a littoral barrier, preventing the sea from reaching the island coast.

Phase F (Figure 2.8) is the most recent phase showing major changes. A thick colluvial layer of lateritic sediment, probably corresponding to intensified activities on the plateau, covered the beach and, at the same time, another beach developed at Roseau. We believe that the lateritic deposits are related to the agricultural development in the late 19th century (production of bananas), whereas the development of new sandy beach may have been caused by the disappearance of the reef in combination with new marine incursions. Perhaps the course of the Pont River was modified, too, but additional surveying is needed here. The humid northern zone is now isolated from the sea and entirely filled up.

Phase G, the last one (see Figure 2.9), corresponds to the present-day situation. It is the result of human redevelopment of the beach with rumble backfill and groin construction in order to protect the beach from further marine erosion.

Conclusion

The phases reconstructed here clearly reflect the littoral development of Roseau beach during the last millennium. The marine deposits found at the bottom of the trenches, below −0.70 m NGG, postdate cal 1000 CE according to the regional curves. We clearly identified the last moments of the stabilization or flattening of the sea level curve related to the postglacial sea rise.

From a geomorphological point of view, the sequence of Phases A–C is clear: Phase A represents sand related to the sea level rise, Phase B shows colluvial matter related to the stabilization at approximately 0.00 m NGG, and Phase C corresponds to the construction

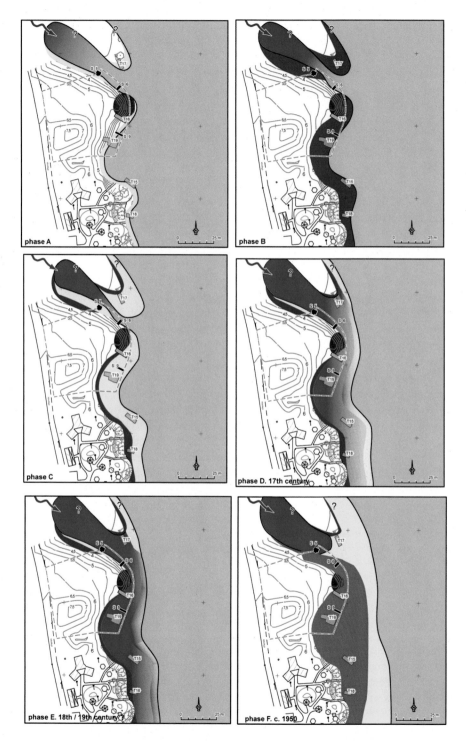

Figure 2.8 Evolution of various phases (A–F) of coastal development at Parking de Roseau beach.
    C. Jorda, Inrap.

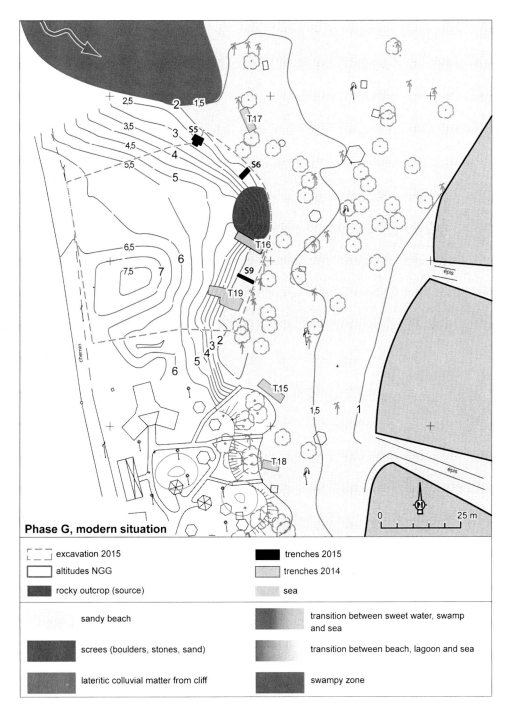

Figure 2.9 Overview of the latest phase (G). C. Jorda, Inrap.

of an emerged beach. Then, however, the landscape changed considerably as Roseau beach turned into a lagoon. The stabilization of the sea level rise and the resurrection of the reef at large probably protected this new environment from the sea. Subsequently, the Roseau area has been subjected to more terrestrial influences, notably the Pont River.

Considering the Amerindian occupation excavated at the plateau, we must conclude that this occupation is not clearly attested for at the beach area. Despite the presence of a few ceramic fragments found in the sediment, attributed to Phases A and B, these elements are not sufficiently present or characteristic to fully appreciate them. A walking surface could be identified at the top of Phase C (S 5), representing the emerged beach. It contained some pottery sherds, charcoal and shells, which might reflect the debris of the occupation excavated at the plateau, but these elements remain undated. In fact, the only true occupation identified at the beach is Phase D. The ceramics and dated horse bone propose an occupation during the 17th century, and we cannot link these data to the Troumassoid village excavated at the plateau. The artifacts related to this Troumassoid village probably washed away, are scarce, or can be found only in deeper layers, which we did not reach due to the reasons mentioned. We can, however, imagine for this period a marine level between −1.00 and −0.50 m NGG with a large beach away from the actual plateau. If we could have observed the gradient of the plateau below the studied formations, we might have synthesized a littoral pertaining to the 12th century and been able to evaluate both the distance from the site to the shore as well as the dimensions and shape of the humid area to the north.

Notes

1   The so-called 5–10% rule is accepted in metropolitan Nouvelle Aquitaine et Outre-mer (NAOM), one of the five interregions of Inrap. However, other interregions have different percentages, and because French Guiana is under NAOM administration, this rule has been applied (uncritically) to the DOM.
2   Burial F 571 is not discussed here as this burial pertains to HL 3, which is not discussed in Chapter 3. This burial is also part of a cluster and its date is recent.
3   Here, we would like to thank Simon Troelstra for his quick scan of the samples considering the diatoms.

3 Site level

In the Lesser Antilles, large-scale excavations opening up an extensive area to map features have been common ground since the excavations at Golden Rock (St. Eustatius) in the early 1980s, but remain scarce. This is probably due to the lack of implementation of the (northwestern, continental) European excavation methodology, or perhaps tradition, in the Antilles, which is shared by the French and Dutch. Secondly, mechanized compliance archaeology is only present within the French and Dutch Antilles (Bonaire, St. Eustatius, and Saba) and in Puerto Rico. Without doubt, the excavations at Golden Rock have opened the eyes of many archaeologists working in the Lesser Antilles to excavate on a larger scale.

When uncovering large surfaces, the subsoil reveals dark-colored spots or features, which represent ancient dug and refilled holes or pits. These holes and pits had been dug to place wooden posts to construct houses, bury the dead, deposit offerings, stock food items, and discard litter. Other features, such as hearths and firing pits, canals, gutters, water- and soil-extraction pits, and ring trenches, do occur at prehistoric sites, but are considered less common. Among the hundreds of features to be found during an excavation, only a certain number have probably functioned simultaneously, representing one particular moment or occupation phase. Villages that have persisted over a few hundred years usually are represented by hundreds to thousands of features, of which only the features within the excavated area are studied. Unraveling this occupational history is challenging, as habitation areas may have been abandoned and reoccupied, or reused as plazas, gardens, and even burial grounds. It is important to state that one must be aware that not all features are to be found and therefore not all occupations will be recognized within an excavated area.

The stripping of archaeological sites, or *décapage* by mechanical shovels, was introduced in the Antilles by the University of Leiden in the late 1980s at Golden Rock, prior to the extension of the airport of St. Eustatius (Versteeg 1989). These excavations were supervised by Aad Versteeg and Kees Schinkel (1992), yielding for the first time the spatial layout of pre-Columbian features and the first identification of "turtle-shaped" Late Saladoid house plans. The first house plans on Guadeloupe were found during the joint DRAC and Leiden University excavations at Anse à la Gourde in the late 1990s, supervised by André Delpuech and Corinne L. Hofman (Delpuech et al. 2001b). This site yielded imbricated circular house plans with numerous burials also dated to the Late Saladoid period (see Morsink 2006). Similar house plans have been found during the excavations at the DRC project (Etrich 2002; Etrich et al. 2003) (see Table 3.1).[1]

Archaeological house plans remain difficult to identify in the field when one is faced with hundreds of features. The larger or central postholes are usually easily detected, but the surrounding posts, often dug in more superficially as wall posts, remain more difficult to untangle and may even have disappeared due to Historic Age and more recent plowing (see

DOI: 10.4324/9781003181651-3

Table 3.1 Overview of house locations on Guadeloupe.

Site	HL	Dimensions	Surface m²	Central posts	Rings	Reference
Moulin à Eau	N	9 x 9	81	2	1	Mestre et al. 2001
Allée Dumanoir	BP 5	11 x 11	121	2	1	Etrich et al. 2003
Allée Dumanoir	BP 6	13 x 13	169	2	2	Etrich et al. 2003
Allée Dumanoir	BP 7	9 x 9	81	0	1	Etrich et al. 2003
Allée Dumanoir	BP 8	13 x 13	169	2	1	Etrich et al. 2003
Allée Dumanoir	BP 9	9 x 8	72	2	1	Etrich et al. 2003
Allée Dumanoir	BP 10	6 x 6	36	2	1	Etrich et al. 2003
Allée Dumanoir	BP 12	10 x 10	100	2	1	Etrich et al. 2003
Allée Dumanoir	BP 13	13 x 13	169	2	1	Etrich et al. 2003
Anse à la Gourde	S 1	11 x 7	77	2	2	Morsink 2006
Anse à la Gourde	S 3	10 x 7	70	2	1	Morsink 2006
Anse à la Gourde	S 4	8 x 2	16	1	2	Morsink 2006
Anse à la Gourde	S 6	11 x 11	121	0	2	Morsink 2006
Anse à la Gourde	S 8	10 x 8	80	4	1	Morsink 2006
Anse à la Gourde	S 10	9 x 7	63	4	1	Morsink 2006
Anse à la Gourde	S 17	18 x 18	324	1	3	Morsink 2006
Anse à la Gourde	S 18	18 x 18	324	2	2	Morsink 2006
Anse à la Gourde	S 20	10 x 10	100	4	1	Morsink 2006
Anse à la Gourde	S 21	20 x 18	360	2	2	Morsink 2006
La Pointe de Grande Anse	1a	12 x 14	168	4	1	van den Bel et al. 2009
La Pointe de Grande Anse	1b	16 x 14	224	1	2	van den Bel et al. 2009
La Pointe de Grande Anse	2	17 x 14	238	4	1	van den Bel et al. 2009
La Pointe de Grande Anse	3	11 x 11	121	2	1	van den Bel et al. 2009
CHU Belle-Plaine	1	11 x 11	121	4	1	van den Bel et al. 2016
STEP Goyave	1	11 x 10	111	8	x	van den Bel et al. 2017
Parking de Roseau	1	12 x 12	144	10	x	van den Bel et al. 2018a
Parking de Roseau	2	15 x 12	180	10	x	van den Bel et al. 2018a
Parking de Roseau	3	12 x 7	84	12	x	van den Bel et al. 2018a

STEP Goyave). Secondly, the shape of a house plan also remains challenging to apprehend when one does not know what to look for: round houses, square ones, two, three, or eight central posts? Did the original inhabitants also have houses on stilts? Eventually, we decided that restricted areas with many postholes and other house-related features, such as circular pits and burials, should be considered a possible house location (HL) when a clear house plan is lacking. These locations probably represented habitation areas in which the basic house configuration cannot be reconstructed due to the erection of multiple houses or extensions on approximately the same spot, creating a palimpsest (see Mans 2012:64, Fig. 3.17).

Another general feature problem is the interpretation of pits—if visible—with complete vessel deposits. Due to soil chemistry of the volcanic soils of Basse-Terre, human bone does not preserve and despite its absence we suspect these pits represent inhumation graves, as witnessed by the morphology of these pits and rare cases of burials in which human bone has been preserved. Chemical analysis of soil samples is an alternative and cheap manner to attest for the presence of bone in these pits (see the phosphor analysis at Parking de Roseau).

In this chapter, we wish to discuss the main features of a habitation site: houses, burials, and circular pits. The combination of these features can be considered as characteristic of pre-Columbian habitation sites reflecting the main unit or house location of (large) villages. Midden areas also play an important role in villages but such waste areas have not been identified during our excavations and tend to be more visible or identifiable on Grande-Terre, where the calcareous soils have better preserved the faunal and shell remains. In addition, continuous plowing may have erased all traces of such middens, which usually manifest themselves as small elevations in the landscape.

3.1   Houses and house locations

Martijn M. van den Bel

The reconstructed house plans are made up by the regular alignment or configuration of posthole features. These plans are to believed the "imprint" of what is left of the house within the subsoil. The features represent the holes in which the wooden posts have been placed ("negative," or below ground level, house foundations) in order to erect the (central) framework, walls, and roof constructions ("positive" house structure, part elevated above the ground). The elevated part remains difficult to reconstruct based solely on the morphology and spatial distribution of the postholes, but attempts have been made by using ethnographic analogies (see Schinkel 1992; Righter 2002b; Samson 2010, 2013; Hofman and Hoogland 2012).

In some cases it has not been possible to reconstruct a definite house plan. Therefore, the less specific house locations will be presented per site. First, however, we need to define two types of postholes, which are found at habitation sites in general, but which date not necessarily simultaneously. This fact, as we shall see, may be the result of architectural traditions (Saladoid *vs* Troumassoid) shifting over time and/or varying house types or functions (dwelling place *vs* activity place). The first type of posthole, or Type A, can be observed at excavation level as a large oval-shaped one measuring generally more than 50 cm in width, 60 cm in length, and deeper than 80 cm (Figure 3.1). They may attain sizes reaching 120×160 cm with a depth of 1.80 cm! When adding the thickness of the removed topsoil, these postholes surpass easily two meters, or about seven feet, in depth. In order to reach such a depth, the hole is generally large enough to fit a person and features most often a step, revealing a holster shape when sectioned. These deeper and larger holes are suspected to bear larger and longer posts representing the central part or framework of the house. We excavated four central ones organized in a square (La Pointe de Grande Anse) and eight in a circle (STEP Goyave). Interestingly, this large type of posthole was not encountered at CHU Belle-Plaine and Parking de Roseau.

The second type of posthole, or Type B, is smaller. At excavation level, this type of feature does not surpass 50 cm in diameter and does not exceed 50 cm in depth either.

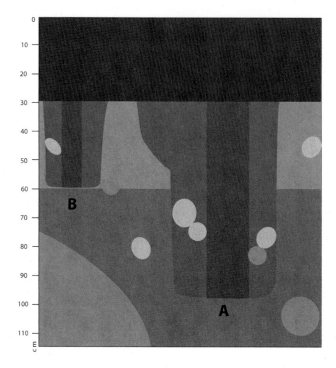

Figure 3.1 Posthole types A and B. Drawing by M. van den Bel, Inrap.

This type of posthole was clearly identified as part of a circle surrounding the central framework at La Pointe de Grande Anse (HL 2). Both types contain pebbles and blocks, which were used to fill up the hole, but were also used to corner the post in the hole, or *calage*, possibly for architectural reasons (position, direction, angles, etc.). The walls of the postholes are straight and the features have a flat bottom; all other kinds of holes, often being very irregular, are, in my opinion, anomalies. Often the location of the actual post (usually 10 to 15 cm in diameter) within the hole can be identified. The burned or rotten post can most easily be recognized. The location of the posthole, however, is less evident when rocks and ceramics are lacking in the fill and the hole left by the post has been back-filled with the same sediment; soil inversion is not observed in the fill of the hole (Figure 3.2).

3.1.1 *La Pointe de Grande Anse*

This excavation yielded 211 features attributable to the pre-Columbian era (Table 3.2). Most of the features are concentrated on the longitudinal summit of the volcanic flow (southeast to northwest). The spatial distribution of the features revealed four house locations where burials, postholes, and pits are clustered (Figure 3.3). Only HL 1 and 2 will be discussed here because radiocarbon samples were taken from these HLs. The third HL, also situated around a burial cluster, did not provide associated postholes of both Type A and Type B.

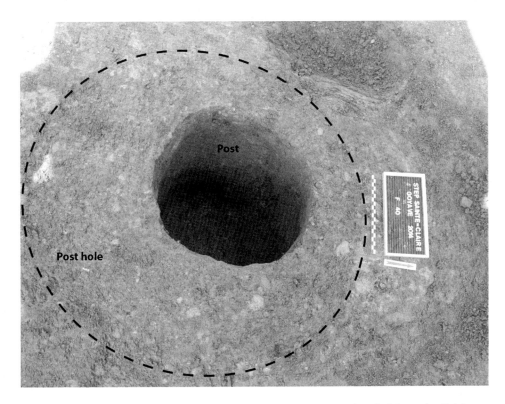

Figure 3.2 Excavated post F 40 and nonexcavated posthole fill (Type B). Photo by M. van den Bel, Inrap.

Table 3.2 Overview of features per site.

Site	Postholes	Postholes (large)	Pits	Burials	Hearths
La Pointe de Grande Anse	150	25	14	16	0
CHU Belle-Plaine	126	0	34	2	10
STEP Goyave	59	19	28	0	0
Parking de Roseau	143	0	32	1	0

House Location 1

This complex house location is situated at the longitudinal summit of the site, slightly to the north of HL 2 (Figure 3.3). HL 1 is represented by a concentration of Type A and B postholes and a cluster of burials. When compared to HL 2, discussed later, this HL has a much higher feature density, blurring the precise identification of the house plan. This is probably due to rebuilding of a later house at nearly the same spot of the first construction, named a "house trajectory" by Alice Samson (2010:7). This has resulted in a "cloud" of posts representing a palimpsest, a typical element of pre-Columbian multicomponent habitation sites in the Lesser Antilles (see Delpuech et al. 2001b).

When compared to HL 2, we consider that the first or oldest plan (HL 1a) of HL 1 consists of four large central posts of which one is probably located outside the excavation perimeter

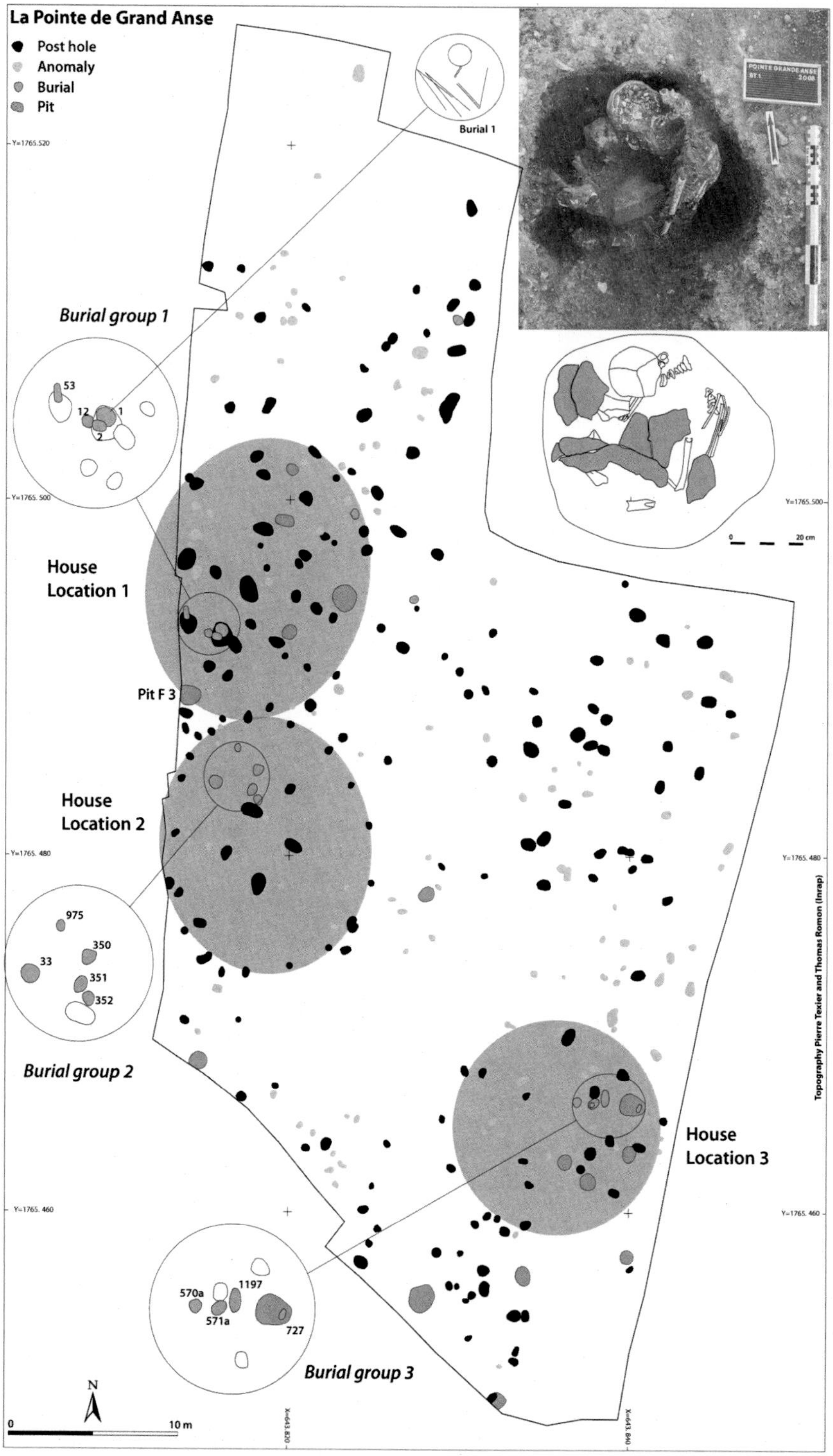

Figure 3.3 House locations and burials at La Pointe de Grande Anse.

Topography and drawing by P. Texier, T. Romon and M. van den Bel, Inrap.

(Figure 3.4). The additional off-center post could be posthole F 210. Its outer ring is touching HL 2 in the south and covers nearly 200 m². In the second stage, the central framework was extended by five posts of which one (F 8b) sections a burial (F 53) and one post was replaced (F 7). The outer ring was extended to the north and its surface was thereby enlarged (HL 1a "extended"). Another outer ring is visible (HL 1b), but no central posts could be ascribed to this arc, which may be an indication for a secondary function of this configuration. They may even have functioned as another extension to HL 1a or 1b. The rebuilding or reconstruction of this house is confirmed by the sectioning of Burial 1, the position of Burial 2 on top of a posthole, and the presence of posthole fills without archaeological material evidencing the first installation at this site.

House Location 2

This house location is exemplary and was recognized in the field (Figure 3.3). Such a "clean" house plan may be considered a rarity in the Lesser Antilles as most house plans are hidden within the clouds of postholes (see HL 1). HL 2 measures 14×17 m and covers a surface of 238 m², consisting of four large central postholes, one off-center posthole, and an outer peripheral circle of at least 17 smaller postholes (Figure 3.4). The four central posts are situated in the middle of the outer circle and form a rectangle of 2.7×2.7 m. The fifth central post is situated 2.5 m to the northeast of the rectangle. The function of this post is probably governed by a particular roof construction, but may be posterior too. The posts of the outer circle are separated by 5 m intervals. Archaeological material was found in abundance in the fills of the central postholes, assigning this house location to a later phase of occupation, which is stressed by its "off-side" position. Interestingly, in the northwestern quarter of the house, five burial pits (one of which contained two individuals) were found grouped together, suggesting that the house and the burials could be contemporaneous.

3.1.2 CHU Belle-Plaine

This excavation yielded 126 features. They have been interpreted as postholes and attributed to the pre-Columbian period (see Table 3.2). About one-third of these postholes are concentrated in the northern zone, constituting a house location with two burials and surrounded by numerous circular pits (Figure 3.5). The average dimensions of these Type B postholes are 32 cm in diameter and 31 cm in depth, suggesting small or light constructions. Holster-shaped holes have also been detected (F 106) and may suggest the presence of a more solid construction. The southern zone is somehow void of postholes, which may be due to its more elevated position, which was flattened, leaving visible the deeper circular pits only.

The house location can easily be spotted, but its configuration is difficult to assess. Despite the low density of postholes, the tentative HL in the northern zone is represented by a circle of posts covering approximately 125 m², having four central posts (F 68, F 93, F 94, and F 115), which form a square area that covers about 25 m² and might represent a small wooden construction too. Within the roundish HL, two burials are present as well as a few circular pits, such as pit F 74, which yielded the oldest radiocarbon date, suggesting this construction was built upon (or next to) a former activity zone.

There is another intermediate zone of exclusively small Type B postholes, possibly stakes, between the northern and southern concentration of pits, but their alignment is irregular. The function of this cluster of postholes is hard to interpret, but several short alignments oriented

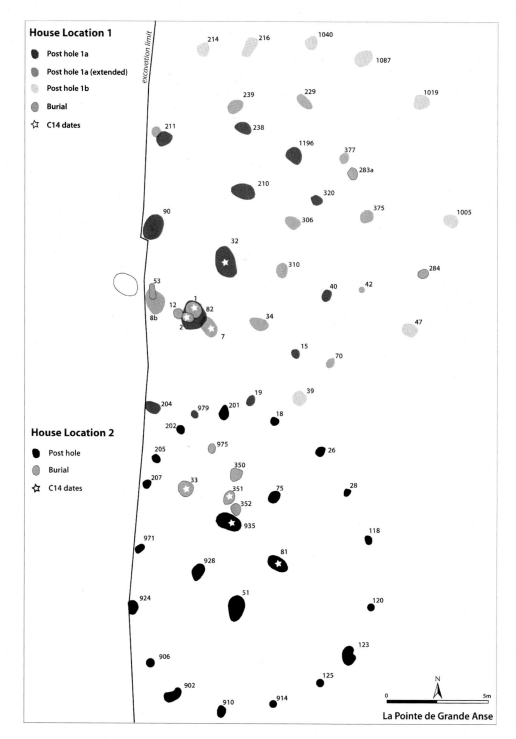

Figure 3.4 HL 1 and HL 2 at La Pointe de Grande Anse.

Topography and drawing by P. Texier, T. Romon and M. van den Bel, Inrap.

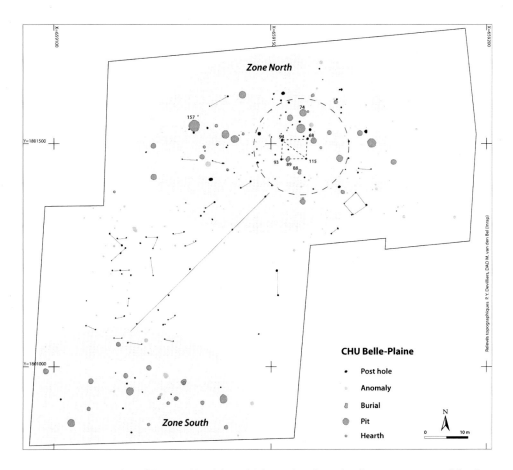

Figure 3.5 Feature plan of CHU Belle-Plaine with house location. Fine lines represent possible alignments of couples of small postholes.

Topography: P.-Y. Devillers, M. van den Bel, Inrap.

SW–NE and doublestakes suggest that it can be identified as a garden to grow on stakes
legumes such as beans (Figure 3.6).

3.1.3   STEP Goyave

This excavation yielded 78 features that have been interpreted as postholes (Table 3.2). The
large majority represents Type B postholes (N=59), which were encountered all over the
morne, whereas the much larger Type A postholes were only found in the western zone of the
excavation (Zone A) (Figure 3.7). The Type A postholes were filled up rapidly, which made
it hard to recognize the features, but an occasional presence of a supporting stone helped us
to find their contours at excavation level (see Figure 3.2).

Only a few features, notably Type A postholes, cross-section each other, such as posthole F
62.2 sectioning pit F 62.1, F 79 sectioning posthole F 56, and pit F 365 or posthole F 415 cutting F 395 and F 398. These cross-cuts may suggest the building of a house, which is perhaps
represented by a circle of eight Type A postholes (F 382, F 56, F 62.2, F 77, F 46, F 40, and

Figure 3.6 Manner of Amerindian gardening in Drake manuscript, c. 1586, f. 121r. Note the stakes on the right for the beans. www.themorgan.org/collection/Histoire-Naturelle-des-Indes/118.

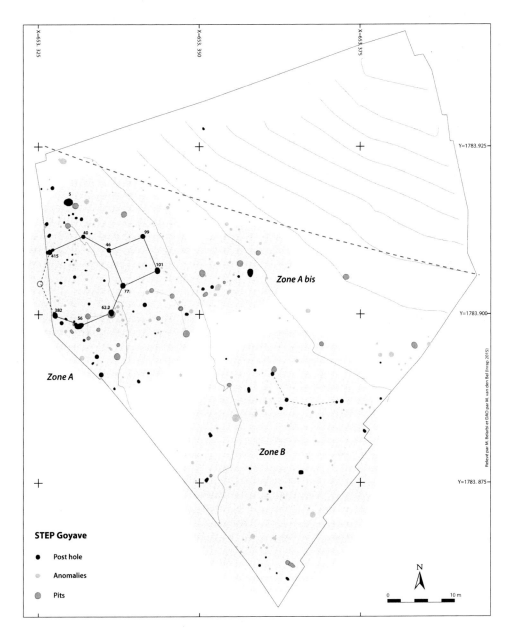

Figure 3.7 Feature plan of STEP Goyave with house location.

Topography: M. Belarbi, M. van den Bel, Inrap.

F 415), spaced every 5 m, and covering 113 m². Unfortunately, one posthole is probably situated outside the excavation perimeter. Only three of these postholes (F 56, F 77, and F 415) have been dated, revealing a date ranging between 950 and 1070 BP, which seems to confirm their contemporaneity. Within the ring of large postholes, there are a few Type B postholes (F 19, F 22, F 54, F 67, and F 309), but as far as we can see altogether they do not reveal any comprehensive configuration related to the ring. This possible plan, however, may certainly represent some kind of construction and/or may also stem from another occupation.

Outside this ring of eight postholes, we did not encounter any peripheral ring of smaller postholes, but there are two Type A postholes (F 99 and F 101) situated just to the northeast of the main ring at a distance of about 5 m from features F 46 and F 77. The latter combination of Type A postholes forms a square covering 25 m². This square may have formed an integrated part of the structure (perhaps to support an entrance) when considering the similar fills, but it may also represent a (later?) extension. This possible house plan is bordered by more large postholes and pits to the east, separating it from the eastern zone or Zone B. Only the very deep Type A postholes F 5 and F 179 appear not to be related to any construction. Zone B did not reveal any regular patterning of features and therefore no houses have been recovered

3.1.4   *Parking de Roseau*

In total 143 features have been interpreted as postholes (Table 3.2). Nearly all postholes are small Type B postholes with an average of 33 cm in diameter at excavation level and 31 cm in depth—the deepest posthole measuring 60 cm. In general, these postholes do not cross-cut each other, but we did notice possible double post fills in one hole (F 264 and F 400) and posthole features close to each other suggesting contemporaneity (F 188 + F 189 and F 194 + F 195). The latter represent perhaps the replacing or renewing of posts, adjustment of the construction, and/or positioning additional posts during the life span or construction phase of the house. We must conclude here that the small dimensions do evoke light constructions, as proposed for CHU Belle-Plaine. Furthermore, it is interesting to note that the concentrations of large circular pits (Assemblage A–E) somehow seem to be associated to three house locations (HL 1–3) identified at this site (Figure 3.8). HL 1 shares terrain with pit Assemblage B; the smaller HL 2, situated between HL 1 and 3, is accompanied by pit Assemblage C and D, and pit Assemblage E is situated aside HL 3. Finally, pit Assemblage A is a bit isolated at the eastern tip of the plateau where the spring is situated.

House Location 1

This house location is situated at the northern limit of the excavation perimeter and flanked by pit Assemblages B and C as well as two intentional depositions of ceramic vessels (F 191 and F 269). The house location and pit assemblages all together measure approximately 30×22 m (660 m²). The depth of the postholes varies between 20 and 40 cm, with a few deeper than 40 cm (Figure 3.8). It is very hard to discern regular configurations of posthole features, due to the significant later plowing disturbances experienced at the more elevated southern part of this house location.

The designation of this house location is based on the few postholes deeper than 40 cm, covering a surface of about 70 m². This central part is surrounded by smaller postholes, roughly spaced 5 m from each other, covering 100 m². This concentration seems to be surrounded again by another series of peripheral postholes, forming an oval axis SE–NW and creating a surface of approximately 1000 m². The latter oval configuration may also represent an enclosure, but it is evident that one may recognize other plans in this dense posthole cloud.

House Location 2

This much smaller house location is situated to the west of the excavation perimeter, between HL 1 and HL 3, and flanked by pit Assemblages C and D; it measures 12×15 m for a surface of 180 m² (Figure 3.9). This house location is primarily defined by a few postholes deeper

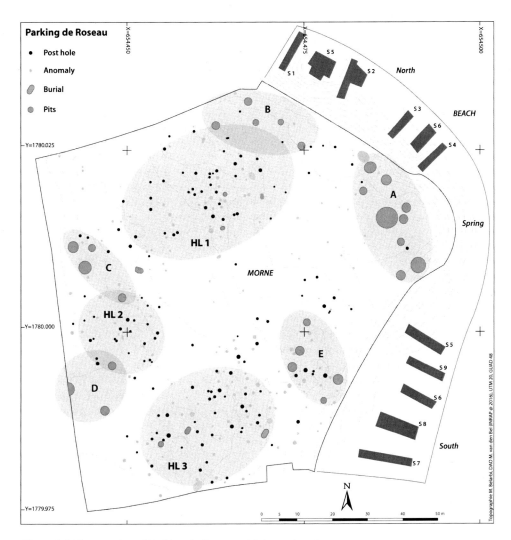

Figure 3.8 Feature plan of Parking de Roseau with house location.

Topography: M. Belarbi, M. van den Bel, Inrap.

than 40 cm, which are surrounded by smaller postholes. This time, however, the surface is much smaller and the general shape is more stretched or slender. It may be possible that this HL 2 is linked to HL 3 to the south. Finally, one notes a small cluster of postholes to the north of pit Assemblage C, which may have been part of a wooden construction; a similar situation is observed to the northeast of pit Assemblage E.

House Location 3

This house location is similar to HL 1; it also has an elongated shape, is oriented NE–SW and covers an area of 425 m² (17×25 m). Within its perimeter are three pits with intentional

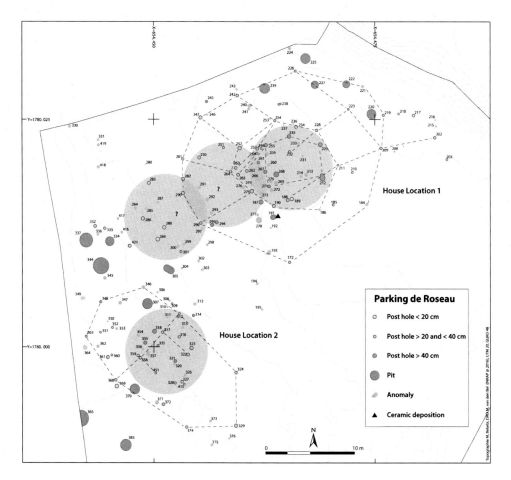

Figure 3.9 HL 1 and 2 at Parking de Roseau.

Topography: M. Belarbi, M. van den Bel, Inrap.

depositions of ceramic vessels, and these pits are flanked by pits to the north. The depth of the postholes varies between 20 and 40 cm. The main element in this house location is represented by a configuration of 11 postholes: it relates to F 118, F 116, F 112, and F 54 in the north and F 389, F 391, F 399 and F 398 in the south, revealing more roundish shapes at the extremities (Figure 3.10). A few postholes are located within this configuration, with F121 and anomaly F 378 possibly forming an interconnected pair. This plan of 11 postholes appears to be surrounded by a larger, irregular alignment of postholes spaced between 2 and 8 m, showing a possible opening to the north, facing the pits; this may represent an enclosure.

This house location probably contained a burial, represented by a rare rectangular pit, F 35, with rounded edges (see Figure 3.10). This shallow pit contained a complete vessel turned upside-down featuring coffee bean eyes (see Figure 4.13). The sediment of this pit was sampled for phosphores analysis in order to test the presence of human bone. The level of phosphor (1220 mg/kg) recorded below the vessel was at least two times more important than the reference sample (1220 *vs* 445 mg/kg), suggesting the presence of (human) bone and most probably representing an inhumation.[2]

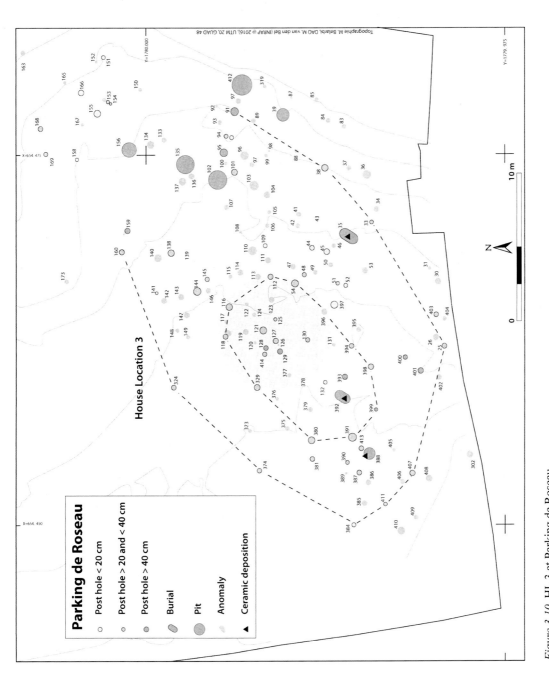

Figure 3.10 HL 3 at Parking de Roseau.
Topography: M. Belarbi, M. van den Bel, Inrap.

The internal and relative chronology of these house locations remains difficult to solve, as we have only a few radiocarbon dates, which all came from one of the pits and not the posthole features. In addition, the small number and deviations of the radiocarbon dates hamper more precise understanding regarding their chronology, suggesting that all house locations could be contemporaneous considering the proposed absolute range. Eventually, we can only state that pit Assemblage A is the oldest and Assemblage D the youngest pit concentration, but we must remark, too, that these pits do not overlap, nor do the features more generally, confirming a contemporaneous and short occupation for this site. This may lead to the idea that HL 1 and HL 3 are contemporaneous, both sharing the same orientation and a common size of approximately 70 m²; HL 1 could be anterior to HL 3. Finally, one must conclude that the excavation perimeter seems too small to fully accommodate spatial and temporal patterning of numerous houses, let alone a complete village. Excavating larger areas and obtaining more radiocarbon dates may in the future provide us with a better data set to study the life span of houses and the internal spatial and temporal organization of villages.

3.1.5   Brief comparison of Amerindian house plans on Guadeloupe

An important criterion to compare the pre-Columbian house plans on Basse-Terre, dating to the second half of the first millennium CE and featuring Late Saladoid and Mamoran Troumassoid ceramics, can be the presence of Type A postholes. These large postholes suggest the presence of solidly build structures, perhaps signifying a communal or central role within the settlement. The central configuration, in either a square (HL 2 of La Pointe de Grande Anse) or a circle (HL 1 at STEP Goyave), suggests an architecturally different building. This can be related to cultural changes and/or to a different function of the constructions. The sites of Belle-Plaine and Parking de Roseau clearly lack Type A postholes and, when comparing the radiocarbon dates, these sites are entirely LCA sites with Troumassoid ceramics only, signifying an important difference with the (slightly) older sites of La Pointe de Grande Anse and STEP Goyave.

Now, we must point to other contemporaneous sites on Guadeloupe attributed to the second half of the first millennium CE, such as Bisdary at Gourbeyre (Romon et al. 2006), La Ramée at Sainte-Rose (Casagrande et al. 2016), and Moulin-à-Eau and L'Allée Dumanoir at Capesterre-Belle-Eau (Mestre et al. 2001; Etrich et al. 2003, 2013).[3] The best-documented and contemporaneous house plans were reconstructed at Capesterre-Belle-Eau site having similar configurations, as found at La Pointe de Grande Anse. The plans at Capesterre-Belle-Eau have a round or slightly oval shape for the outside ring with either 15 (Bâtiment N of Moulin-à-Eau in Mestre et al. 2001:25) or 10 peripheral postholes (BP 8, 9 and 13 at L'Allée Dumanoir in Etrich et al. 2003:82), which were spaced some 5 m apart. Their total surfaces were estimated between 100 and 180 m². Smaller house plans (<10 m in diameter) with eight peripheral posts were also detected at these Capesterre sites (see Table 3.1).

Differences were observed, however, when comparing the position of the central posts. The Capesterre-Belle-Eau plans showed in most of the cases two central posts—or even one—whereas House Location 2 of La Pointe de Grande Anse has at least four. On the other hand, the Anse à la Gourde site, situated in the east of the island of Grande-Terre, clearly showed house plans with four or more central posts in rectangular arrangement (see Bright 2003:17–27; Morsink 2006:19–47). Interestingly, other (even larger) constructions at the latter site have a double peripheral ring and a larger total surface.[4]

The coexistence, however, of different house types at pre-Columbian sites in the Lesser Antilles is a general feature found in large-scale excavations. These differences are generally interpreted as caused by variations in function of the building, status of its dwellers, or reflecting different architectural traditions. For example, the house plans at the Golden Rock site (St. Eustatius), dated to the seventh and eighth centuries CE, and the larger house plans at Anse à la Gourde reveal more complex plans than the ones found at La Pointe de Grande Anse and STEP Goyave. The former also have larger surfaces estimated between 250 and 360 m² and feature secondary peripheralcircles (semicircles), which have been interpreted as passageways, verandas, screens, or walls. According to the excavators, the interior organization of the Golden Rock house plans reflects the cohabitation of multiple families in the same house (Versteeg and Schinkel 1992).

The house plans of La Pointe de Grande Anse fall within the known range of house plans in Guadeloupe for the second half of the first millennium CE, but the contemporary house plan of STEP Goyave represents another type of house plan, which can be added to the register of houses for this period.

Finally, as mentioned in the beginning, the house locations found at CHU Belle-Plaine and Parking de Roseau differ from the ones discussed earlier, despite the fact that they are also flanked by circular pits and share burials. Next to their attribution to the beginning of the second millennium CE, the houses appear to be lighter in construction when compared to the earlier, more sturdy houses as observed by the absence of large Type A postholes. This morphological or architectural difference may also be explained by cultural differences. Cultural changes are considered common ground among Caribbean scholars at the end of the first millennium CE when the Saladoid episode transforms into the Troumassoid one, emphasizing the turn of the ECA into the LCA (Curet and Oliver 1998; Watters 1994; Keegan 2000; Bright 2003; Petersen et al. 2004; de Waal 2006; Hofman et al. 2007).

3.2 Burials

Thomas Romon

The analysis of human skeletal remains offers great potential with regard to the study of (paleo) pathology, diets, disease, and, more recently, genetics and isotope analysis. In addition to the bones themselves, postmortem events also provide important information about different modes of inhumation, which may determine cultural (group) markers. The latter type of research gained more interest at the multiple component site of Anse à la Gourde at La Pointe des Châteaux (Grande-Terre) excavated by the University of Leiden and DRAC Guadeloupe in the mid-1990s (Delpuech et al. 2001b). This important site yielded more than 80 burials, found along house walls and revealing various burial modes of the LCA population of Guadeloupe and the Lesser Antilles in general (Hofman and Hoogland 2013).

Since the programmed excavations at Anse à la Gourde, many other pre-Columbian burials have been identified, nearly all excavated by the present author and of which 19 burials are discussed in this volume (Table 1.4). As referred to in the introduction, volcanic soils do not often yield organic material of any kind, including bones, but for some reason we encountered bone material at pre-Columbian sites situated on Basse-Terre of which La Pointe de Grande Anse and CHU Belle-Plaine are excellent examples. However, the sites of STEP Goyave and Parking de Roseau did not yield any bone material at all.

It must, however, be realized that the shape and dimensions of various pits did remind us of burial pits. These oval or egg-shaped burial pits are quite common on excavations, but there is generally no tangible evidence of bone material such as at STEP Goyave. These pits usually have one fill and contain no artifacts. In some cases, we find one or two complete vessels planked against the pit wall (grave goods) suggesting that the pit might have been used as a burial pit; that is, the absence of human material does not mean there are no burials. The sites situated on the volcanic soils of Basse-Terre are located on various volcanic flows, which might suggest different states of preservation. The preservation of the skeletal remains presented here is in general rather poor and shows only low rates of collagen; hence, the outcomes of the bone material analysis are limited.

3.2.1   *Methods*

All burials presented here have been excavated and recorded by the author according to anthropological methods "employed in the field" (Duday and Sellier 1990; Duday et al. 1990) or known in French as *archéothanatologie* (Duday 2005). The goal of studying human skeletal remains in situ is to identify the funerary modes of inhumation as well. Because of the rather poor state of bone preservation, the principal biological data have been obtained in the field.

   First, the excavation of the burial starts by carefully exposing the skeletal remains with the appropriate tools, such as small trowels, dental picks, and brushes. Taphonomic information is recorded on forms (see Courtaud 1996). In addition, images of the entire burial, detailed pictures of the skeletal remains are made next to drawings on the basis of a zenithal view and georeferenced by four points. The points are materialized by four large metal nails, which dhave been placed on the outside at the extremities of the pit in such a way that two axes are traced with the same height. The altitudes are thus measured, referring to the established axis of which the one at the head is considered the main axis. Finally, the bones are taken out and safeguarded according to anatomical units before being transported to the laboratory.

3.2.2   *La Pointe de Grande Anse*

This site yielded 16 excavated burials. Thirteen are clearly clustered into three distinct spatial units or groups (**Figures 3.3** and **3.4**).[5] The spatial distribution of the remaining three burials appears more random, but this can also be a result of different Amerindian funerary practices. The first group of burials is situated along the western limit of the excavation within the perimeter of HL 1 and consists of four graves. The second group is situated to the south of the first unit and located within the northwestern quarter of HL 2 and consists of five burials. The third group is to be found in the southeastern corner of the excavated area within HL 3 and comprises four burials. The three more randomly distributed burials are situated in the northern part of the excavation. The poor preservation of the bones did not allow for the determination of age, gender, and any biometrical characteristics of the buried individuals. The study of pathologies was impossible too.

   Five of the 16 burials can be considered incomplete, which is due to the poor preservation of the bones and later disturbances. One burial is strictly secondary. Three burials show evidence of skeletal material in both primary and secondary positions, which can be related to Amerindian activities performed on the bone remains after the tissue had decomposed. Seven burials are strictly primary and three burials yielded multiple individuals. The orientation of the burials exhibits variation: six are directed towards the north, one to the south, one to the southeast, two to the west and one towards the northwest. Only one burial (F 1) is associated with a (large) ceramic vessel, which was probably placed upside down over the upper part (head?) of the individual as a lid or cover (Figure 3.11).

Figure 3.11 Burial F1 with ceramic vessel at La Pointe de Grande Anse.
Photo: M. van den Bel, Inrap.

Primary burials

Primary burials are the most common burials at this site and are also most common in the Lesser Antilles. In other words, the Amerindians dug a pit in which they deposited the body and left it there, untouched. La Pointe de Grande Anse yielded seven simple primary burials, while the five incomplete burials can most probably also be placed within this group. This group (N=12) has two individuals who were deposited in semiseated position (see F 1), eight on their back (see F 1197), and two on their side (see F 571). The upper limbs are bent forward and the hands placed on the abdomen. The lower extremities are bent or hyperflexed in a vertical way (N=3); the knees touch the shoulders (N=3); the knees in front of the individual (N=2) on the decubitus side.

Primary burials with secondary disturbances

A primary burial with secondary disturbances represents a burial type that is less frequent than the cases already presented. Once the deceased was buried and the decomposition of the soft tissue was fairly well advanced, the Amerindians returned to the deceased, and moved it and/or removed some of the bones. Interestingly, this kind of activity is mostly encountered at LCA habitation sites (see Anse à la Gourde). The mandible of burial F 1096 was replaced against the left upper limb and the cranium was found (placed) on the left lower extremity, whereas the remainder of the individual was in primary position. Burial F 351 contains an individual in primary position without a cranium and features two craniums in secondary position. It is unfortunately not possible to determine if one of the two skulls belongs to the primary buried individual. The latter is buried on its back, similar to the simple primary burials.

Burial F 33 is a double burial, though the individuals were not buried simultaneously. The first individual was deposited into a pit and—after complete decomposition—this same pit was reused to bury a second individual. In doing so, some bones of the first individual were taken and replaced in the same pit. The remains of the first individual, which were for most part still in primary position, indicate that this person was buried on the back, as in other simple primary burials.

Secondary burials

Burial F 727 is a true secondary burial. The burial pit contains the bones of two individuals that were collected after their bodies had completely decomposed and were reburied together, in the same pit. Whether this pit was one of the original pits is unknown, but all bones are clearly in secondary position. The long bones were gathered in a bundle and placed against the eastern wall of the pit; a cranium and a mandible were found at the center of the pit. The absence of many bones and in particular small-sized ones suggest prior decomposition at a different place. At the moment, it is difficult to attribute this phenomenon with certainty to pre-Columbian burial practices as several burials were disturbed by colonial activities. However, secondary burials in the strict sense are known from other Amerindian sites and are usually dated to the "post-Saladoid" times.

Indications for disappeared items and body preparation

Ten burials possess evidence of items originally present in the burial pit, but which have perished as a result of soil chemistry. These items may relate to organic containers (baskets) or wraps (hammocks) in which the deceased had been placed or covered when buried. Disappearance of these items may have created voids or empty spaces in the pits during decomposition. These voids may have caused items to have moved, and careful study of dislocations of skeletal elements may provide information on the type of containers used. Burial F 1 features such empty spaces: a dislocated cranium and the collapse of the ceramic vessel (see Figure 3.11). This burial also revealed clogged spaces (the thorax was supported to keep it in an upright position) and secondary fillings (sediment between the left humerus and the ribs).

Burial F 2 shows indications for independent constraints having effect on the left side of the body, the upper limb and the lower left extremities. First of all, the left ribs have been moved forward and there is lateral open space under the left elbow. Secondly, the left upper limb forced the radius into an unstable position. Finally, the left lower extremities are maintained in a parallel position according to the body axis and there is lateral space available on top of the left elbow. These observations show that the various segments may have moved in simultaneously as a whole, in one "bloc."

Another example is burial F 571. Here, the position of the upper right limb is somehow maintained in an articulated position in spite of its observed displacement and in this matter is an obstacle between the upper limb and the lower extremities. The item originally holding this together is not present anymore and has been replaced by sediment. This clearly affected the position of the thorax, the upper limbs, and the lower extremities. The residual or final position of the corpse is a position clearly desired by the Amerindians before burying the individual.

Thus, four independent spaces are materialized: the first around the thorax, the second around the upper limbs, the third around the lower limbs and the fourth around the head. The use of the hammock may explain the already mentioned criteria, to wit: first wrapped around the trunk, then the upper limbs, then the lower limbs. Amerindian burials in hammocks are well illustrated by chroniclers of the 17th century. Father Breton stated:

> They dig a round pit of three feet deep and it is in the house so he [the deceased] is covered. They wash the body, dye it with annatto, oil his hair and dress him up nicely just like for their great feasts. They put him in a new bed [hammock] and then put him in the pit, almost in the same position as a child in the belly of his mother, not upside-down, nor with his face against the ground, but upright, the feet below and the head up high, resting on the knees, and [they] covered the pit with a plank.
>
> (Breton 1978:80)[6]

A few remarks must be made here before presenting and discussing the next site. The number of burials remains very modest when taking into consideration the number of people that might have lived and/or died at the site. The absence of pre-adult individuals is striking and may suggest that only part of the population was actually buried at the site. We wonder what factors governed this choice and which fate was reserved for the other part of the deceased population.

3.2.3   CHU Belle-Plaine

This site yielded only two burials. They were separated 4 m from each other and found in the only house location of this site, situated in the northern part of the excavation (see Figure 3.5). No archaeological material was associated with them. In general, the preservation of the skeletal material is rather poor and all recordings of osteological characteristics were done during during excavation in the field. Members of the Laboratory of Anthropology of the University of Bordeaux (UMR 5199) have taken samples for paleogenetic research. In addition, the Bordeaux team also analyzed samples of the La Pointe de Grande Anse site and burials found at the archaeological site of Tourlourous, Capesterre-Belle-Eau de Marie-Galante (see Serrand et al. 2018), but results are lacking for the moment because there is too little collagen preserved in the bones.

The two burials at this site will be presented in detail in order to appreciate the outcome of the field recordings mentioned earlier.

Burial F 88

This concerns a primary burial of an individual of undetermined gender. This person has been put on his back into an oval pit measuring 115×65 cm with the head to the south-west (Figure 3.12). The rump is positioned against the southeastern pit wall, which created a slight uplift of the right flank of the individual with regard to the person's left side. The arms are flexed and the hands positioned near the elbows. The legs are hyperflexed, perpendicular to the axis of the burial, and positioned on the left side of the individual. This burial is heavily disturbed by continuous plowing and, as a result, the skull, the lower left arm and leg are missing. There is minor bioturbation near the left shoulder.

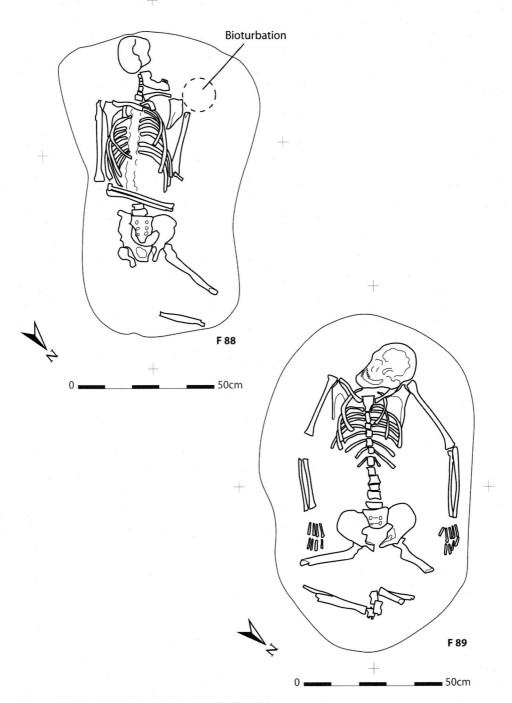

Figure 3.12 Burials F 88 and F 89 at CHU Belle-Plaine.
Drawing by T. Romon, Inrap.

The skull lies on its left side. It is probably still in primary position, but it is in rather poor condition. Only the back of the skull, around the occipital part, and its jaw bone are still preserved; the rest has perished. The atlas is visible on the right lateral side whereas the remains of the rachis show its anterior side. The ribs have dropped towards the front of the individual. The scapulas show their anterior side in close connection to the right with the proximal extremity of the humerus. The right humerus appears with its anterior face up. It rests in a flat position against the exterior limit of the right ribs. The joints of the right elbow are loose. The lower arm is flexed, and the right hand is positioned just below the left elbow. The radius and ulna appear with their posterior face up. They rest in a flat position, parallel next to each other, perhaps a drop of the radius into the body volume of the lower arm. The right hand is heavily disturbed by a movement of the left lower arm as a result of the mechanic shovel touching it during excavation, or *décapage*. The left humerus faces anterior side up.

It rests flat, parallel to the alignment of the body. Its proximal extremity is disturbed by bioturbation. Its distal extremity might have been moved during *décapage*. The left lower arm has also been moved during *décapage* and was ripped off. It is highly probable that it was in flexed position just above the lower right arm. The left hand has been destroyed. The pelvic girdle is closed and it is up showing its anterior side. The lower right arm is also represented by the proximal end of the femur of which the head is to be found in the acetabular cavity of the right coxal. It shows itself on the lateral side and in a flat position. Its distal end is directed to the left flank of the individual. The left leg is represented by the femur and tibia, both flexed on the left side of the individual. The knee has not been preserved. The head of the left femur is located in the acetabular socket of the left coxal. It shows itself by its medial face and rests in a flat position in the same direction as the right femur. The left tibia shows its medial face, too, and rests in a flat position, almost parallel to the left femur. The feet have not been preserved.

To conclude, the poor state of preservation of this burial does not allow for the gathering of detailed information concerning funerary practices. There is some evidence of decomposition in filled-up spaces, as suggested by the dropping of the ribs and perhaps slightly moved position of the pelvis. This person has been buried in a flexed position or a too small pit. The burial pit's fill does not show any signs of postinterment activities.

Burial F 89

This is a primary burial of a single young adult of undetermined gender (see Figure 3.12). There are no burial gifts or other objects associated with this burial. The person is resting on its back in a pit measuring 120×75 cm, with the head to the southwest. The body rests at the center of the pit. Each arm stretches alongside the thorax and the hands are next to the pelvis. The legs are flexed: the right knee to the right of the individual and the left one to the left. The feet are crossed and positioned in front of the pelvis. The knees have been disturbed by plowing and the preservation of the bone is extremely poor.

The skull is seen from its anterior side and the face is crushed by the weight of the sediment. In lies in a primary position at the bottom of the pit with the left ear against the left shoulder. The skull-atlas, atlas-axis and crane-mandible are in a straight connection or alignment. The jawbone has slightly dropped whereas the chin rests on the body of the cervical vertebrae. The rachis is still in connection and it shows itself with the anterior face upwards and rests on the bottom of the pit. There is some sort of twist, without disturbance, of the first five cervical vertebraetowards the left, probably related to the position of the skull to the left. It appears that the ribs have dropped towards the front of the individual (constrictions?) within the body volume.

The scapulae are seen from their anterior side and the connections of the shoulder are straight on both sides. The arms are found in a symmetrical position. The right humerus appears with its anterior face up and rests in a flat position to the right at approximately 12 cm from the exterior limit of the right grill costal. The right elbow has not been preserved. The lower right arm is slightly flexed and the right hand positioned 5 cm to the right of the right coxal. The radius and ulna appear with their posterior sides up. They are in a flat position and parallel to each other; perhaps a drop of the proximal end of the radius into the body volume of the lower arm. The right hand lies flat and in connection at the bottom of the pit, showing its dorsal side. The left humerus shows its anterior side. It also lies flat, 15 cm to the left of the exterior limit of the left grill costal. The connection of the left elbow is loose. The lower left arm is slightly flexed and the left hand situated 5 cm to the left of the left coxal. The radius and ulna are up with their posterior sides. They rest in a flat position, parallel to each other with perhaps a slight drop of the radius in the body volume of the forearm. The left hand is flat and in connection at the bottom of the pit with its dorsal side up.

The pelvic girdle is open. There has been a drop of the two coxals to the bottom of the pit to the exterior of the body volume. Both coxal-femur connections have been preserved. The legs are symmetrical, flexed on each side of the individual, the feet crossed against the pit wall and in front of the pelvis. The right femur appears with the inferior and medial side up. It rests flat, its distal end directed towards the right flank of the individual. The (destroyed) right knee is resting against the pit wall. The right tibia rests upon the right fibula, more or less stretched. Both show their medial side up. The right foot is up with its medial side and rests 10 cm in front of the pelvis upon and slightly in front of the left foot. The connections of the right ankle are straight. The left femur appears with its inferior and medial side up. It rests in a flat position, its distal end directed towards the left flank of the individual. The (destroyed) left knee rests against the pit wall. The left tibia rests on the left fibula in more or less flat position. They show themselves on their medial sides. The left foot appears on its medial side, too, and rests 10 cm in front of the pelvis, below and slightly behind the right foot. The ankle and metatarsic connections are straight.

To conclude, this burial shows evidence of decomposition of perishable materials and the subsequent filling up of the created spaces, as suggested by the position of the hands and feet and the drop of the ribs, as well as the opening of the mandible and that of the scapular girdle. This could be related to voids created by the decomposition of an object made of perishable material, for instance a basket. The position of the arms is remarkable because they are not in a flexed position in front of the abdomen as we observed at La Pointe de Grande Anse. Nonetheless, the position of the legs shows that this individual was buried in its definite position and no further interventions have been identified.

3.2.4   Conclusion

The two pre-Columbian sites presented here, separated in space and in function, yielded burials. The La Pointe de Grande Anse site has at least 16 burials whereas CHU Belle-Plaine, probably excavated completely, only two. The bones are not in good condition, rendering interpretation difficult. The greatest variability in the burial pattern can be observed at La Pointe de Grande Anse, which is certainly related to their numbers. However, it appears that this variability increases during the Late Ceramic Age, notwithstanding that the simple primary burial—that is, the individual placed in hyperflexed position in a small oval pit slightly larger than the deceased—remains the most common burial mode. Manipulation of the decomposed deceased, as observed at La Pointe de Grande Anse, has already been described on the contemporary sites of l'Ilet du Gosier and Anse à la Gourde (Romon and Chancerel 2002; Romon et al. 2003; Delpuech et al. 2001a, 2001b). The same applies to strictly secondary burials. Interestingly, these funeral practices appear to be absent during the Early Ceramic Age, revealing the importance of human remains, which could reflect the emergence of ancestral veneration.

For the primary burials, careful study of the taphonomic of the burial provides information on the preparation of the deceased before interment. This allows for the identification of the presence of certain perishable materials and objects in which the deceased had been placed or wrapped. At first, void areas are newly formed around the corpse, indicating the presence of a perishable wrapping material (other than human flesh). These are also taphonomic aberrations, indicating disappeared items, isolating in this manner the chest from the upper limbs, from the lower limbs, and from the skull, which might move within the pit. They follow the morphology of the different segments or limbs while exerting certain constraints that allow forced positions or "deadlock." These positions cannot be natural: the position of the corpse is intentional and enacted before inhumation. Thus, it varies from one individual to another, but always respects the previously mentioned characteristics.

The use of a hammock can explain these characteristics, and our observations allow us to specify the handling or preparation of the deceased. The deceased was most certainly wrapped in a piece of vegetable fiber (hammock). It is believed that this piece was first rolled around the chest and abdomen. The upper limbs are then arranged and subsequently included in the swaddling. The lower limbs are then integrated, in a flex position, into the swaddling. This preparation is necessarily done before interment for it reduced the volume occupied by the deceased and maintained the position given to the body. It is then placed into a small oval pit, about the same size as the body and its container; hence, the burial now acquires the characteristics of a filled-up space. During the decomposition of the body, voids are formed. These phenomena occur at different times and lead to the movement of skeletal elements, most often by gravity or, on the contrary, to their blocking in positions that can be described as taphonomic aberrations.

The almost complete absence of items is observed at both sites. Only one burial at La Pointe de Grande Anse had a ceramic vessel interpreted as a cover or lid for the deceased. Considering it in this manner, it better can be interpreted as an element of funeral architecture or social status than as personal goods directly associated with the deceased. Goods are more common in Early Ceramic Age burials, such as pearls, amulets, tools, or ceramic vessels. At both sites, the burial pits are clustered into small groups directly associated with habitat structures. The contemporaneity between burials and houses has earlier been discussed for the La Pointe Grande Anse site. It is believed that the former village obtained a special place in the memory and ancestor worship of the communities inhabiting the microregion and that due to this status the site had been turned into a burial ground (see van den Bel and Romon 2010). The location of the burials within the house plan during the Late Ceramic Age is in agreement with the pattern of relocating burial grounds or graves from midden areas or the central plaza during the Early Ceramic Age towards the house, or *carbet* (Keegan et al. 2013).

3.3 Large circular pits

Martijn M. van den Bel

The large circular pits described here will not be presented per site because their morphology and distribution does not vary much and they have also been mentioned in the previous sections. The fact that a whole section is dedicated to pits is unique in Caribbean archaeology where similar pits are rarely found due to the lack of large-scale excavations. Furthermore, the majority of these pits have only two fills and do not contain many ceramics or lithics. For this matter, I called these pits "mysterious" during my 26th IACA presentation, in July 2015 (see van den Bel 2017). This section, in which I present the spatial distribution and morphology of these pits, also represents an introduction to the following chapters with microanalyses performed on these pits; the results of the different analyses will shed some light upon these enigmatic pits (see Figures 3.3, 3.5, 3.7, and 3.8).

3.3.1   *Morphology*

All pits are circular at excavation level and vary in size, from 70 to 300 cm in diameter. Their depths vary as well and range from 20 to more than 100 cm, keeping in mind that these are minimum figures, as in cases their upper part, present in the topsoil, has been bulldozed away (50–100 cm can be missing). This is also true for STEP Goyave but may apply to a lesser extent to the Parking de Roseau site where the topsoil disturbances had been less significant. After the excavation of about 100 large, circular pits at all sites we can distinguish three major pit types: (a) cylindrical pits with straight vertical walls and flat bottoms, (b) convex pits, and (c) "pointed" or conical pits (Figure 3.13). However, neither this morphological distinction nor the study of the various dimensions of these pits yielded any progress in a better understanding of their function or their spatial patterning, as there were no concentrations or alignments of similar pits found at the four sites.

More significant information was available in the sequence of the fills. The majority of the pits revealed only one or two (macroscopically) distinguishable fills. The most voluminous (20–50 cm in thickness) upper fill is relatively sterile and consists of brown sandy loam, whereas the thin (10 cm) lower fill is a darker color and may rarely contain some archaeological material in the form of ceramic sherds. Notwithstanding these few sherds, these pits can be considered nearly void of archaeological material, despite systematic screening on 3 mm. Another noteworthy aspect about these pits is that half of them are filled with rocks (limestone and volcanic boulders), generally found at the bottom of the pit. Among these stones also feature fragments of milling stones.

Only a few pits deviated from the general pattern and had more fills. They contained charcoal and sherd-rich layers, suggesting they were used as dumps, perhaps in their final stage (see Chapter 4). The observations presented here concerning the two-stage filling up of the pits and the sterile top fill suggest these pits had been left open after which they got filled up with colluvial sediment during heavy rainfall. We actually witnessed this process during fieldwork campaign once we had emptied them. This notion was confirmed by the

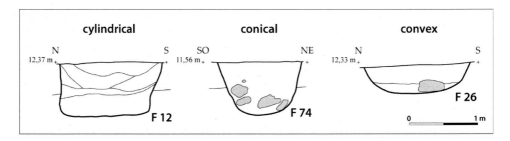

Figure 3.13 Three pit types as defined for the presented sites. Drawing by M. van den Bel, Inrap.

micromorphological analysis conducted by Jeanne Brancier and Cécilia Cammas and combined with phytolith research by Jennifer Watling and Ruth Dickau (see Chapter 5). Following this line of reasoning, it means that the pit had been emptied after it had fulfilled its purpose, and therefore the natural fill does not tell us anything about the function of the pit and what activities might have been done in it (Figure 3.14).

3.3.2 Spatial distribution

As evoked in the section on the house plans, these large circular pits form assemblages or clusters of three, four, or five pits situated in the vicinity of a house location, suggesting a direct spatial and probably therefore contemporaneous link. Contrary to the houses and burials of La Pointe de Grande Anse, this link is evident and radiocarbon dated for CHU Belle-Plaine and Parking de Roseau. This association is more difficult to establish for STEP Goyave and La Pointe de Grande Anse due to long-term habitation at these latter sites spanning multiple occupations.

Within these pit assemblages, we may discern alignments or "batteries" suggesting similar, perhaps simultaneously, repetitive activities. When we, however, compare pit morphology, as already mentioned, we also notice that pit shapes vary within alignments, indicating that although the overall activity may have been similar, subtle differences still may have been present. Interestingly enough, at least at the site of CHU Belle-Plaine, various shallow hearth pits are found. These pits have bowl-shaped profiles of approximately 40–60 cm in diameter and 10 cm in depth. They contained various thin layers of charcoal and glazed orange sand, but no artifacts. According to the radiocarbon dates, the hearth and circular pits functioned simultaneously and probably share a related activity. Sediment has been taken for phytolith analysis (see Chapter 5). The other sites presented here did not feature this kind of shallow hearth, with the exception of STEP Goyave, which showed rather deep orange hearth pits (Figure 3.15). To conclude, the relation between postholes, burials, and circular pits is eminent and one is likely to consider these features to be contemporaneous, forming altogether a larger house location or living unit.

3.3.3 Interpretation

A series of questions now arises. What happened in these pits? What was the content of the pits before it was taken out by the inhabitants and eventually filled up with colluvial sediment—in other words, what was their primary function? At this point, it becomes evident that little research has been done on pits in the Lesser Antilles. The literature reveals that only one excavation on Guadeloupe had microscopically examined pit contents (Table 3.3). It was proposed that these pits were used as latrines (Etrich et al. 2003:46). The applied analysis concerning the identification of coliforms, however, appears to be valid for modern coliforms in "dirty" water, too, and therefore cannot be fully accepted.[7] On the other hand, 20 latrines for a maximum of 200 years may seem reasonable, but one would rather expect here another type of accumulated, dense fill and not the two-step fill as previously outlined.

The archaeological paradox here is that we are searching for something that is not there anymore, but in this case, the answer may perhaps be found in the commonplace of the pits themselves and the location of these pits near houses and sometimes in association with the orange hearths. Indeed, their location close to houses evokes a quotidian/domestic task, which is perhaps supported by the presence of grinding tools (*manos* and *metates*) as well as domestic ceramic ware (predominantly large, open bowls and griddles) (see Chapter 4).

Figure 3.14 Photographs of pit shapes: (a) cylindrical (F 12), (b) convex (F 15) and (c) conical with rocks (F 74) (see also Figure 3.13 for drawings). Note the sculptured stone ball in the profile of F 15 (see also Chapter 4). M. van den Bel, Inrap.

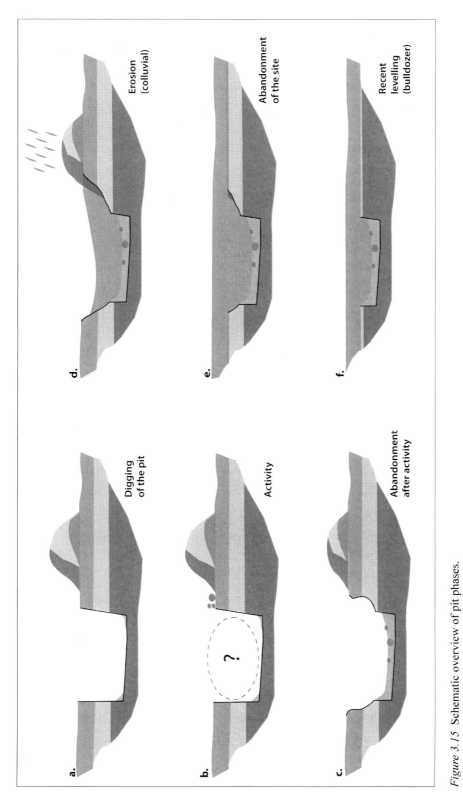

Figure 3.15 Schematic overview of pit phases.
Drawing by M. van den Bel, Inrap.

Table 3.3 Overview of pre-Columbian pits found at different sites on Guadeloupe.

Site on Guadeloupe	Surface m²	N. Pits	Range CE	Interpretation	Reference
CHU Belle-Plaine	6348	34	1000–1200	Storage	van den Bel et al. 2016
Moulin à Eau 2	3000	11	650–1000	Clay extraction or waste pit	Etrich et al. 2013
Yuiketi	4000	9	400–900	Undetermined	Bonnissent 2011
La Pointe de Grande Anse	1784	16	650–1400	Undetermined	van den Bel et al. 2009
Bisdary	5000	17	1100–1400	Unknown	Romon et al. 2006
Rivière du Grand Carbet	960	23	0–650	Waste pits	Toledo i Mur et al. 2004
Fromager	2300	19	650–1100	Waste pits	Toledo i Mur et al. 2003
Allée Dumanoir	6783	53	0–650	Latrines/waste pits	Etrich et al. 2003
Tourlourous	c. 1000	11	300–600	Waste pits	Colas et al. 2002
Anse à la Gourde	1650	2	1000–1300	Waste pits	Delpuech et al. 2001b
Moulin à Eau 1	18,000	24	0–650	Undetermined	Mestre et al. 2001

Combining our observations and ideas, we would suggest that the pits were used for safe-guarding or storing food, either as raw products, half-products, or final products. One could think of corncobs, tubers, beans, and palm seeds, among others. The idea that pulp of grated tubers or seeds for fermentation might also be part of pit storage remains highly speculative and certainly needs further testing in the future.

3.3.4   Final remarks

As mentioned before, there are only a few references available for pits and pit analysis in the Antilles. If we want to verify our idea, we may also look for ethnohistoric and ethnographic analogies, bearing in mind the European point of view of these documents and the changes that occurred in Amerindian society during colonial times, respectively. Mysterious or unexplained archaeological phenomena, as outlined, may indeed benefit from historic or ethnographic input in order to reduce the number of possible interpretations and enrich our understanding and reasoning.

Indeed, a number of chroniclers describe the process of producing tortillas, cassava, tamales, and beer, but, unfortunately, little attention is paid to storage and the use of pits. Perhaps such information was common knowledge or pits were not observed in the villages, as they were absent or kept hidden. Storage pits thus remain elusive in the historic Antilles, but pits are certainly present in pre-Columbian context in the Lesser and Greater Antilles.[8] If we go beyond the Antilles, we come across pits encountered at numerous large-scale excavations in the USA, notably those of Calusa sites in Florida (Wagner 2008). The Calusa houses were surrounded by pits and, according to Wagner (ibid. 293), their villages were semipermanent settlements, created in order to survive the shortage of food in their territory. The excavations of an 18th-century Occaneechi village in North Carolina provide another confirmation for the storage-pit idea.[9] However, eventually, these interpretations are not always fully supported by archaeological data, such as seeds, starch or phytoliths, and rely heavily on historic (written) data.

Regarding the Guianas, pits were used among the Karin'ya of Suriname for softening hard palm fruits in the early 1900s, such as the fruits of the *murisi*, or ité palm tree (*Mauritia flexuosa*):

Murisi epu-po = the morisi fruit. Although the Encycl[opedia] states that these fruits are inedible, they are nevertheless consumed. The Carib digs a small pit on the spot where he expects water, and puts the hard fruits in it; the water running in the pit [is bound] to soften the fruits. He covers the pit with leaves so that the sun cannot harden them again. Within three days they are soft. He peels them and sometimes fills a whole calabash, adds some sugar and consumes them as a thick porridge.

(Ahlbrinck 1931:309)[10]

Although the ité palm (*Arecaceae*) is not endemic to Guadeloupe, other palm trees yielding edible fruits are present. There is the *ti-koko* (*Syagrus inajai*) and *glouglou* (*Acrocomia aculeata*), which grow in swampy areas and along the Belle-Plaine River (see Barfleur 2002). Finally, we focus here on the possibility of stocking in these pits, but it may be evident that one has to look further for other interpretations and gather more archaeological data. Further attention should be paid to these pits from a cultural-chronological point of view as these pits could possibly be markers for the LCA period, or perhaps the post-Saladoid sequence in the Lesser Antilles, suggesting innovation or cultural change in the region.

Notes

1 For an overview of pre-Columbian house plans in the Greater Antilles, see Samson (2010, Table 1).
2 The analysis was performed by Tanguy Leblanc for which we thank him.
3 The latter two sites did not yield evident burials, i.e., with human bones, but rather several oval pits with complete vessel deposits, which have been interpreted as inhumation graves.
4 Here, we would also like to point to the striking resemblance between HL 2 of La Pointe de Grande Anse and Structure 2 of the Tutu site, St Thomas (Righter 2002:291, Fig. 12.5 and Table 12.4). The latter house plan is dated to the 14th century, with four to five deep central posts and an outer circle (64 m²). Both plans can also be compared to the prehistoric longhouse of FAL-7 in the Maticora Valley of western Venezuela, which represents an ovoid longhouse measuring 18×13 m (234 m²), showing four central posts with an outer ring of smaller posts (Oliver 1995:151).
5 HL 3 is not discussed in this publication (only the burials) because no charcoal was sent for analysis, but this HL is situated 30 m to the southeast of HL 2 (see Figure 3.3).
6 "*Ils font une fosse ronde de la profondeur de trois pieds et ce dans une maison, pour qu'il soit à couvert. Ils lavent le corps, le rocoüent tout, luy oignent les cheveux d'huyle et les luy troussent aussy proprement qu à leurs grands festins. Ils l'enveloppent dans un lit de cotton tout neuf, et puis le mettent dans la fosse Presque en la mesme posture que l'enfant est dans le ventre de sa mere, non à la renverse, ny aussy le visage contre terre, mais droit, les pieds en bas, la teste en haut, appuyée sur les genoux, et couvrent le trou d'une planche*"

[translation by MVDB].
7 Steroid analysis was realized by Jago Birk (University of Mainz, Germany) on sediment samples taken from the pits to determine the origins of the organic matter; however, it could not be resolved by this type of analysis. We would like to thank Jago here for his contribution to the report.
8 Here I would like to thank Michael Cinquino for discussing pits on Puerto Rico after my 2015 IACA presentation in St. Martin.
9 See www.ibiblio.org/dig/
10 Translation by the present author of: "*Murisi epu-po = de vrucht van den Morisi. Ofschoon de Encycl[opedie] de vruchten niet eetbaar noemt, worden zij toch veel gegeten. De Karaïb graaft ter plaatse, waar hij water verwachten kan, een kleine kuil, werpt in den kuil de harde vruchten. 't In den kuil loopend water weekt de vruchten. Met bladeren dekt hij den kuil toe, opdat de zon de vruchten wederom niet verharde. Binnen drie dagen zijn zij zacht. Hij krabt ze los, vult er soms een geheele kalebas mede, roert er suiker in om en eet ze als een soort stijve pap.*"

4   Material culture

4.1   Pottery

Martijn M. van den Bel

The Amerindian pottery found at the various sites presented here can be used to provide relative chronological information for estimating its periods of manufacture and relationships to other sites on Guadeloupe and possibly beyond. A cultural chronology is a sequence of archaeological assemblages reflecting ever-changing cultures. The classification of the pottery itself represents the artificial creation or division of groups based on common features, manufacturing techniques, shape, and decoration that can be interpreted as cultural characteristics (Rice 1987:274–275).[1] Pottery is often the most abundant archaeological material at sites, and therefore has received much attention from archaeologists. In addition to a proper description of this material, the general objective of its research is to distinguish a change or evolution in the ceramic repertoire or series that may tell us how its makers lived and what happened to them. In fact, pottery is considered an excellent cultural marker of ancient societies by archaeologists since it is deeply embedded in human history.

4.1.1   Methodology

Although various classification methods can be applied to pottery, predominantly the Fordian and Rousean classifications have been applied in the Antilles, of which the latter has prevailed over the former. The Fordian method was criticized in the sense that the use of a "type" was meaningless (e.g., Shepard 1956:316; Allaire 1977:128) and did not suffice to deal with the large degree of variability and diversity of Amerindian ceramics, as had already been stated by Irving Rouse (1939).[2] Therefore, the latter developed a taxonomic classification based on modes, which is very popular in Caribbean archaeology (Rouse 1939:11–12, 1951, 1960, 1961, 1965, 1983, 1986, 1992, 1995; Rouse and Cruxent 1963; Rouse and Allaire 1978; Rouse and Morse 1999).[3] When Peter Siegel (1996:675) asked Rouse about the procedure of manufacturing pottery, the latter answered that he "coined the term 'mode' to refer to the diagnostic attributes of a class of features, as opposed to the term 'type,' which refers to the diagnostic attributes of a class of whole artifacts." However, the key element is the "feature," which represents any part of the pot "that would have been recognized as being distinct by potters, and therefore a mode is a type of feature."[4] In sum: "Thus Rouse's system begins by grouping these attribute sets, or modes, and then establishes types of attributes rather than types of artifacts" (Petersen et al. 2004:21).

As mentioned in the Introduction, Guadeloupean pre-Columbian ceramics were classified according to the two-step relative chronology and the four Morel phases as defined by Edgar

DOI: 10.4324/9781003181651-4

Clerc (1968). The Rousean chronology was eventually applied to the Guadeloupean ceramic assemblages in the early 1990s by Corinne L. Hofman. Her "attribute" or modal analysis for Saban ceramics, as presented in her dissertation which I was taught at Leiden University, was subsequently applied during her research in the Guadeloupean archipelago (Hofman 1993, Chapter 4). For rim, base, and griddle fragments larger than 5 cm², the combination of various attributes (e.g., lip morphology, wall thickness, firing colors, surface finishing, decoration modes) and vessel shapes, as defined by Anna Shepard (1956:224–251), was used to establish a post-Saladoid sequence for the island of Saba. Dominique Bonnissent (2008:37–39), who took over the excavations on St. Martin from Corinne Hofman in collaboration with the "Association Archéologique de Hope Estate", applied a similar attribute analysis but used a French vocabulary as defined by Hélène Balfet et al. (1989) to describe the large variety of pre-Columbian vessel shapes. In both cases, the goal of the quantitative and qualitative analyses is to define the popularity of the ceramic modes per assemblage and, eventually, to show the variety and change or development between assemblages. The method applied here is a combination of both methods which is influenced by the ceramic analysis as developed and applied by Jérôme Briand to the results of the excavations of the Barrage de Petit-Saut project upon the Middle Sinnamary River in French Guiana in the 1990s (Briand in Vacher et al. 1998:182–183). He also labeled the vessel shapes according to Hélène Balfet et al. (1989), describing rim sherds following the methods of Bernard Debet and Michel Py (1975). Briand made several adaptations to the latter mode of description to apprehend the regional Amerindian modes of decoration, surface finishing as well as other ceramic objects, such as griddles and particular clay objects. Such adaptations were also made by Dominique Bonnissent in her ceramic analysis of the Lesser Antilles (see Bonnissent 2008, Fig. 14). Finally, the combination of these methods is by now adopted by members of Inrap when studying Amerindian ceramic material.

The classification of vessel shapes is primarily based on the rim/lip shape, the principal marker of the vessel shape. Large rim sherds (>5 cm²) permit us to record the orientation and orifice diameter in order to determine a vessel shape. In this manner, the large rims —"constituent elements," or *Éléments Constituants* (EC)—are subsequently isolated, drawn, and inspected in macroscopic detail on texture, temper, firing, surface finishing (technology), and decoration modes in order to establish a "modal series" or *Séries Modales* (SM). This first inventory permits to determine the proportions of the various vessel shapes and principal characteristics of the ceramic assemblage. Quantification of the assemblage is proposed by counting all fragments (i.e., rim, wall and base fragments), per excavation unit (i.e., layer and/or feature), and for the presence of decorative elements such as modeling and slipping. Special attention is paid to the bias between the ceramics found in the archaeological layer and the features, which may reveal multiple occupation or shifting activity areas, but also to the spatial distribution of vessel shapes and fragmentation. The chronocultural interpretation is generally based on the presence of specific typological elements such as morphology, decoration, and/or technology that permit to characterize the ceramic assemblage and eventually an interaction sphere (Boomert 2000:1). Once these typical elements are radiocarbon-dated, an absolute chronology of ceramic production can be established per site. Eventually, when a large body of ceramic data has been gathered in this manner, a valid definition for a particular ceramic complex can be drawn. From this point of view, the concept of "style" or "ceramic style" and "series"—defined by Rouse (1986:7) as "progressively higher levels to trace cultural affinity geographically as well as temporally, where the series are found at the highest level and the subseries and styles at the lower one"—is interesting for comparative ceramic research and needs further application on Guadeloupe.[5] Especially, the post-Saladoid sequence is in need of this comparative research because Guadeloupe and

Marie-Galante seem to be situated upon a cultural divide between the Windward and Lee-ward Islands. By using mainly ceramic material, Rouse (1986, 1992) addressed the timing, geographic distributions, and context of various migrations, focusing almost exclusively on the chronology or temporal-geographic models. However, for many archaeologists this is no longer satisfactory and they also have expanding interests in the complexities of populations, adaptation strategies, gender, interregional interactions, and so forth (see P. Drewett 2000; Righter 2002a; Bonnissent et al. 2013).

4.1.2   *Provenance and fabrication*

Originally I intended to present the ceramic modal series per site, but eventually it was decided to merge the data and present the modal series of each site together, being the main goal of our method. In this manner we present a ceramic register of vessel shapes for the LCA sites in Guadeloupe, or the post-Saladoid ceramic "series," that is, the Mamoran and, to some extent, the later Suazan Troumassoid ceramic "subseries." To do so, a quick scan of the ceramic inventories of the four sites presented here was needed to discard the (Late) Sala-doid ceramics, identified by the presence of Saladoid rims: outward-thickened lips, *lèvres ourlées*, which were recognized only for the site of STEP Goyave and, to a lesser extent, La Pointe de Grande Anse. CHU Belle-Plaine and Parking de Roseau revealed one Saladoid rim sherd. We counted eight Saladoid rim fragments for STEP Goyave, together with one ZIC rim piece, fragments of two potstands or perhaps "incense burners," also known as *fumigateurs*, and a large Barrancoid-like ear-shaped lug. These elements (N=5), however, are eventually of little importance among the total amount of ECs (N=616), leading us to ignore their numbers for this analysis and to treat them separately. More than 12,000 pottery fragments have been recorded (Table 4.1). All this material has been taken from features (postholes, pits, and burials) except for the sherds found at the beach of Parking de Roseau, which were found in various layers. It is important to state here that these assemblages were not taken from midden deposits or the topsoil, which are most often technically problematic from a stratigraphic point of view.[6] Over 600 ECs have been recorded for all sites, permit-ting us to have a significant collection for seriation (Table 4.2). Archaeologically complete vessels were most common at the plateau of the Parking de Roseau site.

The coiling technique was the prevailing technique among the potters of these sites. Griddles, however, were manufactured by pressing two clay slabs upon each other and, if needed, a final coil was added to create an upward-sloping lip. Modeling was used for adjunctions such as handles, legs, feet, spouts, adornos, and the like. Finishing and

Table 4.1 Overview of ceramic count per site.

Site	Weight in grams	Fragmenta-tion	Ordinary	Decorated	Total
LPGA	21396	14	1290	215	1505
CHU Belle-Plaine	37696	15	2319	139	2458
STEP Goyave	37878	18	1750	312	2062
PDR Morne	177974	31	4845	956	5801
PDR Beach	24332	41	529	62	591
	299276	gr	10733	1684	12417

Table 4.2 Overview of *Éléments Constituants* (EC), or Constituent Elements per site.

Site	ECs	Decorated	Rims	Bases	Griddles	Complete Vessels
LPGA	45	19	34	7	7	3
CHU Belle-Plaine	100	27	76	22	6	4
STEP Goyave	86	32	54	15	19	2
PDR Morne	305	104	207	90	32	24
PDR Beach	80	19	61	11	8	0
Totals	616	201	432	145	72	33

decoration techniques vary, from polishing, scratching, smoothing, and incising to grooving and red slipping. However, surface finishing, such as polishing, burnishing, and smoothing has not been recorded for these assemblages when realizing the studies for the reports; hence, we focus on slipping, incising, scratching, grooving, and modeling, representing about 13% of the total general count. Interestingly, the percentage of decoration of all the ECs is higher than that of decoration of the total count (13% *vs* 32%). This difference may be related to the context and quality of conservation of the ceramic material in the features or to our proper observation when cataloging sherds, such as missing small decorated sherds. In general, the quality of the ceramics for all sites is mediocre. This is partly due to the acidity of the volcanic soils, but also to the high level of fragmentation, notably at La Pointe de Grande Anse, which is a long-lived habitation site, as well as STEP Goyave (see Table 4.1). CHU Belle-Plaine is a much smaller habitation site having a similar ratio of fragmentation of about 15 grams per pottery fragment, despite its size. The high ratios for Parking de Roseau seem exceptional knowing that this is also a large habitation site, but a few large pits, which served as waste pits, may have elevated the average weight per sherd. If in doubt, one or various fragments of each EC were chipped off in order to determine firing colors and temper. Firing was recorded according to the color of the section to determine oxidized and reduced firing, as defined by Rye (1981:116, Fig. 104). Temper has been determined with the naked eye, often aided by an 8x (hand) binocular in order to have a better view of the aplastics. We observed two classes of temper: (1) a mineral (sandy) temper (53%), and (2) grog temper (43%). It should be noted that sand is most often also observed in grog-tempered sherds, suggesting rather a mixed temper than a pure grog temper. Other ingredients, notably (3) vegetal matter (3%) and (4) shell (1%), have also been observed but remain unusual aplastics, perhaps not even intentionally added to the clay. In general, one may state that grog-tempered pottery is most often recorded in combination with a reduced firing technique. Microscopic research on temper has been realized by Gilles Fronteau, particularly to acknowledge the presence of grog (see Chapter 5).

4.1.3   The Constituent Elements (ECs)

The EC register consists of 616 elements of which the rim elements (N=432) are most abundant (Table 4.2).[7] This collection, in combination with their context (mainly pits) and radiocarbon dating, permits the establishment of a rather solid series and perhaps the beginning of ceramic catalog for the Late Ceramic Age of Guadeloupe.

The rims

The diversity of the rim collection permitted to establish a morphological division into 13 modal series based on the shape of the rim: straight (SM 1–3), convex (SM 4–6), and concave (SM 7) for open vessels as well as restricted vessels (SM 8–10) according to their inclination of 0°, <45°, and >45°. These vessels are subdivided again according to lip finishing, creating modal subseries, SM 2a–d. It should be noted that it was sometimes difficult to determine the orifice (open or restricted) of convex rim fragments as witnessed by SM 4a *vs* SM 9a, indicating that eventually these modal series can be merged. This is probably due, at least for these modal series, to the large and rapid production of such (shallow) bowls. An exception was made, however, for necks with grooved incisions (SM 10b), small bowls with an orifice diameter of <10 cm (SM 11), and trays (SM 12), which have a specific combination of attributes, allowing to create directly a specific modal series. Unique rims were grouped in SM 13 and Saladoid elements were grouped in SM 14, thus totaling our rim collection to 416 significant elements for the four sites studied (Table 4.3). The open vessels clearly dominate the latter collection (81%) of which SM 2 is the most popular modal series (33%) as well as with regard to the entire rim register (28%). About 40% of the rim elements were decorated, notably by the application of red slip (71%). Finally, it should be noted that some orifices may represent boat-shaped vessels or other polymorphous shapes, which is rather common in the Lesser Antilles.

The open vessels (Figure 4.1)

SM 2. This modal series includes the rectilinear rim profiles inclined <45° towards the exterior. They have different labial treatment (SM 2b and d; or thickened and "banded") and may show a sharply offset upper part (SM 2c). "Banded" rims are rims marked by a pseudo-offset or accentuation of the rim at a few centimeters below the lip. SM 2 represents more than one-quarter of the significant rim collection. Clearly, it forms the most important production

Table 4.3 Modal rim series (SM 1–14).

SM	N	Vessel shape	Profile	Inclination
1	34	Open	Rectilinear	Straight
2	115	Open	Rectilinear	Exterior < 45°
3	47	Open	Rectilinear	Extérieur ≥ 45°
4	37	Open	Convex	Straight
5	46	Open	Convex	Exterior < 45°
6	15	Open	Convex	Exterior ≥ 45°
7	40	Open	Concave	Straight/Exterior ≥ 45°
8	23	Retricted	Rectilinear	Straight/Interior < 45°
9	22	Restricted	Convex	Straight/Interior < 45°
10	21	Restricted	Concave	Straight/Interior < 45°
11	7	Open	Convex	Straight/Exterior < 45°
12	8	Open	Misc	Miscs
13	8	Unique	Misc	Misc
14	9	Open	Saladoid	Divers
Total	432			

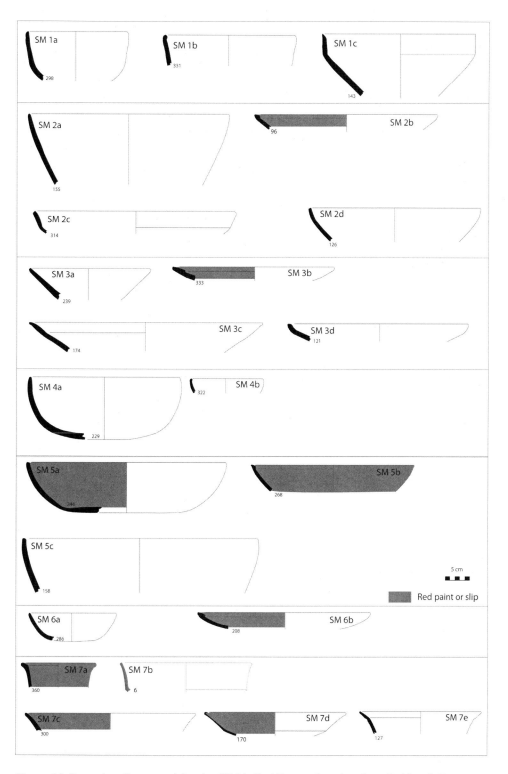

Figure 4.1 Examples of open modal series (SM 1–7). All examples taken from Parking de Roseau.

among the Late Ceramic Age potters of Capesterre. This modal series is affiliated to SM 1 and SM 3 and for this matter makes up half of the EC rim collection.

SM 2a (N=58) easily comprises half of the collection and may represent the same vessel shape which, however, comes in different sizes. When one takes the average (36.9 cm) of the sum of the most frequent number (N=2.51) as a characteristic element of the orifices of this modal subseries, one may distinguish an important peak at 42 cm and smaller peaks at 20, 30, and 36 cm with four or more individuals, thus possibly suggesting the existence of four sizes (Figure 4.2a). About half of the constituent elements are tempered with grog and

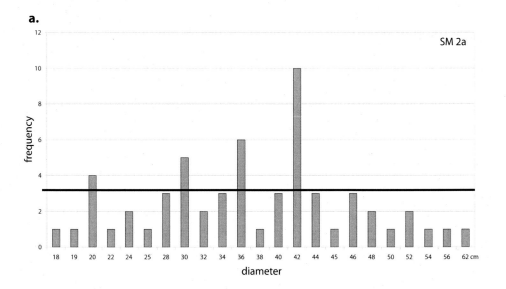

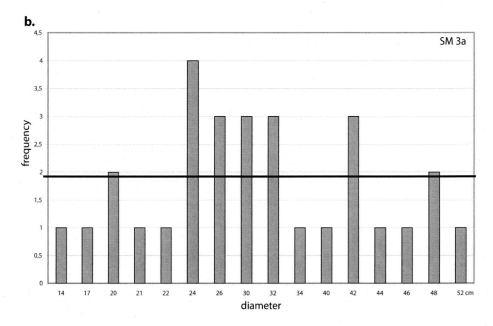

Figure 4.2 Diameter frequency of open vessels: (a) SM 2a and (b) SM 3a.

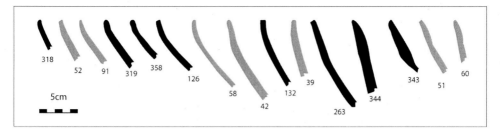

Figure 4.3 Variety at Parking de Roseau for SM 2d. Note that light grey ECs come from the beach area.

the other half with sand of which the latter have received oxidized firing and the former a reduced firing technique, as pointed out in the introduction. About ten individuals received finishing (6%) of which most were red slipped and some were scratched.

SM 2c (N=31) resembles SM 2d (N=15) of which the former has a clearly offset upper part careen and the second a "band" evoking a smoother inflection point (Figure 4.3). Together, they make up 40% of the SM 2 modal series. The outer surface of nearly 40% of SM 2c was finished with red slipping and some scratching, whereas SM 2d did not receive any surface finishing at all. When one takes the average (37.6 cm) of the sum of the most frequent number (N=2.37) as a characteristic element of the orifices of these two subseries, there are two important peaks: one at 28 cm and the other at 46 cm with more than five individuals. Other, smaller peaks are situated in between these peaks with more than three individuals suggesting a range of keeled and pseudo-keeled vessels between 28 cm and 46 cm. Interestingly, the same exercise for the separate subseries shows that the keeled bowls pertain to a wider range of orifices and the pseudo-keels to the smaller range; hence, we might propose that these two series are complementary when regarding their orifices. Temper and firing modes are the same as for SM 2a. Finally, the modal subseries SM 2b (N=6) is different because of the thickened lip applied to the inside of the vessel as well as the presence of red slip on half of the ECs. The orifices range between 24 cm and 34 cm.

SM 3. This modal series includes rectilinear rims inclined ≥45° towards the exterior and have a different labial finishing (N=47). Clearly less popular than SM 2, this class, together with SM 5 and SM 7, is the next most popular modal series. Interestingly, this modal series has not been recorded at STEP Goyave. SM 3a makes up more than half (62%) of this modal series. When one takes the average (31.4 cm) of the sum of the most frequent number (N=1.81) as a characteristic element of the orifices of this modal subseries, an important peak can be distinguished at 24 cm, accompanied by smaller peaks between 26 cm and 32 cm with more than three individuals as well as a small peak at 42 cm (Figure 4.2b). This suggests that SM 3a comes in one size (about 30 cm), but it may also be found occasionally as a larger vessel. Nearly half of the SM 3 population shows red slip, mostly on the interior, whereas some fragments have scratching. Paste and firing are again in equilibrium. The small modal subseries SM 3b (N=9) is different because of the inward thickened lip and the omnipresence of red slip. The mouths vary between 20 cm and 42 cm, proposing average-sized recipients, which can be associated to SM 2b. The other modal subseries (SM 3c and d) are minor subseries just like SM 2c and d.

SM 5. This modal series is represented by convex rims inclined <45° towards the interior without keel but with different lip finishing (N=46) of which SM 5a is dominating this modal series (58%). When one takes the average (3.7 cm) of the sum of the most frequent number

(N=1.63) as a characteristic element of the orifices of SM 5a, an important peak can be distinguished at 28 cm and smaller peaks at 32–34 cm and 46 cm with three or more individuals. This diversity suggests the presence of three vessel sizes for this modal subseries. Paste and firing values are in balance, like SM 3, with a slight preference for grog temper again. Nearly half of the elements are decorated with either slip or scratching. Interestingly, this modal series comprises the most complete vessels of all sites (N=8).

The smaller modal subseries SM 5b (N=13) has an inward thickened lip and shows much red slipping. The medium-sized vessels are affiliated to SM 2b and SM 3b for this matter. SM 5c (N=6) is affiliated with the other "banded" modal subseries.

SM 7. This modal series (N=40) represents the concave rims (SM 7a and b) as well as the concave rims inclined ≥45° towards the exterior (SM 7c–e). They represent about 6% of the constituent elements of which the relatively highly decorated modal subseries SM 7d (42%) is the most important one within SM 7. The latter modal subseries affiliates to SM 2c and SM 3c. The other modal subseries are marked by a thickened lip on the interior (SM 7a), a "banded" rim (SM 7e), and a carinated rim (SM 7b and SM d).

When one takes the average (41 cm) of the sum of the most frequent number (N=1.33) as a characteristic element of the orifices of SM 7d, an important peak can be seen at 28 cm with more than three individuals and two smaller peaks with more than two individuals at 50 cm and 54 cm. This distribution suggests the presence of two vessel sizes for this subseries. Concerning paste, it should be noted that this modal subseries is tempered with grog at Parking de Roseau and at the other sites with mineral matter, while at all sites red slip is common.

The other concave modal subseries SM 7a, SM 7b, and SM 7e (N=16) differ because of labial finishing such as thickened or everted lips towards the exterior, and morphology, i.e. carination (SM 7b), and the presence of a neck (SMa and SM 7e). SM 7c does not feature any such elements.

SM 4. This modal series concerns the convex rims ending in an upright or "straight" position (N=37) of which SM 4a is clearly dominating (81%). The inward thickened lip of SM 4b (N=7) defines the other modal subseries. This modal series is not represented at STEP Goyave and only one specimen has been found at the site of La Pointe de Grande Anse.

When one takes the average (32.2 cm) of the sum of the most frequent number (N=1.67) as a characteristic element of the orifices of SM 4a, one important peak can be witnessed at 30–32 cm with three individuals. This peak, however, is part of a large range, situated between 18 and 36 cm, with two individuals suggesting that this peak is most popular for this larger vessel size range. This modal series is barely decorated, with only two specimens showing red slip. It should be noted that surface finishing is generally rather minimal with smoothing, scratching, and unobliterated coils. Firing and temper are again in equilibrium. This modal series is remarkable for its characteristics and can be affiliated to SM 5a because of its convex rim shape.

SM 1. This modal series represents the rectilinear rims without inclination (N=34). SM 1a and SM 1c have various lip shapes whereas SM 1b only has thickened lips. SM 1c differs again because it has a carinated rim profile. This modal series has not been recorded at La Pointe de Grande Anse.

This modal series is barely decorated except for the carinated version (SM 1c), which features three slipped specimens, but also three specimens with modeled adjunctions such as vertical and rounded small lugs attached to the rim. The latter modal subseries affiliates to SM 2c when considering the sharply offset upper part and the red slip. Finally, this whole modal series is similar to SM 2 and SM 3, but appears less important.

SM 6. This modal series includes the convex rims inclined ≥45° towards the exterior (N=15). The rims with a thickened lip constitute a separate modal subseries (SM 6b). The latter modal subseries also features red slip and the orifice of its members varies between 26 and 34 cm. This modal series has not been encountered at La Pointe de Grande Anse. When one takes the average (29.6 cm) of the sum of the most frequent number (N=1.38) as a characteristic element of the orifices of SM 6a (N=10), an important peak can be distinguished at 26 cm with three individuals and another, less important peak at 34 cm with two individuals. This suggests two different sizes for this modal series. Paste and firing modes are in balance and the SM 6a modal subseries can easily be affiliated to SM 4a and SM 5a.

SM 12. This small modal series (N=6) represents the trays (Figure 4.4). They differ from the griddles in that their base (7.7 cm) and rim (8.8 cm) are thinner, but their height does not surpass about 4 cm either. Mean orifice is 34 cm and for the bases 29 cm, highlighting the tray aspect. They were found exclusively at CHU Belle-Plaine and Parking de Roseau. Despite its small number this is a highly remarkable modal series.

SM 11. Another remarkable modal series is represented by the small (finger) pots having a diameter of less than 10 cm (see Figure 4.13). They come in roundish or tronconical shapes and have been encountered at all sites.

The restricted vessels (Figure 4.4)

SM 8. This modal series represents the rectilinear rims positioned vertically or inclined <45° towards the exterior (N=23). The rims have been subdivided according to their absence (SM 8a) and presence (SM 8b) of which the former is most popular (61%). SM 8c is a unique element and represents a bottle neck; it was the only element found at CHU Belle-Plaine for this modal series. SM 8b is more decorated than SM 8a; half of the modal subseries is slipped red and it also features two different types of adjunctions or handles. Scratching is present in both modal series.

When one takes the average (35 cm) of the sum of the most frequent number (N=1.17) as a characteristic element of the orifices of SM 8a (N=14), an important peak can be distinguished at 40–42 cm with two individuals, suggesting the popularity of this larger vessel shape. SM 8 is closely related to its open counterpart SM 1.

SM 9. This modal series represents the convex rims inclined <45° towards the interior, having received different labial treatments (N=22). SM 9a is most popular (N=19) whereas SM 9b is rare and shows itself by a sharply offset upper part. Scratching (N=6) is more frequent than red slipping (N=4) for this modal series. This modal series is abundant at Parking de Roseau and CHU Belle-Plaine; only one element was recorded at La Pointe de Grande Anse and none at STEP Goyave.

When one takes the average (28.3 cm) of the sum of the most frequent number (N=1.29) as a characteristic element of the orifices of SM 9a, an important peak can be distinguished at 16 cm with more than two individuals, and another combined peak at 28 and 32 cm with two and three individuals, respectively (Figure 4.5). Vegetal and grog temper dominate the mineral temper (73%). This modal series reflects the restricted version of SM 4, but also of SM 5 and SM 6a.

SM 10. This modal series represents the concave rims positioned vertically (SM 10a) and inclined <45° towards the interior (SM 10b), having both different lip shapes (N=21). The latter modal subseries is the most popular one (53%) and is characterized by the combination of red slip and grooved incisions applied to the exterior with folded lips. EC 385 is a fine and exquisite example (see Figure 4.6) of SM 10c. Interestingly, a similar vessel was found at

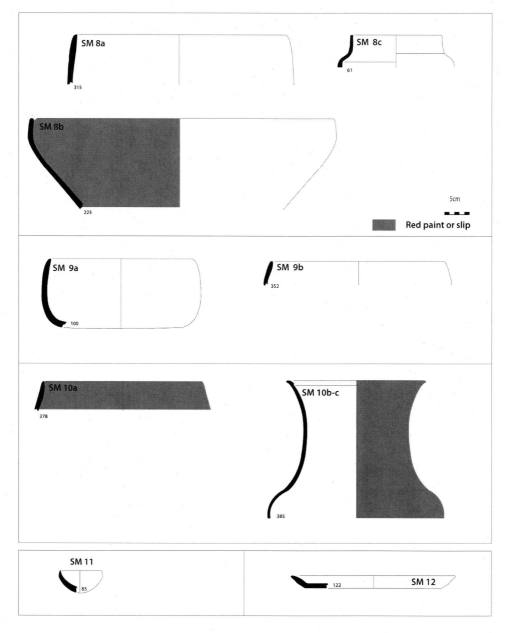

Figure 4.4 Examples of restricted modal series (SM 8–10) and special series (SM 11–12). All examples taken from Parking de Roseau, except for the rare element SM 8c, which is taken from CHU Belle-Plaine.

Les Saintes by members of Inrap (Martias 2008, Annexe B, Plate 2). Mean orifice diameter is 28 cm and 72% is tempered with grog. SM 10b is a most remarkable modal subseries and its rims are easily recognizable when field walking. SM 10a features some scratching and red slipping.

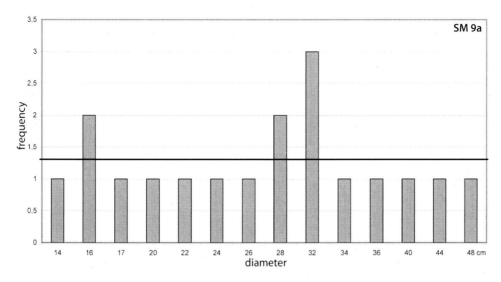

Figure 4.5 Diameter frequency of restricted vessels: SM 9a.

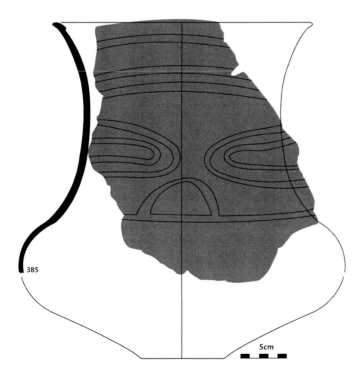

Figure 4.6 Necked vessel of Parking de Roseau (EC 385).

Drawing M. van den Bel, Inrap.

The other vessels

Unique items have been gathered in **SM 13** (N=8); we were not able to attribute them to a series as defined here. **SM 14** represents the Saladoid fragments featuring outward thickened lips, ZIC incisions, and pot stands. All were encountered at STEP Goyave (N=9).

4.1.4   The bases

The base register is composed of 145 individuals, or nearly one-quarter (23%) of the total ECs (Table 4.4). The morphological distribution permitted identification of four general base shapes: flat (SM I), concave (SM II), convex (SM III), and annular/pedestal bases (SM IV) (Figure 4.7). Nearly half of the bases are flat (49%), whereas the others are concave (38%), convex (9%), or annular/pedestal (4%). About one-quarter (27%) are decorated, mainly with red slip which is generally applied to the interior.

The flat and concave bases have been subdivided according to the profile of the first coil departing from the base (*plan d'assise*): rectilinear, convex, concave, or annular. For SM I the rectilinear (N=21) and convex (N=37) ones are most common, whereas for SM II rectilinear (N=17) and annular (N=14) are dominating. The concave profiles are minor elements and show both shapes. Convex and annular/pedestal bases are rare, but remarkable types of which the former revealed the highest number of complete vessels (N=9) and is absent at STEP Goyave. Base diameters vary enormously between 3 and 48 cm with a mean diameter of 13.3 cm and mean thickness of 9.8 cm. This large variation is due to finger pots and trays. However, when one regards the complete vessel shapes, SM III goes well with SM 5a. Other combinations do not provide significant information. Paste and firing values are similar to rim elements, perhaps with a slight advantage for grog.

Table 4.4 Modal base series (SM I–IV). Note that six base fragments were not determined.

Bases		N	Shape	Profile
I	a	21	Flat	Rectilinear
	b	9	Flat	Convex
	c	21	Flat	Very convex
	d	7	Flat	Convex (less thick)
	e	4	Flat	Concave
	f	6	Flat	Annular
II	a	17	Ombilicated	Rectilinear
	b	8	Ombilicated	Concave
	c	9	Very ombilicated	Convexe
	d	14	Ombilicated	Annular
	e	5	Ombilicated	Diverse (less thick)
III		13	Convex	
IV		5	Pedestalled	
Total		139		

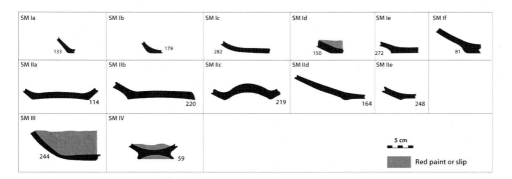

Figure 4.7 Examples of base modal series (SM I–IV).

4.1.5 The griddles

The griddles or *burén* (*plaques à cuire*) are represented by 72 individuals, or about 11% of the total of constituent elements (Table 4.5). First, the rims have been divided into flat (SM A) and elevated or footed (SM B) griddles (Figure 4.8a). Secondly, they were subdivided according to the absence or presence of the last modeled coil or lip, which usually has a triangular shape. They are sometimes "crested" or tipped and may have been positioned a little more towards the interior (i.e., retracted). Elevated (footed) griddles were absent at La Pointe de Grande Anse, but fragments of griddle feet have been identified at this site. Only two specimens (perhaps forming one griddle) were found at STEP Goyave. Traditionally, the pedestal griddles are supposed to be associated to the post-Saladoid ceramic sequence (after c. cal 700 CE) in the Windward Islands (see Allaire 1977:312–313; Bright 2011:185, 191).

The diameter of flat griddles ranges from 24 to 55 cm. Thickness varies between 7 cm and 18 cm with a mean thickness of 10 cm. The mean values of the footed griddles are similar: diameter varies between 15 cm and 54 cm and thickness between 5 cm and 15 cm with a mean of 9.9 cm. When one takes the average (38.5 cm) of the sum of the most frequent number (N=1.47) as a characteristic element of the orifices of SM A, two peaks can be distinguished with three individuals: one peak at 32 cm and another one at 44 cm (Figure 4.9a). These two peaks include two individuals showing a large distribution that cannot be assigned to a particular modal subseries. The diameters of elevated griddles are less variable; when one takes the average (37 cm) of the sum of the most frequent number (N=2) as a characteristic element of the orifices of SM B, one observes a peak at 38 cm with five individuals (Figure 4.9b). This high peak is surrounded by smaller peaks of more than three individuals ranging from 32 to 42 cm, suggesting that the latter sizes are the most common ones. It appears that footed griddles are rather standardized. The foot morphology (rounded or pointed) and the presence of an "underlip" does not seem to matter, but future research is needed on this topic with more complete specimens (see Figure 4.9b). Here we also would like to point out the presence of annular griddles as well as legged griddles (SM B3) for the Parking de Roseau site.

Table 4.5 Modal griddle series (SM A–B).

Griddles	N	Type	Lip	Remarks
A1	4	Flat	Rounded	Smooth
A2	10	Flat	Triangular	Crested
A3	13	Flat	Triangular	
A4	6	Flat	Triangular	Retracted
B1	4	Elevated	N/A	Smooth
B2	29	Elevated	Triangular	Crested
B3	4	Elevated	Pointed	
Total	70			

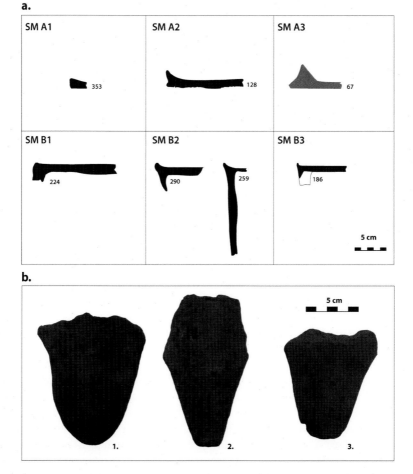

Figure 4.8 Examples of griddles: (a) the modal series (SM A–B) and (b) three griddle feet found in the northern beach area of Parking de Roseau: (1) Trench 2 (US 2–3), (2) Trench 2 (US 3), and (3) Trench 1 (US 4).

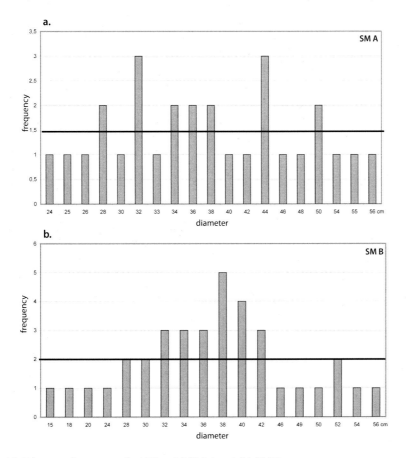

Figure 4.9 Diameter frequency of griddles: (a) SM A and (b) SM B.

4.1.6   *The decoration modes*

The percentage of decorated material for the four sites is 13.6% (see Table 4.1). Again, the decorated ECs constitute an even higher percentage of 32.6% (see Table 4.2). As mentioned earlier, this difference remains difficult to explain. It should be noted that CHU Belle-Plaine has the lowest decoration rates. The decorative repertoire is rather modest at all sites (Table 4.6). The application of red slip is omnipresent (80%), followed at a distance by incisions (7%), scratching (7%)—if one considers the latter as a mode of decoration—and adjunctions (4%). The hue of the applied red slip, apparently a highly important color, varies between 10R 4/4–6 (Weak Red-Red), 2.5YR 4/8 (Red), and 7.5R 3/4 (Dusky Red) (Munsell Soil Color Charts 1990), but may have violet tendencies when it concerns red painting.[8] It has been applied in about equal quantities to the interior, exterior, or both. White slipping is rare and mainly witnessed at Parking de Roseau, whereas polychrome slipping (orange/black and red) was found only at La Pointe de Grande Anse and WOR painting at STEP Goyave. Incisions, simple features, and/or complex motifs are mainly found on the vessel exterior, but also on the interior or lip (Figure 4.10f and i–m).

Table 4.6 Overview of ceramic decoration modes.

Mode		N	Int	Ext	Bif	Lip	
Slip							
	Red	1417	508	418	491	0	
	White	15	12	3	0	0	PDRB
	WOR	4	2	2	0	0	STEP
	Polychrome	3	1	2	0	0	LPGA
Incisions							
	Simple	84	21	50	0	13	
	Complex	37	3	32	0	2	
Scratching		116					
Adjunctions							
	Figuration	16					
	Handle	25					
	Lug	23					
	Other	17					
Total		1757					

A remarkable mixture of complex curvilinear designs with broad incisions or grooving and red slip was found, predominantly at Parking de Roseau, associated with concave rims with folded lips (SM 10b), but were absent at La Pointe de Grande Anse (Figure 4.10a–e, p). Scratching was mainly observed on vessel exteriors; it was sometimes clearly applied with a tool consisting of five or six teeth (Figures 4.10n, r, and 4.10e). Lips with finger-pressed imprints are present at CHU Belle-Plaine and Parking de Roseau (Figure 4.10g–h). Modeled adjunctions are rare, consisting mainly of strapped, looped, and sausage-shaped handles and small lugs (Figures 4.11f, r, and 4.9a, d, f–h, i). Biomorphically and anthropomorphically modeled figurations or adornos are also present but remain rare (Figure 4.9j–l). The Parking de Roseau site yielded a spectacular deposition of a vessel with coffee-bean-shaped eyes (Figure 4.10e). Finally, other modeled objects present are spindle whorls, (body) stamps, a spout, and so on. (Figures 4.8j and 4.11n).

4.1.7   Synthesis

The ceramic register

This typological synthesis is based on 616 constituent elements (EC) and 33 complete vessel shapes in combination with the associated decoration modes. The morphological rim collection shows open vessel shapes with rectilinear profiles, such as SM 2 and SM 3, but also, on a second level, convex (SM 5) and concave (SM 7) profiles. Profile shape and orifice dimension reveal tronconical-shaped basins, which can be deep and shallow. There are also small and shallow bowls. Restricted recipients (SM 8–10) are represented by rectilinear, convex, and concave profiles revealing highly similar but converging shapes (Figures 4.13 and 4.14). Labial treatment varies, but nonmodified (rounded) and thickened lips are most common. Carination and pseudocarination ("banded") are common, too, and altogether make up for the differences in the series. In short, the shape register is fairly modest, containing rather simple

Figure 4.10 Examples of decorated ware.

Photos: M. van den Bel, Inrap.

Figure 4.11 Examples of modeled decorations.

Photos: M. van den Bel, Inrap.

Figure 4.12 Examples of large fragments with profiles.

Photos: M. van den Bel, Inrap.

shapes with flat or concave bases that may be ornamented with red slip. Next to these shapes we must point out the restricted necked pots with folded lips and red slip, most often also having complex grooved incisions (SM 10b) that can be seen as an eloquent marker of the whole register. Elevated or footed griddles slightly dominate the griddle collection where lip treatment is mainly defined by triangular shapes. Interestingly, griddle-like plates or trays (SM 12) occur within this collection and may also represent another possible marker of the register.

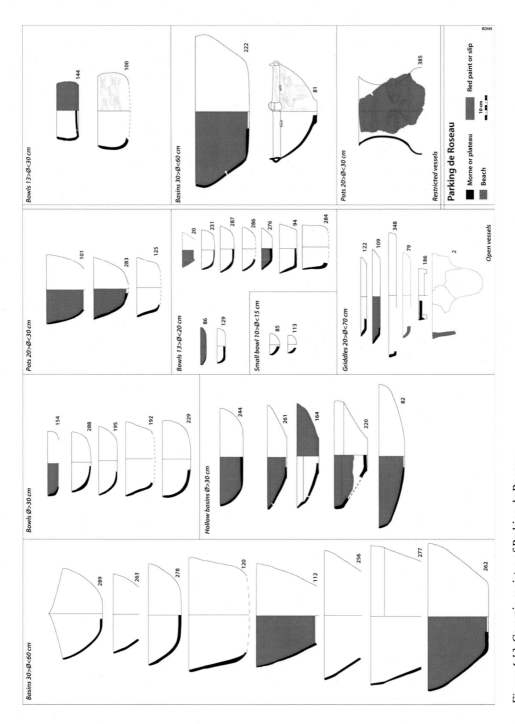

Figure 4.13 Ceramic register of Parking de Roseau.
Drawings: M. van den Bel, Inrap.

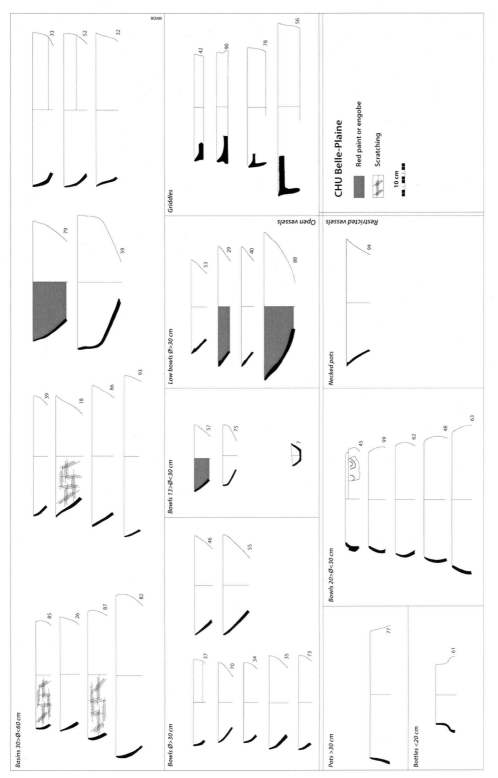

Figure 4.14 Ceramic register of CHU Belle-Plaine.
Drawing: M. van den Bel, Inrap.

Chronology and cultural affiliations

According to the radiocarbon dates, the ceramic register presented here can be attributed to the first quarter of the second millennium (cal 1000–1250 CE). Although older and younger dates have been obtained for the presented sites (with the exception of CHU Belle-Plaine), these can be attributed to previous and later occupations, which are not necessarily present within the excavated limits, with the exception of La Pointe de Grande Anse and STEP Goyave. The latter sites have clear evidence of an earlier occupation (postholes and pits, respectively) but abundant ceramic material seems to be lacking.

The majority of the ceramic assemblage should be attributed to the Mamoran Troumassoid subseries and, to a lesser extent, to the later Suazan Troumassoid subseries. A few elements can be attributed to the Late Cedrosan Saladoid subseries, thus stretching the time-span *lato sensu* of all the assemblages to about 1000 years between cal 500 and 1500 CE. Next to the sites presented here, there are other sites on Guadeloupe that yielded ceramic series attributed to the Mamoran Troumassoid subseries. The majority of these sites are multicomponent sites and have few radiocarbon dates supporting the Late Ceramic Age occupation. Here we point to excavated sites such as Anse à la Gourde at La Pointe des Châteaux (Delpuech et al. 2001b, Chapters 9.4.3–4; Pater and Teekens 2004, Chapters 6.3.2–4) and the site of Tourlourous at Capesterre-de-Marie-Galante (Bonnissent in Serrand et al. 2016, Chapter 6.5.4), which have Troumassoid components attributed to the first quarter of the second millennium. The ceramic material excavated by Gérard Richard at Plage de Roseau has recently been studied by Alice Le Lay (2013), who confirms its attribution to the Troumassoid series and that it also features Cayo ceramics and shows Chican Ostionoid traits (Le Lay 2013:86; Bochaton et al. 2021:8). Other important sites that yielded well-dated ceramic assemblages are Bisdary at Gourbeyre (Romon et al. 2006) and La Ramée at Sainte-Rose (Casagrande et al. 2016). These sites, however, did not provide radiocarbon dates younger than cal 1000 CE, and the material has been firmly attributed to the Late Cedrosan Saladoid subseries. The Early Ceramic Age sites excavated during the DRC project fall within the latter first millennium range, except for Fromager and Moulin-à-Eau 2, as mentioned in the introduction, which have a Late Ceramic Age component.

The majority of the material presented here can be assigned to the Troumassoid (i.e., post-Saladoid) series. When comparing the Late Saladoid ceramic registers from the Bisdary and La Ramée sites to single Troumassoid assemblages, such as Parking de Roseau and CHU Belle-Plaine, which are dated after cal 1000 CE, we must indeed confirm an absence of Saladoid attributes, such as outward thickened lips, hammock-shaped vessels, cartouche incisions on interior vessel rims, polychrome slipping, D-shaped handles, and the like. The differences between these Rousean subseries represent a chronocultural hinge around cal 1000 CE, but also between the Windward and Leeward Antilles, or the Troumassan and Mamoran Troumassoid subseries, respectively (see Rouse 1992:71). Concerning this matter, Guadeloupe pertains to the northern islands where the Saladoid series continue up to cal 1000 CE. This discussion, as mentioned in the introduction, was left by Petersen et al. (2004) and picked up by Hofman (2013:212) more recently, when describing the Late Ceramic Age dynamics as having "fluid boundaries" and "heterogenetic styles" in the Lesser Antilles. Regarding this heterogeneity, we must first compare our register with the post-Saladoid Mamora Bay and subsequent Freeman Bay styles as defined by Rouse and Morse (1999) for the northern Antilles nearly two decades ago. Their ceramic definition and radiocarbon dates (after cal 1000 CE) surely coincide with our series, but remain too restricted or general when compared to the Guadeloupean series. This could be related to the context of the series (midden deposits *vs* closed pits) but could also be interpreted as regional differences or styles as proliferated by the concept of heterogeneity in post-Saladoid times. The heterogeneity is believed to be the result of regional diversion from the Late Cedrosan Saladoid subseries or Mill Reef style into the Mamora Bay style. For decoration, our series show complex grooving, an important Mamoran Troumassoid marker according to Petersen et al. (2004:27), whereas thin-line incisions (with or without punctuations) are far less frequent. This mode is again more important at the site of Stade de José Bade (Bonnissent in Serrand et al. 2016, Fig. 6.44). The lattersite, for example, clearly shares omnipresence for red slipping as well as an abundance of (small) bowls, platters, nonrestricted basins, and restricted pots with folded lips at Parking de Roseau. When regarding radiocarbon dates, however, our series might be a bit younger. When compared to the previous Mill Reef style on Antigua, polychrome, or rather bichrome, painting is absent in the Mamora Bay style (see Bisdary and La Ramée). This trait, however, is present in the Late Cedrosan Saladoid subseries on Guadeloupe and the Troumassan Troumassoid subseries of Martinique or the southern islands in general (see Petersen et al. 2004:27). The inception of the Troumassoid series in the Windward Islands is believed to have taken place during the second half of the first millennium, about 250 years earlier than in the Leeward Islands (see Bérard 2013b:34, Table 1). The Troumassoid is succeeded by the Suazoid series or Suazan Troumassoid subseries, which have different dates of inception as well, i.e. cal 1200 CE and 1100 CE, respectively. It is curious to know that Suazoid sites (i.e. post-cal 1300 CE) are lacking on Guadeloupe, with only a few exceptions to date such as Anse à la Gourde and Morne Cybèle (see Hofman 1999). Indeed, on the one hand, the only precontact radiocarbon dates have been found at La Pointe de Grande Anse, but there is little material evidence to support a possible occupation. On the other hand, the main frame obtained here stops clearly around cal 1200 to 1300 CE, thus omitting the succeeding Suazoid period. At present, little data are known and various ideas suggest a population drop and/or cultural change towards the Greater Antilles, which would explain the noted Chican Ostionoid "influences." Notwithstanding this Suazoid void on Guadeloupe, numerous Mamoran Troumassoid shapes as found at CHU Belle-Plaine and Parking de Roseau are very similar to the "plain ware" of Paquemar and Macabou on Martinique (Allaire 1977, Figs. 38–43; Pinçon 2013), which actually evokes an (early?) Suazoid affiliation (Allaire 1984, 1990a). For example, CHU Belle-Plaine features rare stylistic traits showing influences from the Greater Antilles. The incised *guirlandes* (EC 45) can be found also in the Chican Ostoionoid subseries, as suggested by Louis Allaire for Martinique (1977:183, Fig. 30b; 1990a) or Hofman and Hoogland for St. Vincent (2012:66, Fig. 3d, j, m). This synchronicity shows that the Late Ceramic Age ceramic series of the Lesser Antilles is in continuous need of reassessment. Concerning Guadeloupe, Delpuech et al. (2001b) suggested two Troumassoid occupations for the site of Anse à la Gourde: an early Troumassoid occupation (Phase II) and a late occupation (Phase III), of which the first occupation has been attributed to the Mamoran Troumassoid subseries and the second one to the Suazan Troumassoid subseries (Phase I of Anse à la Gourde concerns a Saladoid occupation). Multiple radiocarbon dates are, however, lacking to provide such a division into two phases or occupations. A similar subdivision was proposed more recently by Dominique Bonnissent for the site of Stade José Bade at Marie-Galante: a first Troumassoid occupation between 950 and cal 1100 CE and a second Troumassoid occupation between cal 1100 and 1250 CE (in Serrand et al. 2016:234). Despite a few more radiocarbon dates, this division lacks typological elements to define such division within the Troumassoid series. The modal series presented here, however, do not favor such division within the Troumassoid series (Early and Late?). As noted earlier, the Basse-Terre sites are slightly different and might be a bit younger as well; hence, the supposed variation may be attributed to regional diversification of the Mamora Bay style. Continuity of this style in the north as the Freeman Bay style or in the south as Suazan Troumassoid is likely, but needs further comparison. According to Reginald Murphy (1999:50), the Freeman Bay style represents the Suazoid series of Antigua, but this "transition" between styles remains difficult to date (see Rouse et al. 1995:449). At the moment, we are experiencing similar problems at Guadeloupe, where future research and microscopic analysis of temper may shed light on the cultural hinge between the Early and Late Ceramic populations.

Only the Parking de Roseau site yielded Cayo ware, but Cayo material appears to be more abundant in the northern part of the site where Gérard Richard excavated (see Le Lay 2013). Again, it was found only in pits excavated on the beach with a possible exception for the vessel showing coffee-bean-shaped eyes that was found upside down in rectangular pit F 35. Only a few other Cayo sites have been encountered on Guadeloupe, such as Anse à la Gourde (Delpuech et al. 2001b) and Anse du Coq at Marie-Galante (Honoré 2014). Other important Cayo sites have been detected in northern Dominica (see Boomert 2010, 2011, 2013), but Cayo remains rather scarce in the Leeward Islands. Although situated in a crab-disturbed stratigraphy at the Parking de Roseau site, the admixture of Cayo wares and European goods, of which the latter are mainly attributed to the beginning of the 17th century (see Chapter 4), suggests a historical phase of this particular beach. This combination has also been encountered at Argyle, on St. Vincent, where an entire Kalinago village was excavated by Leiden University (Hofman and Hoogland 2012).

4.2   Lithics

Sebastiaan Knippenberg

This chapter discusses the lithics that have been found during the different excavations. The fair amount of stone artifacts at the various sites attests to the significant role stone played in the pre-Columbian societies of the Caribbean. As the indigenous people of this archipelago were not familiar with the use of metals, they still had to strongly rely on lithic tools in many common household activities. Especially, tasks requiring sharp, hard, or tough implements, such as cutting, scraping, drilling, grinding, abrading, engraving, and polishing were done with a series of hard rock utensils made from a variety of rock materials (Hofman et al. 2007; Knippenberg 2006; Lammers-Keijsers 2008; Rodríguez Ramos 2001). In addition to this practical purpose, stone and minerals were also valued for their decorative qualities. The Amerindians adorned themselves with beautifully polished beads and pendants, made of a special selection of rocks and minerals likely signifying their possessors' wealth, status, gender, and origin (e.g., Chanlatte Baik 1984; Watters and Scaglion 1994; Queffelec et al. 2018; Falci et al. 2020). Even stone was worshipped, as exemplified by the manufacture of very typical *cemí* three-pointer stones, a unique Caribbean artifact, reported by the early Spanish chroniclers to be related to the veneration of the deified ancestors and magical power in general and assumed to enhance agricultural fertility in particular (Oliver 2009; Pané 1999; Siegel 1997; Walker 1997). As a result of this wide range of purposes, many of the pre-Columbian lithic assemblages from the Caribbean islands display a large variety of raw materials and a highly diverse set of artifact types (see Knippenberg 2006; Rodríguez Ramos 2001; Walker 1980).

Access to proper rocks and minerals varies greatly within the Antillean archipelago owing to the region's diverse geological build-up. This is recurrent especially within the Lesser

Antillean island arc, with neighboring islands having different geological formation histories and as a result offering totally different rock materials to the communities that inhabited them (Tomblin 1975; Wadge 1994; see also Knippenberg 2006). Guadeloupe can be considered one of the most striking examples, the main land body actually being made up of two separate islands, a volcanic (Basse-Terre) and a limestone one (Grande-Terre). Furthermore, the small islands immediately surrounding it include the islet of La Désirade, a geologically unique island within the entire Lesser Antilles hosting a special suite of rocks. This means that the Amerindian communities living on Guadeloupe faced totally different lithic environments according to the island they lived on. Those who inhabited the island of Grande-Terre, where only relatively soft and often brittle calcareous rock is available, were forced to make trips to neighboring islands to obtain harder and more flakeable materials. On Basse-Terre the suite of available rocks is more extensive, and by exploiting their direct surroundings the local communities were able to obtain a large portion of their required materials.

4.2.1   Research questions

The archipelagic nature of the region and its geological interisland diversity offer the archaeologist studying stone procurement and use of lithics some great potential for understanding intercommunity interaction and interisland travel (Knippenberg 2006). Also, the relatively small size of the Lesser Antilles contributes to this potential, as it facilitates a quick and proper overview of raw material sources. These are often very localized in space and unique in characteristics, making possible distinction between raw materials from different islands and even from different locations on the same island (Knippenberg 2006, 2011a). Finally, the stone tool manufacturing process is subtractive in nature, and therefore it leaves clear traces in the archaeological record. This enables us to obtain a relatively in-depth insight into the transport-reduction sequence of raw materials and tools (Knippenberg 2006; Torrence 1986). In other words, it allows for proper identification of places where tools were being manufactured, in which form lithic materials were distributed, and where tools were being used and discarded. Given this potential, the study of the lithic assemblages from the four sites was aimed at answering the following questions:

(1) Which types of raw stone materials did the inhabitants of the different sites use for the making of their stone tools and other artifacts?
(2) Can natural sources be identified for these materials and how did the different communities obtain these materials? Did that occur by means of direct procurement or can exchange with neighboring communities be held responsible for this?
(3) In what state of reduction did the different rock materials arrive at the various sites, and which steps of the manufacturing process took place onsite? How can the different technologies of working the material be characterized?
(4) What was the aim of the production for each raw material?
(5) What was the function of the tools used at the different sites?
(6) How do the stone artifact assemblages compare to one another and how do they relate to other sites on Guadeloupe and its surrounding islands?

In order to assess these research questions, the methodology used for my Ph.D. dissertation research has been followed (Knippenberg 2006). The lithic artifacts from the different assemblages have systematically been analyzed following a predefined set of attributes (Knippenberg 2006) that was designed particularly for the analysis of Caribbean lithic assemblages, bearing in mind the questions listed. It has been used for the study of samples from many additional sites within the region (see Knippenberg 2006, 2009a-b, 2011a-b, 2012a), making detailed intersite comparisons possible.

In summary, the following attributes have been described on all artifacts: (a) raw material, (b) specific subclass of raw material, (c) artifact type, (d) length, (e) maximal dimension, (f) width, (g) thickness, (h) weight, (i) macroscopic traces of use-wear, (j) traces of burning, (k) cortex count, and (l) probable source. For better understanding of the form in which the material arrived at the site and the characteristics of the reduction and technology at the site, all flakes and flake cores have been studied on: (m) reduction/modification, (n) scar count, (o) platform type, (p) distal end, and (q) flaking technique. I refer to Knippenberg (2006) for a complete presentation of the attribute list.

4.2.2   Lithic samples

The archaeological work at the four different sites produced varying quantities of lithics. At most sites the number of rocks that have been uncovered, labeled, and bagged is larger than the actual number of stone pieces that can be classified as artifacts. In this study I consider a piece of stone to be an artifact when it was modified by humans and/or when it was brought to a site by humans if it does not naturally occur in the site area. I regard modification here in the broadest sense. This includes not only general stone working techniques such as flaking, pecking, grinding, and sawing but also related modifications as a result of abrading, hammering, and polishing, as well as modifications in shape and color due to intentional burning of the piece of rock (Knippenberg 2006:93). Despite the clear definition of an artifact, it was in some cases not straightforward to separate artifacts from natural rock. This especially applies to water-worn rock at the sites of La Pointe de Grande Anse and Parking de Roseau, as both sites border pebble beaches. Close inspection of the site areas, however, revealed that these pebbles are rare and probably do not naturally occur in the substrate.

At CHU Belle-Plaine most stone material collected and bagged during excavation can be considered natural. This applies to strongly weathered igneous rock as well as a fine-grained limestone variety. The former has changed color and turned into relatively soft material, representing the different stages in the transformation the underlying bedrock experienced during soil formation. Using the above definition, the excavations at Parking de Roseau yielded the largest assemblage of lithic artifacts with 773, followed by La Pointe de Grande Anse and STEP Goyave with, respectively, 425 and 257 lithics (Table 4.7). The assemblage from CHU Belle-Plaine is considerably smaller, with only 59 artifacts identified.

To a certain degree these differences in quantity reflect the lithic richness of each site. CHU Belle-Plaine can be considered an especially poor site, as the lithic assemblage is small, despite systematic mesh-screening of feature fills. That these quantitative differences may to a certain extent be biased is shown by the La Pointe de Grande Anse site, where the feature fill of one pit yielded the majority of material. Also the differences in area that have been excavated and variation in period and intensity of occupation may have influenced these numbers.

4.2.3   Raw materials

All four sites yielded a variety of rock materials originating from different areas and localized sources. A broad distinction can be made between groups of rock types of which each group can be associated within a specific set of interrelated artifacts, being part of the same

Table 4.7 Number of lithic artifacts according to raw material per site. For Parking de Roseau the material is grouped following different collection methodologies.

	Parking de Roseau								Points de Grande Anse				CHU Belle-Plaine		STEP Goyave	
	Features				Other contexts		Total		>1 cm		<1 cm		Total		Total	
	Hand-collected		Mesh-screened		Hand-collected											
Rock type	N	%	N	%	N	%	N	%	N	%	N	%	N	%	N	%
Flint	48	8.7	54	29.8	5	11.6	107	13.8	12	6.3	37	15.7	6	1.2	10	3.8
Chalcedony	14	2.6	53	29.3	1	2.3	68	8.8	15	7.9	57	24.2	5	1.0	1	0.4
Carnelian	1	0.2	–	–	–	–	1	0.1	–	–	–	–	–	–	–	–
Jasper	–	–	1	0.6	–	–	1	0.1	13	6.9	30	12.7	–	–	1	0.4
Chert	2	0.4	3	1.7	–	–	5	0.6	5	2.6	12	5.1	–	–	1	0.4
Quartz	–	–	4	2.2	–	–	4	0.5	–	–	6	2.5	–	–	2	0.8
Igneous rock	479	87.2	66	36.5	36	83.7	581	75.2	138	73.0	82	34.7	402	79.4	242	92.7
Augite crystal	–	–	–	–	–	–	–	–	–	–	1	0.4	–	–	–	–
Tuff	–	–	–	–	–	–	–	–	1	0.5	–	–	–	–	–	–
Limestone	1	0.2	–	–	–	–	1	0.1	–	–	–	–	91	18.0	–	–
St. Martin greenstone	2	0.4	–	–	1	2.3	3	0.4	2	1.1	–	–	–	–	–	–
Green rock	–	–	–	–	–	–	–	–	1	0.5	–	–	–	–	–	–
Fine-grained rock	–	–	–	–	–	–	–	–	1	0.5	–	–	1	0.2	1	0.4
Jadeitite	–	–	–	–	–	–	–	–	–	–	–	–	–	–	–	–
Metamorphic rock	1	0.2	–	–	–	–	1	0.1	–	–	–	–	–	–	–	–
Red ochre	–	–	–	–	–	–	–	–	–	–	1	0.4	1	0.2	4	1.5
Ironrich rock	1	0.2	–	–	–	–	1	0.1	–	–	–	–	–	–	–	–
Unidentified	–	–	–	–	–	–	–	–	1	0.5	10	4.2	–	–	–	–
Total	**549**	*100*	**181**	*100*	**43**	*100*	**773**	*100*	**189**	*100*	**236**	*100*	**506**	*100*	**261**	*100*

chaîne opératoire. Siliceous stone comprising cryptocrystalline quartz (SiO_2) rock, such as flint, jasper, and chalcedony, as well as macrocrystalline vein quartz and rock crystal, make up a significant part of the assemblages in number (see Table 4.7). Given their fine grain size, their considerable hardness and their conchoidal fracture, these rocks are predominantly associated with chipped stone aimed at the production of flake tools.

The largest portion, both in number and weight, however, consists of igneous rock present in a variety of types and grain sizes. These rocks are primarily associated with water-worn pebbles and cobbles in all shapes and sizes that had been used as core tools. Among the remainder a whole series of rare rock types occur that are predominantly associated with a limited set of tools, including axe heads and polishing stones.

Igneous rock

The largest group, both in number as well in weight, is made up by igneous rock at all four sites (see Table 4.7). The igneous rocks found display a large variety in color, grain size, and in the type and abundance of phenocrysts (mineral inclusions) (see Plates 6–16). A proper classification of igneous rocks using general petrological terminology (see Winter 2005) was beyond the scope of this study, as this requires geochemical and thin-section analysis. The rocks, however, have been grouped on the basis of their variation in presence and nature of phenocrysts, following earlier work by Christian Stouvenot (2003). The grouping was to some degree hampered by the weathering that has affected a portion of the rocks. This weathering has often changed the rock's outer color from dark hues towards lighter ones blurring the original matrix color of the rock (see, for example, Plates 4e, 6a–d, 7a, 9a, 10b, 11a-b, 12b, 16c-d, 17a–c, 18c, and 19c-d). In particular, igneous rock within the CHU Belle-Plaine and, to a lesser degree, the STEP Goyave assemblages has clearly suffered from this alteration (Plates 4e, 16c, 17b, 19c-d). Recent cleavage or minor damage to some specimens, however, has in some cases revealed the inner core, allowing for better study of the igneous rock ground mass (Plate 17a).

Despite this, it can be stated that almost all rocks are very dense, lacking vesicles. Only at STEP Goyave has a single vesicular rock been found resembling scoria or pumice. The ground mass of most igneous rock used at all sites generally exhibits an intermediate grey to bluish color tending towards mafic types, which are rocks, by definition, mainly composed of dark colored biotite, hornblende, pyroxene, and olivine (Plates 7b, 8a, 10a, 12a, 14b, d, 15, 17a, and 18c). However, true mafic igneous rock with a dark grey ground mass is rare (Plates 4a and 6e) and light-colored igneous rock, also referred to as felsic with predominantly quartz, plagioclase, feldspar, and muscovite, is almost absent.

The largest group consists of igneous rock with a mixture of light-colored (feldspar and quartz) and dark-colored phenocrysts (mafic minerals), corresponding to Stouvenot's type B (Plates 7b, 10a, 12a, 14b, and 15). CHU Belle-Plaine deviates from this as the majority of igneous rock is made up by varieties lacking clearly discernable phenocrysts.

Among the La Pointe de Grande Anse and Parking Roseau assemblages, light-colored minerals generally predominate, with a minor portion exclusively containing these felsic phenocrysts. At STEP Goyave rock with a predominance of dark-colored minerals is more abundant. Concentration of phenocrysts at all three sites exhibits considerable variation, most of the specimens possessing a moderate density, although differences between the sites are noticed. Rare specimens have a coarser mineral texture, almost grading into plutonic rock (Plate 14a-b). These can be grouped among Stouvenot's type C. True plutonic rocks, such as diorites, have, however, not been identified among the samples from the different sites.

Among type B rock great variation in cleavage behavior is noticed. A minor portion gives a regular conchoidal fracture, whereas fracture of many specimens is very irregular. In general it can be said that the higher the abundance of phenocrysts, the more irregular the rock's cleavage. Type C rock almost without exception produces irregular cleavage. Apart from these varieties displaying phenocrysts, all four sites have yielded fine-grained homogeneous rock that lacks discernible minerals (Plate 6a). These correspond to Stouvenot's type A. Especially at CHU Belle-Plaine and STEP Goyave, large portions of the igneous rock are among this type. The dark grey mafic rock variety predominates among this type at STEP Goyave. This is also the case at La Pointe de Grande Anse and Parking de Roseau, whereas at CHU Belle-Plaine the rock has a lighter hue. Stronger degree of weathering at CHU Belle-Plaine, however, might have biased this pattern. Due to their homogeneity and lack of larger mineral inclusions, most of the rock belonging to this group gives a regular conchoidal fracture and this makes it a proper material to be reduced and worked by percussion flaking.

Acquisition

Without having made an in-depth petrographic study using thin-section and geochemical analysis, it can still be stated that the listed groups of igneous rocks fall within the range of rocks that can be found locally on the volcanic island of Basse-Terre (Stouvenot 2003). The majority of the material, especially the B and C types, consists of water-worn pebbles and cobbles in different shapes and sizes. Many have somewhat irregular shapes, suggesting they had been acquired from river beds (**Plates 10a-b, 14d, 17a-b,** and **19c-d**); others possess very regular and symmetrical oval to round forms indicating that also cobble beaches had been visited for the acquisition of material (**Plates 6a, 7a-b, 8a-b, 9b, 14b, 16d,** and **20a-b**). At three sites both contexts are nearby. At La Pointe de Grande Anse, the little river Grand Anse drains through an area where the magmatic deposits of the Madeleine Soufrière massif surface (Stouvenot in Toledo i Mur et al. 2004). Its riverbeds offer a whole range of pebbles and cobbles, as well as the nearby cobble beach. Making a personal comparison of the naturally available igneous rock with the artifacts, I learned that the similarity is striking and that the community of La Pointe de Grande Anse explored their nearby surroundings for the acquisition of proper pebbles and cobbles to be used as tools.

Also, the Parking de Roseau site has both contexts nearby. A small stream, Pont Ravine, runs approximately 200 m to the north of the excavated area; the larger Rivière de Sainte-Marie can be found around 500 m more north. At both, rock in all sizes can be collected. In addition to this, extensive parts of the shoreline contain water-worn pebbles and cobbles. Limited inspection of all these contexts revealed that igneous rock types cover most of the range that can be found at the site. At Goyave the stream of the Petite Rivière de Goyave runs approximately 100 m north of the site and is the most likely place from where the local communities collected the igneous rock. The nearest coastal occurrences are approximately 500 m to the southwest.

Only at CHU Belle-Plaine was igneous water-worn rock unavailable in the direct site surroundings. In order to obtain this, the CHU Belle-Plaine community had to explore the cobble beaches along the north coast of Basse-Terre. This easy availability of igneous rock at the first three sites applies to the B and C types. The fine-grained igneous rock of type A was probably harder to find. Inspection of the Pointe de Grande Anse surroundings showed that this type of igneous rock is very rare. Stouvenot (2003) notes that this rock type can be found to the north of the Pérou River, where magmatic deposits of the Matéliane-Piton de Bouillante surface.

Cryptocrystalline quartz rock

In contrast to the abundant local availability of proper igneous rock at many of the sites, cryptocrystalline quartz rock, often grouped under the general term "chert" (Leudtke 1992), can be considered absent in the immediate site surroundings. Still, all four sites yielded fair numbers of different varieties of chert, including flint, chalcedony, and jasper (Tables 4.7–4.8). Each variety and its likely provenance will be discussed in the following paragraphs.

Flint

The nodular type of chert that forms in banks within fine-grained homogeneous limestone is called flint (Knippenberg 2006; Leudtke 1992). It was generally a much desired raw material for its often superb quality. Within the four assemblages, different varieties of flint have been identified. By far most abundant and occurring at all four sites is Long Island flint (see Table 4.15). Other varieties include Coconut Hall and Blackman's Point flint, both from Antigua, in addition to an unknown light grey–brown flint variety found at Roseau.

LONG ISLAND FLINT

Making up around 50% or more of all cryptocrystalline quartz rock in all four assemblages is Long Island flint, originating from a small islet off the north coast of Antigua (Knippenberg 2006; van Gijn 1996) (Figure 4.15). Here it is present as round nodules and tubers in fine-grained limestone (mudstone) of the Antigua Formation dating from the Oligocene, which outcrops on the island, as well as in extensive secondary occurrences covering almost the entire northern part of this islet (Knippenberg 2006; van Gijn 1996). Both its high quality as well as its easy accessibility must be held responsible for its popularity during Amerindian times. In the Archaic and in the Ceramic Age, it was the most utilized raw material for the manufacture of flake tools in the northwestern Lesser Antilles (Bonnissent 2008; deMille 2005; Hofman and Hoogland 2003; Knippenberg 1999a, 1999b, 2006). Ceramic Age sites on Guadeloupe often display a high abundance of this material (Knippenberg 2006, 2009b, 2012a).

The Long Island flint artifacts discovered at the four sites in this study display colors ranging from dark grey to light brown, to yellowish brown (also referred to as honey brown) and have a very fine grain size and homogeneous texture (Plates 1a, c, j, l, and 2b-c, e, h–k). Based on the type of cortex still present on a portion of the artifacts, it has become clear that secondary material was collected. The cortex was either (water) worn or displays patinated surfaces, resulting from natural breakage of the flint, and the broken surface being exposed to chemical and mechanical weathering when being buried in the soil. This variation in cortex types suggests that both cobble beaches along the northern shore and more inland surface scatters were exploited.

COCONUT HALL AND BLACKMAN'S POINT FLINT

Other recognized flint includes the Coconut Hall (Plates 1h, 2d-e) and Blackman's Point varieties (Plate 1i). Coconut Hall flint has been found in small quantities at Parking de Roseau, Pointe de Grande Anse, and STEP Goyave, whereas Blackman's Point flint has only been identified once, at Parking de Roseau. Both are flint varieties that originate from the same Oligocene limestone formation on Antigua as Long Island flint does. Coconut Hall

Table 4.8 Number of crypto- and macrocrystalline artifacts by subvariety per site.

Rock variety	Parking de Roseau								Pointe de Grande Anse				STEP Goyave		CHU Belle-Plaine	
	Features				Other contexts		Total		>1 cm		< 1 cm		Total		Total	
	Hand-collected		Mesh-screened		Hand-collected											
	N	%	N	%	N	%	N	%	N	%	N	%	N	%	N	%
Flint																
Long Island	41	63.1	37	32.2	3	50.0	81	43.5	11	24.4	37	26.1	9	64.3	5	55.6
Coconut Hall	3	4.6	6	5.2	–	–	9	4.8	1	2.2	–	–	1	7.1	–	–
Blackman's Point	1	1.5	–	–	–	–	1	0.5	–	–	–	–	–	–	–	–
Unspecified	1	1.5	4	3.5	1	16.7	6	3.2	–	–	–	–	–	–	–	–
Burnt (unspecified)	1	1.5	7	6.1	1	16.7	9	4.8	–	–	–	–	1	–	1	11.1
Total	**47**	**72.3**	**54**	**47.0**	**5**	**83.3**	**106**	**57.0**	**12**	**26.7**	**37**	**26.1**	**10**	**71.4**	**6**	**66.7**
Chalcedony																
Dull	7	10.8	21	18.3	–	–	28	15.1	3	6.7	2	1.4	1	7.1	3	33.3
White with grey glaze	–	–	–	–	–	–	–	–	4	8.9	19	13.4	–	–	–	–
Transparant	6	9.2	21	18.3	1	16.7	28	15.1	1	2.2	7	4.9	–	–	1	11.1
Transparant brown	–	–	–	–	–	–	–	–	–	–	8	5.6	–	–	–	–
Transparant dark grey	–	–	–	–	–	–	–	–	4	8.9	21	14.8	–	–	–	–
Siliciied wood	1	1.5	1	0.9	–	–	2	1.1	–	–	–	–	–	–	–	–
Other	1	1.5	10	8.7	–	–	11	5.9	3	6.7	–	–	–	–	–	–
Total	**15**	**23.1**	**53**	**46.1**	**1**	**16.7**	**69**	**37.1**	**15**	**33.3**	**57**	**40.1**	**1**	**7.1**	**4**	**44.4**
Carnelian																
Total	**1**	**1.5**	–		–		**1**	**0.5**	–		–		–		–	

(Continued)

Table 4.8 (Continued)

Rock variety	Parking de Roseau								Pointe de Grande Anse				STEP Goyave		CHU Belle-Plaine	
	Features				Other contexts		Total		>1 cm		<1 cm		Total		Total	
	Hand-collected		Mesh-screened		Hand-collected											
	N	%	N	%	N	%	N	%	N	%	N	%	N	%	N	%
Jasper																
Red Terres-de-Bas	–	–	–	–	–	–	–	–	11	24.4	22	15.5	–	–	–	–
Red	–	–	–	–	–	–	–	–	2	4.4	8	5.6	–	–	–	–
Other	–	–	1	0.9	–	–	1	0.5	–	–	–	–	–	–	–	–
Total	–	–	**1**	**0.9**	–	–	**1**	**0.5**	**13**	**28.9**	**30**	**21.1**	–	–	–	–
Chert (unspecified)																
Total	**2**	**3.1**	**3**	**2.6**	–	–	**5**	**2.7**	**5**	**11.1**	**12**	**8.5**	**1**	**7.1**	**1**	**11.1**
Quartz																
Milky quartz	–	–	3	2.6	–	–	3	1.6	–	–	6	4.2	1	7.1	–	–
Rock crystal	–	–	1	0.9	–	–	1	0.5	–	–	–	–	1	7.1	–	–
Total	–	–	**4**	**3.5**	–	–	**4**	**2.2**	–	–	–	–	**2**	**14.3**	–	–
Total	**65**	**100**	**115**	**100**	**6**	**100**	**186**	**100**	**45**	**100**	**142**	**100**	**14**	**100**	**11**	**100**

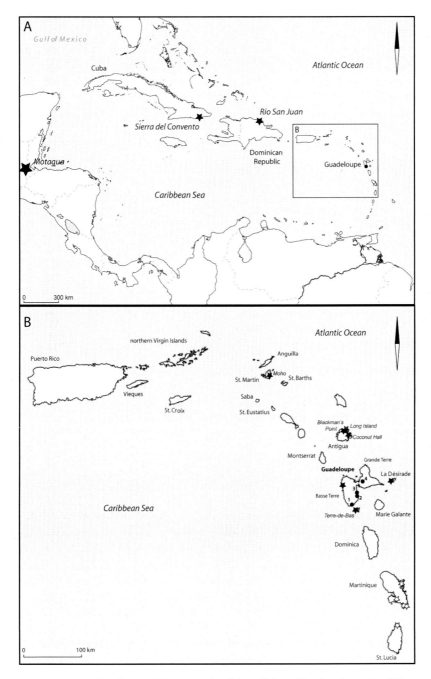

Figure 4.15 Maps showing the possible source localities of the utilized rocks at the different sites: A. Map of the Caribbean showing the locations of the three known jadeitite occurrences (black stars) (after García-Casco et al. 2013; Schertl et al. 2018). B. Map of the northern Lesser Antilles showing the source locations (black stars) and the sites discussed in this work (black dots). White stars give the locations of the main jasper sources in the southern Lesser Antilles. Archaeological sites: 1. La Pointe de Grande-Anse; 2. Parking de Roseau; 3. STEP Goyave; 4. CHU Belle-Plaine.

flint can only be found in secondary form. Its occurrence is very localized, situated at the Coconut Hall peninsula along Antigua's northeastern coast, and consists of a surface scatter of differently sized cobbles (Knippenberg 2006) (see Figure 4.15). The flint often has a heterogeneous appearance, with clearly visible fossil fragments and different-colored zones, often grading from light (greyish) brown to brown. It has a fine-grained texture, which is slightly coarser than the Long Island variety. This flint material was exploited only during the Ceramic Age, notably in its later phase (cal 800–1500 CE), and can be considered less popular than Long Island flint (Knippenberg 2006, 2011a). It is often found in very low quantities at sites surrounding Antigua (Knippenberg 2006, 2011a).

Blackman's Point represents the third flint variety from Antigua. Similar to Coconut Hall, the Blackman's Point source represents a secondary occurrence of differently sized flint cobbles at the Blackman's Point peninsula of Antigua's northern coast, facing Long Island (Knippenberg 2006) (see Figure 4.15). The flint is fine grained, although on average its grain size is coarser than that of the Long Island material. In general it has a relatively homogeneous matrix without many discernible fossils or other clasts. A small portion, however, may contain clearly visible clasts, giving the rock a heterogeneous appearance. Similar to Coconut Hall, the color hues are in general light, grading from light pink to yellow to light reddish brown to light brown. Also, this flint variety was used only during the Late Ceramic Age and displays a similarly infrequent usage on Antigua and the surrounding islands (Knippenberg 2006, 2009b, 2011a).

Chalcedony

As a rock type chalcedony is generally referred to as a translucent variety of cryptocrystalline quartz (Bates and Jackson 1984), although it may grade into more dull types within single outcrops. When banded it is called agate, and the name "carnelian" is used to refer to orange varieties of chalcedony (Bates and Jackson 1984). Chalcedony can form in limestone, but its occurrence in igneous rocks as vein or cavity fillings precipitated from silica-bearing solutions is predominant (Hamilton et al. 1992). Due to this manner of formation, chalcedony occurrences can be numerous, small, and isolated.

Chalcedony has been identified at all four sites in varying amounts (see Table 4.8). At La Pointe de Grande Anse it is the most abundant cryptocrystalline rock variety, whereas at Parking de Roseau and CHU Belle-Plaine it is the second most numerous variety, after flint. At STEP Goyave it is relatively rare. The artifacts exhibit a variety in color and translucency (Plates 1d-e, g, and 2g, l). Most pieces possess some degree of translucency and are light in color, grading from white to light yellow brown, to light grey or even to light pink. Also, petrified wood at Parking de Roseau and silicified coral at Pointe de Grande Anse have been identified, as well as a single orange translucent artifact of carnelian at Parking de Roseau (Plate 1b). The small size of the artifacts and small number for each group make it difficult to evaluate to what extent this variation actually reflects the use of different source localities or whether the internal variation among single chalcedony pieces or varieties can be held responsible for this diversity.

Within the Caribbean, the formation of chalcedony is often associated with hydrothermal processes in igneous rock, although it is rarely reported in other contexts as well (Bérard and Vernet 1997; Knippenberg 2006; 2011a). Given the volcanic nature of the Lesser Antillean archipelago it is found on many islands, often in very localized and small outcrops (Bérard 2004; Bérard and Vernet 1997; Knippenberg 2006, 2011a; Westercamp and Tazieff

1980:29). With many of these, petrified wood is associated as well (Knippenberg 2011a; Westercamp and Tazieff 1980:29).

Basse-Terre, the volcanic part of Guadeloupe, has very rare secondary occurrences of chalcedony, including silicified corals (Stouvenot, pers. commun. 2009, 2015). It can be found in lapilli deposits along with other nonigneous rocks that were transported during volcanic outbursts. It can be collected occasionally from one of the cobble beaches along the northwestern shore, between Bouillante and Deshaies (personal observation 2015, 2016).

However, it is more abundant on the neighboring islands to the south, notably Martinique and St. Lucia, and to a lesser extent Dominica (Bérard 2004; Bérard and Vernet 1997; Honeychurch 1995; Knippenberg 2006, 2011a).[9] On the former two islands it is associated with relatively extensive jasper occurrences, and the material exhibits a great diversity there. On Dominica occurrences are rarer and seem to be less abundant. Antigua has chalcedony as well, and the only occurrence of carnelian in the Lesser Antilles is hypothesized to be situated on this island, although the exact location has not been found yet (Murphy et al. 2000). The presence of a possible carnelian artifact may point to the use of an Antiguan occurrence. Given the high abundance of chalcedony at Parking de Roseau and Belle-Plaine compared to jasper (see next section), it suggests occurrences were visited that did not provide abundant jasper. This supports the use of a local Guadeloupean or Dominican source.

Jasper

Jasper, an often dull red, but also yellow, brown, and green cryptocrystalline rock, can form near iron ores or in veins in igneous rock as a result of hydrothermal alternation and silica precipitation (Bates and Jackson 1984). Similar to chalcedony, its occurrence may be very localized, although jasper in the Antilles is often more predominant in these hydrothermally altered igneous rock areas than is chalcedony (Bérard 2004; Bérard and Vernet 1997; Knippenberg 2011a). Jasper is much less abundant than chalcedony at the studied sites, Pointe de Grande Anse being the only exception (see Table 4.8). Here both varieties occur in almost equal quantities. At Parking de Roseau only a single piece has been found, whereas at Belle-Plaine and Goyave jasper is absent. At Pointe de Grande Anse, most jasper is a characteristic dull red variety, often also including grey and brown areas (Plate 2a). This material varies in grain size and may contain small cavities, making it a mediocre rock for flaking. Other jasper at Pointe de Grande Anse is clearer red with a fine grain size. The only jasper piece found at Parking de Roseau is from a multicolored variety (Plate 1k). It has a dark red color in the core, grading to yellow-brown on the outside.

It is unknown from where these jasper varieties originate. Most of the previously mentioned islands, including Guadeloupe (Basse-Terre), Martinique, and St. Lucia, that have chalcedony occurrences also possess significant jasper sources (Bérard and Vernet 1997; Knippenberg 2011a; Stouvenot, pers. comm. 2009, 2015). The clear red single piece found at Pointe de Grande Anse bears similarities with red varieties found at the main jasper sources on Martinique and St. Lucia, but it also looks similar to the less common red jasper that can be found scattered at the cobble beaches of the northwestern shores of Basse-Terre (Guadeloupe), where chalcedony is also found. In the paragraph on chalcedony it was suggested that the Parking de Roseau and Goyave communities might have exploited these more local occurrences, which indicates that jasper could have been collected as well. The absence of the yellow variety of jasper, which is abundant on Martinique and St. Lucia, is another indication that this material did not derive from these more distant sources.

However, the predominant jasper variety found at Pointe de Grande Anse and the piece at Parking de Roseau do not bear any similarity with the known varieties of any of these three islands. Christian Stouvenot has reported an even higher abundance of similar material at the d'Anse Pajot site on Terre-de-Bas, Les Saintes, a small island facing Pointe de Grande Anse (Stouvenot in Toledo i Mur et al. 2004). The high abundance at these two closely located Ceramic Age sites and the absence or low occurrence at other Ceramic Age sites on Guadeloupe, suggests that this jasper must have had a more local origin. Its source has been hypothesized to be likely on the small island of Terre-de-Bas, taking into account that the material is most abundant at d'Anse Pajot (Figure 4.15).

Other chert

Apart from the previously presented cryptocrystalline rock, a dull light-green chert found at Goyave should be mentioned. It is fine-grained and has a very homogenous texture and matrix without any visible inclusions (Plate 2f). This makes it likely that it does not represent a flint. Its source, however, remains unspecified.

Quartz (macrocrystalline)

Different varieties can be grouped under macrocrystalline quartz. Most common are quartz fillings in veins, often also referred to as milky quartz due to its white color. If cavities or veins have enough space and there is enough time for material to crystallize, crystal quartz or rock crystal may be formed, often exposing the characteristic hexagonal rhombohedral crystal form. The name "rock crystal" is reserved for the translucent varieties of such quartz, whereas amethyst, rose quartz, and smoky quartz are names used for colored varieties (Hamilton et al. 1992; Schumann 2001).

Both milky quartz and rock crystal have been identified in small numbers (see Table 4.8). Parking de Roseau and Goyave yielded both quartz types (Plate 5f). The crystal variety has also been seen among the mesh-screened material from La Pointe de Grande Anse within the fraction less than 1 cm. It should be questioned whether this material can be considered to be artifacts. An alternative explanation is that these pieces represent small natural mineral grains weathered out of igneous rock.

Specifying a source for these materials is difficult to almost impossible, as milky quartz especially is found widespread as vein infillings among the Lesser Antilles, notably in association with plutonic rock bodies (e.g., Virgin Gorda of the British Virgin Islands and some of its surrounding islets), although sometimes in very small and localized settings. Small, secondary water-worn cobbles have been seen along the same northwestern shores of Basse-Terre where some of the jasper and chalcedony is found (personal observation 2015), and these may well be where the communities at Goyave and Parking de Roseau gathered it. Rock crystal is less frequent on the islands. I do not know of any occurrences on Basse-Terre, but this does not exclude its presence on this volcanic half of Guadeloupe. I have seen a true occurrence in El Yunque forest, in Puerto Rico; on Canouan, of St. Vincent and the Grenadines; and on St. John, one of the US Virgin Islands. It is also reported to occur on Antigua (Murphy et al. 2000).

St. Martin grey-green tuffaceous mudstone

At the sites of Point de Grande Anse and Roseau five artifacts are made of a very characteristic rock called St. Martin greenstone. It is a much used and distributed rock type among the Lesser Antilles (Knippenberg 2006). Earlier research has shown that it represents a grey-green mudstone containing a volcanoclastic component in the form of wind-blown plagioclase minerals and possibly tuff (Knippenberg 2006). It very characteristically weathers into a white, corroded chalky-looking rock, as is also the case for the Parking de Roseau and Pointe de Grande Anse artifacts (Plates 3b-c and 4b-c). The extent of weathering, however, can vary a lot, from completely corroded specimens, to partly corroded pieces exposing limited areas of original grey-green nonweathered fine surface, to rare, only somewhat weathered axes.[10] The Parking de Roseau specimens have been weathered completely into white corroded rock, whereas in the Pointe de Grande Anse assemblage one artifact still exposes a portion of the light grey-green, fine-grained rock (Plate 4c). Apart from a difference in appearance, the weathering has affected the entire rock in the case of two artifacts at Parking de Roseau, as both have become very light in weight. This is probably related to the dissolution of the calcite fraction in the rock as a result of the local acid soil conditions at this site.

Due to its fine grain size and significant weathering, it has been difficult to classify the rock and as a result it has received various names, including chalky chert, radiolarian limestone, cherty carbonate, as well as *cherto-tuffite* in French reports (Haviser 1987, 1999; Knippenberg 1999a, 2004, 2006; Stouvenot 2003). Since my Ph.D. work it has been called St. Martin greenstone to emphasize its color, which likely played a role in choosing this material for artifact manufacture. It has to be emphasized that the term "greenstone" is not used here in a geological sense, as it is a metamorphosed basic igneous rock mainly composed of chlorite, actinolite, or epidote (Bates and Jackson 1984).

Petrographic and archaeological work has shown that this sedimentary greenstone originates from the Middle to Late Eocene Pointe Blanche Formation on St. Martin, hosting a bedded sequence of fine-grained (recrystallized) green and white tuffs, calcareous tuffs, and cherts (Christman 1953; Knippenberg 2006). The distribution of outcrops of this rock type are numerous on the island and can be extensive. Especially along the southeastern coastline, impressive rock sections are present at Little Bay, Point Blanche, Red Pond, Devils Cupper, and Cole Bay. Whether these locations functioned as sources for this material has to be doubted. Preliminary geochemical work of St. Martin greenstone artifacts from the Early Ceramic Age site of Anse des Pères has revealed limited variation in trace-element composition, suggesting the exploitation of localized outcrops that exposed only a limited range of beds (Knippenberg 2006:89–92). Outcrops at Moho may have been such a location (see Figure 4.15). Recent survey work has discovered a workshop site of this material along the small Ravine de Moho (Fouéré 2006; see also Bonnissent 2008, I:207, Fig. 478).

La Pointe de Grande Anse excavations yielded a third artifact that may originate from the same Pointe Blanche Formation. It is a fine-grained, grey-green to light-green layered rock, less cherty in appearance than the nonweathered parts of the St. Martin tuffaceous mudstone discussed earlier (Plate 4d). It also lacks the typical weathering. However, its color and grain size as well as the layering fall within the range of bedded rock being part of the Pointe Blanche Formation.

Metavolcanics

SMALL WATER-WORN PEBBLES

Apart from the abundant amounts of igneous rock and the variation they exhibit in grain size and mineral contents, there is a small portion of material that is different in nature and bears evidence that it has undergone some form of metamorphism. Recurrent is a group of small water-worn pebbles with a fine-grained matrix, in texture resembling quartzites, in which some larger minerals float (Plate 5a). They vary in color from light green to blue. These rocks have been found at Parking de Roseau, STEP Goyave, and CHU Belle-Plaine. To some degree they exhibit similarity with fine-grained metavolcanics found on the island of La Désirade (see Figure 4.15) (Bouysse et al. 1983; see also Knippenberg 2006). More in-depth petrographic analysis, however, should clarify whether they actually came from this small island northeast to Grande-Terre.

STEP Goyave yielded one water-worn pebble fragment of which the fine grain size did not allow for proper identification of the rock type. It has a very light green color and does not contain any inclusions. It may represent a very fine tuff, a noncarboneous siltstone or mudstone, a metavolcanic, or even a chert.

DARK GREY METAVOLCANIC

The Parking de Roseau assemblage includes an axe head made of a fine-grained dark grey rock possessing an extensive milky quartz vein, making up a large part of the artifact (Plate 3d). Based on the characteristic fine-grained, sugary texture and presence of milky quartz vein, it probably represents a mafic meta-volcanic rock. Also, this rock probably originates from somewhere outside Basse-Terre. Petrologic work is needed to characterize this rock and evaluate its possible origins. It is known that dark-colored metavolcanics have been produced abundantly on the Greater Antilles (see, for example, Knippenberg 2012b) and an origin from one of these islands should be considered as a possibility.

Jadeitite

The Pointe de Grande Anse site has yielded a flake fragment that was struck from a ground stone artifact, likely an axe head, made of jadeitite, the rock primarily composed of the rare mineral jadeite (Plate 5a). This identification has been made only by macroscopic inspection using a hand lens. Experience with other assemblages that have received more in-depth petrographic, mineralogical, and geochemical analyses has shown that jadeitite artifacts in the Caribbean stand out and can fairly easily be distinguished from other rocks (Hardy 2008; Harlow et al. 2006; García-Casco et al. 2013; Knippenberg et al. 2012; Schertl et al. 2018).

It is also through these works that it has recently become evident that jadeitite was frequently and widely used as a raw material for axe heads in the Lesser Antilles and Virgin Islands (Hardy 2008; Harlow et al. 2006; García-Casco et al. 2009, 2013; Knippenberg et al. 2012; Rodríguez Ramos 2010, 2011; Schertl et al. 2018). Sources of this material can be found in the Río San Juan area of the northern Dominican Republic, the Sierra del Convento, in southeastern Cuba, and the Motagua Valley, in Guatemala (see Figure 4.15) (Harlow 1993; Harlow et al. 2011; García-Casco et al. 2009; Schertl et al. 2012). Preliminary results from in-depth mineralogical, petrologic, and geochemical analyses on the provenance of axe heads found in the Lesser Antilles and the Virgin Islands, as well as from studied samples found in Puerto Rico and the Dominican Republic, demonstrate that pinpointing a source is difficult, but that potentially all three source regions might have been of significance to the distributed jadeitites in the eastern Caribbean. In particular, the Río San Juan and Motagua source materials exhibit strongest similarities with these artifacts (Harlow et al. 2006; García-Casco et al. 2009, 2013; Schertl et al. 2018), making the Dominican Republic source the most likely origin given its closer proximity and based on the co-occurrence of Ceramic Age settling of this island and distribution jadeitite in the Antilles.

Felsic igneous rock

The Parking de Roseau assemblage includes another unique material associated with the use of axe heads. It relates to a light-green, possibly felsic igneous rock variety (Plate 3a). Many small mineral grains can be discerned under magnification. Among them quartz and black mafic minerals can be differentiated. The rock also possesses a very thin white vein that exhibits minor evidence of weathering. Based on the latter feature, it likely is feldspar, rather than quartz. This rock possibly originates outside Basse-Terre as well. Its exact provenance, however, cannot be specified for now due to lack of reference material.

Lithified coral

The Parking de Roseau assemblage includes a single piece of lithified coral. Likely this specimen was obtained locally as coral reefs occur along the coast.

4.2.4   Artifacts

Ceramic Age lithic assemblages in the Caribbean often display a wide variety of lithics, including artifacts that can be associated with both flaked and ground stone technologies, in addition to a whole series of use-modified tools, as well as manuports and items modified only due to intentional burning (Knippenberg 2006). The lithic assemblages discussed in this work largely include this range. Flaked stone aimed at the manufacture of flake tools, often the most numerous part within Ceramic Age lithic assemblages, includes approximately one-third of the total number of stone artifacts at most sites. True ground and polished stone tools, such as axe heads, are rare in the collections, other shaped tools (certain types of querns) are also rare, and only at the Parking de Roseau site has a polished bead been found.

Use-modified tools, to the contrary, including a whole range of water-worn pebbles and cobbles in different shapes and sizes utilized for a variety of purposes, form a significant part of the large assemblages of Parking de Roseau (~16%), Pointe de Grande Anse (~17%), and STEP Goyave (~12%). They are rare at CHU Belle-Plaine. Unmodified water-worn pebbles or fragments thereof without any signs of usage or other forms of artificial modification are numerous at, again, the three largest assemblages (~45%). Finally, burned rock makes up only a small portion at the four sites.

Flaked stone

All four assemblages include a relatively large number of flakes, cores, and related debitage, clearly showing rock had been worked at all four sites. At three sites a clear distinction can be made between two sets of flaked stone for which the reduction followed separate *chaînes opératoires*. The largest group is related to the local reduction of cryptocrystalline rock, including milky quartz (Plates 1 and 2), and the other group is related to the reduction of igneous rock, predominantly in pebble or cobble form (Plates 4a, 6c–e, and 16a–c). Both groups display clear differences in reduction sequence, flaking characteristics, and size of the material. Only the CHU Belle-Plaine assemblage deviates from this. At this site almost all flaked stone is associated with chert and quartz, whereas only a single igneous rock flake has been found, indicating that the reduction of igneous rock did not form a structural element.

REDUCTION OF CRYPTO- AND MACROCRYSTALLINE QUARTZ ROCK

The presence of flakes, flake cores, shatter (blocs), and other waste, or *débitage*, clearly suggests crypto- and macrocrystalline quartz rock was reduced at all four sites (Tables 4.9 and 4.10). The absence of blades shows that reduction was directed towards producing flakes as the main basic tool form. This is in agreement with other Lesser Antillean Ceramic Age lithic assemblages, where the manufacture of blade tools did not occur (Bérard 2004, 2008; Crock and Bartone 1998; DeMille 1996; Fouéré 2003, 2006; Knippenberg 2006; Walker 1980).

The significant differences in the number of artifacts recovered may bias our views on the characteristics of the local reduction at each site. The low number of cryptocrystalline quartz flaked artifacts at the STEP Goyave and CHU Belle-Plaine severely limits the information we can obtain on raw material acquisition, cobble reduction, tool manufacture, and tool use for these two settlements. In this respect, Parking de Roseau provides the best data, having yielded 183 artifacts. Still, the amount of flaked stone at this site is relatively small when compared to other lithic assemblages from Ceramic Age sites in the surrounding region (see, for example, Crock and Bartone 1998; DeMille 1996; Knippenberg 2006; Rodríguez Ramos 2001), much owing to the restricted use of mesh screens during excavation. An elaborate description of the Parking de Roseau material will be presented first, followed by a short presentation of the material from the other sites.

PARKING DE ROSEAU

At Parking de Roseau the cryptocrystalline artifacts are on average small in size, with most artifacts ranging from 1 cm to 4 cm (Figure 4.16). It is noticed that the flint material is larger than the chalcedony artifacts (Figures 4.17 and 4.18). Taking a closer look at the cores, it becomes clear that except for a chert specimen with a maximum dimension of 5.7 cm, all cores are smaller than 3.5 cm. Most pieces have been exhaustively reduced. This makes proper evaluation of the original size of the unworked material difficult. The largest Long Island flake, of 6.9 cm (Plate 1l), provides a minimum dimension for unworked raw material. It is noticed that the largest flake among the chalcedony is only 3.7 cm, again suggesting that originally this type of cryptocrystalline rock was smaller.

Study of the cortex or natural outer surface shows that secondary material was collected (that is, material that had eroded out of its primary context) and could have been collected from surface scatters. The flint cortex and patinated natural cleavage planes on the Long Island and Coconut Hall pieces are in most cases characteristic of material that can be picked up from inland surface scatters. This material can be found in abundance at the edge of the northern shore of Long Island where erosion exposes eluvial flints that are buried in the topsoil (see Knippenberg 2006). At Coconut Hall natural scatters are more inland, bordering the local settlement site. The chalcedony material lacks the formation of cortical rinds, so typical for flints, and as a result, the outer surface primarily consists of patinated surfaces.

Cortex count data were used to evaluate whether the flint and chalcedony entered the Parking de Roseau site as unworked cobbles or as preworked cores (see also Knippenberg 2006). Only the sample of Long Island flint flakes is large enough to properly evaluate this. The diverse nature of the chalcedony material bears many uncertainties with it. It is unclear whether the material pertains to a single source or whether it represents multiple varieties from different origins following various transport-reduction trajectories.

Around 55% of the Long Island flint flakes still possess the cortical surface (see, for example, Plate 1j, l), including 6% with more than 75% of the dorsal face covered with

Table 4.9 Parking de Roseau: number of cryptocrystalline flaked stone artifacts by type variety.

Artifact type	Parking de Roseau									
	Long Island flint	*Coconut Hall flint*	*Blackman's Point flint*	*Flint (unspecified)*	*Chalcedony*	*Carnelian*	*Jasper (unspecified)*	*Quartz*	*Chert (unspecified)*	*Total*
Non-utilized flakes										
Complete flake	25	3	1	–	25	–	1	–	–	**55**
Split flake	3	–	–	–	–	1	–	–	–	**4**
Proximal fragment	3	3	–	1	6	–	–	–	–	**13**
Medial-distal fragment	6	3	–	–	3	–	–	–	1	**13**
Fragment	1	–	–	1	2	–	–	–	–	**4**
Other debitage										
Waste	14	–	–	2	15	–	–	–	1	**32**
Shatter	7	–	–	7	9	–	–	3	1	**27**
Utilized artifacts										
Complete flake	4	–	–	–	1	–	–	–	1	**6**
Split flake	1	–	–	–	–	–	–	–	–	**1**
Medial-distal fragment	5	–	–	–	1	–	–	–	–	**6**
Shatter	1	–	–	–	–	–	–	–	–	**1**
Retouched implements										
Complete	–	–	–	–	–	–	–	–	–	–
Medial-distal fragment	1	–	–	–	–	–	–	–	–	**1**
Drill on core	1	–	–	–	–	–	–	–	–	**1**
Flake cores										
Single platformed	–	–	–	–	–	–	–	–	–	–
Double platformed	–	–	–	–	–	–	–	–	–	–
Multiple platformed	2	–	–	–	–	–	–	–	–	**2**
Discoid	1	–	–	–	–	–	–	–	–	**1**
Conical	–	–	–	–	–	–	–	–	–	–
Bi-directional bipolar	3	–	–	1	3	–	–	–	–	**7**
Tri-directional bipolar	1	–	–	–	–	–	–	–	–	**1**
Shapeless	2	–	–	1	4	–	–	–	1	**8**
Unmodified rock										
Waterworn pebble	–	–	–	–	–	–	–	–	–	–
Crystal fragment	–	–	–	–	–	–	–	–	–	–
Total	**81**	**9**	**1**	**13**	**69**	**1**	**1**	**3**	**5**	**183**

Table 4.10 La Pointe de Grande Anse, STEP Goyave, and CHU Belle-Plaine: number of cryptocrystalline flaked stone artifacts by type variety.

Artifact type	Pointe de Grande Anse							STEP Goyave						CHU Belle-Plaine			
	Long Island flint	Coconut Hall flint	Chalcedony	Terre-de-Bas jasper	Jasper (unspecified)	Chert (unspecified)	Total	Long Island flint	Coconut Hall flint	Chalcedony	Quartz	Chert (unspecified)	Total	Long Island flint	Flint (unspecified)	Chalcedony	Total
Non-utilized flakes																	
Complete flake	3	–	6	3	1	–	13	3	1	1	–	1	6	1	–	1	2
Split flake	2	–	–	–	1	1	4	–	–	–	–	–	–	–	–	–	–
Proximal fragment	–	–	–	–	–	2	2	–	–	–	–	–	–	–	–	–	–
Medial-distal fragment	–	–	–	3	–	1	4	1	–	–	–	–	1	1	–	–	1
Fragment	–	–	1	–	–	–	1	–	–	–	–	–	–	–	–	–	–
Other debitage																	
Waste	–	–	–	–	–	–	–	2	–	–	–	–	2	–	1	1	2
Shatter	–	–	6	1	–	–	7	–	–	–	–	–	–	–	–	1	1
Utilized artifacts																	
Complete flake	2	–	–	–	–	–	2	–	–	–	–	–	–	1	–	–	1
Split flake	1	–	–	–	–	–	1	–	–	–	–	–	–	–	–	–	–
Medial-distal fragment	1	1	–	–	–	–	2	2	–	–	–	–	2	–	–	–	–
Shatter	–	–	–	–	–	–	–	–	–	–	–	–	–	–	–	–	–

Retouched implements																	
Complete	—	—	—	—	—	—	—	—	—	—	—	—	—	1	—	—	1
Medial-distal fragment	—	—	—	—	—	—	—	—	—	—	—	—	—	—	—	—	—
Drill on core	—	—	—	—	—	—	—	—	—	—	—	—	—	—	—	—	—
Flake cores																	
Single platformed	2	—	2	—	—	—	2	—	—	—	—	—	—	—	—	—	—
Double platformed	—	—	—	1	—	—	1	—	—	—	—	—	1	—	—	1	1
Multiple platformed	1	—	1	—	—	—	1	—	—	—	—	—	1	—	—	—	1
Discoid	—	—	—	—	—	—	—	—	—	—	—	—	—	—	—	—	—
Conical	1	—	—	—	—	—	1	—	—	—	—	—	—	—	—	—	—
Bi-directional bipolar	1	—	—	—	—	1	1	1	—	—	—	—	1	—	—	1	1
Tri-directional bipolar	—	—	—	—	—	—	—	—	—	—	—	—	—	—	—	—	—
Shapeless	1	—	1	1	—	—	3	—	—	—	—	—	—	—	—	—	—
Unmodified rock																	
Waterworn pebble	—	—	—	—	—	—	—	—	—	1	1	—	1	—	—	—	—
Crystal fragment	—	—	—	—	—	—	—	1	—	—	1	—	1	—	—	—	—
Total	11	1	15	11	2	5	45	9	1	1	2	1	14	5	1	5	11

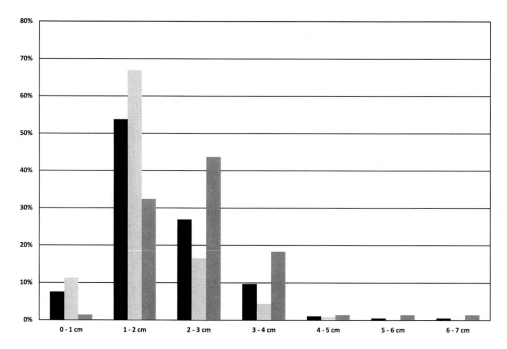

Figure 4.16 Parking de Roseau. Size distribution for all cryptocrystalline flaked stone artifacts (N=186). Black bar: all material. Light grey bar: mesh screen sample. Dark grey bar: other material.

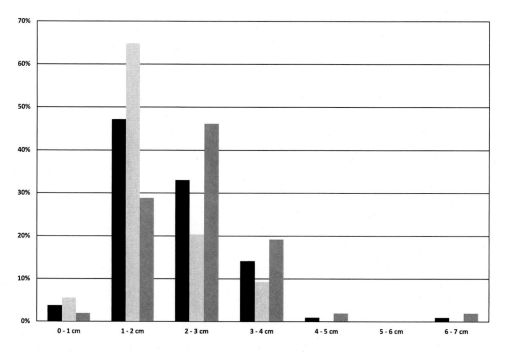

Figure 4.17 Parking de Roseau. Size distribution for all flint artifacts (N=106). Black bar: all material. Light grey bar: mesh screen sample. Dark grey bar: other material.

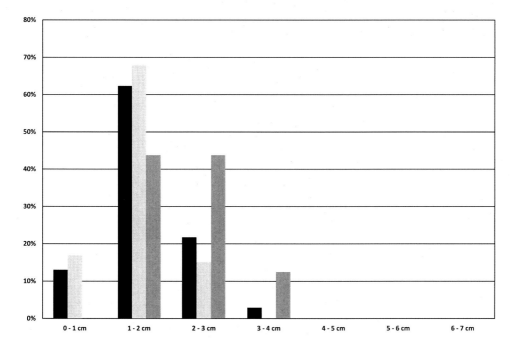

Figure 4.18 Parking de Roseau. Size distribution for all chalcedony artifacts (N=69). Black bar: total. Light grey bar: mesh screen sample. Dark grey bar: other material.

cortex. Based on a comparison with the cortex count data from replicative experiments by Jeff Walker (1980) using Long Island flint, these figures are suggestive of the arrival of unworked material at the site (Knippenberg 2006). Among most of the experiments, cortical flakes sum up to only 43%, which is much lower than in the case of Parking de Roseau.

It can be stated that the artifacts display features that are generally found among the flaked stone flint and chert assemblages within the Ceramic Age sites of the Lesser Antilles, which are classified as expedient (Bérard 2004, 2008; Crock and Bartone 1998; DeMille 1996; Fouéré 2003, 2006; Knippenberg 2006; Walker 1980). Local reduction of the material did not follow a well-defined and very standardized sequence. As a result, cores exhibit a great variety in the manner they were worked. This may to some extent be biased as the cores are exhaustively reduced (Plate 1c-d) and this predominantly provides information about the later stages of reduction, not about the entire sequence. It should be noted that the typically flat bipolar cores, or *pièces esquilliées*, representing this stage, are numerous. A significant part of the cores consists of specimens classified as shapeless, without any preferred direction, signifying the unstandardized nature of the reduction.

Studies elsewhere, on larger assemblages with more data on earlier reduction stages, have shown that during the late Ceramic Age core reduction was very opportunistic and did not follow a predefined trajectory. Scar negative characteristics among flakes and cores, as well as percussion characteristics among flakes, all point to the use of the direct freehand percussion and bipolar flaking techniques. Among the flakes more can be classified to the former, whereas among the cores, bipolarly reduced specimens predominate (Plate 1c). This relates well to the notion that the cores represent exhaustively reduced small artifacts, for which the bipolar technique was the only means by which these still could be worked. Following this line of reasoning, it can also be deduced that many flakes were struck off during earlier reduction stages. This correlates well with the notion, based on cortex count data, that all reduction stages are present at the site.

Close inspection of the flakes showed that they formed the aim of the reduction, as many exhibit evidence of being utilized as tools. Tool manufacture can be classified as expedient, according to which useful edges rather than predefined tool types were aimed at. Flakes generally were put to use without a prior secondary working or shaping stage. Utilized flakes as a result exhibit great variety in shape. In many cases the edges were not intentionally retouched; they exhibit fine edge damage only due to usage. Only a few show evidence of an edge actually being modified to better serve its function.

The Parking de Roseau assemblage includes in all 16 artifacts with evidence of use-wear. This number is a conservative estimate of the actual number of the artifacts being put to use, as certain activities can leave very subtle use-wear traces that can be identified only with microscopic techniques. Among the 16 used specimens, only one is present that has an edge that was preshaped into a point, suggesting that this artifact was utilized as a drill (Plate 1a). This is the only piece for which the primary form was not a flake. In addition to this modified piece, flakes shaped as points that were put to use as drills in an opportunistic fashion have also been identified. These display only subtle use-wear on the pointed end.

Another secondarily worked flake shows an edge that was shaped into a steep curvate (Plate 1f). This artifact was likely used to scrape thin and elongated objects. The assemblage includes only one other scraper with steep edges exhibiting use-wear. The remainder of the tools have thin edges (Plate 11), with either unifacial or bifacial use-wear, likely the result of a cutting activity.

LA POINTE DE GRANDE ANSE

At Pointe de Grande Anse the number of artifacts associated with the local reduction of cryptocrystalline rock is much smaller than at Parking de Roseau (45 pieces). Many similarities with the larger Parking de Roseau sample, however, can be put forward. First of all, similar secondary material from inland scatters on Long Island were used. The high percentage of cortex-bearing flakes among the Long Island material exhibits similarities with that of Parking de Roseau and the Long Island flaked stone samples from other Lesser Antillean Ceramic Age sites (Knippenberg 2006). This suggests that at Pointe de Grande Anse the Long Island flint entered as unworked cobbles as well.

A similar line of reasoning can be put forward regarding the jasper material that presumably came from Terre-de-Bas, Les Saintes. Among this material, the percentage of cortex-bearing flakes is also around 50%. Other similarities include the average small size of the material, the unstandardized reduction sequence as shown by a large variation in types of flake cores, the use of freehand and bipolar reduction techniques, and the ad hoc use of flakes. The assemblage lacks flakes being secondarily modified into a specific tool type. The number of expedient tools with evidence of use-wear is low, with only six artifacts: five flakes and one flake core. All flakes have unifacial use-wear on the thin edges, suggesting they were used as cutting implements.

STEP GOYAVE AND CHU BELLE-PLAINE

At both these sites the number of cryptocrystalline flaked stone artifacts is very low, with 12 and 11 pieces, respectively. At CHU Belle-Plaine they represent the only flaked stone material, flakes and associated débitage among the igneous rock being basically absent. The characteristics of both small samples clearly fall within the range encountered at Parking de Roseau and there is no reason to assume the material was reduced significantly differently. Characteristic features recognized at both sites include the overall small size of the material, the ad hoc use of flakes, and the application of both the direct freehand and bipolar percussion techniques. At STEP Goyave also the reduction of a flake as a core has been seen.

The nonstandardized reduction sequence at CHU Belle-Plaine is clearly manifested also in the variation exhibited by the three flake cores. One can be considered double platformed, with both platforms being perpendicular. The second core is an angular shaped piece with three platforms (Plate 2j), and the third specimen is a bidirectional core, also referred to as a *pièce esquillée*. All are relatively small and point to the exhaustive reduction of the cryptocrystalline quartz rock.

To what extent preworked or unmodified material entered the sites cannot be specified with these small samples. The small cores indicate that the later stages of reduction occurred at both sites. Larger material, however, is also present, as is shown by a large core-on-flake at STEP Goyave, measuring 4.1×3.8×0.9 cm (Plate 2i) and having a 75–99% cortex cover on its dorsal face, and a large flake at CHU Belle-Plaine, measuring 7.4×3.5×1.2 cm (Plate 2k). These pieces may have been part of the earlier reduction stage. Both small samples include two utilized flakes each. At STEP Goyave it relates to two specimens with similarly used curvate edges exhibiting edge damage (Plate 2h). Both tools were probably used to scrape thin elongated objects, such as wooden arrow shafts. The CHU Belle-Plaine site includes one relatively large flake with minor edge damage along one of its long edges, which was probably used as a cutting tool (Plate 2k). The other flake has a pointed end, which was carefully chipped. Most likely this piece was used as a drill or burin.

Igneous rock flaked stone

The assemblages from Parking de Roseau, Pointe de Grande Anse, and STEP Goyave all include significant numbers of igneous rock flakes, shatter (angular debris), and, to a lesser extent, waste and core artifacts (Table 4.11). Similarly to the chert material, the co-occurrence of these artifact categories suggests igneous rock was locally reduced at all three sites. The determination of the aim of this local reduction, however, is less straightforward than in the case of the chert material. This is due to the considerable variation in igneous rock types present and the diversity in the characteristics of the artifacts, suggesting that the working of igneous rock can be categorized into different *chaînes opératoires*.

For a significant portion of the material, a co-occurrence of reduced core artifacts, flakes, and other débitage exists. At Parking de Roseau and Pointe de Grande Anse, this applies to predominantly fine-grained, dark-colored igneous rock (Plates 4a and 6e). At STEP Goyave, among both fine-grained and coarser, more porphyritic rock, this co-occurrence is present (Plate 16a–c).

At all three sites some reduced core artifacts exhibit characteristics of being angular flake cores, with clearly created platforms from which multiple flakes were detached. At STEP Goyave and, to a lesser extent, Parking de Roseau variation is most significant, with some pieces possessing only a few scar negatives and others being more profoundly reduced. Among the latter group at STEP Goyave, a flat, irregularly shaped pebble was bifacially reduced from two sides (Plate 16c). With the other, a natural cleavage face was used as a platform from which flakes were detached.

This suggests that these cores were reduced to obtain flakes, similar to the reduction of the cryptocrystalline quartz rock. Unfortunately, this notion cannot be backed up by the clear identification of flakes actually having been used as tools. Careful inspection of edges reveals that none of the flakes were intentionally retouched into a tool. One specimen at STEP Goyave possesses some crude chipping. It is, however, unclear whether this actually should be considered to represent true retouching with the aim of creating a workable and durable edge. Unfortunately, this macroscopic study of use-wear is to a great extent hampered by post-depositional weathering, which most of the igneous flakes underwent, blurring any subtle edge damage or polish. This accounts especially to the material at STEP Goyave.

A clear difference between the igneous rock flaked stone and the cryptocrystalline material concerns the much larger size of the igneous rock flakes. First of all, this shows that the natural raw material was much larger, which relates well with the common occurrence of cobbles and pebbles of all shapes and sizes close to the sites. In contrast to the cryptocrystalline quartz reduction, size and availability was not restricted (Figure 4.19). Whether this unrestricted availability completely explains the size difference or whether the larger flakes served different functions when compared to the chert flake tools remains unanswered, given the difficulties with identifying the actual use-wear on the igneous rock flakes.

Apart from this creation of large flakes, La Pointe de Grande Anse also yielded a fragment of a smaller, bifacially reduced core piece with dimensions of 48×35×19 mm (Plate 4a). It resembles a petaloid axe in shape and may be interpreted as an axe pre-form. It shows flaking along all sides. Flaking was unsuccessful in many cases, as evidenced by severely battered parts and small flake scars. Flakes made from not the exact same but a similar fine-grained igneous rock type also occur at the site, suggesting local axe head manufacture might have taken place. Finished axe heads from the same material, however, have not been found at Pointe de Grande Anse to back this up. Petaloid axes made of fine-grained dark-colored igneous rocks, on the

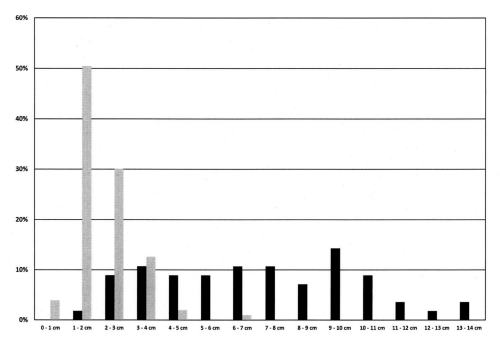

Figure 4.19 Parking de Roseau. Size distribution of chert (cryptocrystalline quartz) (black) and igneous rock flakes (light grey).

other hand, are known from other sites on Guadeloupe (Knippenberg 2006), including those of STEP Goyave and CHU Belle-Plaine. At the other sites, no true preforms have been identified. Given the varied nature of the igneous rock flakes, with some varieties lacking any core pieces, the possibility remains that some of this material derives from local axe head manufacture. However, any axe head making must have been limited in scale.

The Parking de Roseau assemblage also includes ten strongly weathered igneous rock flakes. The absence of any related core artifacts poses the problem of how to interpret the presence of these flakes. In general, they represent relatively large specimens that possess flake scars on their dorsal faces, suggesting they were struck from already worked rock. The extensive weathering the igneous rock has undergone may indicate that these artifacts date from an older occupation at the Parking de Roseau location. Similarly flaked stone has been found at other sites on Basse-Terre, where it was hypothesized to date to the Archaic Age (F. Casagrande, pers. comm. 2015).

At all three sites one group, predominantly including coarse porphyritic igneous rock, is made up almost entirely of flakes with the dorsal faces completely or largely covered with water-worn natural surfaces, indicating that these flakes were detached from water-worn pebbles and cobbles (Plate 6c-d). Use-wear can be discerned on the dorsal faces of some, suggesting that they were struck from hammerstones or hammer-grinders. These flakes may be seen as erratic débitage that is unintentionally formed during usage due to the wrong angle being applied when the tool was struck. Apart from flakes being struck from tools during usage, there are a number of coarse-grained flakes from water-worn rock without use-wear on the dorsal faces. These flakes may be associated with minor shaping or the reshaping of large slabs to be used as querns or grinding stones (see next section).

Ground stone: axe heads

Axe heads, or simply axes, are one of the most recurring true ground stone tools within the Caribbean Ceramic Age lithic assemblages (Knippenberg 2006). Adzes with plano-convex cross sections and more slender shaped chisels were made as well, but these woodworking tools are generally rare (Knippenberg 2006, 2012a; Rodríguez Ramos 2001). The manufacture of these implements usually involved a flaking stage, followed by pecking, grinding, and polishing. This separates them from querns and grinding stones, which often are also considered ground stone tools, but which in the Caribbean context generally did not undergo these different stages in their manufacturing process (see Knippenberg 2006). Their ground and sometimes even polished surfaces primarily derive from their often extensive use life. They will therefore be discussed in a later section.

As mentioned earlier, the occurrence of limited local axe head manufacture was suggested for the Parking de Roseau site by the presence of a preform and possibly associated débitage. Unfortunately, finished axes from the same raw material have not been found at that site. The four sites, however, have yielded finished axes and one adze, all made out of other materials (see Table 4.11).

In almost all of these cases the rock materials represent rare varieties that are associated only with the use of these ground stone woodworking tools and are not local to the site areas. The STEP Goyave and CHU Belle-Plaine sites may have produced the only exceptions, as they include axe fragments of fine-grained igneous rock that may be local to the site area or local to Basse-Terre.

Parking de Roseau is again the richest site with five axe heads, followed by La Pointe de Grande Anse with two axe fragments, one rare adze specimen, and an axe flake. The STEP

Table 4.11 Number of artifacts by type and by raw material for the noncryptocrystalline quartz portion of the assemblage per site.

Artifact type	Parking de Roseau					Pointe de Grande Anse						
	Igneous rock (fine-grained)	Igneous rock (porphyritic)	St. Martin greenstone	Metamorphic rock	Total	Igneous rock (fine-grained)	Igneous rock (porphyritic)	St. Martin greenstone	Fine-grained green rock	Jadeitite	Unidentified fine-grained rock	Total
Flake	28	28	–	–	**56**	22	25	–	–	1	1	**49**
Blade	–	1	–	–	**1**	–	–	–	–	–	–	**–**
Shatter	8	8	–	–	**16**	–	10	–	–	–	1	**11**
Waste	3	2	–	–	**5**	3	–	–	–	–	–	**3**
Flaked item	7	1	–	–	**8**	4	4	–	–	–	–	**8**
Axe	1	–	2	1	**4**	–	–	–	–	–	–	**–**
Axe fragment	–	–	1	–	**1**	–	–	2	–	–	–	**2**
Adze	–	–	–	–	**–**	–	–	–	1	–	–	**1**
Axe preform	–	–	–	–	**–**	1	–	–	–	–	–	**1**
Flake from axe	–	–	–	–	**–**	–	–	–	–	–	–	**–**
Sculptured stone head	–	–	–	–	**–**	–	–	–	–	–	–	**–**
Quern	–	13	–	–	**13**	–	3	–	–	–	–	**3**
Quern fragment	1	15	–	–	**16**	–	4	–	–	–	–	**4**
Mortar	–	2	–	–	**2**	–	–	–	–	–	–	**–**
Passive grinding stone	–	1	–	–	**1**	–	1	–	–	–	–	**1**
Hammerstone	3	48	–	–	**51**	1	9	–	–	–	–	**10**
Hammerstone fragment	–	4	–	–	**4**	–	4	–	–	–	–	**4**
Abrader	1	5	–	–	**6**	–	–	–	–	–	–	**–**
Abrader fragment	1	1	–	–	**2**	–	–	–	–	–	–	**–**
Pestle	–	1	–	–	**1**	–	1	–	–	–	–	**1**
Hammer-grinder	1	7	–	–	**8**	–	2	–	–	–	–	**2**
Polishing stone	5	–	–	–	**5**	–	–	–	–	–	–	**–**
"Engraver"	1	–	–	–	**1**	–	–	–	–	–	–	**–**
Multi-purpose tool	–	11	–	–	**11**	–	5	–	–	–	–	**5**
Unspecified tool fragment	1	1	–	–	**2**	–	3	–	–	–	–	**3**
Netweight	–	1	–	–	**1**	–	–	–	–	–	–	**–**
Waterworn pebble	25	223	–	–	**248**	–	19	–	–	–	–	**19**
Waterworn pebble fragment	14	73	–	–	**87**	1	14	–	–	–	–	**15**
Total	**100**	**446**	**3**	**1**	**550**	**32**	**104**	**2**	**1**	**1**	**2**	**142**

Table 4.11 (Continued)

Artifact type	STEP Goyave					CHU Belle-Plaine				
	Igneous rock (fine-grained)	Igneous rock (porphyritic)	Metamorphic rock	Unidentified fine-grained rock	Total	Igneous rock (fine-grained)	Igneous rock (porphyritic)	Limestone	Unidentified fine-grained rock	Total
Flake	26	20	–	–	**46**	1	–	–	–	**1**
Blade	–	–	–	–	–	–	–	–	–	–
Shatter	4	6	–	–	**10**	–	–	–	–	–
Waste	9	3	–	–	**12**	–	–	–	–	–
Flaked item	2	5	–	–	**7**	–	1	–	–	**1**
Axe	1	–	–	–	**1**	–	–	–	–	–
Axe fragment	–	–	–	–	–	1	–	–	–	**1**
Adze	–	–	–	–	–	–	–	–	–	–
Axe preform	–	–	–	–	–	–	–	–	–	–
Flake from axe	1	–	–	–	**1**	–	–	–	–	–
Sculptured stone head	–	–	–	–	–	–	1	–	–	**1**
Quern	1	5	–	–	**6**	–	–	–	–	–
Quern fragment	1	9	1	–	**11**	5	–	–	–	**5**
Mortar	–	–	–	–	–	–	–	–	–	–
Passive grinding stone	–	–	–	–	–	–	–	–	–	–
Hammerstone	1	4	–	–	**5**	–	1	–	–	**1**
Hammerstone fragment	–	1	–	–	**1**	–	–	–	–	–
Abrader	–	3	–	–	**3**	1	–	–	–	**1**
Abrader fragment	–	3	–	–	**3**	2	–	–	–	**2**
Pestle	–	1	–	–	**1**	–	–	1	–	**1**
Hammer-grinder	–	–	–	–	–	–	–	–	–	–
Polishing stone	–	–	–	–	–	1	–	–	–	**1**
"Engraver"	–	–	–	–	–	–	–	–	–	–
Multi-purpose tool	1	–	–	–	**1**	–	–	–	–	–
Unspecified tool fragment	2	–	–	–	**2**	–	–	–	–	–
Netweight	–	–	–	–	–	–	–	–	–	–
Waterworn pebble	16	60	2	–	**78**	14	2	3	–	**19**
Waterworn pebble fragment	14	23	1	1	**39**	8	3	2	1	**14**
Total	**79**	**143**	**4**	**1**	**227**	**33**	**8**	**6**	**1**	**48**

Goyave assemblage has one incomplete axe and an axe flake, and CHU Belle-Plaine yielded only a single axe fragment.

St. Martin tuffaceous greenstone is predominant among this axe material. Three specimens derive from Parking de Roseau (Plate 3b-c) and two from Pointe de Grande Anse, in addition to a possible third one (Plate 4b–d). Other materials include a dark grey metavolcanic and a light-green igneous rock at Parking de Roseau (Plate 3d), jadeitite at Pointe de Grande Anse (Plate 5e), fine-grained dark grey and grey igneous rock at STEP Goyave and CHU Belle-Plaine, and a weathered, fine-grained igneous rock at STEP Goyave (Plate 4e).

None of the recovered adze and axe heads can be considered complete. Four specimens, three at Parking de Roseau and one at STEP Goyave, are incomplete, missing only the edge bit. One medial-distal and a proximedial example derive from Parking de Roseau and Pointe de Grande Anse, respectively. Parking de Roseau also yielded a distal fragment or butt part, whereas the adze from Pointe de Grande Anse is the medial fragment. CHU Belle-Plaine and Pointe de Grande Anse include unspecified fragments, and the latter site and STEP Goyave also produced an axe flake.

When we take a closer look at these woodworking tools, we can notice that the petaloid or tear-dropped celt shape, the most common type of axe, predominates. Variation within this type is present, with relatively straight specimens and axes being more tapered.

The two almost complete St. Martin greenstone specimens are more slender and lack the clear widening at the proximal end. Their sizes are 92×45×31 mm (Plate 3b) and 88×36×19 mm (Plate 3c). In addition, their faces are more convex, whereas for the other two these are almost flat. The light-green igneous or tuffaceous rock petaloid celt is similar in size (84×51×24 mm) and also misses its edge bit (Plate 3a). The dark metavolcanic one must have been larger originally, the medial-distal recovered piece already measuring 86×62×32 mm (Plate 3d).

At CHU Belle-Plaine the only axe found is represented by a small fragment made of a grey, fine-grained igneous rock that exhibits a faceted surface with clear, dense parallel striations, suggesting it came from a ground stone artifact. Part of its face exhibits an abraded, pitted zone, suggesting the piece was also used as a pestle-like tool. This combination of characteristics is often found among reutilized axes (for example, see Knippenberg 2006; Lammers-Keijzers 2008).

La Pointe de Grande Anse and STEP Goyave yielded small flakes detached from axes, as both also have striations on their dorsal face. The specimen from Pointe de Grande Anse is made of jadeitite, a material that has been used exclusively for the manufacture of axes, adzes, and chisels in the Caribbean (Plate 5e) (García-Casco et al 2013; Knippenberg 2012b). The one from STEP Goyave is made of a fine-grained dark igneous rock variety.

STEP Goyave also yielded an exceptionally large axe measuring 185×106×45 mm, made of a strongly weathered igneous rock variety (Plate 4e). It represents a complete petaloid-shaped axe of which the edge-bit was removed by bifacial flaking. The large size as well as the igneous rock variety resembles the simple type of large axes often referred to as ceremonial axes, which are very common on Guadeloupe (Harris 1983). Its proximal end possesses flake scars on both faces, suggesting the piece has been worked, probably to reshape its edge. This reworking, however, has never been finished. Also, the butt part has scar negatives. They may have resulted from usage, when the axe was used as a wedge and was hit on the butt. The scar negatives are rather worn, suggesting the artifact underwent mechanical weathering following this reworking stage. This mechanical weathering probably also blurred any traces of the grinding process, which cannot be identified.

La Pointe de Grande Anse yielded the only example of a possible adze (Plate 4d). It is the proximedial fragment of a tool with a plano-convex cross section. It is made of a fine-grained grey-green rock variety, resembling certain rock varieties from the Pointe Blanche Formation but lacking the characteristic weathering crust found on the most exploited raw material from this bedded sequence of rocks.

REUSE OF AXE HEADS

Three axe fragments exhibit evidence of reuse as a hammer-grinder or pestle. The dark grey metavolcanic specimen from Parking de Roseau is the clearest example of such reuse (Plate 3d). This artifact completely lacks its edge part. The cleavage plane was utilized as a hammer-grinder or pestle-like tool, with this plane and its edges possessing the clearly abraded pitted areas typical of such a type of tool. As a pestle, it can be considered to represent a complete tool.

Reuse as hammer-grinders or pestles is a common feature found among the stone axes in the Caribbean (Knippenberg 2006; Lammers-Keijzers 2008). In particular, igneous and metamorphic axe heads often exhibit evidence of such reuse. St. Martin greenstone axes, however, almost completely lack this evidence. This association with the former two rock classes can to a large degree be attributed to the toughness of most igneous and especially some of the metamorphic rock varieties. This makes these tools very shock resistant, a highly preferred feature when using them not only for wood chopping but also as hammers or pounding implements.

Other ground stone artifacts

Apart from axes, the number of other types of true ground stone artifacts is very limited. Only the Parking de Roseau site yielded another ground stone item. It represents a complete bead, which was collected during mesh-screening of the fill from pit F 339. The bead is made out of a colorless translucent quartz crystal variety often referred to as rock crystal (Plate 5f). Following Beck's classification scheme (1981), adopted by Watters and Scaglion (1994) in their study on the beads from Trants, it can be categorized as a straight long bead with a circular cross-section. It has a height of 8 mm and a diameter of 5 mm. It was drilled from one end (uniconically), with this end having an aperture of 3 mm, whereas the diameter of the other opening is only 2 mm. The side of this cylindrical bead has been completely ground and polished, giving it a very shiny appearance. Both ends lack this finishing and still exhibit irregularities as well as small damages around the edges. The quartz is clearly translucent, displaying internal cracks and fissures. It is not known whether these cracks were formed naturally or caused by the drilling of the hole.

Other core tools

The lithic assemblages of all four sites include a wide series of core tools that did not undergo an extensive reduction and shaping stage before being used. Most were not artificially shaped at all and were put to use directly. A small portion was shaped to only a minor degree. Regarding the first group, a whole range of water-worn pebbles and cobbles in all shapes and sizes were collected by the Amerindians to serve different functions. In most cases the extent of used surface is so limited that it allows us to definitely determine that these rocks have not been worked to shape them in the proper tool form.

Plate 1 Cryptocrystalline quartz flaked stone from Parking de Roseau: a. Long Island flint drill; b. carnelian flake; c. Long Island flint *pièce esquillé*; d. translucent chalcedony core; e. translucent chalcedony flake; f. chert flake with curvate edge; g. white chalcedony waste (casson); h. Coconut Hall flint flake; i. Blackman's Point flint flake; j. Long Island flint flake; k. red jasper flake; l. Long Island flint flake with use-wear.

Source: Photos: S. Knippenberg.

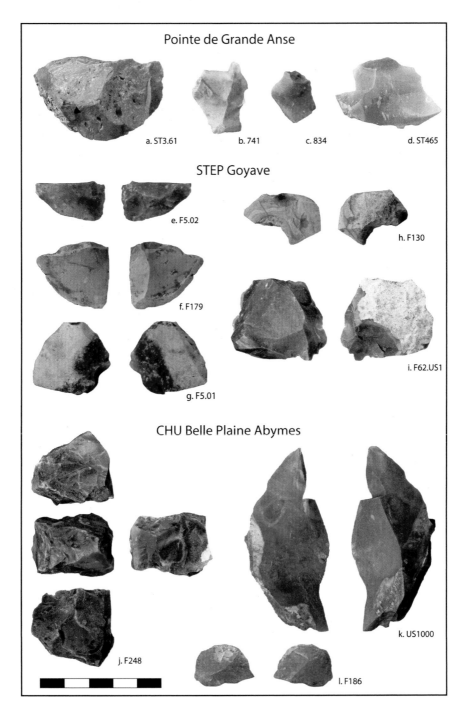

Plate 2 Cryptocrystalline quartz flaked stone from Pointe de Grande Anse: a. red jasper flake core: b-c. Long Island flint flake; d. Coconut Hall flint flake. STEP Goyave: e. Coconut Hall flint flake; f. green chert flake; g. white chalcedony flake; h. Long Island flint flake with curvate used edge; i. Long Island flint core-on-flake. CHU Belle-Plaine: j. Long Island flint flake core; k. Long Island flint flake with use-wear; l. chalcedony flake.

Photos: S. Knippenberg.

Plate 3 Axe heads from Parking de Roseau: a. light-green igneous rock re-utilized axe head; b. St. Martin greenstone axe head; c. St. Martin greenstone axe head; d. dark metamorphic reutilized axe head.

Photos: S. Knippenberg.

Pointe de Grande Anse

a. ST748.36   b. ST121   c. ST212

d. ST3.13

STEP Goyave

e. F112

Plate 4 Axe-related artifacts from Pointe de Grande Anse: a. igneous rock flaked item, possibly fragment of a preform; b. Saint Martin greenstone proximal axe fragment; c. Saint Martin greenstone distal axe fragment; d. medial adze fragment from fine-grained green rock; e. igneous
rock incomplete axe (STEP Goyave).

Photos: S. Knippenberg.

Plate 5 Miscellaneous artifacts from Parking de Roseau: a. meta-volcanic polishing stone; b-c. igneous rock polishing stone; d. igneous rock engraver; e. Jadeitite flake fragment from an axe (Pointe de Grande Anse); f. rock crystal (quartz) bead.

Photos: S. Knippenberg.

Parking de Roseau

a.F178.US2.16

c.T2N.US5.1

d.T2N.US5.3

b.F399.US1

e.F178.US4.27

Plate 6 Igneous rock hammerstones and flaked stone from Parking de Roseau.: a-b. hammerstone; c-d. igneous rock flake; e. flake core.

Photos: S. Knippenberg.

Parking de Roseau

a.F135.US1.1

b.F174.US3.3

Plate 7 Igneous rock hammerstones from Parking de Roseau.

Photos: S. Knippenberg.

Plate 8 Igneous rock active abrading stone (a) and pestle (b) from Parking de Roseau.
Photos: S. Knippenberg.

Plate 9 Igneous rock hammer abrader (a) and hammerstone with indentations (b) from Parking de Roseau.

Photos: S. Knippenberg.

Plate 10 Igneous rock quern (a) and quern—anvil (b) from Parking de Roseau.
Photos: S. Knippenberg.

Parking de Roseau

a.Decap C.1

b.F102.1

Plate 11 Igneous rock quern (a) and mortar (b) from Parking de Roseau.

Photos: S. Knippenberg.

Parking de Roseau

a.F178.US2.29

b.F334

Plate 12 Igneous rock fragment of a (shaped) quern (a) and almost complete quern (b) from Parking de Roseau.

Photos: S. Knippenberg.

Parking de Roseau

a.F156.US5.4

b.F412.US5.4

Plate 13 Igneous rock quern—anvil (a) and grinding stone (b) from Parking de Roseau.
Photos: S. Knippenberg.

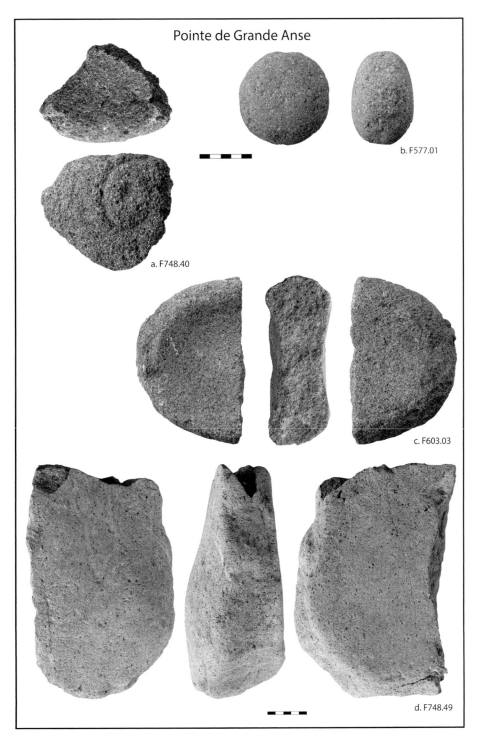

Pointe de Grande Anse

a. F748.40

b. F577.01

c. F603.03

d. F748.49

Plate 14 Pointe de Grande Anse: a. coarse igneous rock mortar fragment with incision; b. igneous rock hammerstone; c. coarse igneous rock quern fragment; d. igneous rock quern.

Photos: S. Knippenberg.

Plate 15 Igneous rock passive grinding stone from Pointe de Grande Anse.

Photos: S. Knippenberg.

Plate 16 Igneous rock artifacts from STEP Goyave: a-b. flakes; c. flaked item; d. pestle; e. quern with opposite used faces.

Photos: S. Knippenberg.

Plate 17 Igneous rock passive tools from STEP Goyave: a. quern; b. anvil and grinding stone; c. quern fragment.

Photos: S. Knippenberg.

STEP Goyave

a. F186

b. F77

c. F62.20

Plate 18 Igneous rock tools from STEP Goyave: a. active grinding stone or quern; b. hammerstone; c. passive grinding stone with evidence of re-shaping.

Photos: S. Knippenberg.

Plate 19 Igneous rock artifacts from CHU Belle-Plaine Abymes: a. stone head; b. quern; c-d. quern fragments.

Photos: S. Knippenberg.

CHU Belle Plain Abymes

a. F144

b. F10

c. F247

Plate 20 Tools from CHU Belle-Plaine Abymes: a. igneous rock hammerstone; b. igneous rock polishing stone; c. limestone pestle.

Photos: S. Knippenberg.

In the case of some large querns and mortars as well as passive grinding stones, this is less evident, as usage of extensive surfaces may have blurred any earlier working of the rock by, for example, pecking. The flat and sometimes angular shape of some of the latter tools suggests that crude shaping had likely occurred (Plate 12a). This shaping involved limited flaking followed by a more subtle pecking stage in which surfaces intended to be used were made more regular. Many of the querns also possess evidence of pecking that was applied to reroughen an already used grinding surface. Some of the mortars are more bowl-shaped with deeply concave used surfaces (Plates 11b, 14a, c). This shape is not common among natural rock and especially regarding this tool type, the shape of the rock must have been modified prior to its use. A decorative incision was made on one specimen, signifying that also other forms of modification occurred.

Based on the type of macroscopically visible use-wear as well as the shape of the rock and the used surface, a number of tool types have been identified. Querns, mortars, grinding stones, and anvils have been distinguished among the passive tools that rested on the ground (see Table 4.11). The active (hand-held) tools could be divided into hammerstones, hammer-grinders, grinding stones, and polishing stones (see Table 4.11). It has to be stressed that determining the tool type without performing microscopic use-wear analysis limits the detail to which different tools can be identified and distinguished (see Lammers-Keijsers 2008). This is particularly true for regions such as the Lesser Antilles, in which water-worn rock served as raw material and tools were not shaped into predefined or standardized tool forms (Knippenberg 2006). For example, a distinction between a grinding stone used for grinding lithic implements (*polissoir*) such as axes or lapidary items, and a quern or milling stone (*meule*), used for grinding food, is not always evident, especially when small fragments of tools are under consideration. Both tools have clear flat to concave abraded used faces. In this study a distinction between the two is made on the basis of the shape of the used zone and the nature of the use-wear. Grinding stones preferably have an elongated used zone, with a clear orientation in any striations present. They generally also have a smoother and more regularly abraded used face than querns.

The fact that tools could serve different functions complicates this even more. Grinding stones and querns especially also bear evidence that occasionally they were used as anvils (*enclume*). To prove whether such multiple uses occurred simultaneously is often difficult. Many cases of multiple use concern artifacts that originally were intended to be used as querns or grinding stones and were reused as anvils subsequently, or, if fragmented, as active tools, mirroring the use-life of an axe head that after having become useless as a wood-chopping tool, was put to use as a hammer-grinder or a pestle.

QUERNS AND MORTARS

Passively used querns, sometimes also referred to as milling stones or metates, constitute a significant portion of the identified core-tools among the four assemblages (see Table 4.11). This type of tool has been identified often, especially at Pointe de Grande Anse and Parking de Roseau. Mortars are much rarer. Both tools were used for grinding food and other vegetal substances. Querns are considered tools with a flat to slightly concave used face, whereas mortars show a used surface with very pronounced cavity, in some cases giving the tool the shape of a bowl. Still, examples exist for which it is hard to say whether they relate to querns or mortars, owing to the different ways querns were used, from tools where solely a grinding motion was applied to slabs against which both grinding and pounding motions were applied, more equaling mortars.

QUERNS

Querns are exclusively associated with igneous rock. Clearly discernable phenocrysts predominate in the more porphyritic varieties of this type of tool. The inhabitants of the Pointe de Grande Anse, Parking de Roseau, and STEP Goyave sites collected properly shaped flat, water-worn stone slabs from the near surroundings to serve as querns. Many of these slabs must have had natural shapes that approached the desired tool form, as most of the querns do not possess significant evidence of having been shaped before usage.

Most of the surfaces not intended to be used do not bear any evidence of working or reshaping. Preshaping in many cases involved only slightly adjusting the surface to flatten it, so that it could be used as the grinding face. This might have involved flattening or creating slight concavities by pecking the surface. For many, however, it probably only involved pecking to roughen the surface in order to create a proper surface for grinding food substances. Exactly determining the nature of this preshaping of the used surface is in most cases impossible, as later use-wear blurred or completely erased any of the earlier shaping evidence.

QUERNS AT PARKING DE ROSEAU

The Roseau assemblage includes a total of 28 large water-worn cobbles that have been interpreted as milling stones or querns (Plates 10a-b, 11a, and 12a-b). All querns are made of igneous rock, almost exclusively of the porphyritic type (97%). The igneous rock varieties with a high density of phenocrysts are relatively more abundant (43%) among these tools than among the other artifact categories (~20%), clearly indicating that density of phenocrysts resulting in a coarser texture was a desired quality for use as a quern. Only one-third (N=9) is complete, while another third (N=8) is incomplete with more than half of the tool remaining. The remainder (N=11) is fragmented to varying degrees. Shape and size of these cobbles vary considerably (Figure 4.20). The smallest complete tool measures 12.7×9.9×3.6 cm and has a weight of only 0.8 kg, whereas among larger examples sizes and weights occur of 40.9×27.2×21.2 cm and 28.8 kg, and 44.6×33.3×22.9 cm and 29.3 kg.

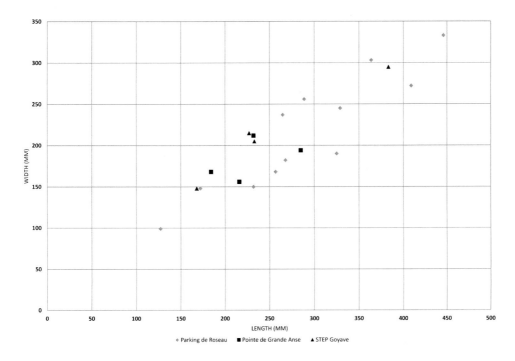

Figure 4.20 Length and width dimensions of querns.

The largest recovered specimen, however, could unfortunately not be studied in detail, as its exceptional size did not allow for storage at the Inrap research lab. It relates to a large, irregularly shaped, somewhat water-worn, dark-colored igneous rock river boulder. Its maximal dimension must be larger than 50 cm and its weight must be greater than 100 kg. The flattest face was used as grinding surface, as is suggested by its very regular and smooth abrasion and the presence of remnants of the pecking process to (re)-roughen this face. Given its exceptionally heavy weight, it is not likely that it was moved around a lot within the house or settlement.

Despite the variation in shape and size, it is evident that the Amerindians were selective in choosing the proper water-worn cobbles for use as querns. Most querns can be considered flat (width > 2×thickness) (Plates 10a-b and 12b) and it is noticed that oval shapes are recurrent. In cases of more irregularly shaped cobbles, the presence of at least one flat surface must have been decisive in picking them out (Plates 11a and 12b).

Many pieces exhibit only minor abrasion and it can be stated that in many of these cases unmodified water-worn rock was used (Plate 11a). Some show flake scars, but these are associated with post-usage reduction of the tools for yet unknown purposes.

Only a small portion of the tools, however, were shaped prior to use. They have a relatively regular flat shape with more angular straight sides, a feature that is not commonly found among natural rock. The extensive use-life of these specific tools, however, resulted in significantly abraded and worn artifacts, blurring any traces of an earlier shaping stage.

More than 50% of the tools (N=15) exhibit abrasion on both opposing flat to concave faces (Plates 10a-b and 12a-b). In most of these cases (N=12), one face is clearly less abraded than the other one (Plates 10b and 12b). These less abraded faces are generally also flatter or even slightly convex. This distinction in wear is a common feature among querns and other passively used tools with a presumed long use-life. Use-wear studies elsewhere (see, for example, Verbaas and van Gijn 2007) have shown that the face with the less extensive wear in this case represents the lower face of the tool that was not used, but that became abraded due to the rubbing of the tool against the surface on which it was placed. Three tools lack this differentiation and have extensive use-wear on both faces, resulting in the formation of two clearly concave surfaces (Plates 10a and 12a). Both must have been used in an alternating sequence.

Comparing the used faces of the different tools, clear variation exists in the extent to which they have been abraded. Many tools exhibit only minor abrasion, usually restricted to a smaller central zone of the flat face. It is further noticed that these used faces did not become very concave. These tools were probably used for a short or less intensive period.

Seven tools possess traces of pecking on their used faces (Plates 10a-b and 12a). Generally these traces are present at the perimeter or the deeper parts of the tools' used zone (Plates 10a-b and 12b). They clearly represent the remnants of the roughing or reroughing stage, as they were formed prior to the abrasion. With deeply abraded tools it can be inferred that these tools were roughened multiple times in order to keep the tool useful for grinding vegetal substances.

QUERNS AT LA POINTE DE GRANDE ANSE

La Pointe de Grande Anse site yielded a more limited number of querns and quern fragments than Parking de Roseau. Similar to the latter site, all specimens are made of porphyritic igneous rock varieties. Large, flat shaped water-worn cobbles were chosen to serve as this type of tool. As can be expected from this smaller sample, the size range is much more restricted than at Parking de Roseau (see Figure 4.19). The largest one measures 28.5×19.4×12.8 cm, and the smallest specimen 18.4×16.8×8.5 cm. Apart from their size and shape, the tools at La Pointe de Grande Anse also bear similarities in the use-wear they possess and the location of these traces. First of all, the complete tools do not exhibit extensive use-wear (Plate 14d). Many have only slightly concave faces. Most tools have been used on only one face, the other face possessing the typical minor abrasion that results from the friction of the tool with the subsurface it was positioned on. There are also tools with both concave faces having been used as food-grinding surface (Plate 14c).

QUERNS AT STEP GOYAVE

At STEP Goyave a considerable number of querns have been identified, in all 17 artifacts. Similar to the other sites, the querns are exclusively made of igneous rock, among which porphyritic varieties predominate (88%) (Plates 16e, 17, and 18c). Only one-third are complete; the remainder has been fragmented to varying degrees. Shape and size of these cobbles vary considerably. The smallest complete tool measures 16.8×14.8×5.5 cm and weighs only 1.5 kg, whereas the largest example has a size of 38.3×29.5×12.5 cm and weighs 15.0 kg. Many specimens exhibit only minor abrasion, and often unmodified water-worn rock was used, probably collected in river beds (Plates 17a-b and 18c). Some have flake scars, but these are associated with post-usage reduction of the tools for yet unknown purposes (Plate 18c).

Most of them are relatively flat, possessing at least one flat to slightly concave face. Seen from above, oval shapes have been recognized (Plate 17a), but also more angular to irregular shapes occur (Plates 17b and 18c). Among the latter an exceptionally thick block is present. Similar to the other sites, some of the tools exhibit abrasion on both opposing flat faces (Plate 18c), with one face being less abraded than the other one, suggesting that the latter represents the lower face that got abraded due to friction with the surface on which it rested.

Querns with both faces being used as grinding surfaces for vegetal material occur at STEP Goyave as well (Plate 16e). Similar to Parking de Roseau, these are rare. The high frequency of querns exhibiting minor abrasion is another similarity with Parking de Roseau. This suggests that they were used for a short or less intensive period.

QUERNS AT CHU BELLE-PLAINE

This assemblage includes only one complete quern and four fragments. The complete specimen is a flat water-worn pebble with one naturally formed flat face (Plate 19b). This face exhibits minor abrasion, suggesting that it was used to grind matter. The oval shape of the used surface, the absence of a clear directionality, and the minor abrasion suggest that the artifact was used as a tool for food grinding, rather than one for processing tools or other objects.

Two other tools exhibit more significant abrasion. One is a side fragment of a flat, water-worn cobble with one deeply abraded used face (Plate 19d). The other one represents a medial fragment of which both flat faces have been used as they are slightly concave and exhibit clear abrasion (Plate 19c).

A third fragment was originally part of a passive grinding stone, but was probably used as an active implement in a later stage. It shows a clearly concave grinding surface. It got broken and the cleavage plane, which runs perpendicular to this used surface, exhibits abrasion too. The final fragment is rather small and not more can be said than that it possesses a slightly concave abraded surface.

MORTARS

Mortars are much less common than querns at the different sites, with only the lithic assemblages of Parking de Roseau and Pointe de Grande Anse having two mortars each. In most cases the pieces are fragmented. All four tools possess a deep concave or deep indentation with evidence of use-wear (Plate 11b). The indentations clearly formed due to repetitive grinding and pounding activities. In all cases it can be noted that the igneous rock materials they are made out of are very coarse-grained granular varieties with dense concentrations of phenocrysts grading towards plutonic rocks.

At Parking de Roseau both tools represent complete blocky specimens with rough to slightly worn outer surfaces, suggesting they had not been collected from riverbeds or cobble beaches. Both have similar size ranges and weigh more than 9 kg. The F 162 mortar has two opposing flat faces of which one was used.

The other specimen has only one flat, slightly concave utilized face, the opposing face being irregular and significantly convex. Therefore, this tool must have been buried in the ground to some extent in order to provide a horizontal flat surface when it was used. The diameter of the used indented area varies from 16 cm on the F 162 specimen to 12.5 cm on the other.

At La Pointe de Grande Anse both mortars are fragments of tools with a deep cavity, almost resembling flat bowls. As with Parking de Roseau the igneous rock is unique among the assemblage and very granular, with a coarse mineral structure containing small vesicles. Both pieces are thick at the perimeter of the tool and thin in the center. The largest fragment (ST 748.42) is 7 cm thick on the side, whereas in the center its thickness is only 1.8 cm, where the tool has been broken. Their bowl-shaped form suggests that these tools were artificially shaped. The granular texture of the rock material as well as the tools' intensive use inhibits proper evaluation of the manufacturing process. Clear traces of grinding to shape them have not been identified. Most likely the shaping involved only fine pecking.

Specimen ST 748.40 has a unique feature. On the outside of the tool a design motif has been created by pecking (Plate 14a). As the tool is fragmented, this motif is most likely incomplete. It represents a concentric circle. Similar simple abstract motifs are known from petroglyphs within the region (Dubelaar 1984, Fig. 33). This motif is also known to form part of complex engravings on the late-prehistoric stone ball belts found in the Greater Antilles and Virgin Islands (Oliver 2009, Fig. 23).

PHYTOLITH ANALYSIS OF A QUERN AND MORTAR

Regarding the function of these tools, it has been hypothesized that most specimens probably functioned as food-grinding implements. The predominant use of querns at the various sites discussed relates well with that at other sites, where additional use-wear or starch grain analyses supported the macroscopic interpretation (see, for example, Pagán-Jiménez 2012). To elaborate on this, phytolith samples have been taken from a quern (F 156 US 4.3; Plate 10a) and a mortar (F 162) from the Parking de Roseau site in order to determine the type of plant material that was processed on the tool (see contribution by Pagan-Jiménez). This analysis showed that the residue samples contained mostly phytoliths of grasses, herbs, and aboreal taxa, but no human-grown or economically used plants. They are interpreted to reflect the background vegetation at the time that the pit in which the tool was found filled up, and do not inform us about the function of the tool. Only the sample from the mortar contained a phytolith of a palm species (Arecaceae) that was ground on the tool or stored in the pit in which it was found.

GRINDING STONES

The number of grinding stones used for abrading and polishing axe heads and possibly other ground stone artifacts is much lower than that of querns, signifying the important role of the latter in food processing (see Table 4.11). La Pointe de Grande Anse, Parking de Roseau, and STEP Goyave are the only sites where this type of tool was found. At these three sites specimens occur that served different purposes and can be considered multifunctional tools. They will be discussed in a separate paragraph. Leaving out the latter tools, La Pointe de Grande Anse and Parking de Roseau are the only sites with grinding stones explicitly used for the purpose of processing ground stone tools or objects.

At Parking de Roseau only one large water-worn cobblestone has been classified as a passive grinding stone on the basis of the shape of the used zone and the nature of the use-wear (see previous discussion). It relates to a 35.8×22.3×19.3 cm sized thick elongated pebble, which has become damaged due to burning (Plate 13b). It has at least four flat to slightly convex faces that have become abraded due to usage. On three faces the use-wear is minor and these were probably only used for a short period. The fourth face, on the other hand, shows very regular and smooth abrasion marks and this face exhibits clear polish and very fine striations parallel to the longest side of the used zone. This face clearly was used to grind objects. Given its elongated shape and minor concavity, flat objects such as axe heads may have been likely candidates.

At Pointe de Grande Anse the only grinding stone (ST 748.45) is a complete flat shaped water-worn cobble made of a porphyritic blue igneous rock measuring 34.6×33.0×6.4 cm and weighing 7.7 kg (Plate 15). Its face used for grinding has an elongated oval, slightly concave abraded zone. The elongated shape of the abraded zone makes it likely that tools or other large objects were ground on it. Similar to many other passively used slabs, the opposing flat face is slightly convex to flat, but also exhibits less abrasion. Part of this abrasion is probably the result of the friction of this face against the underlying surface on which it rested. The central part, however, exhibits stronger abrasion and this may suggest this particular zone was utilized as a grinding surface as well.

Active tools

HAMMERSTONES

Hammerstones comprise the largest group among the hand-held actively used tools. Actually it is the most numerous tool type out of all use-modified tools at all sites except for CHU Belle-Plaine (see Table 4.11). These tools have been identified by the presence of small pits or pitted zones at one or multiple locations on the rock. The formation of the pits is the result of the rock hitting a hard surface or object. Hammerstones might have been used as percussion tools when reducing flint, chalcedony and jasper for the manufacture of flake tools, or when producing the igneous rock flakes. They could also have served as pecking tools in more finely shaping axe heads, or the shaping and resharpening of the flat faces of querns and polishing stones. Finer examples might have been used in creating petroglyphs or related pictographic rock. Crushing rock for creating temper can also be mentioned as a possible function.

At Parking de Roseau 55 specimens have been identified, including five fragmented ones. The number at La Pointe de Grande Anse is 14, including four fragments; at STEP Goyave it is six, including one fragment; whereas at CHU Belle-Plaine only one specimen has been identified. At all sites igneous rock pebbles exclusively served as raw material. Porphyritic varieties are by far predominant (95%).

Shape and size variation is extensive (Figure 4.21). Most pebbles have an elongated shape, varying from oval "eggs" and "tear drops" to more slender tools almost resembling cylinders with tapered ends. Typically ball-shaped hammers are rare. At Parking de Roseau the length varies between 4.7 cm and 20.2 cm, whereas the width and thickness are 3.4–8.2 cm and 2.0–5.8 cm, respectively. The smaller Pointe de Grande Anse sample of hammerstones exhibits a similar range in size as that at Parking de Roseau. At STEP Goyave the hammerstones are on average larger, but still fall within the range of Parking de Roseau. At Roseau most hammerstones (N=30) have multiple pitted areas. In many cases, these used zones are on both ends of one or more sides (Plate 6b). More randomly scattered zones also occur (Plate 6a, 7b). The next frequent type has pits on a single end (N=12) followed by bidirectional hammers with pits on both ends (N=9) (Plate 7a). Hammers with pits on only one of the sides are rare, and there is only one specimen of which the flat face has been used.

Some hammers deserve special mentioning. A 19.3 cm long specimen from Trench 9 with an almost circular cross-section (7.6×7.0 cm) has very localized pitted zones on both tapered ends (Plate 9b). In addition, it has damage within a slender zone all around the centre of the piece. The cause of this damage is unclear. It may have been applied in order to allow a firmer grip.

Another interesting example is represented by a small hammer with deeply pitted areas on both faces and both sides (F 178 US 4.18). The indented areas on the sides make this tool similar to water-worn artifacts found at sites in the Greater Antilles, which have been interpreted as fishnet weights. It may have served this purpose in its final stage of usage.

At La Pointe de Grande Anse, hammers with multiple used zones are most common (Plate 14b), followed by those with only one used zone. This site also yielded two specimens with use-wear all over the tool. This latter type has also been found at CHU Belle-Plaine, the only

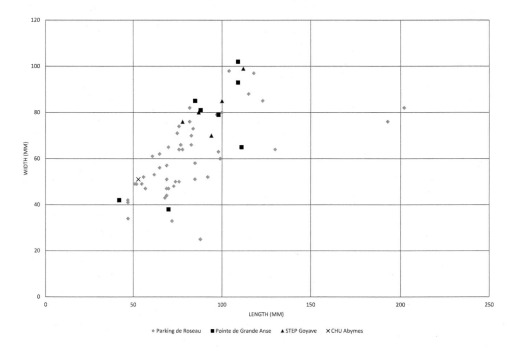

Figure 4.21 Length and width dimensions of hammerstones.

hammerstone within the assemblage. It is a small water-worn pebble of which only the flatter faces do not possess use-wear. The tool was probably held at these faces. At STEP Goyave the bidirectional type is the most common one, with pitted zones on both ends of the tool (Plate 18b). All the other hammerstones have pits on more and varying faces. A broken one deserves mentioning, as this specimen was used after breakage, allowing the edge of the cleavage plane to serve as the utilized area.

ACTIVE ABRADING OR GRINDING TOOLS

The lithic assemblages of three sites include tools that were hand-held and actively used to grind, abrade, or rub material (see Table 4.11). Again it has to be stressed that microscopic use-wear is needed for proper identification of what exactly was ground in order to better understand their function. Probably the majority can be considered to represent the hand-held tools that were used to rub or grind food substances against a quern, in Spanish often referred to as a *manos*.

The Parking de Roseau collection includes eight specimens, at STEP Goyave six have been found, and CHU Belle-Plaine yielded only one fragment. They are all made of porphyritic igneous rock varieties. At Parking de Roseau round to oval water-worn pebbles had been chosen that could easily be hand-held (Plate 8a). Pebble shape varied more at STEP Goyave. In addition to round pebbles, an elongated specimen with an angular cross-section occurs (Plate 18a).

These pebbles exhibit different degrees of abrasion and smoothing, and on one example fine parallel striations were noticed. The more abraded specimens might have been used as the hand-held implements that were rubbed against passive milling stones during food grinding. True edge-grinders, on which one of the sides has been heavily abraded and even faceted (Rodríguez Ramos 2005), have not been recognized among the assemblage. This suggests that the tools were used for grinding food substances that were oily or greasy, resulting in less abrasion.[11]

HAMMER-ABRADERS OR HAMMER-GRINDERS

More or less similar to the tools presented in the former paragraph, the assemblages also include actively used tools with which both a pounding and a grinding motion had been applied against the querns. They can be considered as different types of food-grinding tools than the true *manos*, and may have been used in cases where food substances had to be crushed and subsequently ground. According to these use-motion characteristics, they also resemble pestles (Plate 9a). They differ from these tools because of their shape: they are generally thicker and shorter.

Only Parking de Roseau, with eight specimens, and La Pointe de Grande Anse—with one example—yielded this type of tool (see Table 4.11). All are made of porphyritic igneous rock pebbles. At Parking de Roseau pebbles vary in size between 12.1×6.8×2.1 cm and 6.4×5.6×2.9 cm. Most tools (N=4) have use zones on both ends of the tool. Two have only one end that was used, while the two remaining specimens have a utilized zone on one end as well as one or multiple sides. The example from La Pointe de Grande Anse is larger, with dimensions of 13.1×12.5×5.8 cm, but it has only minor use-wear. In addition to these unmodified pebbles, axe heads were reutilized as hammer abraders. Their similar size and shape as well as their toughness made these specimens excellent candidates for this purpose (see previous discussion).

PESTLES

In many ways resembling a hammer-grinder, the pestle represents an elongated slender version with evidence of pounding and grinding on one or both ends. A single specimen of this tool has been found only at three sites: Parking de Roseau, STEP Goyave, and CHU Belle-Plaine (see Table 4.11). At Parking Roseau and STEP Goyave, the Amerindians chose igneous rock, at CHU Belle-Plaine limestone.

Both at Parking de Roseau (Plate 8b) and STEP Goyave (Plate 16d) elongated igneous rock pebbles, weighing 1.1 kg, were selected and used on both ends, displaying the typical use-wear according to which pitted zones also exhibit abrasion. Both have similar sizes, of 17.5×6.8×5.0 cm and 15.3×7.4×7.1 cm.

The specimen from CHU Belle-Plaine is a worn, somewhat odd-shaped elongated limestone rock measuring 8.3×5.8×4.7 cm (Plate 20c). It has one almost completely flat regular end showing possible use-wear in the form of abraded pits. In shape, it clearly resembles a pestle. Limestone material, however, is rather soft for a pounding tool, making it difficult to specify for what purpose this piece was intended to be used, most likely for very soft materials.

ACTIVE POLISHING STONES

A small number of pebbles has been classified as polishing stones (see Table 4.11). These natural water-rounded rocks possess polished zones showing fine parallel striations which can be discerned when studied with a hand lens. Generally speaking, these artifacts are regarded as tools in polishing or smoothing ceramics. Hard inclusions in the clay matrix, such as sand grains or small rock particles used as temper, caused the formation of the many fine striations.

Polishing stones have been identified only at Parking de Roseau and CHU Belle-Plaine, the former site yielding five specimens whereas the excavations at the latter site produced only a single tool. All the Parking de Roseau specimens are made of fine-grained igneous varieties, including two possible meta-volcanics (Plate 5a–c). The fine grain size distinguishes these polishing stones from most other water-worn rocks used as tools. The polishing stones at Roseau vary considerably in size, from 2.2×2.1×1.5 cm to 9.7×6.2×1.9 cm, and have relatively symmetrical and regular shapes. The CHU Belle-Plaine example is a relatively large, also regularly egg- to oval-shaped water-worn pebble with dimensions of 7.1×5.1×3.4 cm. In addition to fine parallel striations, which can be discerned when studied with a hand lens, it also possesses polished zones.

A UNIQUE TOOL

The Parking de Roseau assemblage includes a unique artifact, made of a light-greenish, fine-grained igneous rock (Plate 5d). It is difficult to determine the exact purpose it served. It is a very flat (0.9 cm) tool with one side running into an edge. Both the flat faces and the edged side seem to have been modified or shaped. Unfortunately, the specimen is fragmented, but it can clearly be seen that the edged side has been used. It possesses a brown shiny residue or wax cover on both faces, giving the tool a smoother feel at this side. The surface of this shiny cover extends itself over a length of 7.1 cm with a greatest width of 0.9 cm on both faces, indicating the contact between the tool and the material it worked was extensive. This suggests that it was used to make deep grooves into materials. The side opposite to the edge is flat and has fragments of a black residue in the deeper part of the stone. This residue might have served as an adhesive to attach the tool to some sort of hafting device. Black residues have been found on different types of lithics at

Anse à la Gourde and Morel (Lammers-Keijzers 2008; see also Knippenberg 2006). In all cases, it has been hypothesized that the material served as a glue (see, for example, on this black matter Serrand et al. 2018).

Multifunctional tools

A number of tools exhibit evidence they served multiple functions (see Table 4.11). In the introductory paragraph it was mentioned that distinguishing true multifunctional tools from reused tools is sometimes difficult. In this work, complete tools that bear evidence of having had multiple functions are considered multifunctional tools. Fragmented tools that served a different purpose after having been broken are considered to represent reused tools; such is the case with the axe heads being reutilized as hammer-grinders. Multifunctional tools have been identified at three sites. Most pieces derive from the Parking de Roseau assemblage (N=12), followed by La Pointe de Grande Anse (N=3) and STEP Goyave (N=1). The following combinations of functions have been distinguished among the multifunctional tools:

- Anvil and quern/mortar (N=9);
- Anvil and passive grinding stone (N=1);
- Quern and grinding stone (N=2);
- Hammerstone and passive/active grinding/milling stone (N=5);
- Anvil, hammerstone, and passive/active grinding/milling stone (N=1).

The combination of use as a quern or mortar with that as an anvil is found most frequently, six times at Parking de Roseau, two at La Pointe de Grande Anse, and one at STEP Goyave (Plates 10b and 13a). In many cases these tools can be considered querns that in a final stage served as anvils. They generally possess at least one flat to concave abraded face that also has a localized zone with pits. These pits generally override the abraded area. One exceptional piece from Parking de Roseau has two opposing deeply concave faces due to long-term use as a quern/mortar, with one of these faces possessing a pitted zone in the center. Its use as an anvil eventually caused the tool to be broken into two.

At La Pointe de Grande Anse a flat water-worn cobble has been found with one flat face bearing evidence of having been used as a quern while the opposing flat face shows a very localized pitted zone that became indented due to a prolonged period of use. The latter face may have been used to crack nuts or crush small pieces of rock.

Use as both a passive grinding stone and an anvil has been identified only once at Parking de Roseau. It relates to a flat oval pebble with an elongated, very smoothly abraded used zone (F 412 US 5.1). The opposing flat face has pits within a very localized area.

At Parking de Roseau and Pointe de Grande Anse, slabs have been identified that were used as querns as well as grinding stones. The specimen from Parking de Roseau weighs 12.4 kg and represents a large, flat water-worn slab with one regular, concave abraded face and a more irregularly shaped opposite face with a strong elongated concavity that exhibits abrasion. The former face likely was used as a quern surface; the latter concavity may have served as grinding surface. The remainder of this face also exhibits minor abrasion that may have been the result of rubbing against the surface on which it was placed.

La Pointe de Grande Anse yielded another exceptional piece (ST 748.5). It is a large, flat angular shaped water-worn cobble that possesses four used faces. The two opposing flat faces bear evidence of being used as querns. In the center of one of these faces a localized concave pitted zone points to use as an anvil for cracking or crushing nuts or other small matter. Two of its elongated sides are also abraded due to usage. The long and slender shape of these used faces and the clear parallel direction that is visible within the use-wear suggests that these sides were used as surfaces for grinding axe heads. These sides also have small pits suggesting they also functioned as anvils.

Three tools (F 196.6, F 220 US 1.2, and F 365 US 3.8) from Parking de Roseau and two pieces from Pointe de Grande Anse show evidence of having been used as grinding or abrading stones as well as hammerstones. Two specimens at both sites have been used only as active tools, whereas the third one from Parking de Roseau was passively used as a quern and actively as a hammerstone. This latter one has pits only on one end and one flat face being abraded. The other four tools have multiple pitted areas and show only one face or side used as an active abrading stone. Only one water-worn pebble (F 156 US 5.1) from Parking de Roseau has use-wear indicating that it was utilized as an anvil, hammerstone, and quern. It is a sizable pebble with a limited pitted zone on one of its sides, suggesting occasional use as a hammerstone. This seems in accordance with its large size, making it not a practical rock to be used as an active hammer. One of its flat faces was flattened by pecking before having been used as a quern, as is evidenced by the abrasion it underwent. This face also exhibits a slight polish all over. The opposing face has a localized zone with pits, suggesting use as an anvil.

A unique sculptured artifact at CHU Belle-Plaine

One of the most intriguing finds from the CHU Belle-Plaine excavations consists of a rounded igneous rock cobble with dark-colored phenocrysts (Plate 19a; and see Figure 3.14b). It measures 9.5×8.9×7.7 cm and has a weight of 651.5 g. The exceptional feature relates to the incision of a human face. The face consists of two round eyes and one horizontally lined mouth underneath. Three lines have been applied on its head, one running in the middle from the forehead towards the back, the other two forming a loop along both sides of the head. Both the eyes and the various lines must have been engraved using the pecking technique with the help of a very thin stone tool. The lines especially exhibit irregularities in their deeper parts, indicating that they were not ground but pecked.

The simple form of the face itself exhibits much resemblance with some of the faces found among the many petroglyphs in the Trois-Rivières area on Basse-Terre. In a sense it can be considered to represent a miniature petroglyph. When compared closely to the petroglyphs from Basse-Terre it reveals another similarity: petroglyph B at the Petroglyph Park, also known as *les Capitaines*, depicts persons with very simple headdresses, made up by a central elongated shape accompanied on both sides by two bended lines (Delpuech 2001:98–101). This exhibits broad similarity with the three lines that have been pecked on the head of the face of the Belle-Plaine cobble. These three lines may represent the equivalent of this type of headdress in sculptured form, in which depicting a headdress is more difficult and much restricted by the shape of the rock.

Its major difference with regard to the other petroglyphs is its portable character. Portable stone faces are very rare in the Lesser Antilles and the only examples known to the author have been found at the Late Ceramic Age sites of À l'Escalier, on La Désirade (de Waal 2006:231) and Island Harbour, on Anguilla (Crock and Petersen 1999, Fig. 54). The artifacts from La Désirade and Anguilla are flatter in shape and the face exhibits differences in the manner in which the eyes and mouth have been portrayed. However, it is similar in the simple overall depiction of the face. Similarities in the way the face has been depicted can also be found on the elaborate *cémi* three-pointer stones, for example, found at Sandy Hill on Anguilla (Crock and Petersen 1999, Fig. 72). Other portable depictions of heads and faces are the well-known shell *guaízas*, or masks (Mol 2007). These often have more elaborate faces showing additional features such as headdresses. Given the many forms in which *cemí* invested objects are represented and also the common occurrence of sculptured heads among these forms, both as single heads as well as being part of elaborate *cemí* three-pointer stones (see Oliver 2009), the sculptured head from CHU Belle-Plaine may be seen as a *cemí*, or more correctly formulated as an object possessing the power of *cemí*.

Other material

MANUPORTS

Significant parts of the assemblages from the different sites consist of water-worn pebbles or fragments thereof that do not possess any signs of modification in the form of working traces (flake scars or pecked surfaces) or use-wear (pits, striations, abrasion, etc.). Because at most sites the underlying substrate does not contain any water-worn rock, these specimens must have been brought to the site by its inhabitants. The size of the pebbles exhibits a significant variation, partly overlapping with the size range of the various use-modified tool types already described. However, it should be noted that the majority of these nonmodified rocks is smaller than the size range of the identified tools. This suggests that at least a portion was brought to the site with other intentions.

The abundant occurrence of nonmodified water-worn pebbles is a common characteristic of Ceramic Age sites in the Lesser Antilles (Knippenberg 2006). Study of the Early and Late Ceramic Age Morel and Anse à la Gourde assemblages revealed that a significant portion of the small pebbles functioned as fishnet weights, as evidenced by the presence of thin lines of black residue around the artifacts, interpreted as remnants of adhesive (Knippenberg 2006; Lammers-Keijsers 2008). Since these adhesives easily weather from the rock, especially in acid soils such as those of Basse-Terre, any evidence of this fishing net usage has disappeared and this may explain why the small pebbles found at the sites in this study do not bear any signs of being used.

BURNED ROCK

A small portion of the unmodified igneous rock at the different sites exhibits signs of being burned or heated. Percentages range between 7% at the La Pointe de Grande Anse and 13% for the Parking de Roseau site. Most rocks that exhibit signs of being burned or heated are water-worn pebbles and cobbles without any other evidence of modification. At all sites this water-worn rock is predominant. Rarely, cobbles used as querns, but also hammerstones, possess these signs. Finally, angular natural rock is also present among this material. An overall interpretation for this material is that these stones were placed in hearths or used as cooking stones for heating liquids. This especially accounts for the water-worn rock, of which it is obvious that these stones were brought to the site. This and their association with signs of heating and burning implies that they were deliberately collected for only this purpose. Whether this is also true for the more angular natural rock is more difficult to say, as these stones relate to naturally occurring rock material in the substratum of the sites. Their signs of burning may be unintentional. With regard to the flat metate tools, they may also be considered as a type of baking plates, especially when it is realized that they are overrepresented among the tools exhibiting signs of burning or heating.

4.2.5   Spatio-temporal distribution

At three sites the majority of lithics came from a very limited number of features. Especially at Pointe de Grande Anse and Parking de Roseau, a few pits stand out due to their rich lithic inventories, suggesting that some pits functioned as waste locations. At STEP Goyave the variation is not so significant and the richest feature turned out be a posthole and not a pit. It is noteworthy that many of the large tools such as querns, mortars, and grinding stones were discarded in pits.

At CHU Belle-Plaine the pattern is different, as the actual number of lithics per feature is very low despite the fact that the fills of many pits were mesh-screened.

The large assemblage from Parking de Roseau and its long period of occupation allowed for comparison of earlier contexts with the later ones. Radiocarbon dating of three features (F 174, F 178, and F 197) showed that the western cluster of pits is older than the northwestern cluster of which only one pit has been dated (F 337). The western pits further represent an extensive time span, from about cal 780–980 CE to cal 1170–1270, whereas pit F 337 likely dates between cal 1260 and 1295 CE.

Comparing the different samples collected from these dated pits shows that they exhibit great similarity in the rock varieties and tool types they produced. This is concurrent with the general pattern that the use of stone materials and tools is a firmly rooted aspect of these small-scale societies and does not exhibit many changes through time (Knippenberg 2006). Some differences, however, could be noted. A few pits (F 174, F 337, F 365, and F 412) contained predominantly active tools, whereas in most others passively and actively used tools occur in more equal amounts. These differences more likely reflect functional differences between the pit samples rather than changes in tool use through time, as the pits with active tools do not cluster in certain periods.

The only difference that may have been time-related is the absence of Long Island and other flints in the three youngest pits (F 156, F 337, and F 365), which most likely date to the late 13th and early 14th centuries. These pits only contained chalcedony flaked stone, which may have had a local Basse-Terre origin. This may suggest that during this period access to the Long Island and other Antigua materials had terminated.

4.2.6   Discussion and conclusions

The four lithic assemblages include in varying degrees a wide variety of lithic artifacts that fit well within a settlement context. In particular, Parking de Roseau, La Pointe de Grande Anse, and STEP Goyave have yielded significant numbers of tools associated with food processing that commonly occur in household settings, such as large slabs used as querns and active (hammer) abraders or grinders used as hand-held food-preparation tools.

The lithic assemblage of the CHU Belle-Plaine site can be considered as rather poor, with only 54 true artifacts and manuports. This low number of artifacts stands out when it is also compared to that of other Late Ceramic Age sites (Knippenberg 2006, 2009a). To a great part this difference may be explained by the preservation of the site at which artifact-rich find deposits were completely disturbed and got lost by Historic Age and recent agricultural activities. At CHU Belle-Plaine the only undisturbed contexts are formed by the feature fills, particularly those within the pits.

Apart from this preservation bias, the composition of the assemblage is also different from what we normally find at Late Ceramic Age sites (Knippenberg 2006). The most notable differences are the low number of flaked stone–related artifacts and the low number of axe heads found. Flaked stone is often especially abundant at Late Ceramic Age sites. Again, the disappearance of deposits with finds may to some extent be held responsible for this low occurrence, although it should be realized as well that none of the mesh-screened features fills yielded significant numbers of flaked stone. This suggests that in the surroundings of most of these features, stone working probably did not take place.

A third reason for the relative scarcity of lithics, when compared to the other three sites of this work, concerns difficult access to suitable stone raw materials. Parking de Roseau, La Pointe de Grande Anse, and STEP Goyave all are close to cobble beaches and small river-beds providing a whole range of proper igneous rock material, whereas the direct surroundings of CHU Belle-Plaine lack such rock sources. Consequently, the low numbers can be explained by a combination of poor conservation, short-term settlement, and larger distance to suitable rock material.

That access to igneous rock raw material was not restrained at Parking de Roseau, Pointe de Grande Anse, and STEP Goyave is shown not only by the high number of use-modified tools found but also by the less exhaustive use of these tools at these sites. Most quern slabs exhibit only minor abrasion marks, and this seems to point to short-term usage. Furthermore, many specimens are still intact. This, for example, contrasts to similar tools found at Anse à la Gourde, a site on Grande-Terre's northern coast in an area exclusively composed of limestone (Knippenberg 2006). Here the tools on average possess many abraded utilized surfaces. It is further noticed that the number of tools is lower and that they are more frequently fragmented.

Exotics

In addition to these locally obtained rocks, all four assemblages have lithics that are made out of exotic stone varieties. The cryptocrystalline rock used for making flake tools does not naturally occur in any of the four sites' direct surroundings and must have come from farther localities. Given the relatively high abundance of chalcedony at Parking de Roseau, La Pointe de Grande Anse, and CHU Belle-Plaine, especially when compared to other sites in the Lesser Antillean region (see Knippenberg 2006, 2011a), it is hypothesized that this material most likely came from somewhere on the volcanic island of Basse-Terre, or perhaps Dominica. Also, the characteristic jasper found at Pointe de Grande Anse was probably acquired from relatively nearby, the isle of Terre-de-Bas, Les Saintes.

A specimen of one of the other jasper varieties found at Parking de Roseau does not resemble any of the common types on the main jasper islands of Martinique and St. Lucia. It can be hypothesized that this piece is local to Basse-Terre, the volcanic island of Guadeloupe, although similar varieties have not been seen at the few places where jasper can naturally be found on Guadeloupe (personal observation).

Given the presumably relatively close distance these chalcedony and jasper varieties originate from, it is likely that the inhabitants of the different sites went to the localities where these materials occur and collected the material themselves. However, the rare as well as isolated presence of chalcedony and jasper on the island and the diverse nature of especially the chalcedony hamper proper understanding of the source areas of the various materials, and this leaves open the possibility of alternative trajectories by which the material got to the different sites.

It is exactly known from where the three identified flint varieties originate. Furthermore, how they got distributed is well understood (Knippenberg 2006, 2011a). The Long Island, Coconut Hall, and Blackman's Point flint sources all are situated either on an islet north of

Antigua or on the north coast of Antigua itself (Knippenberg 2006). Long Island flint has been used at all four sites and is relatively abundant, from around at 25% at Pointe de Grande Anse to 72% at Goyave. This is a common feature for Ceramic Age settlement sites in the northern Lesser Antilles, as regional comparative analysis has shown (Knippenberg 2006).

Fall-off analysis plotting the abundance of this flint variety against the distance from Long Island indicates that sites on the north coast of Guadeloupe are situated in the direct access area or supply zone, which implies that the communities of these sites either visited and collected the material themselves or interacted with the communities on Antigua that controlled the source (Knippenberg 2006). Based on the unique composition of the flint varieties within neighboring settlement sites, it has been hypothesized that the former option was the case during the early phase of the Ceramic Age (cal 500 BCE to 400 CE), whereas subsequently, particularly between cal 400 and 1250 CE, smaller abundances concurrent with settlement on Long Island itself suggest that the source was locally controlled, making direct access for outside communities more difficult (Knippenberg 2006).

Only the Parking de Roseau assemblage and, to a minor degree, the material from Pointe de Grande Anse contain sufficient quantities of Long Island flint to soundly compare the data with other sites. When set against some contemporaneous sites from Guadeloupe (Knippenberg 2006), both former sites yield moderate percentages of Long Island flint as part of the total of cryptocrystalline rock, respectively 33% and 25%.[12] At the northern Grande-Terre sites of Anse à la Gourde and Anse Trabaud these percentages are 58% and 85%, respectively. The lower percentage at the former sites may suggest that Parking de Roseau and La Pointe de Grande Anse were not situated in the direct access area or supply zone of the Long Island flint distribution. This implies that these communities interacted with an intermediate community, likely the sites on the northern Grande-Terre shores, to obtain Long Island flint. This is different from the situation in the early phase of the Early Ceramic Age, for which fall-off analysis shows that sites on Basse-Terre were still within the direct access area or supply zone of the Long Island flint distribution (Knippenberg 2012a).

The presence of Coconut Hall flint at both Parking de Roseau and La Pointe Grande Anse, and Blackman's Point flint at only the Roseau site more directly attests to interaction with either local Antiguan communities at Coconut Hall and Blackman's Point or intermediate ones on Grande-Terre. In fact, it is believed that the use of these flint materials was strongly tied to and controlled by these Antigua settlements adjacent to both sources during the Late Ceramic Age (Knippenberg 2006, 2011a). Also, the fact that they occur much less at the sites discussed in this study as well as at other sites on Guadeloupe is already an indication that access was more restricted when compared to that of Long Island flint. Only the Parking de Roseau assemblage allows for an evaluation of the use of Long Island flint through time. Comparing early and late contexts within the site shows that the Roseau community stopped using these varieties during the last phase(s) of occupation, around the end of the 13th century and the beginning of the 14th century. In this period only chalcedony, presumed to be (more) local, was used. From this it can be concluded that access to the nonlocal flint materials had ceased, and this suggests that the relationships with the communities of Antigua or intermediate ones had terminated or at least changed to such a degree that exchange did not occur anymore.

Items of exchange

Apart from the Antigua flints there are other rock materials that were acquired through inter-community exchange. One of the best-studied examples is represented by the St. Martin greenstone, of which fragmented axe heads have been found at Parking de Roseau and Pointe de Grande Anse.

Regional research has shown that St. Martin greenstone axes were manufactured only within a localized region, including St. Martin and its surrounding neighbor islands Anguilla, St. Eustatius, and likely St. Barthélémy and Saba (Knippenberg 2006). Sites outside this region yielded only finished items, suggesting the axes were obtained from one of the communities making them. It was a highly esteemed material, as recent studies have shown that it became distributed all the way to Carriacou, one of Grenada's Grenadines, at a distance of approximately 680 km to St. Martin (Knippenberg in prep.). It has been found at many sites of Guadeloupe, sometimes in large quantities, as work at Anse à la Gourde has shown (Knippenberg 2006). This richness may suggest that the communities on Guadeloupe were in direct contact with one of the axe manufacturing sites, those on St. Eustatius being the closest and therefore the most likely candidates. The further distribution of the material was likely the result of down-the-line exchange. The communities on Guadeloupe may have passed these axes on to communities more to the south in exchange for desired commodities from the Windward Islands.

Only recently it has become clear that with the acquisition, manufacture, and distribution of jadeitite axes a similar mechanism must have operated, though much more extensive in scale (Knippenberg 2012b; Knippenberg et al. 2012; Schertl et al. 2018). Pinpointing a source for the different axes found in the Lesser Antilles, Virgin Islands, and Puerto Rico, using in-depth mineralogical, petrographic, and geochemical analyses, has thus far turned out to be very difficult owing to the large variation jadeitite can exhibit within each source and the considerable overlap in mineralogical and petrographic characteristics that exists between the three known source regions (see Harlow et al. 2006; García-Casco et al. 2013; Knippenberg et al. 2012; Schertl et al. 2018).

Recent archaeological work at the Ceramic Age settlement site of Playa Grande in the northern part of the Dominican Republic has shown that locally axes, and possibly also chisels, were manufactured of jadeitite (Knippenberg 2012b; Schertl et al. 2018). The site is closely situated to the Río San Juan jadeitite source, one of the three major sources of this jade variety in the Circum-Caribbean region. Mineralogical, petrographic, and geochemical analyses have shown that the locally manufactured jadeitite axes are similar to the nearby source material, and this makes a strong case for the Río San Juan source being of significance to the Lesser Antilles material.

Pointe de Grande Anse is not the only site on Guadeloupe where jadeitite has been found, as eight specimens have been recovered during large-scale excavations at Anse à la Gourde (García Casgo, personal communication 2011; Knippenberg in prep.). Similar trajectories can be put forward to explain the presence of some of the other unique axe heads found at the sites discussed. This applies to a dark grey metamorphic axe and a light-green igneous axe found at Parking de Roseau, and an adze made from a light-green fine-grained material found at Pointe de Grande Anse. However, first proper rock identification is needed in order to pinpoint possible source regions, and subsequently the rock materials need to be petrologically compared to actual source materials.

In case of the dark grey metamorphic axe found at Parking de Roseau, a provenance somewhere in the Greater Antilles should be considered as these islands host many suitable materials. The presence of jadeitite at the Guadeloupe sites shows that material from the Greater Antilles, or from even farther, traveled all the way to the eastern Lesser Antilles, and this leaves open the possibility that the dark grey axe got distributed through the same network. The grey-green adze may have originated from St. Martin and may have been transported through the same network as the St. Martin greenstone. For the light-green axe from Parking de Roseau a provenance is unknown. That these tools were highly valued is also expressed in their long use-life. Both the dark grey and the light-green axes exhibit evidence of reuse as a hammer-grinders or pestles.

Lapidary artifacts

Despite the presence of exotic tools and flaked stone, the four sites can be considered very poor in lapidary artifacts such as beads and pendants. Parking de Roseau yielded only one translucent quartz rock crystal bead, whereas at the other three sites beads and pendants are totally lacking. This poverty of lapidary items can to a certain extent be explained by the applied excavation strategy, during which screening was executed only on samples from fills belonging to a limited series of features. However, this low frequency also fits the Late Ceramic Age pattern for the Lesser Antilles. This late period has a much lower occurrence of stone lapidary items within settlement sites than, for example, the earliest phase of the Ceramic Age (cal 400 BCE to 400 CE) (Knippenberg 2006; Hofman et al. 2007). Besides, it has become obvious as well that some of the rarer and more exotic rock and semiprecious stone varieties had disappeared and that now beads and pendants were primarily manufactured from local, more widely available materials such as quartz, but also calcite and diorite (Knippenberg 2006).

Cemí *three-pointer stones and other ritual objects*

The absence of *cemí* three-pointers at any of the four sites is striking, because it has become clear that these ritual objects became abundantly present in the Late Ceramic Age, as the archaeological research at Anse à la Gourde and Anse à l'Eau has shown (Knippenberg 2006). Sample bias may be an issue, as these objects still have to be considered relatively rare artifacts. This especially accounts for CHU Belle-Plaine.

Fieldwork at the two mentioned sites on Grande-Terre's northern coast, however, has shown that within a sample of similar and even smaller size to those of Parking de Roseau, La Pointe de Grande Anse and STP Goyave, they still occur. The sample of 25 artifacts at Anse l'Eau includes one stone three-pointer. The larger sample from the test-unit excavations at Anse à la Gourde (N~950) has a total number of seven *cemí* three-pointers. Extrapolating a similar richness at Parking de Roseau, La Pointe de Grande, and STEP Goyave would result in the finding of at least five at Parking de Roseau to two at STEP Goyave and one at Pointe de Grande Anse. Especially for the Parking de Roseau site, this makes a strong case that this community had much less access to these highly valued religious objects.

Despite the absence of *cemí* three-pointer stones at all four sites, the CHU Belle-Plaine site yielded a unique sculptured stone head that may be considered to represent a different form of *cemí*. The way the head was sculpted resembles the head depictions of many of the petroglyphs in the southern part of Basse-Terre. In addition, Pointe de Grande Anse yielded a unique stone artifact showing engravings. It represents a quern or mortar fragment with a concentric circle on the outside. The engraving signifies that this food-grinding tool may have had an important, perhaps ritual function. In the Lesser Antilles we are not familiar with engraved querns or mortars. However, in the Greater Antilles, elaborate pestles, the active counterparts of mortars, are recurring artifacts (Bercht et al. 1997:113, 122, 145, 149).

4.3   European wares from Parking de Roseau

Fabrice Casagrande

Before being conquered by different northwest European powers, the Lesser Antilles were called on by the Spanish and later on by other European sailors during their voyages towards the New World. In the 16th and early 17th century, the Lesser Antilles were mainly considered places of maritime rendez-vous but also as harbors to meet and exchange with the local population, commonly called Caribes. In exchange mostly for fresh food, the Europeans gave the Amerindians *pacotilla* or batches of mirrors, bells, and glass beads and all other stuff imaginable (Bodinier 1992). Once filled up, the ships or fleets continued their voyage either towards the Americas or towards the homeland. This so-called contact period ended for Guadeloupe in 1635 when the French decided to settle the island of Basse-Terre.

The excavations at Parking de Roseau yielded a few objects that can be attributed to this latter period. They have been found predominantly in the upper sandy layers of the Roseau beach where several trenches were dug at the foot of the volcanic cliffs. In addition to a few glass beads (see Chapter 4), these trenches yielded 34 fragments of European ware: 25 wall fragments, two rims and one handle. All fragments can be attributed to Spanish jars or so-called olive oil jars. In general, their paste is composed of sand containing some larger quartz particles as well as some mica fragments, which are visible to the naked eye. The hues are yellow to salmon.

Two rim fragments are neck components and coated with a lead glaze. The first was discovered during the SRA survey (Stouvenot 2013), and has a beveled rim with a thickened outer arc—perhaps for a lid? (Figure 4.22). The interior features a dark grey anthracite glaze with silver reflections. We were not able to trace this glaze in the existing literature, which provided solely the application of green and yellow glazes on the interior. The dimensions and shape of these kinds of amphorae vary much from one to the other, and at first all rims look alike; however, according to the typochronology established by George E. Avery (1993), the neck fragment found at Parking de Roseau can be attributed to the second quarter of the 17th century (Figure 4.23).

Two Spanish shipwrecks have been excavated at the Dry Tortugas, an archipelago situated to the west of the Florida Keys (USA). They sank during a hurricane in September 1622. A large quantity of Spanish jars has been found in the cargo of these ships (Kingsley et al. 2012). Two types of amphorae have been recognized (Figure 4.23). Type 1 includes jars of a large size having an oblong shape, whereas Type 2 represents smaller globular vessels (Figure 4.24). Both types have proper rims (Avery 1993). The rim found at Parking de Roseau can thus be attributed to Type 2 of this chronology.

A sunken cargo found on the leeward side of Martinique yielded, among others, a glazed pot from Catalonia (Amouric et al. 2012). A similar fragment was found at Parking de Roseau (Figure 4.26). It is noteworthy that the Kalinago site of Argyle, on St. Vincent, features at least one fragment of a Spanish jar (see Hofman and Hoogland 2012).

The second Spanish jar component is entirely different from the one already described. The rim curves inward and its upper part is covered in a green lead glaze, whereas the rest of the fragment is covered in a transparent glaze applied to a white engobe that shows a few green speckles of green glaze (Figure 4.25). Without doubt, this fragment can be attributed to the "early" Spanish jar types. Its globular shape with two opposite handles applied to the neck refers to the first model that can be found in the Americas.

The production centers of these early models are believed to have been located in southern Spain, such as in Seville or Cadiz, but the exact origins of these vessels might be more

Figure 4.22 Collar of Spanish jar found at the beach of Roseau by SRA. After Stouvenot 2013.

Photo: F. Casagrande, Inrap.

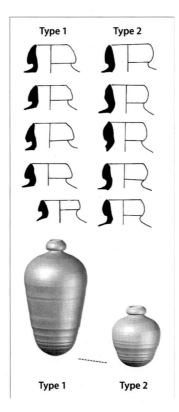

Figure 4.23 Collars of Spanish jars found on the Dry Tortugas.

Adapted by F. Casagrande after Avery 1997.

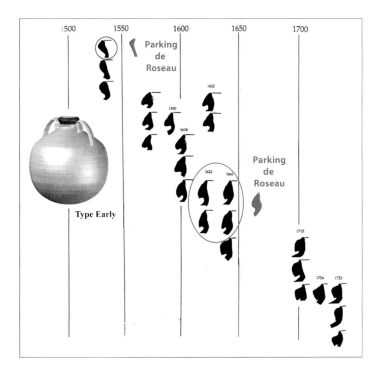

Figure 4.24 Typochronology of collars of Spanish jars.

Adapted by F. Casagrande after Avery 1993.

Figure 4.25 Complete Spanish jar found at large on the Windward side of Martinique at the bottom of
the sea (jar held by the Musée Paul Gauguin, Le Carbet, Martinique).

Photo: F. Casagrande, Inrap.

Figure 4.26 Rim with a transparent glaze from Catalunia found at the beach of Parking de Roseau.

Photo: F. Casagrande, Inrap.

Figure 4.27 Early type rim of a Spanish jar found at the beach of Parking de Roseau.

Photo: F. Casagrande, Inrap.

variable (Carter 1982). Traditionally, these vessels are believed to have contained and stored olive oil, but they could also have contained other victuals, such as olives in vinegar, honey, or wine (Goggin 1960; Martin 1979). Some authors believe that the lead glaze applied to its interior is related directly to the product it might have contained (Goggin 1968). Here, we want to add that these containers might as well have been recycled to serve as freshwater containers and that these Spanish jars might also have ended up in the cargoes of other European ships (see Carter 1982).

In fact, the natural springs at Roseau beach (see Chapter 2), along the seaside where fresh water flows out of the cliffs, is exactly the place where the Spanish jars were found mixed up with Amerindian ceramics. One specimen can be attributed to the first half of the 16th century, whereas the other is dated about a century later, thus covering the 16th and early 17th centuries; hence, the period during which many Europeans called on Roseau to fetch water and exchange goods with the Amerindians.

4.4   Glass beads from Parking de Roseau

Karlis Karklins

Six glass beads were encountered at the Parking de Roseau site (Figure 4.28). Two were recovered from the fill of pits F 178 and F 412, while the rest came from archaeological test trenches on the beach (see Figure 3.8). All are of drawn manufacture (made of segments of glass tubes drawn out from a gather of molten glass) and include both tubular (unaltered segments) and globular (heat-rounded) varieties. These are identified using the Kidd and Kidd (2012) classification system as expanded by Karklins (2012) (Table 4.12). The bead marked with an asterisk (*) is not recorded in the Kidd and Kidd system.

Table 4.12 The Parking de Roseau glass beads.

Variety	Description	Provenience	Figure
Ib*	Tubular; opaque shadow blue (burned; difficult to determine original color) with an undetermined number of red stripes	Trench 9, US 3	a
Ib23	Tubular; translucent bright navy blue with 3 opaque red stripes	Pit F 178, US 1–2	b
Ibb1 (?)	Tubular; opaque red with 3 (?) blue-on-white stripes; fragment	Trench 9, US 3	c
IIa40	Globular; opaque robin's-egg blue	Trench 9, US 3	d
IIb56	Globular; translucent robin's-egg blue with 3 opaque white stripes	Trench 6, US 3	e
IVk7	Globular; chevron bead with five starry layers: transparent green exterior/opaque white/opaque red/opaque white/translucent blue core	Pit F 412, US 2	f

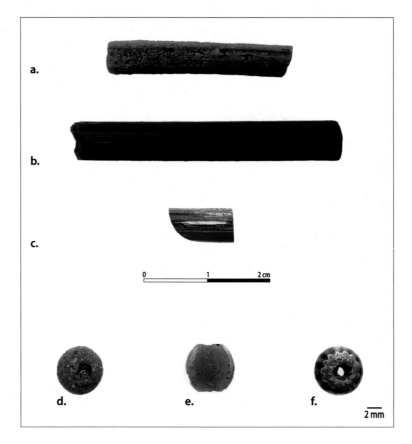

Figure 4.28 The Parking de Roseau glass beads: (a–c) tubular, (d–f) globular.

Photos: T. Romon, Inrap.

4.4.1   *Dating*

Dating the Roseau beads is a bit problematic. Based on the revised chronology for 16th-century glass beads in the American Southeast prepared by Keith Little (2010), the three globular specimens may all be attributed to his Complex 2 (cal 1550–1600 CE). Elsewhere, however, these three varieties have much longer temporal ranges. For example, globular robin's-egg-blue beads (IIa40)—known as "early blues" in the southeastern United States—are widely distributed over eastern North America. They appear as early as 1600 in the Mohawk region of New York State and continue in use there until 1750. In the same region, variety IIb56 dates to about 1580–1659 (Rumrill 1991).

Rounded green chevron beads (IVk7) are relatively scarce, but have been encountered at several sites in eastern North America that are attributed to the 1620–1700 period (see Blair et al. 2009; Garrad 2001; Mouer 1992). While it is possible that the beads date back to as early as about 1550, it is unlikely that they postdate the 1635 occupation of Basse-Terre by the French.[13] Two datable rim fragments from Spanish olive jars recovered from Trenches 7 and 9 are attributed to roughly 1550–1575 and the second quarter of the 17th century, respectively, tending to substantiate this (see Chapter 4). The three tubular beads cannot be accurately dated at present, but their styles are certainly in keeping with those of the three globular varieties. That they date to the same period is supported by the fact that two of them were recovered from the same stratigraphic level in Trench 9.

4.4.2   Comparisons

Early contact-period glass beads are relatively scarce at sites in the Antilles. The earliest beads thus far recovered were excavated at the Long Bay site on San Salvador Island, The Bahamas. Many believe this is where Christopher Columbus first set foot in the New World, giving the people he encountered various trifles, including glass beads. Interestingly, among the few European items excavated at Long Bay are ten whole and fragmentary ring-shaped beads, 2.5–3.6 mm in diameter, with relatively large perforations. Of wound manufacture, all are transparent green except for one pale-yellow/amber specimen (Brill et al. 1991:250). While it is known that Columbus' store of goods included "green and yellow glass beads," there is no direct proof that the recovered beads came from him and, consequently, Hoffman (1991:242) cautiously assigns them to the 1492–1560 period.

The excavation of a sugar mill dating to the early 16th century at Sevilla la Nueva, Jamaica, yielded 23 glass beads including tubular Nueva Cadiz types in red, blue, and green with round (Ia), square (Ic), or twisted-square (Ic') bodies. They are associated with 12 large, faceted blue chevrons (IVk) (Woodward 2006:187).

A variety of drawn glass beads were encountered at Puerto Real, a Spanish town on the north coast of Haiti that existed from 1502 to 1578. The inventory includes blue chevrons with both faceted and heat-rounded forms (IVk), as well as tubular blue chevrons with five layers (IIIk3); Nueva Cadiz varieties with plain (IIIc) and twisted (IIIc') bodies; dark blue beads with spiral white stripes (IIb'); and purple ones with white stripes (IIb) (Deagan 1987:172–173). Deagan (1987:166) also mentions the presence of large and very large (up to 55 mm in length) faceted blue chevron beads at Concepción de la Vega in the Dominican Republic. This was a Spanish settlement that grew around a fort established by Columbus in 1492. It was destroyed by an earthquake in 1562 and subsequently abandoned. Such beads were also present at the site of Casa de Engombe, a 16th-century sugar mill complex at the western edge of Santo Domingo (Deagan 1987:164).

Excavations conducted at El Cabo San Rafael, a Taíno settlement situated at the eastern tip of the Dominican Republic, produced five glass beads. Three are Nueva Cadiz types described as having square cross-sections and "iridescent blue/green/white in colour." The two intact specimens are 30 mm long. Also found were two fragments of a cobalt-blue bead with faceted ends (Samson 2010:284–285). The site, occupied since about cal 800 CE, was abandoned around 1504 as a result of wars with the Spanish. A cave site on Isla de Mona, one of the islands of the Puerto Rican archipelago, produced a blue, square-sectioned Nueva Cadiz bead. The recovered artifacts span the period from 1493 to 1590 (Cooper et al. 2016:1057).

At the southern end of the Antilles island chain, the Argyle site on St. Vincent yielded a handful of beads, which include a small faceted blue chevron (IVk), a blue (IIa40) specimen, a large greyish-blue bead with six red stripes (likely IIb61), and a large black bead (IIa6), as well as a white seed bead (IIa14) set into the rim of a Cayoid vessel (Hofman and Hoogland 2012). These beads may all be assigned to the late 16th to early 17th centuries, a date supported by the recovered Spanish and Portuguese ceramics. Of all the sites discussed here, this is the only one, which has a correlative (IIa40) among the Roseau beads.

4.4.3   Conclusions

Based on comparisons with beads recovered from early contact sites in the Antilles and the eastern United States, the indication is that the Parking de Roseau beads arrived with Spaniards visiting Guadeloupe between 1550 and 1635. The beads were likely made in either Holland or France, production tubes and rejects of varieties Ibb1(?), IIa40, and IIb56 having been recovered from factory wasters dating to the early 17th century in both Amsterdam (Bradley 2014:56) and Rouen (Karklins and Bonneau 2019). Of course, Venice, the dominant bead-making center for most of the historic period, cannot be ruled out entirely as it probably produced similar varieties as well.

4.5   Invertebrates: daily activities and regime

Nathalie Serrand

Of the four sites presented in this volume, only three yielded invertebrate assemblages; no remains were found at La Pointe de Grande Anse site. The three invertebrate series are very small: 39 remains at CHU Belle-Plaine, 72 remains at STEP Goyave, and 484 remains at Parking de Roseau. However, at the latter two sites, these numbers (three specimens at STEP Goyave and 49 at Parking de Roseau) can only partially be associated with the reconstructed Amerindian occupations.

4.5.1   State of preservation: altered and quite unrepresentative assemblages

The small size of the invertebrate assemblages is not surprising, given the geographic area where the sites are located. This is characterized by acid volcanic soils, which rarely yield abundant archaeological faunal remains, if any. The remains found, illustrated in Figure 4.29, witness a very damaged, weathered, and decalcified state for most shell pieces.

While preservation is not good, the lack of systematic sieving can also be added as a factor for the small quantities of shell, resulting in very small series, mainly consisting of the harder pieces of the most resistant species: they consist of solid parts (mostly columella) of queen conch shells (*Lobatus gigas*) and fragments of coral that show advanced states of acid dissolution (Figure 4.29). This clearly reveals that other, more fragile remains and species probably dissolved in the sediments and are lost to science.

At Parking de Roseau, there is a slight difference between the remains from the plateau and the lower beach areas. Shells found in the latter area appear to be less dissolved and some specimens show a typically bluish patina, probably resulting from deposition in the clayish silts of the lagoon (Figure 4.29j). This area yielded numerous complete queen conchs (Figure 4.29g–j) as well as other species, including land crabs (Tables 4.13 and 4.14). Given the advanced alterations and partial preservation, the assemblages cannot be considered as representative assemblages. Therefore, discussion of the importance of invertebrates as an alimentary resource or as a raw material at these sites is impossible. Such an analysis can be made more easily of the assemblages found on the calcareous island of Grande-Terre, which represents an important difference between Basse-Terre and Grande Terre.

4.5.2   Methods, materials, taxonomic compositions

Invertebrate remains were collected while digging and screening the features at CHU Belle-Plaine and Parking de Roseau. All species were identified (Pointier and Lamy 1998; Warmke and Abbott 1961) and quantified using the number of individual skeleton pieces

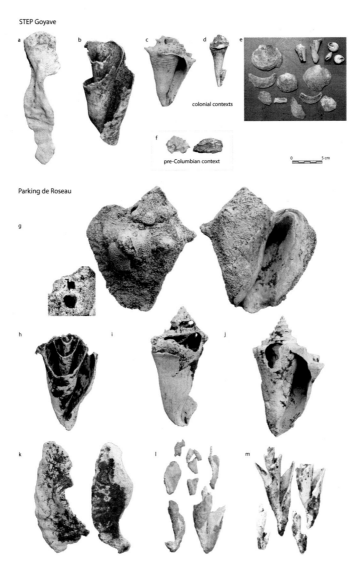

Figure 4.29 STEP Goyave: a. *Lobatus gigas* lip of an adult/mature individual (lower area US 1106); b. *Lobatus gigas* subcomplete shell of an adult individual (lower area US 1025); c. *Lobatus gigas* subcomplete shell of a subadult individual (beach area US 1050); d. *Lobatus gigas* subcomplete shell of a juvenile to subadult individual (beach area US 1078); e. Fragments of clam *Codakia orbicularis*, queen conch *Lobatus gigas*), and land snails *Pleurodonte josephinae* and *Bulimulus* cf. *guadelupensis* (beach area, US 1043); f. Coral fragment (Upper area, pre-Columbian context, pits F 211 and F 401) Parking de Roseau: g. *Lobatus gigas* complete shell of a mature individual with an extraction hole (beach area, Trenches 6–7 South US 3); h-i. *Lobatus gigas* subcomplete shells subadult and adult individuals (beach area, Trench 6 South US 3); j. *Lobatus gigas* subcomplete shell of a subadult individual (beach area, Trench 6 South US 4); k. *Lobatus gigas* detached lips of mature individuals (beach area, Trench 6 South US 3); l-m. *Lobatus gigas* columella decalcified parts (plateau, pits F 337 and F 365).

Photos: N. Serrand, Inrap.

Table 4.13 List of species in NISP, weight, and MNI counts for all assemblages.

Family	Species	Parking de Roseau			STEP Goyave			CHU Belle-Plaine*		
		NISP	Weight	MNI	NISP	Weight	MNI	NISP	Weight	MNI
		361	36596	160	70	1397	38			
MOLLUSCS										
Gastropods		**308**	**36424**	**112**	**21**	**1259**	**12**	7		
FISSURELLIDAE	Fissurella nimbosa	1	4	1						
	Fissurella sp.	1	1	1						
TROCHIDAE	Cittarium pica	115	4570	40						
TURBINIDAE	Lithopoma tuber	4	23	3						
NERITIDAE	Nerita tessellata	1	1	1						
	Neritina punctulata	24	41	23						
STROMBIDAE	Lobatus gigas	161	31774	42	19	1256	12			
	Lobatus cf. gigas				1	2				
	Lobatus costatus							3		
	Lobatus sp.							4		
MURICIDAE	Thais=Mancinella deltoidea	1	10	1		1				
unidentified gastropod					1	1				
Bivalves		**11**	**90**	**7**	**35**	**111**	**12**	27		
LUCINIDAE	Lucina pectinata	1	34	1						
	Codakia orbicularis	6	29	4	34	109	12	8		
	Codakia sp.				1	2				
OSTREIDAE								12		
ARCIDAE								7		
CHAMIDAE	Chama sp.	1	6	1						
TELLINIDAE	Arcopagia fausta	3	21	1						
Land snails		**42**	**82**	**41**	**14**	**27**	**14**	3		
BULIMULIDAE	Bulimulus cf. guadalupensis	8	4	8	2	1	2	2		

PLEURODONTIDAE	*Pleurodonte josephinae*	33	76	32	12	26	12
PLANORBIDAE	*Biomphalaria* cf. *glabrata*							1
	Pomacea glauca	1	2	1			
CRUSTACEANS							
Decapods		**16**	**20**	**5**			
GECARCINIDAE	*Cardisoma guanhumi*	6	10	2			
	Gecarcinus sp.	2	2	1			
	Gecarcinid	8	8	2			
CORALS		**107**	**3509**	**6**	**2**	**12**	**2**	**2**
Anthozoa							
ACROPORIDAE	*Acropora cervicornis*	1	18	1			
	Acropora palmata	6	448	1			
	Acroporidae	2	8				
FAVIDAE	*Solenastrea* spp.	2	244	1			
	cf. *Solenastrea*	6	1293				
	Diploria spp.	1	107	1	1	8	1
MEANDRINIDAE	*Dichocoenia* spp.	1	144	1			
PORITIDAE	*Porites* cf. *porites*	57	447	1			
	Porites sp.	15	318				
	Poritidae	5	123				
	unidentified invertebrate	11	359		1	4	1
Total		**484**	**40125**	**171**	**72**	**1409**	**40**	**39**

* Weight and MNI data are not available for this site

Table 4.14 Provenience of species in NISP counts for the CHU Belle-Plaine assemblage (after S. Grouard). Weight and MNI data are not available for this site.

CHU Belle-Plaine, invertebrate
NISP (S. Grouard)

Family	Species	Features							
		F20	F73	F186	F213	F215	F216	F218	TOTAL
MOLLUSCS		1	2	1	1	4	27	1	37
Gastropods		1	2	1		2	1		7
STROMBIDAE	*Lobatus costatus*	1	1	1					3
	Lobatus sp.		1			2	1		4
Bivalves						2	25		27
LUCINIDAE	*Lucina pectinata*						8		8
OSTREIDAE						1	11		12
ARCIDAE						1	6		7
Land snails					1		1	1	3
BULIMULIDAE	*Bulimulus* cf. *guadalupensis*						1	1	2
	Pomacea glauca				1				1
CORALS							2		2
Anthozoa							2		2
Total		1	2	1	1	4	29	1	39

(NISP, including complete shells and fragments), the weight of remains in grams, and the frequency of the Minimum Number of Individuals (MNIf).[14] The MNIf has been estimated, for each species, combining the most frequent unique element, which can describe only one individual (Poplin 1976a-b). No invertebrate remains were found at the site of La Pointe de Grande Anse. Yet, the amount of vertebrate fauna studied from one pit (F 3) at this site is significant. Of 38 different taxa, 3,429 remains were recovered, but they account for only 82 individuals (see Chapter 4). It is quite surprising that not even one single shell specimen was found during the excavation!

At the site of CHU Belle-Plaine, vertebrates and invertebrates were studied in one assemblage by Sandrine Grouard (see Chapter 4). This assemblage is close in number to that from La Pointe de Grande Anse, with 3,701 remains of which 2,236 were studied. These include only 39 remains of invertebrates, or 1% of the total NISP (Tables 4.13 and 4.14). They consist of two pieces of eroded, unidentified coral (pit F 216); two specimens of land snails of the Bulimulidae family (pits F 216 and F 218); one specimen of freshwater mangrove snail of the Planorbidae family (*Biomphalaria* cf. *glabrata*; pit F 213), seven pieces of the marine gastropods *Lobatus costatus* and *Lobatus* sp. (pits F 20, 73, 186, 215, and 216), and remains of three bivalve families, Lucinidae, Ostreidae, and Arcidae (pits F 215 and F 216). The latter are the most abundant, with (in all) 27 bivalve remains. Pit F 216, to the south of the excavated area, yielded by far the maximum number of remains (29 remains of five different taxa).

The invertebrate assemblage at the STEP Goyave site is rather small, with only 72 remains accounting for 40 individuals (total weight: 1409 g) (Tables 4.13 and 4.15). All remains are weathered and decalcified (Figure 4.29a–f). Furthermore, only a slight amount is directly

Table 4.15 Provenience of species in NISP counts for the STEP Goyave assemblage.

STEP Goyave, invertebrate NISP

Family	Species	Beach area											Morre			Total
		1008	1025	1042	1043	1050	1056	1066	1078	1106	1078?	total	211	401	total	
MOLLUSCS		**3**	**1**	**20**	**13**	**20**	**1**	**3**	**5**	**1**	**1**	**68**	**1**	**1**		**70**
Gastropods		**3**	**1**	**4**	**2**	**2**		**1**	**4**	**1**	**1**	**19**	**1**	**1**		**21**
STROMBIDAE	*Lobatus gigas*	3	1	4	2	2			4	1	1	18	1	1		**19**
	Lobatus cf. *gigas*						1									**1**
Unidentified gastropod							1	1				1				**1**
Bivalves				**5**	**8**	**18**	**1**	**2**	**1**			**35**				**35**
LUCINIDAE	*Codakia orbicularis*			5	8	18		2	1			35				**34**
	Codakia sp.						1									**1**
Land snails				**11**	**3**							**14**				**14**
BULIMULIDAE	*Bulimulus* cf. *guadalupensis*			1	1							2				**2**
PLEURODONTIDAE	*Pleurodonte josephinae*			10	2							12				**12**
CORALS																
Anthozoa													**1**	**1**		**2**
FAVIDAE	*Diploria* spp.												1		1	**1**
Unidentified invertebrate														1	1	**1**
Total		**3**	**1**	**20**	**13**	**20**	**1**	**4**	**5**	**1**	**1**	**69**	**2**	**1**	**3**	**72**

associated with the Amerindian contexts, probably not more than the three remains found in the upper area in two pre-Columbian features (pits F 211 and F 401). Indeed, the 69 other remains have been found in the stratigraphic units of the lower area where a colonial water mill was excavated. Nevertheless, it is possible that some remains found in these units may represent specimens that had eroded from the upper area of the site. The latter remains are mainly represented by parts of queen conch *Lobatus gigas*, clam *Codakia orbicularis* and the land snail *Pleurodonte josephinae* (Figure 4.29a–e and Table 4.16). In any case, the three more likely Amerindian remains are one piece of the queen conch *Lobatus gigas*, one fragment of the coral *Diploria* sp., and one unidentified fragment.

Finally, the site of Parking de Roseau is the only one that yielded a real, but not consequent, assemblage, of 484 remains accounting for 171 individuals (total weight: 40 125 grams) (Table 4.13). However, as for STEP Goyave, the link between the majority of the shell remains and a strict Amerindian context is not evident. In general, this may be considered an overall issue for this site, which has an upper area, or plateau—where most features are attributed to the pre-Columbian occupations—and a lower, or laguna-beach area, where European and pre-Columbian material has been found to be mixed. Due to a high water level and absence of continuous pumping, there was no possibility to excavate this area properly and therefore it was not possible to identify the exact stratigraphic position of these artifacts (see Chapter 2).

About 90% of the remains derive from the trenches dug in the beach (Table 4.16). Only 49 remains are from seven features on the plateau: F 178, 197, 204, 337, 344, 365, and 412 (Figure 4.30a). Interestingly, these features containing invertebrate remains are among the largest features found at the site. This suggests that these large quantities of material, particularly the abundance of other artifacts, may have contributed to the exceptional and partial preservation of the shell remains. Indeed, pit F 178, the largest of all pits, yielded 31 of the 49 shell remains found on the plateau (63.2%). Therefore, it is difficult to draw conclusions on the distribution of the shell remains for this part of the excavation, knowing that their preservation is due to the particular context of the remains. Moreover, the only remains found on the plateau belong to the queen conch *Lobatus gigas* (NISP = 46) and this shell is represented almost exclusively by columella parts and ends (>93% NISP), the most resistant parts of the conch shell. They are complemented by three coral fragments attributed to the Acroporidae family and the genus *Dichocoenia*. The coral clearly confirms that only the toughest parts of the most resistant species were preserved in a few optimal contexts.

The beach yielded the other 435 remains (90% NISP) (Figure 4.30a). This assemblage is also dominated by conch shells and corals but, in addition, contains a variety of other species: seven marine gastropods, four marine bivalves, three land snails, and, finally, two species of land crabs (Table 4.16). This ensemble indicates that this muddy-sandy beach context ensured a better preservation of invertebrate remains than the plateau (Figures 4.29g–m and 4.30b–f). According to NISP importance, the species are conchs, topshells *Cittarium pica*, corals, and land snails, ahead of *Neritina punctulata*, land crabs, *Codakia orbicularis*, *Lithopoma tuber*, *Arcopagia fausta*, *Fissurella* sp., *Nerita tessellata*, *Mancinella deltoidea*, *Lucina pectinata*, and *Chama* sp. Nevertheless, the relatively high numbers of land snails (represented by the species *Pleurodonte josephinae*, *Bulimulus* cf. *guadalupensis*, and *Pomacea glauca*), Gecarcinid land crabs (*Cardisoma guanhumi*, *Gecarcinus* sp.), and a variety of corals suggest that in this profile some taxa may be of natural origin. On the one hand, the isolated fragments of fissurellas (2), *Nerita tessellata* (1), and purple-shell *Mancinella deltoidea* (1) may have been included in the muddy-sandy matrix of the beach area by the Amerindians whereas, on the other hand, the land snails could have been naturally occurring

Table 4.16 Provenience of species in NISP counts for the Parking de Roseau assemblage.

Parking de Roseau, invertebrate NISP

Family	Species	5	6	1 nord	2 nord	4 nord	5 sud	6 sud	7 sud	9 sud	canal [1]	canal [2]	canal entre 6 et 7 nord	total	178	197	204	337	344	365	412	total	TOTAL
MOLLUSCS		**18**	**0**	**1**	**3**	**34**	**172**	**29**	**39**	**3**	**2**	**10**	**4**	**315**	**29**	**1**	**3**	**3**	**2**	**7**	**1**	**46**	**361**
Gastropods		**16**	**0**	**1**	**3**	**24**	**141**	**21**	**37**	**3**	**2**	**10**	**4**	**262**	**29**	**1**	**3**	**3**	**2**	**7**	**1**	**46**	**308**
FISSURELLIDAE	*Fissurella nimbosa*				1									1									**1**
	Fissurella sp.				1									1									**1**
TROCHIDAE	*Cittarium pica*	11				14	62	4	19	2		3		115									**115**
TURBINIDAE	*Lithopoma tuber*				1		1	1	1					4									**4**
NERITIDAE	*Nerita tessellata*							1						1									**1**
	Neritina punctulata			1			19		3	1				24									**24**
STROMBIDAE	*Lobatus gigas*	4				10	58	15	14	1	2	7	4	115	29	1	3	3	2	7	1	46	**161**
MURICIDAE	*Thais Mancinella deltoidea*									1				1									**1**
Bivalves		**1**	**0**	**0**	**1**	**6**	**2**	**1**						**11**	**0**	**0**	**0**	**0**	**0**	**0**	**0**	**0**	**11**
LUCINIDAE	*Lucina pectinata*				1									1									**1**
	Codakia orbicularis					1	4	1						6									**6**
CHAMIDAE	*Chama* sp.	1												1									**1**
TELLINIDAE	*Arcopagia fausta*	1					1	1						3									**3**
Land snails						9	25	6	1	1				**42**	**0**	**0**	**0**	**0**	**0**	**0**	**0**	**0**	**42**
BULIMULIDAE	*Bulimulus cf. guadalupensis*					1	6	1						8									**8**

(Continued)

Table 4.16 (Continued)

Parking de Roseau, invertebrate NISP

Family	Species	Beach area													Morne or plateau								TOTAL
		5	6	1 nord	2 nord	4 nord	5 sud	6 sud	7 sud	9 sud	canal 1	canal 2	entre 6 et 7 nord	total	178	197	204	337	344	365	412	total	
PLEURODONTIDAE	*Pleurodonte josephinae*	1				8	18	5	1					33									33
	Pomacea glauca		1											1									1
CRUSTACEANS **Decapods**		0	0	0	0	1	14	0	1	0	0	0	0	16	0	0	0	0	0	0	0	0	16
GECARCINIDAE	*Cardisoma guanhumi*						5		1					6									6
	Gecarcinus sp.						2							2									2
	Gecarcinid					1	7							8									8
CORALS **Anthozoa**		19	1	1	2		36	7	35			2		104	2	0	0	0	0	1	0	3	107
ACROPORIDAE	*Acropora cervicornis*						1							1									1
	Acropora palmata						2	1	2					6							1		6
	Acroporidae													2							2	2	2
FAVIDAE	*Solenastrea* spp.						2							2									2
	cf. *Solenastrea*		6											6									6
	Diploria spp.											1		1									1
MEANDRINIDAE	*Dichocoenia* spp.																				1	1	1
PORITIDAE	*Porites* cf. *porites*	19				1	23	2	24					70			3	3	2	8			70
	Porites sp.						1		1					2									2
	Poritidae	1							4					5									5
Unidentified invertebrate		1				1		3	4	2				11									11
Total		37	11	1	4	37	222	36	75	3	2	12	4	435	31	1	3	3	2	8	1	49	484

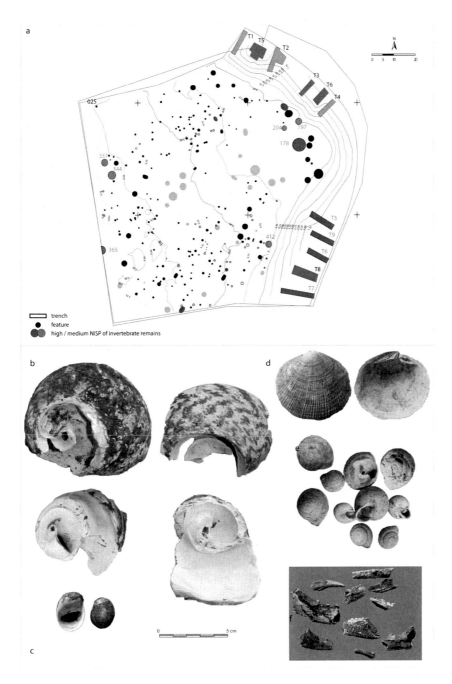

Figure 4.30 Parking de Roseau: a. Distribution of invertebrate remains in the trenches at the beach area and features at the upper part or plateau; b. Typical *Cittarium pica* type of remains found at the beach area (Trench 6 South, US 3); c. *Neritina pucntulata* complete shell found at the beach area (Trench 6 South US 6); d. *Codakia orbicularis* complete shell found at the beach area (Trench 6 South US 6); e. *Pleurodonte josephinae* shells found at the beach area (Trench 6 South US 3); Gecarcinid land crab remains found at the beach area (Trench 6 South US 4).

Photos: N. Serrand, Inrap.

in the site's environment (i.e., one very fresh *Pomacea glauca*). Furthermore, most land crabs and corals may have been naturally present in the excavated layers without totally excluding some anthropogenic introductions. Numerous present-day Gecarcinid crab holes were observed during the excavations in the lower area, which is now a humid sandy beach. This bioturbation is partly responsible as well for the fact that the stratigraphic provenience of the artifacts in the lower area cannot be totally trusted. In addition, the state of preservation of the crab remains did not help us in discriminating more or less ancient remains.

As for corals, the species variety differs from what is usually observed at pre-Columbian sites, with a high proportion of Poritidae (72% corals NISP), while the Acroporidae, the most utilized species, are not well represented. Besides, no coral element was used or modified; they appear mostly as raw fragments, which suggests that they were incorporated in dead state after tides and storms at the foot of the plateau.

Thus, the beach assemblage, at least queen conchs (*Lobatus gigas*), topshells (*Cittarium pica*), maybe nerites (*Neritina punctulata*), and a few bivalves (*Codakia orbicularis*, *Lucina pectinata*, *Arcopagia fausta*) may be related to the pre-Columbian use of invertebrates at Parking de Roseau, unless these taxa are related to the early colonial occupation of the Capesterre region (see Chapter 4).

4.5.3   Conclusion

The three sites discussed did not bring forward much information about the pre-Columbian Amerindian use of invertebrates: there is unfortunately very little material and it is sparse, altered, and decalcified. The states of alteration suggest partial and uneven preservation of remains depending on the portions and contexts of the sites. Only a few elements can be associated without doubt to the pre-Columbian occupation. Only the species with the most resistant shells have been found at the sites, notably and not surprisingly, the queen conch and West Indian topshell. Possible complementary taxa may be land snails (*Pleurodonte* genus), a few bivalves such as *Codakia orbicularis* or *Lucina pectinata*, and possibly land crabs, but their stratigraphic contexts are uncertain.

Finally, these data cannot be considered as representative and unfortunately discussion on the importance of invertebrates as alimentary resource or raw material at these sites is impossible, illustrating the difficulties of studying invertebrates on the volcanic islands of the Lesser Antilles. Luckily, the calcareous islands can make up for this loss.

4.6   Faunal remains: daily activities and regime

Sandrine Grouard and Noémie Tomadini in collaboration with

Marine Durocher, Eric Pellé, and Brigitte David

The main goal of the archaeozoological studies carried out at the CHU Belle-Plaine, La Pointe de Grande Anse, and Parking de Roseau sites was to complete the cultural, chronological, and environmental knowledge of Guadeloupe's pre-Columbian societies (Grouard and Pellé 2009; Grouard 2016; Tomadini and Grouard 2018). Indeed, faunal spectra allow us to analyze diets, as well as technological and /or cultural responses, plus territorial management.

Simultaneously, subsistence strategies are at the heart of a long-standing debate on the Saladoid and Troumassoid sites in the Lesser Antilles (Keegan 2000; Wing 2001; Delpuech and Hofman 2004). In these island environments, which are generally characterized by a low specific diversity of terrestrial fauna and by the absence of large terrestrial vertebrates, Amerindian societies have been able to take advantage of the marine and coastal ecosystems, which represent the most productive environments compared to the terrestrial ones.

The analysis of the faunal remains of past populations allows us to determine the real proportion of each resource. These animal resources can be for alimentation, but also cultural, technical (raw materials, ornaments, etc.), or symbolic (animal burials, taming), and cosmogonic (zoomorphic ceramics, rock art). These studies together make it possible to evaluate the large-scale human-animal relationships, as well as territorial management, navigation, fishing, and hunting practices.

4.6.1 Material and methods

The numerous pits at the CHU Belle-Plaine and Parking de Roseau sites were wet-screened; however, at La Pointe of Grande Anse site, the material was exclusively collected by hand. Unfortunately, the STEP Goyave site did not yield any vertebrates.

At CHU Belle-Plaine, between 10 and 20 liters of sediment per pit (F 15, F 20, F 66, F 73, F 74, F 149, F 157, F 168, F 186, F 188, F 200, F 213, F 215, F 216, F 221, and F 248) were sieved with 2.7 mm mesh in the field. In addition, a few liters from pits F 20, F 73, F 216, and F 221, were sent to AASPE laboratory for 1 mm mesh sieving.

At Parking de Roseau, only trenches 7 and 9 were sieved with 5 mm mesh during the field phase. All sieved residues were checked in the laboratory under binocular and magnifying glass with neon. This step is important because of the difficulty of separating the fragments from each other without prior training for skeletal recognition. Without this training, the most spectacular ones only are recovered: mandibulas, skulls, femurs, humerus of tetrapods, and vertebrae of large fish, which all together represent only 20% of the vertebrate remains from the sieve.

The faunal remains were identified to their lowest taxonomic levels using comparative collections from the Laboratoire d'Anatomie Comparée and the "Caraïbes/Caribbean" collection stored in UMR 7209: Archéologie, Archéobotanique: sociétés, pratiques et environnement, of the Muséum national d'Histoire naturelle (MNHN) in Paris.

The Number of Identified Specimens (NISP) and the Minimal Number of Individuals by combination (cMNI), which takes into account the ages, sizes, and sexes of the animals, were quantified for each taxon (S). Each of these methods has its own advantages and disadvantages, which have been discussed previously (see Chaplin 1971; Ducos 1975; Poplin 1976a-b, 1977; Grayson 1984; Lyman 1994; Grouard 2001), and have been used on an ad hoc basis according to each case.

The subsistence strategies of the pre-Columbian populations were studied by analyzing the faunal spectrum per sample, taxa distribution, and abundance. Abundance is perceived through taxonomic richness, obtained directly by the number of taxa (S), and also estimated by applying the Margaleff index (dI; 1958, cited by Bobrowski and Ball 1989). This index was calculated using the formula $dI = (S - 1) / LogN$ where S is the number of species and N is the total NISP; the higher the index, the richer the sample. Diversity, or heterogeneity of taxa distribution, was estimated by using the Simpson Reciprocal index (H'), and calculated by applying the formula $H' = 1/\Sigma pi^2$ where $pi = ni/N$, ni = NISP per taxon, and N = total NISP. The higher the index, the more diversified is the sample (Grayson 1984:160). A spectrum that offers both high wealth and high diversity reflects a generalized subsistence economy (Leonard and Jones 1989). To test the human selection in carcasses, as well as differential turning down and provisioning to sites, we used the Percentage of Representation of Skeletal Parts, developed by Dodson and Wexlar (1979) and Korth (1979). For each sample collected, the bones are classified by anatomical part and the percentage of representation (PR) is defined per ratio: PR = (FO × 100) / (FT × MNI), where FO represents the frequency observed for each skeletal lateral element for each taxon identified, and FT represents the expected frequency of representation for each lateral skeletal element for each individual taxon (referential). The profile of each assemblage is reproduced graphically when the number of remains allows it.

Of course, a number of biases, which are not due to taphonomic processes or human selection, should be taken into account in the results, such as the differential sampling during excavation, the absence of sieving or the size of the sieve mesh, and the difficulty of identifying certain bones (e.g., fish axonostes and baseostes), which are therefore not taken into account in the percentages. Finally, we quantified traces of cutting, thermal alterations, and traces left by nonanthropogenic agents before and after burial.

4.6.2   *Richness, diversity, and faunal assemblage*

A total of 7,460 remains have been studied at these three sites (see Table 4.13). The sites of CHU Belle-Plaine and La Pointe de Grande Anse yielded the majority of the material (4,005 and 3,429 remains, respectively). The low number of identified specimens at the Parking de Roseau site (NISP = 26; see supra study by Nathalie Serrand) is explained by the taphonomic dissolution of the vertebrate remains induced by climatic and edaphic processes and by the acid sediment. It should be noted, however, that other faunal remains (including rice rats) were discovered in 2001 and 2002 during the excavation of a small area 300 m north of the excavation (Richard 2004, 2005), but these elements could belong to different chronological periods, as the stratigraphy was not clear.

Among the 2,372 specimens identified to their lowest taxonomic levels, 44 families and 61 species, representing 220 individuals, have been determined (Table 4.17). Of all the assemblages, mammals dominate in NISP (42.9%), followed by fish (34.1%). On the other hand, the trend is reversed when considering the MNI (30.1 *vs* 42.9%) as well as the number of species for these two zoological classes (33 *vs* 8). In this case, squamates, marine turtles, and birds are represented by eight taxa each, gastropods and bivalves by three taxa each, and finally, lissamphibians and corals by one species each. The dominant zoological classes differ among the sites. At CHU Belle-Plaine, rodents (Mammalia, Rodentia) are represented by two species: the rice rat (Oryzomyini)[15] and the agouti (*Dasyprocta* cf. *leporina*), which dominate both in NISP (910) and MNI (27 and 24, respectively). At La Pointe de Grande Anse, fish are the best represented remains (NISP = 514; NMI = 63). At Parking de Roseau, marine turtles dominate in the number of remains (NISP = 14), but mammals are more diversified (S = 5) and more abundant in terms of individuals (MNI = 6).

Richness indices (dI) calculated for the CHU Belle-Plaine and La Pointe de Grande Anse sites show the very rich subsistence economy at these two sites (11.6 and 12.05, respectively). However, the diversity index (H) indicates that the population living at CHU Belle-Plaine was "specialized" (H = 5.21), notably on rice rats and agouti, contrary to that at the La Pointe de Grande Anse site, where the subsistence economy was quite "open" (H = 10.53) and diversified. Richness and diversity indices were not calculated for the Parking de Roseau site, because its pre-Columbian levels were disturbed by later occupations, indicated by the discovery of several skeletal parts of domestic mammals introduced by Europeans (e.g. cow, pig, caprines, and equids). Indeed, the equid metatarsus discovered

Table 4.17 Faunal spectrum of CHU Belle-Plaine, La Pointe de Grande-Anse, and Parking de Roseau according to chronology, NISP, and MNI.

Family	Species	Common name	CHU Belle-Plaine		Pointe de Grande-Anse Trois Rivières		Parking de Roseau		NISP total	MNI total
			NISP	MNI	NISP	MNI	NISP	MNI		
Anthozoa	Anthozoa	Coral	2	2					2	2
Total Anthozoa			**2**	**2**					**2**	**2**
Strombidae	*Lobatus costatus*	milk conch	7	3					7	3
	Lobatus sp.	conch	2						2	0
Bulimulidae	Bulimulidae	land snails	4	2					4	2
Planorbidae	*Biomphalaria straminae*	Ram's horn snail	1	1					1	1
Total Gastropoda			**16**	**6**					**16**	**6**
Arcidae	Arcidae	ark	106	7					106	7
Ostreidae	Ostreidae	oyster	79	12					79	12
Lucinidae	Lucinidae	lucina	8	8					8	8
Total Bivalvia			**193**	**27**					**193**	**27**
Elopidae	*Elops saurus*	ladyfish			8	1			8	1
Albulidae	*Albula vulpes*	bonefish	1	1					1	1
Holocentridae	*Holocentrus* spp.	squirrelfish			10	2			10	2
	Holocentridae	squirrelfish	12	1					12	1
Exocoetidae	*Exocoetus* sp.	flying fish	7	1					7	1
Belonidae	*Tylosurus crocodilus*	houndfish	98	3	8	2			106	5
	Strongylura spp.	needlefish	2	1	30	3			32	4
Carangidae	*Decapterus* cf. *afuerus*	shortfin scad			4	1			4	1
	Caranx crysos	blue runner			1	1			1	1
	Caranx ruber	bar jack			13	3			13	3
	Caranx hippos	crevalle jack			15	3			15	3
	Caranx spp.	jack	22	3					22	3

(*Continued*)

Table 4.17 (Continued)

Family	Species	Common name	CHU Belle-Plaine		Pointe de Grande-Anse Trois Rivières		Parking de Roseau		NISP total	MNI total
			NISP	MNI	NISP	MNI	NISP	MNI		
	Trachinotus cf. *goodei*	palometa			2	1			2	1
	Carangidae	jack			44				44	0
Mullidae	*Pseudupeneus maculatus*	spotted goatfish			6	2			6	2
Scombridae	*Scomberomorus cavalla*	king mackerel			3	2			3	2
	Scomberomorus maculatus	Atlantic Spanish mackerel			17	3			17	3
	Thunnus atlanticus	blackfin tuna			33	6			33	6
	Katsuwonus pelamis	skipjack tuna	8	1	65	3			73	4
	Scombridae	mackerels/tunas/bonitos	3	1	3				6	1
Labridae	*Bodianus rufus*	Spanish hogfish			2	1			2	1
	Halichoeres bivittatus	slippery dick			1	1			1	1
	Labridae	wrasses			1				1	0
Scaridae	*Scarus* spp.	parrotfish			2	1			2	1
	Sparisoma viride	stoplight parrotfish			2	1			2	1
	Sparisoma spp.	parrotfish	11	2	3	1			14	3
	Scaridae	parrotfish	3		15				18	0
Centropomidae	*Centropomus undecimalis*	common snook			27	2			27	2
	Centropomus spp.	snook	38	2					38	2
Serranidae	*Cephalopholis fulva*	coney			1	1			1	1
	Epinephelus spp.	grouper	9	2	1	1			10	3
	Mycteroperca sp.	grouper			1	1			1	1
	Serranidae	grouper			120	5			120	5
Haemulidae	*Conodon nobilis*	barred grunt	13	2	9	3			22	5
	Haemulon spp.	grunt	9	1	25	3			34	4

Lutjanidae	*Lutjanus* spp.	snapper	6	18	24		3
	Lutjanidae	snapper	16	3	16		3
Perciformes	Perciformes		34		34		0
Acanthuridae	*Acanthurus* spp.	doctorfish	18	12	30		6
Sparidae	*Calamus* sp.	porgy	9	3	8		2
Ostraciidae	*Acanthostracion* sp.	cowfish		1	1		1
Balistidae	*Balistes vetula*	queen triggerfish	9		9		1
	Balistes sp.	triggerfish	1	1	2		1
	Melichthys niger	black triggerfish	1	1	1		1
Diodontidae	*Chilomycterus* sp.	burrfish		7	7		1
	Actinopterygii	fish unidentified	718	141	813		0
Total Actinopterygii			**1048**	**655**	**1653**		**94**
	cf. *Leptodactylus fallax*	cf. "mountain chicken"	2	1	2		1
cf. Leptodactylidae							
Total Lissamphibia			**2**	**1**	**2**		**1**
Iguanidae	*Iguana* sp.	iguana	7	9	16		2
cf. Dactyloidae	cf. Dactyloidae	anole	2	1	2		1
cf. Teiidae	cf. *Pholidoscelis* sp.	ameiva	3	1	3		1
	cf. Teiidae	ameiva	2		2		0
Dipsadidae	cf. *Erythrolamprus juliae*	leeward groundsnake		4	4		1
Serpentes	Serpentes	snake	3		3		1
Lacertilia	Lacertilia	lizard	3		3		0
Squamata	Squamata	lizard	13		13		0
Total Squamata			**33**	**13**	**46**		**6**
Cheloniidae	*Caretta caretta*	loggerhead turtle		86	86		1
	cf. *Eretmochelys imbricata*	Atlantic hawksbill turtle		2	2	1	1
	Chelonia mydas	common green turtle	45		42	12	1
	Cheloniidae	sea turtle			12	2	0
Total Testudines			**45**	**86**	**142**	**14**	**3**

(Continued)

Table 4.17 (Continued)

Family	Species	Common name	CHU Belle-Plaine		Pointe de Grande-Anse Trois Rivières		Parking de Roseau		NISP total	MNI total
			NISP	MNI	NISP	MNI	NISP	MNI		
cf. Phoenicopteridae	cf. *Phoenicopterus ruber*	greater flamingo					1	1	1	1
Columbidae	cf. *Zenaida* sp.	dove	16	2					16	2
Procellariidae	*Puffinus lherminieri*	Audubon shearwater			90	6			90	6
Passeriformes	Passeriformes	"passerine"	48	3					48	3
Aves	Aves	birds	49	2					49	2
		Aves grand	large bird	3	1			3		6	1
Total Aves			**116**	**8**	**90**	**6**	**4**	**1**	**210**	**15**
Trichechidae	*Trichechus manatus*	West Indian manatee					1	1	1	1
Dasyproctidae	*Dasyprocta* cf. *leporina*	red-rumped agouti	397	24	50	4			433	28
Oryzomyini	Oryzomyini	rice rat	512	27	50	5			554	32
Rodentia	Rodentia	rodent	188						188	0
Phyllostomidae	*Monophyllus* cf. *plethodon*	insular single leaf bat			1	1			1	1
Equidae	*Equus* sp. *	horse/donkey/hybrids					1	1	1	1
Suidae	*Sus scrofa domesticus* *	pig					1	1	1	1
Bovidae	*Bos taurus* *	cow					1	1	1	1
	Caprinae *	sheep/goat					2	1	2	1
Mammalia	Mammalia moyen	medium mammals					1		1	0
Total Mammalia			**1098**	**51**	**101**	**10**	**7**	**5**	**1183**	**66**
Tetrapoda	Tetrapoda				84				84	0
Vertebrata	Vertebrata		1452		2400		2		3853	0
Total Vertebrata			**1452**		**2484**		**2**		**3937**	**0**
Grand Total			**4004**	**131**	**3429**	**82**	**26**	**7**	**7459**	**220**
Number of taxa (S)			37		36		7		62	

during the 2014 survey dated to the 17th century (UBA-125187: 254 ± BP or cal 1631–1670 CE; see Table 4.16). Furthermore, the saw-cut traces of a caprine's radius (TR 6 South US 3) as well as the cervical vertebra of a cow (TR 5 South US 3; Figure 4.31) clearly show that these remains are later than the 17th century, because traces of this particular butcher's tool appear only in the Antillean zooarchaeological assemblages of the 18th century (Tomadini 2018). The presence of numerous terrestrial crab (e.g., *Cardisoma guanhumi*) galleries within the stratigraphy seems to be at the origin of its disturbance. Only one unidentified bone from pit F 178 of this site has been dated to the Troumassoid period *stricto sensu* (KIA-84387: 870± 30 BP or cal 1045–1250 CE; see Table 4.16). Skeletal parts of indigenous taxa recognized in the disturbed levels, such as the Atlantic hawksbill turtle (*Eretmochelys imbricata*), the greater flamingo (*Phoenicopterus ruber*), and the West Indian manatee (*Trichechus manatus*), may have been discarded during the Troumassoid occupation or later, but it is rather difficult to establish their exploitation during the pre-Columbian occupation of the site. Thus, for a more coherent data set, the Parking de Roseau site was not considered in the following discussion.

4.6.3 Modality of animal exploitation

Fish

Most of the skeletal parts of fish were absent at the CHU Belle-Plaine and Pointe de Grande Anse sites (Figure 4.32). For example, otoliths were totally absent from the remains. Is this a taphonomic phenomenon or is it due to the sorting of sieve residues? It must be remembered that otoliths, because of their aragonite composition, are often confused with molluscs. However, apart from this particular anatomical part, most of the cranial bone is absent in the samples, except for a few skeletal elements of the mouth (quadrate, articulary, dentary, maxillary, premaxillary, and pharyngeal elements; 1–22% PR; see Figure 4.32). Finally, within the axial elements, the vertebrae are particularly well represented with regard to all families. This shows a rejection of the fleshiest skeletal elements; thus, the heads could have been cut when fishing or prepared elsewhere at the site, and only the bodies may have been thrown into the pits.

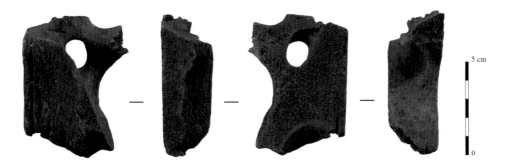

Figure 4.31 Sixth cervical vertebrae from cow (*Bos taurus*) with saw cut (Parking de Roseau—TR 5 south US 3).

Photo: N. Tomadini, MNHN.

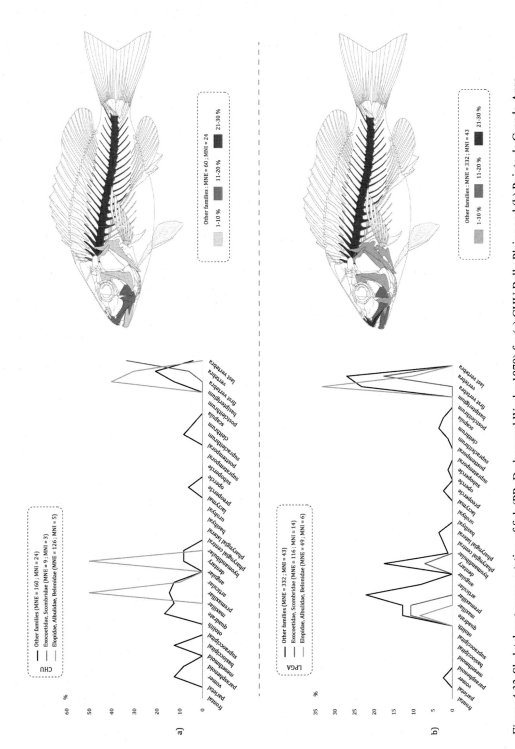

Figure 4.32 Skeletal part representation of fish (PR; Dodson and Wexlar 1979) for (a) CHU Belle-Plaine and (b) Pointe de Grande-Anse. Adapted by S. Grouard after Dodson and Wexlar 1979.

Turtles

Each site yielded bones belonging to a species of sea turtle: a loggerhead turtle (*Caretta caretta*) at Pointe de Grande Anse and a green turtle (*Chelonia mydas*) at CHU Belle-Plaine. These two species live near the coast where they feed on the surrounding benthic beds and regularly return to lay their eggs on sandy beaches. Thus, they can be caught easily by turning them over when they are spawning. Although they are represented by only a few bones, it seems that these animals were taken whole to the habitation area, considering that the whole skeleton is represented. In addition, two artifacts produced from dorsal turtle shell were discovered at the CHU Belle-Plaine site. First, a small fragment being a tool or an ornament with very sharp edges, polished on both sides, was found in pit F 73 (Figure 4.33a). This type of artifact, always fragmented, is common at pre-Columbian sites, but its purpose or use is still unknown. It could have been an ornamental breastplate, for example.

A second tool/ornament was found in the lower fill of this same pit, F 73 (Figure 4.33b-a). It appeared to be burned, black in color and, in addition to polishing, it has a very sharp edge. It could be a fragment of an adze similar to those made from conch lips, which are commonly found at Amerindian sites (Serrand 2002). Comparable examples have been made of manatee (*Trichechus manatus*) ribs, such as the specimen discovered at Macabou in southeast Martinique (Grouard 2008, 2016) (Figure 4.33c).

Rodents

Due to the persistence of deciduous premolar 4 throughout the life of some agoutis (*Dasyprocta* cf. *leporina*), it is impossible to evaluate for the moment the age of these animals from their stage of tooth wear (pers. commun. Pierre-Olivier Antoine). New methodological

Figure 4.33 a: Polished artifact made of dorsal turtle shell (Cheloniidae) (CHU–pit F 73), b: Polished and burned artifact made of a dorsal turtle shell (Cheloniidae) (CHU—pit F 73-inf.), c: Adze made from a manatee (*Trichechus manatee*) rib (Macabou site, Martinique; Sondage 15, Layer 1, Level 1–2, M² D1d).

Photo: S. Grouard, MNHN.

approaches are currently being tested to overcome this inconvenience (Grouard and Durocher 2019; Durocher 2021). For Oryzomyini, this type of analysis could be carried out only on seven individuals from the Belle-Plaine site. With regard to dental abrasion rates, it seems that the population of this site captured juvenile animals (stage 1 = 2 individuals), but also older ones (stage 4 = 1 individual) and even very old animals (stage 5 = 4 individuals). This distribution could either indicate anthropogenic pressure on these rodents or correspond to a generalist capture method. The sample, too succinct, does not allow one to decide on either of these hypotheses. However, the teeth (especially incisors) as well as the forelimb and hind limb of both rodent species are the best-represented skeletal parts at all sites. With the exception of the calcaneus and talus, the feet and spinal elements (vertebrae and ribs) are, to the contrary, very poorly represented (Figure 4.34). This pattern reveals either a search or preference for the fleshy limbs, but it also shows a differential conservation effect.

Methods of preparation of these rodents have been observed at the site of Belle-Plaine, where 60 remains bear traces of fire. Some bones appear to have been affected for more than 50%, such as distal tibias, calcaneum, pelvis, incisors, and molars. It is likely that the latter were roasted over a fire, letting the flames lick the fleshy bones, probably on a grill, or *boucan*, as represented in a drawing by Theodore de Bry from the late 16th century (Le Moyne de Morgues and de Bry 1591, Plate XIV). Finally, it should be noted that a bead made of the diaphysis of an agouti tibia was found in pit F 168 at the same site. About 4 cm long and 1 cm in diameter, it has very fine small chips on its edges. The cortical surface of the bone is polished at various spots and shows slight traces of polishing at other places.

4.6.4   Selected ecosystems

According to their geological, geographic, edaphic, and climatic characteristics, Guadeloupe's twin islands harbor an unevenly distributed great diversity of ecosystems and environments. The distance from the sites to each ecosystem, the abundance of taxa in each biotope, as well as the size of the individual faunal species are phenomena related to the profusion or rarity of the latter, their facility of harvesting, and accessibility. Moreover, they are all evidence of land management and cultural choice. Using an analogous approach with the data on the food and life habits of terrestrial and marine animals in the current scope of Caribbean research, we have attempted to reconstruct a number of selected ecosystems. It can be stated generally that the Amerindians predominantly exploited the ecosystems close to their villages (Figure 4.35).

As a matter of fact, at the CHU Belle-Plaine site, particularly the forests (69% NISP, 49% MNI, and 47% S) and mangroves (9% NISP, 23% MNI, and 21% S) located in the direct vicinity of the site were visited by the Amerindians (Figure 4.35).

The ecosystems characterizing the Grand Cul-de-Sac Marin, such as foreshore areas, sandy bottoms and seagrass beds, and coral/rock bottoms (15% NISP, 27% MNI, and 39% S) were exploited intensively as well. On the other hand, the surface waters along the coasts and the deep-water channels were exploited only sporadically (7% NISP, 6% MNI, and 12% S). Conversely, the main ecosystems exploited on the La Pointe de Grande Anse site are represented by deep waters, such as the Canal de Saintes (23% NISP, 22% MNI, and 17% S), as well as the coral reefs and rocky bottoms (30% NISP, 38% MNI, and 44% S; Figure 4.35). Many so-called coral species easily adapt to rocky spots when coral reefs are absent. The inhabitants of Trois-Rivières may also have gone to Les Saintes or even to the very

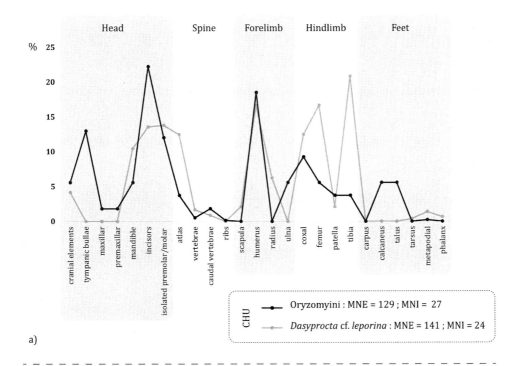

a)

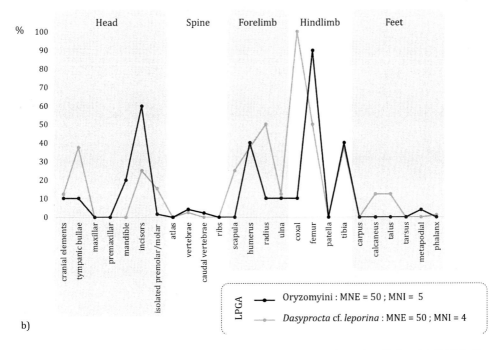

b)

Figure 4.34 Skeletal part representation of rodents (PR; Dodson and Wexlar 1979) at (a) CHU Belle-Plaine, and (b) Pointe de Grande-Anse.

Adapted by S. Grouard after Dodson and Wexlar 1979.

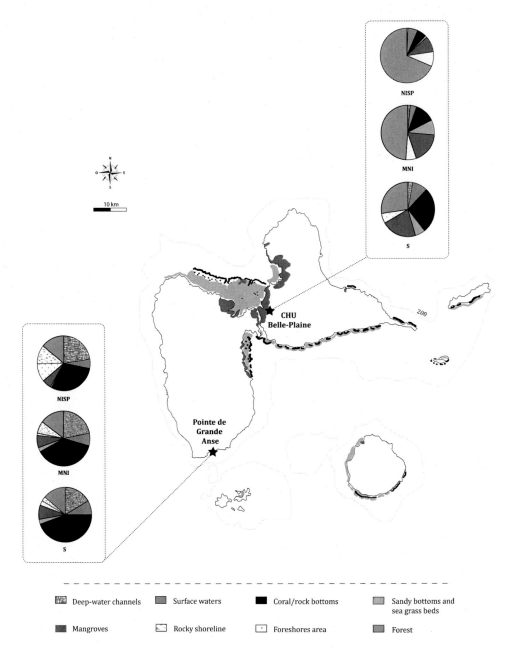

Figure 4.35 Map of the main marine ecosystems of Guadeloupe: mangroves (dark green), seagrass beds (grey), and coral reefs (black); and the main ecosystems (pie charts) exploited by the pre-Columbian Amerindians at the CHU Belle-Plaine and La Pointe de Grande-Anse sites After Bouchon et al. 2002, 2008; Tomadini 2018.

small islands of Petite-Terre, situated within sight and accessible by canoe. Finally, brackish waters (mangroves and sandy bottoms) are also well represented (6% NISP, 9% MNI, and 11% S) as well as foreshore areas (11% NISP, 1% MNI, and 3% S), rocky coastlines (11% NISP, 7% MNI, and 3% S), and forests (14% NISP, 15% MNI, and 14% S) as shown by the large number of marine turtles, puffins, and rodents.

4.6.5 Conclusion

The diet at the CHU Belle-Plaine and La Pointe de Grande Anse sites was similar to that of the other Troumassoid sites in the French West Indies, based on rich subsistence economies with a specialization on one or two taxa, such as pelagic fish at the La Pointe de Grande Anse site and rodents (rice rats and agoutis) at the CHU Belle-Plaine site. Consequently, the eco-systems exploited are located close to the sites, including the coral/rock bottoms and deep-water channels at La Pointe de Grande Anse and the forest areas at the CHU Belle-Plaine site. However, the Troumassoid sites in the West Indies generally yielded 80–90% of fish, with terrestrial tetrapods being a more minor component of food consumption (10–18%) (Grouard and Perdikaris 2019). On the other hand, the terrestrial tetrapods are abundant in the Early Saladoid levels (33%). Yet, mammals (rodents) dominated subsistence (60%) at the CHU Belle-Plaine site, as at a Saladoid site, which is surprising for this period.

Notes

1 The word "ceramic(s)" derives from the Greek word *keramos*, which means "burned stuff," "earthenware," and "fired product." The terms "ceramics" and "pottery" are used synonymously in archaeology, but according to Longman's *Dictionary of Contemporary English* (1989), there is a difference between ceramics ("the making of pots, tiles etc. by shaping pieces of clay and baking them until they are hard, or articles produced in this way") and pottery ("the work of a potter or other objects made of baked clay"), although the two terms are fairly similar. In the Lesser Antilles we are dealing with low-fired, relatively coarse cooking and serving utensils and other objects made of earthenware clays, making the choice for the term "pottery" understandable. However, the terms "earthenware" or "ware" are also used by various authors. Although some researchers use "ceramics," the fact remains that "pottery" fits the Antillean material best. Here, we use "pottery," even when referring to the chemical analysis of the pottery. However, in some cases the use of "ceramics" is unavoidable, for example when discussing chronology, in using designations as Early and Late Ceramic Age, or typological terms such as "ceramic series."

2 It is noteworthy that when conducting his Haitian research Rouse actually applied both the modal and typological methods (Rouse 1939:42–56), as did Roosevelt (1980:193) for Parmana. Rouse also received severe critique, notably by Thomas Patterson (1991:4), who stated that Rouse focused too much on "the products of observable behavior . . . rather than the social relations, actions and circumstances that structure and constrain this behavior."

3 There are many methods of classification, which can be considered as a basic procedure by which a discipline and its data are structured. It is not the goal of any science: the objective of most classificatory systems is to create types (Rice 1987:275).

4 An attribute can be described as a "minimal characteristic of an artifact such that it cannot be further subdivided." It can be seen as a property, characteristic, feature, or variable of an entity. It often involves aspects of form, style, decoration, color, and raw material (Renfrew and Bahn 1996:539; Rice 1987:275). However, according to Rice (1987:276), a type is "a cluster of items, a group or class of items that is internally cohesive and can be separated from other groups by one or more discontinuities in attribute states."

5 The classic Rousean terminology, however, defines "style" as synonymous with "complex" or "phase" as the entire repertoire which is based on various assemblages of a people made during a single cultural period in a particular geographic location (Rouse 1972, 1985:385, 1992:175; see also Cruxent and Rouse 1958:23). A "series" is a group of styles related throughout space and time

that are known to have descended from a common ancestor (Rouse 1986, 1992:183–184). Other definitions of ceramic style are proposed by Roosevelt (1997:87–88), or Zucchi et al. (1984:159): *"Combinaciones unica de pasta, forma y decoración [halladas en quatro alfalfarias (A–D)], nos llevaron a proponer que estas probablemente corresponden a diferentes entidades sociales a las cuales hemos denominado componente cerámicos."*

6   Ceramic study and the chronocultural chart of the Antilles is primarily based on the excavation of midden deposits. Having studied important middens at St. Martin (van den Bel in Sellier-Ségard et al. 2020), the present author prefers to study ceramics from (pit) features that have a more reliable stratigraphy, a rather short and closed context that assures the contemporaneity of the pit content as well as the liability of the radiocarbon dates. Middens have a larger variety but show a less important number (ECs) of vessel shapes. In short, variation is more important in midden deposits, whereas the quality of the sample prevails in features.

7   All ECs have been drawn, with the exception of Parking de Roseau EC 123, EC 177–178, as well as five bases >5 cm^2.

8   The present author believes that only chemical analysis can determine the origins of the various red hues. See, for example, the chemical analysis conducted by J. Moretti (2003) of more than 20 red dyes mastered by the Kali'na of coastal French Guiana.

9   Honychurch mentions the occurrence of flint on Dominica. After personal communication and observation of some Dominican nodules sent by Honychurch, it has to be concluded that this material is white to colorless translucent chalcedony (see also Knippenberg 2006).

10 Some of these completely corroded pieces may have lost this weathered outer crust, exposing an irregular surface of the original, fine-grained grey-green rock. No technological features can be discerned on this surface.

11 Examples of active food-grinding tools are known from the Dutch Early Neolithic (LBK) that were used for grinding peas. These tools are very smooth, but do not exhibit much abrasion (Knippenberg and Verbaas 2012).

12 These percentages are based on the mesh-screened samples from both sites.

13 It is noteworthy that a 16th-century French penny was found during the excavations of Moulin-à-Eau at Capesterre-Belle-Eau, which can be interpreted as an heirloom or fetish object of an early French settler planting tobacco at this site (Mestre et al. 2001).

14 All remains have been considered, whatever their ways of being brought to the site. The remains of invertebrates collected dead, intrusive species, or remains that were used as raw material are dealt with specifically afterwards.

15 Work currently underway suggests the presence of two morphotypes in Continental Guadeloupe, differentiating between the Oryzomyini of Basse-Terre and those of Grande-Terre. These two morphotypes would probably belong to the large Oryzomyini. Thus *Oryzomis megalomys* from Grande-Terre of Guadeloupe and Marie-Galante (Barbotin 1970; Pregill et al. 1994) [syn. *Megalomys* sp. (Trouessart 1885; Pinchon 1967), syn. *Megalomys audreyae* (Forsyth Major 1901; Hopwood 1926)] could be a synonym of the *Antillomys rayias* described later by Brace et al. 2015 for Antigua and Grande-Terre (Grouard and Durocher 2019; Durocher et al. 2020; Durocher 2021).

5 Microanalysis

By the end of the second millennium, specialization in additional, most often microscopic, analysis got *en vogue* among Caribbean archaeologists, as witnessed by the "Crossing Borders" publication by Hofman et al. (2008). Highly specialized laboratory-analyzed or computer-analyzed metadata, also called "archaeological sciences," represented by sciences such as starch, phytolith, chemical analysis, and LiDAR, landscape and interconnection analysis, respectively, made up for the lack of large-scale excavations, which are now principally realized by project-led archaeology. In addition to the introduction of this commercial archaeology, scientific research is apparently now more than ever propelled by immediate scientific success instead of long-term dirt archaeology campaigns at sites such as Macabou and Vivé, on Martinique, Hope Estate, on St. Martin, Anse à la Gourde, on Guadeloupe, Golden Rock, on Statia, and Tanki Flip, on Aruba. This trend towards specialization, already visible in the seminal monograph on the Tutu archaeological village site (Righter 2002a) becomes clearer through the Ph.D. research of Sebastiaan Knippenberg (2006) and Jaime Pagán-Jiménez (2007), who paved the road for further regional and environmental analyses.

The following chapters also provide results based on microscopic research addressing clear questions such as: How was a pit filled up over time? What is the function of a circular pit? What was ground on this particular stone? Can we identify grog in this sherd? Although the answers may sometimes be negative, the results always raise more questions, but point in new directions.

5.1 Micromorphology of a circular pit at CHU Belle-Plaine

Jeanne Brancier and Cécilia Cammas

The feature map of CHU Belle-Plaine reveals 34 circular pits, which have few or no equivalents in the literature of the LCA Lesser Antilles (see previous chapter). The function or role of these pits within a village remains difficult to understand and it is often quite complicated to observe with the naked eye different layers of their content. For this matter, micromorphology may help to identify and describe these features and their soil components and provide evidence for analysis and subsequent interpretation of these enigmatic circular pits. One pit was chosen for analysis.

The micromorphological sample was collected from pit F 157, situated in the northern part of the excavated area (Figure 5.1). As discussed previously, this particular area has two pit assemblages flanking one house location with two burials. The sediment core was taken with a plastic half-pipe (42×5 cm) which was inserted into the pit profile from top to bottom (see Figure 5.1). The pits were dug by the Amerindians into the volcanic bedrock.

DOI: 10.4324/9781003181651-5

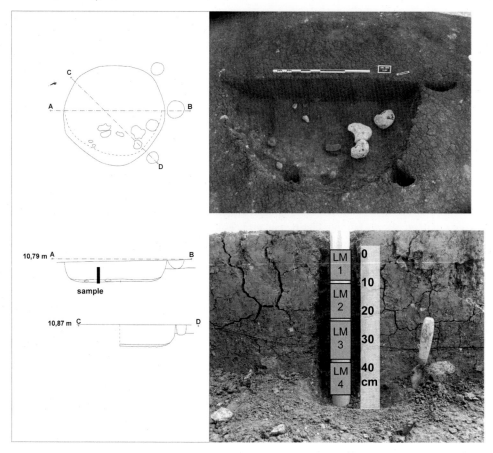

Figure 5.1 Circular pit F 157 and sample location.

Photos: C. Cammas, Inrap, and J. Brancier.

Interestingly, during the excavations we observed that the excavated pits filled up completely with sediment after one weekend with heavy rainfall.

From the sediment core, four thin sections were prepared in the laboratory of the Micromorphology Unit of Inrap, hosted by UMR EGC (Environment & Grande Culture) of AgroParisTech, in Grignon, France. The thin sections were prepared according to the standard protocol established by Guilloré (1985): (i) soil samples were dry-heated at 50°C maximum; (ii) impregnated with polyester resin under vacuum to harden them; (iii) the solid blocks formed were cut in the shape of a waffle, which was fixed temporarily to a slide; (iv) subsequently, the exposed face of the waffle was flattened, polished down, and stuck permanently to a glass slide; and (v) the second face was thinned to a thickness of 2–30 μm and then covered with a glass film. The finished thin sections measured 12×6 cm. They were observed under a polarizing petrographic microscope (Nikon E200 Pol-×20 to ×400), in plane-polarized light (PPL), in cross-polarized light (XPL), and in oblique incident light (OIL). Our micromorphological descriptions are based on the terminology of Bullock et al. (1985) and E. Fitzpatrick (1993), and their interpretation is made by following Courty et al. (1989);

Goldberg and Macphail (2006); Cammas and Wattez (2009); Stoops et al. (2010); and Brancier et al. (2014).

The results are presented in the form of a synthetic table in which we describe and interpret the microstratigraphy from top to bottom of the profile (Table 5.1 and Figure 5.2). When doing micromorphological analysis, it is possible to observe and describe microstratigraphic units (UMiS) of the soils. These units are defined according to their texture, structure and constituents.

5.1.1 Results

General characteristics of sediments

The sediment appears heterometric and is poorly sorted. It consists mainly of iron concretions forming concentric nodules and, to a lesser extent, of basaltic minerals and lithorelics resulting from the alteration of the local volcanic bedrock. The fine fraction is abundant, globally massive to massive-fissural, brown to grey-brown, more or less dark and subisotropic.

The clay coatings, birefringent in XPL, are present in greater or lesser quantities depending on the horizons. They are shaped in fairly angular clay papules of yellow to orange limpid color when in the mass and in the form of microlaminated coatings when in porosity. These pedological features express episodes or phases of leaching. The presence of iron in the fine fraction in the form of isolated elements or shaped as concretions indicate a poorly drained environment. Coatings and impregnations around voids characterize alternating waterlogging phases with better drainage, which may be typical of a groundwater level (Cammas et al. 2012) (Figure 5.3).

General characteristics of anthropogenic features

Microfragments of mixed clay (Figure 5.4). In XPL, some clay aggregates, oriented, appear orange to red, indicating combustion of the clayey matrix in an oxidizing condition. The different oblong constituents are parallel to the cracks or fissures of the matrix, which reveal modification of the basic clay material (kneading, strong compaction). Because of their intrinsic properties, these aggregates are related to microceramic fragments.

Microfragments of burned plants (Figure 5.4). In the matrix, we observed numerous microfragments of burned plants, appearing as black shiny dots in OIL. This indicates that these dots are microcharcoals.

Burned aggregates (Figure 5.4). These aggregates are relatively easy to observe in the matrix because their color and shape indicate that they are exogenous elements of the matrix. They have generally a subrounded shape, with a dark red to brown color in PPL that can be confused with ferruginous concretions. But in OIL, their color oscillates, from brick-ocher red on the outside to black in the middle, riddled with brilliant, shiny black microdots, like the charcoals. They do not have any particular internal organization and some of them contain carbonized plant microfragments evoking rootlets. These aggregates are highly similar to those observed and defined at some pre-Columbian archaeological sites with clayey subsoils in French Guiana (Brancier et al. 2014; Brancier 2016). In French Guiana they are interpreted as fragments of burned soil surfaces. In this particular pit in Guadeloupe, these burnt soils may originate from the few small fireplaces discovered at the site. For example, the fireplace may have been scraped by the Amerindians in order to clean the area, and the scrapings then thrown into the studied pit, which subsequently explains the subrounded form of the aggregates, typical of rolled elements. In short, these burned aggregates clearly show the presence of human activity around the pits.

Table 5.1 Synthetic description of the microstratigraphy of the thin section.

Thin section	UMiS	Depth (cm)	Structura and textural characters	Microartifacts	Pedological features	Interpretations
LM 1	1	0–6 cm	Clayey matrix grey-brown (orange-yellow in OIL), rather dusty, compact and composed with subangular blocks separated by more or less fine channels, and by a high porosity (about 30%).	Few damaged roots	Aggregates with quite limpid orange to microlaminated clay coating, oriented in all directions. Ferruginous concretions in nodules distributed by "pockets." Scarce bioturbation with some channels resulting of roots digested by enchytraeids (earthworms).	Humectation/desiccation and redistribution of clay particles related to seasonal changes, dry/wet, and heavy rains that can fill in the pit.
LM 2						Upper level of infilling whose significant porosity is related to roots degradation and to the passage of soil fauna (enchytraeids/earthworms).
LM 3	2	6–9 cm	Massive-fissural clayey matrix, orange-brown (ferruginization) to grey-brown, enriched in black microparticles.	Few subvertical and subhorizontal roots forming a scarce developed porosity around 5%.	In some places, massive soil aggregates are very rich in different kind of clay coatings: limpid microlaminated yellow to orange, taken in the porosity without particular orientation. Ferruginous concretions nodules are present in all the matrix (approximately 5–10%); some lithorelics of the substratum remain (2%). Scarce bioturbation with some channels completely filled with enchytraeids (earthworm) excrement.	Clay particles reorganization/reworking by humectation/ desiccation, and pedological evolution of soils (Stoops et al. 2010): ⇒colluvium associated with waterlogging and episodes of water saturation.
LM 4						

Thin section	UMiS	Depth (cm)	Structura and textural characters	Microartifacts	Pedological features	Interpretations
	3	9–30 cm	Same matrix as above but more fissural, with cracks oriented rather anarchically forming a microporosity around 10–15%.	Microfragments of charcoals (subangular to subrounded) and abundant burnt plants (between 0.5 mm and 0.7 cm size). Some charcoals are surrounded by a rusty eddy due to ferruginization. Burned aggregates, dark red to black in PPL and orange to red or black in OIL (between 1mm and 1 cm in diameter), pottery sherds (3 mm diameter) and limpid yellow (in PPL) microbones.	Orange to dark-red clay papules, taken in the matrix; microlaminated (within the matrix) and/or limpid clay coating linked to the microporosity Ferruginous concretions nodules (about 5–10%); some substratum minerals remain (2%). Scarce bioturbation, using subvertical channels, leaving enchytraeids (earthworm) excrement.	Anthropogenic discharges with regular recovery as bioturbation is not very developed. Water circulation: ⇒ Fireplace discharges? Black mass composed with an abundance of charred plant material, and black nodules = burnt soils ⇒ Chemical reactions between heated/burnt residues and the water that fill the pit, forming red-ferruginisation rises/edge. Pre-Columbian use phase of the pit as a discard area remained open, with a fast recovery because it is massive with few traces of bioturbation.
	4	30–33 cm	Clayey-silty matrix, birefringent in XPL, with fissural porosity mainly subhorizontal: 10–20% of porosity.	One microcharcoal fragment, oriented subhorizontally in the mass. Numerous fragments of unburned plants like roots, subhorizontally oriented.	Abundant clayey papules, yellow to bright orange, taken in the mass. Ferruginous clay coatings in porosity, oriented downward in crescent, limpid yellow to dusty microlaminated orange. Some fissured ferruginous concentric nodules and lithorelics (10–20%) from the substratum.	Roots must have broken on this layer, not being able to pass through the lower level, which is too indurated/dense. Clues of water bolts by ferruginous oxidation features.

(*Continued*)

Table 5.1 (Continued)

Thin section	UMiS	Depth (cm)	Structura and textural characters	Microartifacts	Pedological features	Interpretations
	5	33—38	About 50% of lithorelics (around 20% of 3 mm size) embedded in a compact with subhorizontal fissural microporosity, silty-clayey matrix, pale yellow (very discolored), slightly micropunctuated by black residual particles.		Orange-yellow ferruginous impregnations around the coarse grains fraction, with no birefringence in XPL. Some ferruginous impregnations forming nodules in the mass.	Fast infilling because the biological activity is invisible. Water circulation ⇒ oxidation features in the porosity: water bolts. Substratum on which there was a quick recovery.
	6	38—41	More than 50% of lithorelics smaller than above (2% around 4 mm size and the rest around 1 mm size), embedded in a compact matrix between the coarse grains fraction, lightyellow punctuated by black micromineral fragments.		Same as above, UMiS 5	Water circulation ⇒ oxidation features in the porosity: water bolts.

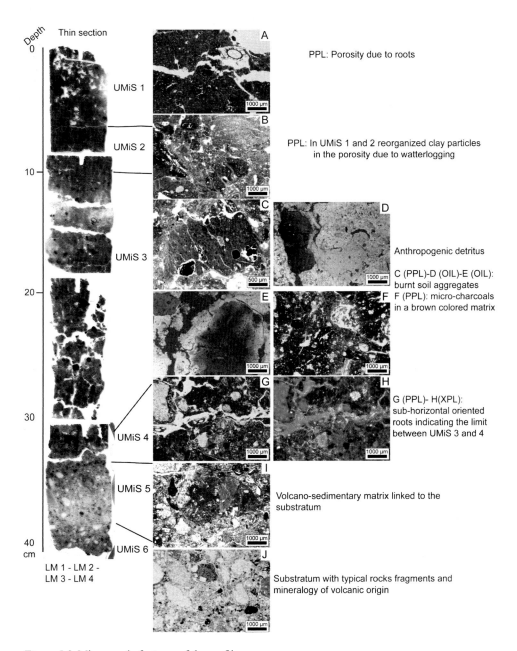

Figure 5.2 Microscopic features of the profile.

Photos: C. Cammas, Inrap, and J. Brancier.

5.1.2   *Chronological description*

After the identification of pedological and anthropogenic features, which allowed us to better understand the studied context, it was possible, thanks to the microscopic analysis, to highlight the different phases of digging and filling of the pit. These are now presented in chronological order, from bottom to the top of the sequence.

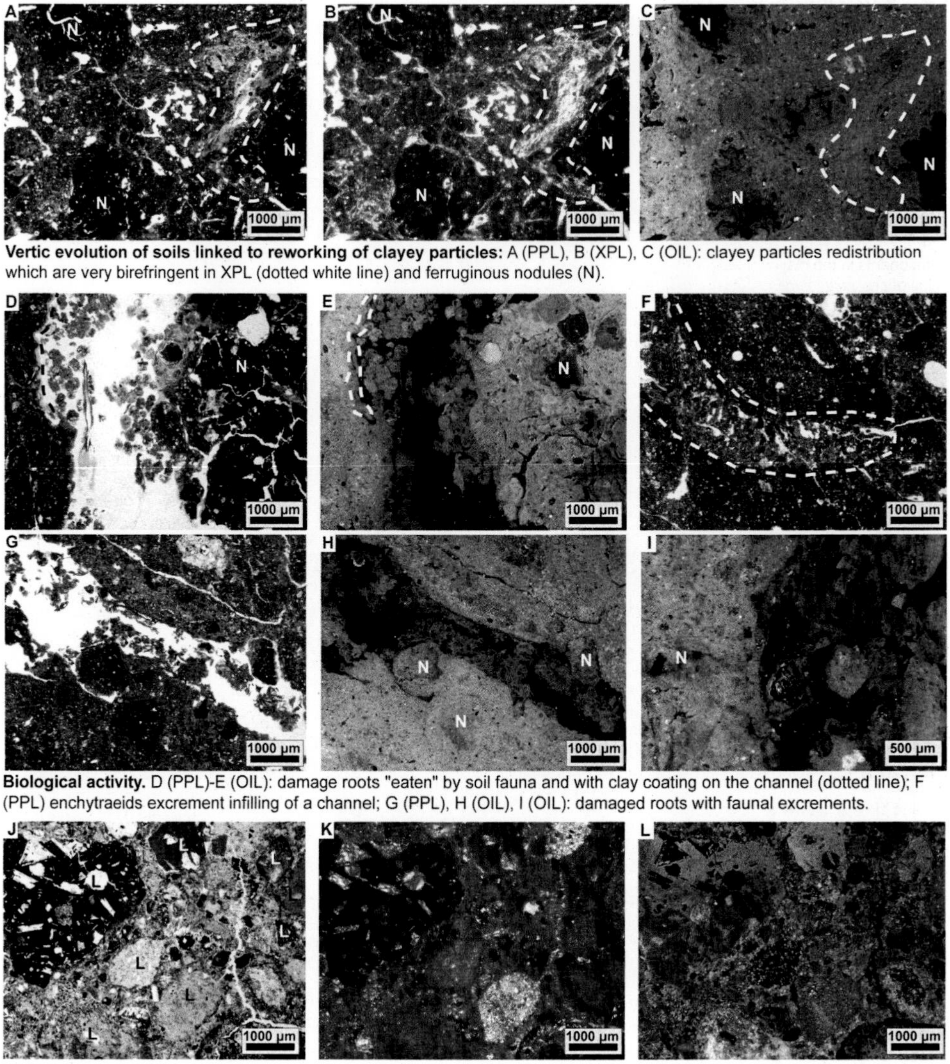

Vertic evolution of soils linked to reworking of clayey particles: A (PPL), B (XPL), C (OIL): clayey particles redistribution which are very birefringent in XPL (dotted white line) and ferruginous nodules (N).

Biological activity. D (PPL)-E (OIL): damage roots "eaten" by soil fauna and with clay coating on the channel (dotted line); F (PPL) enchytraeids excrement infilling of a channel; G (PPL), H (OIL), I (OIL): damaged roots with faunal excrements.

Substratum with typical mineralogy of volcano-sedimentary origin (UMiS 5). J (PPL), K (OIL), L (OIL): note that the matrix is not birefringent in XPL. L is lithorelic.

Figure 5.3 Microphotographs of general soil characteristics.

Photos: C. Cammas, Inrap, and J. Brancier

Bottom of the pit (LM 4; UMiS 5 and 6). The Amerindians dug the soil until the bedrock appeared at the bottom of the pit, around 35 cm in depth. It consists of conglomerates in a silty-clayey matrix and has a bleached color (see Figure 5.3). Numerous basaltic lithorelics can be observed, generally bigger than 2 mm, forming in this manner the volcanic conglomerate (MacKenzie et al. 2017). The lithorelics are surrounded by ferruginous impregnations testifying of an alternation phase between waterlogging and a better-drained environment in this horizon, which is considered typical of fluctuating water levels.

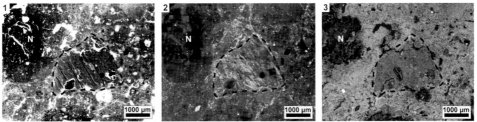

Pottery sherds (dotted lines) (UMiS 3): 1 (PPL), 2 (XPL), 3 (OIL). In PPL, we can observe a preferential orientation of the components in the clayey matrix, with a birefringence in XPL, typical of reductrice combustion. In OIL we see the micro-particles of charcoals in black. N is ferruginous nodules.

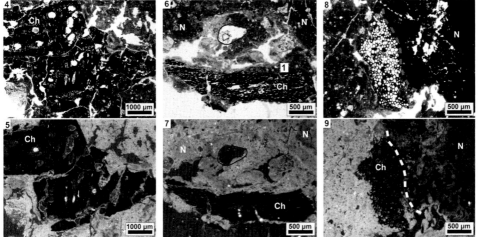

Micro-fragments of charcoals (Ch) (UMiS 3) in PPL and OIL view. 4 (PPL)-5 (OIL): note the fracturation due to the compaction and biological activity, and the rust-colored of iron-clay coating in the charcoal cells; 6 (PPL)-7 (OIL): sub-horizontal orientated fragmented charcoal; 7 (PPL)-9 (OIL): charcoal next to a ferruginous concretion. Here we can also see the usefullness of OIL view to distinguish charcoal from ferruginous features.

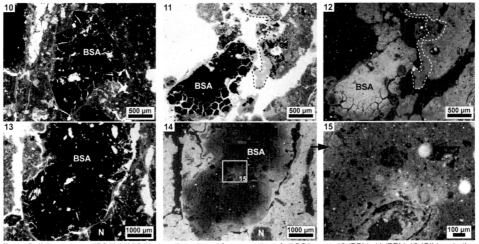

Burnt Soil Aggregates (BSA) (UMiS 3): note the external fragmentation of all BSA crust. 10 (PPL); 11 (PPL)-12 (OIL): note the limpid clay coating around the BSA and the channel (dotted line); 13 (PPL)-14 (OIL): bottom part of a BSA. Note the color gradient between outside (orange) and inside (black) in OIL; 15 (OIL): 14 zoom, note the micro-particles of charcoals being black and the oxidized plant fragments in orange.

Figure 5.4 Microphotographs of anthropogenic components.

Photos: C. Cammas, Inrap, and J. Brancier

Main phase (LM 2, LM 3; UMiS 3 and LM 4; UMiS 4). The microlimit between the bedrock and the first filling (UMiS 4) appears quite clearly at 2 to 3 cm: it is materialized by many subhorizontally oriented roots. Indeed, roots that penetrated into the pit were probably blocked by the bedrock, forming a bioturbated and fossilized microunit at this level (cf. Figure 5.4). In the UMiS 3, the sediment is clayey-silty, quite massive, and has fissure porosity. This microunit is mainly composed of an accumulation by anthropogenic features like burned soil aggregates, microcharcoals, and a few bone splinters as well as numerous pedological components such as ferruginous concretions. The absence of sorted sediment at about 20 cm indicates a rather anarchic filling-up over a long period, suggesting colluvium in which the artifacts were "captured" into the matrix (discharge). The porosity, related to the bioturbation, is rather tenuous but still visible in this UMiS 3. It also shows that the filling up took a long time with relatively slow recovery. Consequently, this filling represents an anthropogenic input that may come from fireplaces and perhaps activities related to food consumption or production: it has a darker fine matrix with microfragments of charcoal and burned soil aggregates containing potsherds and microbone fragments.

Last phase (LM 1 and 2, UMiS 1 and 2). The limit between UMiS 3 and UMiS 2 is quite diffuse. However, two main features indicate the transition from one to the other: the absence of anthropogenic components and the microstructure of the matrix. The latter appears more massive than below (porosity around 5% *vs* 15% below). Ferruginous nodules are still present and some minerals of the substratum remain (around 2%). At the top, the matrix of UMiS 1 has a more developed porosity (about 30%) than below, probably due to the important passage of many roots, and the biological activity abundant in this horizon, typical of a surface layer. UMiS 1 and 2 are characterized by a reorganization of the clay particles (clay coatings). It indicates for these two top layers a pedological evolution of the soil like slickensides, typical of clayey soil in the context of water-level fluctuations as can be found in ponds with waterlogging episodes (Cammas et al. 2012). Clay particles are weathered, undergoing seasonal alternations with heavy rain periods, in which the pit was full of water, and drier periods; such events may be the origin of the reorganization of the clay particles. The biological activity is sparsely developed, however, as some channels are filled entirely with enchytraeids' excremental pellets (Bullock et al. 1985; E. Fitzpatrick 1993). These could have been developed during episodes of better drainage.

5.1.3   Conclusions

Micromorphological analysis revealed a very slim microstratigraphy, indicating two main phases of filling for pit F 157. It confirms the macroscopic observations in the field in a handsome way. During the first phase, which was indeed the most important moment, it was filled up for about 20 cm. This episode was associated with the period of pit use by the Amerindians over a quite long time. Leaving the pit open allowed a continuous filling, with a regular cover, formed at the same time with anthropogenic discharges and natural colluvium, all taken up by the active bioturbation. Anthropogenic discharges include domestic artifacts, such as pottery sherds or scarce microbones, as well as products of combustion, such as charcoal and burned soil aggregates, which can be associated with fire activities, emanating directly from a fireplace area and/or from a soil-cleaning activity (Brancier 2016). The second phase of filling is composed by the last 10 cm and corresponds to the end of the utilization phase of the pit. It presents the question of whether this abandonment phase of the pit is connected with the abandonment of the site or only related to the use of another one. In either case, the pit was clogged by colluvial phenomena.

Finally, the interest of a micromorphological analysis in solving this type of archaeological problems relates to the additional information it provides that cannot be detected directly in the field. This type of analysis on humid tropical pre-Columbian anthrosol contexts, however, has been done at only a few sites, so comparative data are very limited. Furthermore, it would have been highly interesting to be able to microscopically study a similar sequence of samples within one of the fireplaces that were situated in the vicinity of the pits. This would have permitted us to test the hypothesis regarding the origin of the burned soil aggregates observed in pit F 157. Archaeological micromorphology is still quite recent in the Antilles (Todisco and Cammas 2011; Cammas 2013; van den Bel et al. 2016; Jegouzo et al. 2018; Brancier et al. 2018), and for this reason a regional reference collection of anthropogenic features has to be built in order to provide more precise information on ancient human activities.

5.2   Microbotanical analysis

Ruth Dickau and Jennifer Watling

A total of 14 samples were analyzed for microbotanical remains from two different sites (Table 5.2). Eight of these were bulk sediment samples from the Belle-Plaine site originating from eight archaeological features: six circular pits, one hearth, and one hearth within a pit. These were analyzed for phytoliths by J.W. at the University of Exeter, in the UK.

The remaining seven samples were from the Parking de Roseau site. Six samples from pit features were analyzed for phytoliths: four bulk sediment samples and two previously extracted residue samples from a quern and a mortar stone. In addition, an unwashed griddle

Table 5.2 Provenience table of microbotanical samples analyzed from the CHU Belle-Plaine and Parking de Roseau sites.

Site	Sample no.	Type	Location	Analysis	Notes
CHU Belle-Plaine	15.1	Bowl pit	North	phytolith	
CHU Belle-Plaine	66.1	Bowl pit	North	phytolith	Rich in organics
CHU Belle-Plaine	216	Bowl pit	South	phytolith	Contains shell fragments; very compact
CHU Belle-Plaine	248.3	Bowl pit	South	phytolith	Contains shell fragments
CHU Belle-Plaine	73.4	Square pit	North	phytolith	Contains shell fragments; rich in organics
CHU Belle-Plaine	157.2	Square pit	North	phytolith	
CHU Belle-Plaine	218.4	Hearth	South	phytolith	Contains charcoal; rich in organics
CHU Belle-Plaine	140	Hearth	South	phytolith	
Parking de Roseau	156 US 4.3.A	Quern	Level 4	phytolith	Sample from quern used face, from pit feature F156
Parking de Roseau	162.1.A	Mortar	Level 1	phytolith	Sample from mortar used face, from pit feature F162
Parking de Roseau	239	Pit	Level 2	phytolith	
Parking de Roseau	344	Pit	Level 2	phytolith	
Parking de Roseau	383	Pit	Level 2	phytolith	
Parking de Roseau	239	Pit	Level 2	phytolith	
Parking de Roseau	200	Burén fragment	Level 2	starch	

fragment from one of the pits was analyzed for starch grain residue as a preliminary test of this technique in Guadeloupe. Samples from Parking de Roseau were analyzed by R.D. at HD Analytical Solutions, Inc., in London, Canada.

These microbotanical analyses were undertaken to investigate the function of the pits at CHU Belle-Plaine and Parking de Roseau and to identify possible plant foods or materials stored within them and used generally at the sites. Previous macrobotanical analysis from these same pits had yielded only wood charcoal.

5.2.1   Rationale

Microbotanical analyses, specifically of starch grains and phytoliths, are a well-developed method of archaeobotanical investigation. They have been applied extensively throughout the American tropics, particularly through the pioneering work of Deborah Pearsall, Dolores Piperno, and other scholars (e.g., Ball et al. 2016; Chandler-Ezell et al. 2006; Dickau et al. 2012; Iriarte et al. 2010; Pearsall 1982; Pearsall and Piperno 1990; Piperno 1989, 2006; Piperno and Holst 1998b; Piperno and Pearsall 1998a; Watling and Iriarte 2013). Microbotanical analysis has not been used as extensively in the Caribbean islands as it has on the Central and South American mainland, but work by several researchers, particularly Pagán-Jiménez, is promoting microbotanical analysis in the Caribbean and demonstrating its utility, especially in contexts where macrobotanical preservation is poor (see Berman and Pearsall 2008; Mickleburgh and Pagán-Jiménez 2012; Pagán-Jiménez and Carlson 2014; Pagán-Jiménez et al. 2015, 2019; Rodríguez Suárez and Pagán-Jiménez 2008).

Phytoliths are bodies of biosilica, formed in the cells or cell walls of certain plants. These plants take up dissolved silica from groundwater and deposit them in certain tissues for structural support, physiological functions, or protection against herbivores and fungi (Sangster et al. 2001). The formation of phytoliths is under genetic control, and only occurs in certain plant taxa (Piperno 2006). Concentrated work by many researchers on major domesticates and economic species has resulted in the identification of diagnostic morphotypes for many of these taxa, such as maize (*Zea mays*) cob rondels, squash (*Cucurbita* spp.) rind scalloped spheres, and arrowroot (*Maranta arundinacea*) seed phytoliths (see comprehensive review in Ball et al. 2016). Because phytoliths are made of silica, they preserve well in most contexts. They may be recovered from artifact residues, dental calculus, and terrestrial sediments where they are deposited after the decay of plant material, or lake cores where they are introduced from the surrounding vegetation.

Starch grains are microscopic particles used by plants to store energy, usually for regrowth or germination. They are made up of alternating layers of amylose and amylopectin, which gives them a quasi-crystalline molecular structure that causes birefringence (the formation of an interference cross) under cross-polarized light when undamaged (Blanshard 1987; Gott et al. 2006). Starch grains have been found to preserve for long periods of time on the surface of archaeological artifacts (stone, pottery, and organic finds) used in processing plant material, presumably in microcrevices where they are protected from enzymatic degradation (Fullagar 2006; Haslam 2004; Loy et al. 1992). They have been recovered from human dental calculus as well (e.g. Henry and Piperno 2008; Mickleburgh and Pagán-Jiménez 2012; Piperno and Dillehay 2008), and occasionally within soils (see Barton and Matthews 2006; Haslam 2004). Their morphology can be diagnostic to the level of genus or species, permitting taxonomic identification of the plants used and processed by people in the past (Piperno and Holst 1998a; Reichert 1913; Torrence and Barton 2006).

5.2.2 Methods

Phytolith methods

Phytolith extraction from bulk sediment samples and artifact surface sediment samples followed the standard protocols described in Piperno (2006). The samples were first pretreated to remove clays through deflocculation, agitation, and gravity sedimentation. In order to maximize the recovery of important phytoliths of different size classes, such as those that derive from the rinds of *Cucurbita* fruits and leaves and cobs of maize, archaeological sediments were separated by wet-sieving into silt (2–50 μm) and sand (50–250 μm) fractions. Carbonates were removed with hydrochloric acid (37%) and organics with nitric acid (60% at University of Exeter, 70% at HD Analytical) and potassium chlorate. Phytoliths were floated using heavy liquid with a specific gravity of 2.37 g/cm^3 (zinc bromide at University of Exeter, sodium polytungstate at HD Analytical). Extracted phytoliths were dried with acetone before being mounted in Entellan (University of Exeter) or Permount (HD Analytical) to permit three-dimensional rotation and viewing. Slides were scanned using a transmitted light microscope equipped with digital imaging. A minimum of 200 phytoliths were counted for statistical frequency of morphotypes within the silt (A) fraction (Piperno 2006). The entire sand (C) fraction was mounted and scanned for diagnostic phytoliths. Taxonomic identifications were made using published sources (Bozarth 1992; Dickau et al. 2013; Iriarte 2003; Iriarte and Paz 2009; Piperno 1989, 2006; Piperno and Pearsall 1998b; Watling and Iriarte 2013) and by comparison with in-house phytolith reference collections.

Starch methods

Starch analysis methods were based on published protocols (Loy 1994; Pearsall 2000; Torrence and Barton 2006). The unwashed griddle fragment was placed into a beaker using sterilized tongs and covered with distilled water. Two milliliters of sodium hexametaphosphate was added to help deflocculate clays. The artifact was sonicated for 5 minutes and then gently brushed with a sterilized toothbrush to facilitate dispersal of adhering sediment. The artifact was then further sonicated for another 5 minutes. The resulting sediment was concentrated through centrifugation, and the water decanted. Starch grains were separated from the residue sample by heavy liquid floatation using sodium polytungstate heavy liquid, prepared to a density of 1.75 g/cm^3. The supernatant containing any floating starch grains was decanted into a new, labeled, sterile centrifuge tube. Distilled water was added to the extracted supernatant to lower the density and allow starch to fall out of suspension. The extract was centrifuged and rinsed several times with distilled water, and mounted in a 10% glycerin solution on microscope slides. Slides were analyzed using a transmitted-light compound microscope equipped with polarization and digital imaging camera. During processing and analysis, various laboratory protocols were implemented to mitigate and control for modern starch contamination (Crowther et al. 2014), including: sterilization of all equipment, testing of all consumables, barring food and modern plant material from the lab, minimal handling of the artifact with sterilized forceps, and processing a blank control sample alongside the artifact. This control sample tested negative for starch.

5.2.3   Results

CHU Belle-Plaine

Globular granulate phytoliths (GGs, Figure 5.5), produced in the wood and bark of trees and shrubs, accounted for more than 80% of the phytolith assemblages (Figure 5.6). When assemblages are dominated by a single morphotype such as this one, it is common practice to extend the phytolith count to capture other patterns in the archaeobotanical data that might otherwise be missed (Pearsall 2000). Thus, an additional 200 non-GGs were counted for each sample where possible and the results presented separately (Figure 5.7). Phytolith representation was especially poor in samples 15.1 (N=48) and 216 (N=140) (both bowl-shaped pits), which meant that the initial count of 200 was not fulfilled. Only sample 218.4 (the hearth/pit feature) yielded 200 non-GGs in the extended count. The other five samples contained only 14 to 90 non-GGs, probably the result of both poor phytolith representation and the dominance of GGs in the assemblages. Following Dickau et al. (2013), relative frequencies were not calculated for samples where n<50. Instead, phytolith presence or absence data is provided in Figure 5.7.

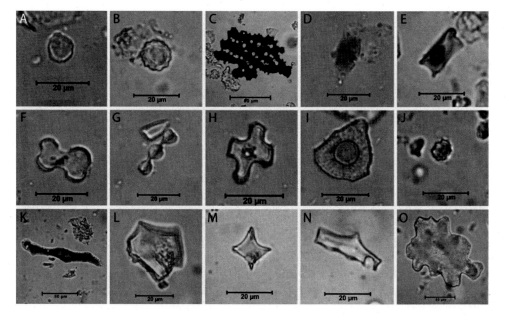

Figure 5.5 Selected phytolith morphotypes: A) Arboreal globular granulate, CHU Belle-Plaine; B) Arecaceae echinate globular, Parking de Roseau; C) Asteraceae opaque perforated plate, Parking de Roseau; D) *Heliconia* trough body, CHU Belle-Plaine; E) Poaceae rondel, Parking de Roseau; F) Panicoideae bilobate, CHU Belle-Plaine; G) Panicoideae polylobate, CHU Belle-Plaine; H) Panicoideae cross body (Variant 1), CHU Belle-Plaine; I) *Cyperus/Kyllinga* achene body, CHU Belle-Plaine; J) Marantaceae nodular globular, Rose-aude Roseau; K) Arboreal sclereid (burnt), Parking de Roseau; L) Arboreal faceted body, Parking de Roseau; M) Bambusoideae collapsed saddle, Parking de Roseau; N) cf. Olyreae complex shortcell, Parking de Roseau; O) cf. Marantaceae granulate irregular lobed, Parking de Roseau.

Photo: R. Dickau and J. Watling.

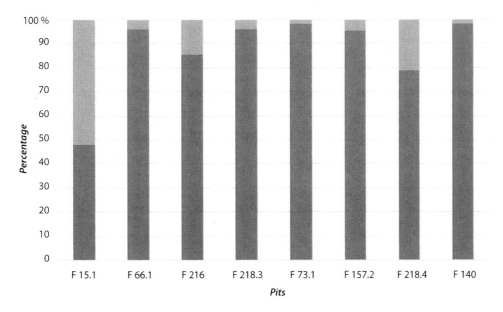

Figure 5.6 Histogram showing relative abundance of GG phytoliths in the CHU Belle-Plaine samples. Blue bar: GGs. Orange: other.

PITS

The data show little difference between the phytolith assemblages from the bowl- and square-shaped pits, implying that if the two did serve separate functions, it was probably not in relation to the types of plant material that were stored within them. Furthermore, the absence of phytoliths of domesticated crops or other economic species suggests they were unlikely to have been used to store vegetable foods.

Samples 15.1, 216 and 157.2 contained <50 phytoliths in the extended count. Among those non-GG phytoliths present were: Arecaceae (palms) (globular echinate type, Figure 5.5B), Poaceae (grasses) (rondels [Figure 5.5E] and bulliforms), and the herbs Asteraceae (Figure 5.5C) and *Heliconia* (Figure 5.5D), all of which generally prefer open environments. Samples 66.1, 248.3, and 73.4 contained these same phytoliths (but no *Heliconia*), alongside other arboreal types (faceted bodies, tracheids, and sclereids) and trace amounts of phytoliths belonging to the Panicoideae (warm- and wet-adapted) grass subfamily (bilobates, polylobates, and crosses (Figure 5.5F–H). Aside from GGs, rondels, bulliforms and an unidentified type of long cell were the most dominant morphotypes in these samples (up to 40%, 35% and 40%, respectively). The taxa represented in these samples, if indicative of local standing vegetation, are suggestive of a clearing within a predominantly forested environment. It is possible, however, that some or perhaps most of the GGs originated from wood used for building materials which later decomposed upon site abandonment. The high frequency of postholes, many of which were located very close to these pits, gives strength to this interpretation.

HEARTH FEATURES

The phytolith assemblages from the two hearth features (218.4 and 140) were generally more diverse than those from the pits, and their composition differed from one another. GG phytoliths were 15% less abundant (though still dominant) and grass phytoliths (bilobates

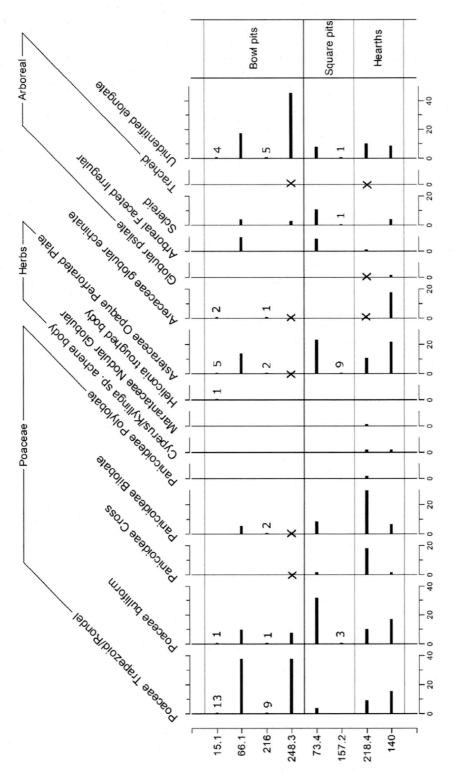

Figure 5.7 Percentage frequency diagram of non-GG phytoliths in the CHU Belle-Plaine samples. Numbers indicate absolute phytolith counts where n < 50; x = emphasizes rarer morphotypes (<2%).

and crosses) more common in sample 218.4 than in sample 140. Furthermore, sample 140 contained more than double the amount of Asteraceae (20%) than sample 218.4 and up to 20% palm phytoliths, which were found at <1% in sample 218.4. Cross phytoliths produced in the leaves of maize can be differentiated from those produced by wild Panicoideae grasses by their size and three-dimensional morphology. Following Piperno (2006), discriminate function analysis was performed on 30 cross-shaped phytoliths from sample 218.4 and the presence of maize leaf in the assemblage was confirmed (Table 5.3). This evidence indicates that the inhabitants of Belle-Plaine were practicing maize cultivation and suggests that people discarded the leaves in domestic hearths like those represented by these features.

Small quantities of the wetland reed *Cyperus* sp. were identified in both samples (Figure 5.5I). These plants may have been consumed or used as construction material, and were presumably naturally abundant in the wetlands close to the site. Species belonging to the Marantaceae family grow in both wetland environments and forest understories. Arrowroot (*Maranta arundinacea*), a root crop cultivated in the lowland neotropics, belongs to this family, but the particular phytoliths diagnostic of this species were not encountered.

Parking de Roseau

Table 5.4 presents a summary of the phytolith morphotypes recovered from the two artifact samples and the four bulk sediment samples from Parking de Roseau and their taxonomic associations. Figure 5.7 presents these results graphically, as a frequency diagram, and Figure 5.8 summarizes these results, comparing grasses, herbs, and arboreal taxa (including palms). Unlike at Belle-Plaine, no domestic crops were identified in the phytolith assemblage from any of the samples from Parking de Roseau. Generally, the diversity of phytoliths suggests that the assemblages represent background vegetation around the features or vegetation that found its way into the fill of the pit features, through cultural or natural means. However, there are some significant differences in frequencies between the samples, discussed later.

Sample 156 was a sediment or residue extraction from the used face of a quern. Phytolith extraction yielded a large volume of amorphous fragmentary silica. The origin of these silica is undetermined. It may be related to volcanic activity (tephra), highly fragmentary biosilica (broken phytoliths and silicified epidermal tissue, diatoms, or other biosilica), or weathering products from the surface of the stone artifact. Because of the amount of this material, obtaining a minimum 200 count of identifiable phytoliths was difficult, and only 182 phytoliths were documented. The phytolith assemblage was dominated by GG phytoliths (87.9%) from woody taxa, with smaller amounts of grass phytoliths (10.4%), and three Marantaceae nodular globular phytoliths (Figure 5.5J). The phytolith assemblage of the mortar sample was the most diverse of all the samples analyzed. Arboreal GGs were the

Table 5.3 Discriminant function analysis of cross-shaped phytoliths from hearth feature F 218.4. Maize leaf presence is determined by size and quantity of Variant 1 compared to Variant 5/6 panicoid cross phytoliths (*sensu*Piperno 2006).

N	X Var 1 (µm)	X Var 5/6 (µm)	% Var 1	Maize*	Wild†
30	12.85	10.85	86.7	0.660542	0.339458

*−1.96669+(0.1597589*X Var 1)−(0.0126672*X Var 5/6)+(0.00820956*% Var 1)

† 2.96669−(0.1597589*X Var 1)+(0.0126672*X Var 2)−(0.00820956*% Var 1)

Table 5.4 Summary of phytolith frequencies (percent) from the Parking de Roseau site samples. Phytolith frequencies calculated as a percent of total phytoliths counted per sample.

Morphotype	Taxonomic Association	Sample					
		156	162	200	239	344	383
Cross Body	Poaceae	0.5	4.5	0.0	0.0	0.0	0.4
Trapezoid/Rondel	Poaceae	9.9	23.5	8.5	60.8	1.0	36.6
Bilobate	Panicoideae	0.5	9.5	0.5	7.4	1.0	2.1
Thin Bilobate	Poaceae, cf. *Aristida* sp.	0.0	0.0	0.0	0.5	0.0	0.0
Collapsed Saddle	Bambusoideae	0.0	9.0	10.8	24.0	6.2	14.8
Complex Shortcell	Bambusoideae, cf. Olyreae	0.0	0.5	0.0	0.0	0.0	0.0
Nodular Globular	Marantaceae	1.6	0.0	0.0	0.0	0.0	0.0
Granulate Irregular Lobed	cf. Marantaceae	0.0	9.0	0.0	0.5	0.0	0.0
Opaque Perforated Plate	Asteraceae	0.0	1.0	1.4	0.0	0.0	4.1
Granulate Globular	Woody eudicot	87.9	26.0	78.9	6.4	91.9	2.1
Echinate Globular	Arecaceae	0.0	0.5	0.0	0.0	0.0	0.0
Sclereid	woody eudicot	0.0	0.5	0.0	0.0	0.0	0.0
Faceted Irregular	woody eudicot	0.0	1.5	0.0	0.0	0.0	0.0
Domed Granulate		0.0	1.0	0.0	0.0	0.0	0.0
Hair Cell		0.0	0.0	0.0	0.0	0.0	0.4
Unidentified		0.0	1.5	0.0	0.5	0.0	0.0
Total Phytoliths Counted		**182**	**200**	**213**	**204**	**209**	**243**

most frequent (26.0%). Other arboreal phytoliths were present in small quantities, such as a sclereid (Figure 5.5K), a small number of faceted irregular phytoliths (Figure 5.5L), and a palm (Arecaceae) echinate globular phytolith (Figure 5.5B). This palm phytolith was the only one observed from Parking de Roseau. Palms are abundant phytolith producers, and the phytoliths are quite robust, typically preserving very well. The isolated occurrence of this phytolith may represent intentional use of palms, such as processing on the tool or storage within the pit feature, rather than background vegetation. The grass phytolith assemblage on the mortar was comprised of cross bodies, trapezoid/rondels, Panicoideae bilobates, Bambusoideae collapsed saddles (Figure 5.5M), and an Olyreae (a tribe of Bambusoideae) complex shortcell (Figure 5.5N). This was the only sample to yield an Olyreae phytolith, and based on modern reference work on surface sediments from under specific vegetation biomes in South America, Olyreae was determined to be indicative of humid evergreen tropical forest (Dickau et al. 2013). In addition, the sample had a number of large granulate irregular lobed phytoliths (N=51) (Figure 5.5O). The taxonomic associate of these phytoliths is unknown. The sample also yielded Asteraceae opaque perforated plate phytoliths (Figure 5.5D), and several unknown phytoliths.

Among the bulk sediment samples, samples 200 and 344 were dominated by GG phytoliths (>78%), suggesting a predominantly forested environment. However, samples 239 and 383 were dominated by grass phytoliths (67% and 39%, respectively, excluding Bambusoideae, which is predominantly a forest taxon). The difference between these samples and Samples 200 and 344 is notable. It is possible that the vegetation near these pits was disturbed and open at the time of sediment deposition or infilling, or that grasses were intentionally used in the pits for cultural reasons, although no domesticated or economic species were identified. Interestingly, more than 90% of the recorded phytoliths in samples 239 and

383 were burned. There was no taxonomic patterning to the occurrence of burnt phytoliths; all morphotypes had high frequencies of burnt specimens. In addition to burnt phytoliths, Sample 239 also exhibited a significant amount of particulate micro-charcoal in the extract. Asteraceae phytoliths were present in Sample 383 in their highest frequency (4.1%) out of all the samples. A small number of Asteracaeae phytoliths were also identified in Sample 200. Although Asteraceae is usually considered an indicator of open or disturbed habitats, some species can be found in forested environments. In summary, comparison of the phytolith assemblages from the six samples of Parking de Roseau shows that Samples 156, 200, and 344 all come from features with high amounts of arboreal phytoliths, and low amounts of grass and herb phytoliths (Figures 5.8 and 5.9). These phytolith assemblages are comparable to those in the CHU Belle-Plaine pit sediments, and suggest that either woody species were

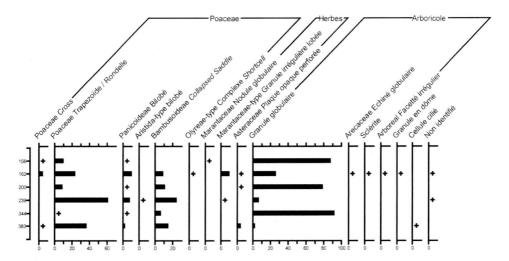

Figure 5.8 Diagram of phytolith frequencies by major morphotype groups. Frequencies calculated as a percent of total counted phytoliths. Frequencies <2% shown by a plus symbol (+). Diagram produced in C2 (Juggins 2010).

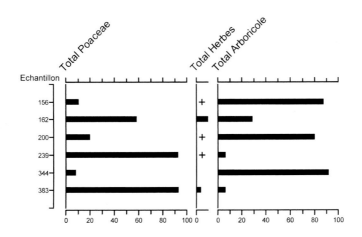

Figure 5.9 Summary diagram of total frequencies of grasses, herbs, and arboreal taxa.

introduced into the pits or the local area near the pits was forested when sediment filled in the pits. In contrast, Samples 383 and 239 both show higher frequencies of grass phytoliths, low frequencies of arboreal phytoliths, and high amounts of burnt phytoliths. These factors suggest that either burnt grasses and herbs were introduced into the pit or the local vegetation was more open or disturbed at the time the pit sediments were deposited. Sample 162, from the face of a mortar tool, stands out as the most diverse sample, and distinctive from the two groups previously discussed. Numerous morphotypes were observed in this sample that were not observed in any other sample, but none were from domesticated species.

GRIDDLE FRAGMENT

Starch extraction and analysis of the griddle fragment yielded a total of 42 starch grains. Two lenticular starch grains measuring 17.6 μm and 23.5 μm in diameter, with a depressed center and no fissures or lamellae, are consistent with those produced in chili pepper fruits (*Capsicum* sp.) (Perry et al. 2007) (Figure 5.10A-B). Maize was represented by a polygonal starch grain measuring 19.2 μm with a centric hilum and Y-shaped fissure (Figure 5.10C). The starch grain did not exhibit any extinction cross under cross-polarized

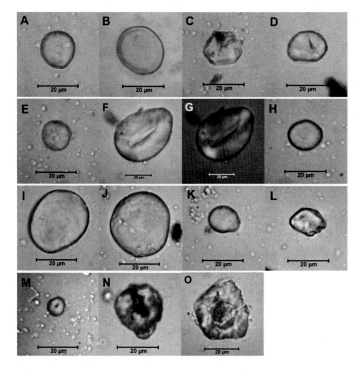

Figure 5.10 Selected starch grains recovered from the griddle fragment (Cat. #200). A) *Capsicum* sp.
B) *Capsicum* sp., C) *Zea mays*, D) cf. *Zea mays*, E) cf. *Xanthosoma* sp., F) unidentified damaged ovate with eccentric hilum, cf. tuber starch G) same starch grain, under cross polarized light, H) small unidentified lenticular (<25 μm), I) large unidentified lenticular (>25 μm), J) unidentified large dimpled lenticular, K) unidentified starch with nub at end, L) unidentified, M) unidentified, N) unidentified damaged, O) unidentified damaged. Scale bar: 20 μm.

light, suggesting it was damaged from processing or cooking (Henry et al. 2009). Two additional starch grains were tentatively identified as maize, but lacked all the characteristic features to make a secure identification (Figure 5.10D). A single dome-shaped starch grain with an open centric hilum (14.7 μm) was tentatively identified as cocoyam (*Xanthosoma* sp.) (Figure 5.10E). Unfortunately, this morphotype is similar to those seen in several other tuberous taxa, and identification remains tentative without a larger assemblage. Another tuberous species was represented by a large (50.2 μm), ovate starch grain with lamellae and eccentric hilum. A large, open longitudinal fissure shows that the starch was damaged, preventing taxonomic identification (Figure 5.10F-G). The most common starch morphotype was a lenticular or discoid grain with centric hila and diffuse birefringence. Several of these (N=4) ranged between 15 and 25 μm (Figure 5.10H), but the majority (N=12) were larger, ranging from 26 to 31 μm (Figure 5.10I). Many had small initial fissures or shadows at the centric hilum area, and several had lamellae. These starches are not consistent with lenticular forms observed in *Capsicum* sp. and remain unidentified. Another unidentified morphotype was a small oval starch with slightly eccentric hilum and a nub at one end (Figure 75.10K). In addition to several unidentified starch grains, the sample also included five starch grains that exhibited processing damage (Figure 5.10N-O).

5.2.4 *Conclusions*

Starch analysis on the ceramic griddle fragment from Parking de Roseau revealed the use of maize, chili pepper (*Capsicum* sp.), possibly cocoyam (*Xanthosoma* sp.), and at least three other unidentified taxa, including an undetermined type of tuber or root. Some starch grains showed evidence of processing or cooking alteration, which is not surprising given that they were recovered from an artifact used to cook food. These starch residues indicate that cultivated food, and therefore horticulture, was part of the subsistence economy of the Parking de Roseau inhabitants. Likewise, phytoliths from maize leaves in the sediment from Hearth Feature 218.4 show that maize was used at CHU Belle-Plaine. Unfortunately, phytolith analysis of sediments from the pit features of both sites did not yield any evidence of economic plants, with the exception of trace numbers of palm phytoliths. If the pit features were being used to store crops, then these were taxa or specific plant parts that do not produce abundant diagnostic phytoliths. However, phytoliths were recovered from all of the pit samples, demonstrating that phytoliths were preserved in the sediments. The recovered phytoliths represent mainly non-economic taxa (grasses, herbs, and arboreal taxa) that were either introduced into the pits intentionally or represent local vegetation from the immediate vicinity of the site. If the latter premise is correct, then the variation observed between the samples from the Parking de Roseau site indicates that the pits were either situated in different environments or that the contexts sampled were deposited at different times and vegetation changed significantly over time. This hypothesis can be evaluated by ascertaining relative or absolute dates of the samples. There was less variation observed among the CHU Belle-Plaine pits, and it appears that these were situated either in a more forested environment or close to wooden stakes that, upon decomposition, contributed an "arboreal" phytolith signature. Future use of phytolith analysis within the Lesser Antilles will improve resolution of local palaeovegetation reconstruction and refine interpretations of human-environment interactions.

5.3   Starch analysis

Jaime Pagán-Jiménez

Starch grain research became common ground in the Lesser Antilles in the last two decades (Berman and Pearsall 2008; Newsom and Wing 2004; Pagán-Jiménez 2011). Hitherto the interpretations of the pre-Columbian botanic culture in the region relied mainly on 16th-century Spanish documents. They created, in combination with a large amount of ethnographic botanical information, a three-step "metatheory" concerning the evolution of human adaption and agriculture in the Antilles, in which the last step represents the Saladoid adaptation to the insular environment and population (Pagán-Jiménez 2013:391–392). Until recently, Guadeloupe provided little information on this general evolution in the Lesser Antilles (Mickleburgh and Pagán-Jiménez 2012), revealing the presence of maize (*Zea mays*) among the Late Ceramic Age population and other root crops such as coontie or marunguey (*Zamia* sp.) and sweet potato (*Ipomoea batatas*). The Troumassoid sites presented here provided nine samples for starch analysis taken from lithic artifacts (Table 5.5).[1]

Table 5.5 General description of the discussed starch samples.

Site	Artifact #	Sample ID	Lab. No.	Provenience (pit features)	Artifact type and sampling area	Weight (g)	Volume (ml)
CHU Belle-Plaine	1a	CHU-157 A	IN-01	F 157	Passive grinding stone fragment, used face	0.002	0.01
CHU Belle-Plaine	1b	CHU-157 B	IN-02	F 157	Passive grinding stone fragment, side	0.008	0.04
CHU Belle-Plaine	2	CHU-231	IN-03	F 231	Passive grinding stone fragment, used face	0.017	0.09
STEP Goyave	3	F113. US4.1.A	IN-04	F 113	Complete passive grinding stone, used face	0.084	0.2
STEP Goyave	4	F55.1.A	IN-05	F 55	Complete passive grinding stone, used face	0.047	0.15
STEP Goyave	5	F255.1.A	IN-06	F 255	Complete passive grinding stone, used face	0.092	0.2
STEP Goyave	6	F174. US1.1.A	IN-07	F 174	Passive grinding stone fragment, used face	0.188	0.35
Parking de Roseau	7	Roseau	IN-08	F 102.1.A (102, 2nd half)	Grinding mortar, Used concavity	0.206	0.47
Parking de Roseau	8	Roseau	IN-09	F 222.1.A	Grinding mortar, Used concavity	0.101	0.22

5.3.1 Materials and methods

Extraction of samples

Table 5.5 shows the basic information on the extracted samples and the provenances of the studied artifacts. A total of one sediment/residue sample per artifact was extracted, specifically in areas with recognizable use wear (a facet produced by the grinding of materials). Sample extraction was done by Inrap personnel and Sebastiaan Knippenberg, following detailed protocols previously developed by Pagán-Jiménez. First, the workspace for the extraction procedures was thoroughly cleaned. A sterile paper sheet was placed on the working surface where each tool was to be sampled. Next, sediment residues (direct scraping, dry method) were extracted in the used faces of the artifacts using a sterilized metal pick (see also Pearsall et al. 2004; Perry 2004). Before a new sample was taken, the work space was cleaned again, materials were replaced, and the metal pick was sterilized with distilled water and heat. The extracted sediments for each tool surface were first placed on sterile white paper sheets and then were deposited in new zip lock bags. All the residue-sediment samples were processed for the separation of starch grains with cesium chloride (CsCl), as discussed in the next section.

Starch separation from sediments

The following protocol was applied, modified from Atchison and Fullagar (1998), Barton et al. (1998), and Pearsall et al. (2004). After placing each sample into a sterile plastic microcentrifuge tube of 1.5 ml, a solution of CsCl with a specific gravity of 1.79 g/cm^3 was added. The objective was to separate the starch grains through flotation and to isolate them from other particles, as starches are known to have an average specific gravity of 1.5 g/cm^3 (Banks and Greenwood 1975). The separation was effected by a microcentrifuge running at 2500 rpm and lasting for 15 minutes during the first phase. The supernatant, where the starch grains would be contained, was decanted and poured into a new sterile microcentrifuge plastic tube.

The next step was to add distilled water to the sample and agitate the mix for ten seconds. This process reduced the specific gravity of the mixture through the dilution of salt crystals with the objective of eliminating, with repeated washes, their presence. This last step was repeated two more times (three times in total), adding less water in each successive step, and running each sample through the microcentrifuge at 4500 rpm for 15 minutes. The remaining solution with the residues was then placed on a sterile slide for microscope analysis. Half a drop of liquid glycerol was added and stirred with a stick or needle in order to increase the viscosity of the medium, to enhance the birefringence of the starch grains, and to rotate them when necessary during the analysis.

Taxonomic ascription of the recovered starch grains

The study of starch grains in archaeology provides a valuable means to address questions about plant use. As other studies have shown, starch residues can preserve for a long time in the imperfect, irregular (pores, fissures, cracks) surfaces of lithic, ceramic, and shell tools related to the processing and cooking of plant organs (Haslam 2004; Loy et al. 1992; Pagán-Jiménez 2005, 2007; Pearsall et al. 2004; Piperno and Holst 1998a). If starch grains can be extracted from a tool and correlated to the starch of a known plant, then a direct link can be established between the implement and the starch-rich plant or plants that it processed.

At present, we have assembled a comparative reference collection of starch grains obtained from modern economic plants of the Neotropics (specifically from the Caribbean, northern South America, and the Andes) and the Old World. It includes more than 140 specimens that have been formally described (Pagán-Jiménez 2007, Appendix B; Pagán-Jiménez 2015). The detailed morphometric description of the features of modern starches allow us to identify the taxa of archaeological starches through comparison as long as these grains exhibit the necessary diagnostic traits in sufficient quantities. The latter have been established according to the descriptive analysis of modern samples in the reference collection. If these conditions are not met by the archaeological starch grains, then the taxonomic identification is unfortunately less secure. In such cases, we use the categories "cf." (in reference to the closest tentative classification) and "not identified." A reliable or secure identification will not be established if archaeological starch grains exhibit traits that are not documented in our reference collection or in the published literature consulted for this study (see, for example, Table 5.6; Pearsall et al. 2004; Piperno 2006; Piperno and Holst 1998a; Piperno et al. 2000; Perry 2001, 2002a, 2002b, 2004, 2005; Reichert 1913; Ugent et al. 1986). Other research that includes starch grain analysis is currently in progress regarding northeastern South America, specifically French Guiana (McKey et al. 2010; Pagán-Jiménez 2011, 2012). These publications and the ancient starch grains previously recovered in the region were consulted for comparative purposes.

Table 5.6 Dimensions of some starch grains from various modern plants of Pagán-Jiménez's comparative collection and other selected published sources, and comparison with ancient starches recovered in this study.

Taxa	Range of measures in µm (minimum and maximum length for groups of starch grains)	Mean in µm (if available, standard deviation of the mean are in parenthesis)	No. of measures	Recoverd starches (this study)
Domesticates				
Maize (*Zea mays*), Races:				
a. Pollo	2–28	13 (±3.9)	116	Cluster tentatively identified in artifact #1 ranges between 5 and 11.5 with a mean of 8.5 µm.
b. Early Caribbean	3–20	13 (±3.6)	101	Single starch in artifact #2 is 11.58 x 9.14 µm
c. Negrito de Colombia	5–20	12.3 (±3.3)	107	
d. Cateto cristalino	3–18	10.3 (±3.1)	107	
e. Chandelle	2–20	12.3 (±3.2)	89	
f. Tuśon	1–18	12 (±3.2)	109	
Bean (*Phaseolus vulgaris*)	10–40	20 (±6.1)	111	Fabaceae starches in artifact #1 are 31.35 x 23.58 µm; 20.32 x 8.03 µm, 28.57 x 22.18 µm, and 22.32 x 15.48 µm. *Phaseolus* tentative identification in artifact #1 is 30 x 24.17 µm.

Taxa	Range of measures in μm (minimum and maximum length for groups of starch grains)	Mean in μm (if available, standard deviation of the mean are in parenthesis)	No. of measures	Recoverd starches (this study)
Poroto (*Phaseolus lunatus*)	8–48	30	? (Reichert 1913)	
Chili pepper (*Capsicum chinense, habanero*)	16.4–40	26.6	25 (Perry et al. 2007)	Single starch tentatively identified in artifact #1 is 20.16 × 19.01 μm
Chili pepper (*Capsicum baccatum baccatum*)	13.5–41.7	25.1	25 (Perry et al. 2007)	
Cultivars				
Cocoyam (*Xanthosoma sagittifolium*)	5–13	8 (±2)	52	
Purple cocoyam (*Xanthosoma violaceum*)	5–15	10 (±4.5)	44	Cocoyam starches (tentative and secure identifications) in artifact #1 are 9.89 × 8.84 μm and 8.78 × 8.46 μm, respectively
Yautía de palma or elephant's ear (*Xanthosoma undipes*)	3–7	4 (±1.1)	49	
Malanga or cocoyam (*Xanthosoma* cf. *daguense*), Ecuador	4,5–16	11.1 (±2.87)	20	
Yampee (*Dioscorea trifida*)	10–47	33 (±7.16)	63	
Wild				
Jack bean (*Canavalia rosea*)	10–53	28 (±8)	109	
Habichuela parada or wildbush bean (*Macroptilium lathyroides*)	3–28	17.5 (±3.9)	122	
Chili pepper (*Capsicum annum aviculare*)	2-2-6.1	3.5	50 (Perry et al. 2007)	
Dunguey (*Dioscorea altissima*)	15–75	38 (±13)	63	
Ñame or yam (*Dioscorea* spp. 4)	9.21–48.45	24.10 (±9.45)	20 (Pagán-Jiménez 2015)	

The identification of the archaeological starch grains was realized with an Olympus BX-53 (with polarizer), employing a 10x eyepiece and a 40x objective. The principal diagnostic, but not a unique element to discern starch grains from other residues, is the presence of the "extinction" or Maltese cross observable under polarized light. The slides with the archaeological samples were examined and their X and Y coordinate positions were annotated in order to facilitate location and perspective in later inspections. Almost all the starch grains recovered were photographed in different positions (when possible) through rotation. After the analysis, the slides were stored in new standard cardboard slide-holders at the Pagán-Jiménez laboratory.

5.3.2   *CHU Belle-Plaine*

Two lithic grinding tools from this site represent artifacts that were apparently used for the processing of plant material (see Table 5.5). Important domestic plants and cultivars such as beans (Fabaceae, probably *Phaseolus* sp.), chili pepper (*Capsicum* sp.), maize (*Zea mays*), and cocoyam (*Xanthosoma* sp.) were identified in two different areas, and separated samples, of artifact No. 1 (used face and side area), while only one starch could be retrieved and positively identified as maize in artifact No. 2.

Table 5.7 and Figures 5.11–5.14 synthesize the results obtained by this study. It should be noted that in Table 5.7, ubiquity (expressed in %) combines approximate (or "cf.") and secure identifications and refers to the occurrence of the identified taxa between the sample spectra. Species richness also combines both approximate and secure identifications per sample.

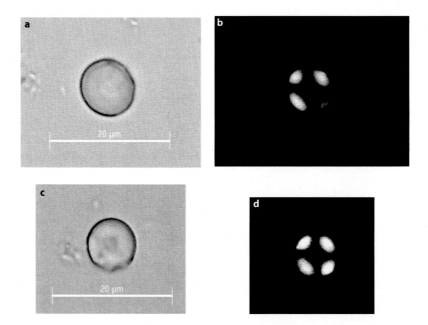

Figure 5.11 Tentative (a, b) and definite (c, d) identifications of cocoyam starches. Images in (b) and (d) are micrographs of the same starches shown in (a) and (c), though with dark field and polarized light.

Photo: Pagan Jiménez.

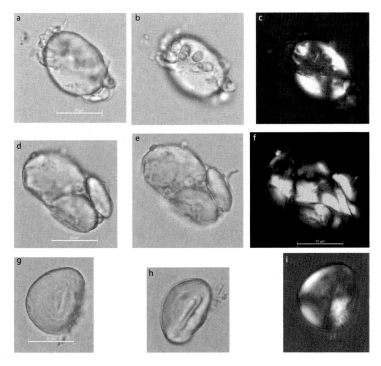

Figure 5.12 Starches ascribed to Fabaceae (a) and (d) and to *Phaseolus* sp. (g). Images in (b) and (c), (e) and (f), and (h) and (i), are different aspects (refocus, dark field polarization, or rotation) of the starches shown in images (a), (d) and (g).

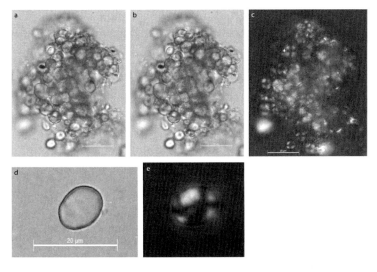

Figure 5.13 Cluster of starches tentatively ascribed to maize (a), and a single starch identified as maize (d). Images in (b) and (c) are different aspects of the starch cluster shown in image (a). Image in (e) is the same starch as (d) but in dark field and with polarized light.

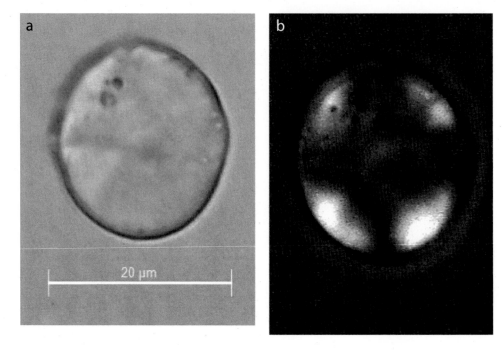

Figure 5.14 Starch grain (a) identified as one of chili pepper (*Capsicum* sp.). Image in (b) is the same one, but in dark field and with polarized light.

Cocoyam

Two starch grains, one tentatively ascribed and the other securely identified as cocoyam on artifact No. 1, have sizes and morphological traits that fit well with those registered in modern comparative collections of economically important cocoyams (Tables 5.6 and 5.7; Figure 5.11). These starches also count with small distal pressure facets and Maltese crosses that are typical of the genus *Xanthosoma*, though the tentatively identified starch has a central depression produced by pressure that does not allow a clear enough view of the Maltese cross for the researcher to be completely sure of its identification. Based on the previous characteristics observed on these starches, it seems reasonable to believe that both derive from one of the *Xanthosoma* cultivars such as *X. sagittifolium* or *X. violaceum*. Wild species of this genus produce starches with smaller size ranges and mean sizes, different from those documented here (see Pagán-Jiménez 2015).

Beans (Fabaceae)

Starches identified to the family level as Fabaceae on artifact No. 1 have morphometrical characteristics that are typical in many domestic and wild species of this family (Tables 5.6 and 5.7; Figure 5.12). However, noted size ranges and diverging shapes after rotation (like the diagnostic kidney shape) are more common in useful Fabaceae specimens of the genera *Phaseolus* (from which bean derives) and *Canavalia*. Both plant genera produce seeds that are edible after submitting them to various ways of processing, such as grinding (to make

Table 5.7 Starch grain distribution, ubiquity of taxa, and species richness by samples for CHU Belle-Plaine.

	Artifact #1a, used face	Artifact #1b, side	Artifact #2, used face		Total Starches	Ubiquity (%),
	(IN-01)	(IN-02)	(IN-03)			
	Passive grinding stone		Passive grinding stone			
Corms						
Cocoyam (*Xanthosoma* spp.)		1			1	33.3
Cocoyam (cf. *Xanthosoma* spp.)		1			1	
Seeds/Grains/Fruits						
Bean (cf. Fabaceae, nondiagnostic, attached to bigger Fabaceae starches)	18				18	66.6
Bean (Fabaceae)	4	1			5	
Bean (cf. *Phaseolus* spp. [*vulgaris/lunatus*])		1			1	33.3
Zea mays			1		1	66.6
cf. *Zea mays*		Cluster, c. 100 starches			c. 100	
Chili pepper (cf. *Capsicum* spp.)	1				1	33.3
Not identified	1	1			2	—
Total starches	24	5 + c. 100	1		c. 130	—
Species richness	2	3	1		—	—

flour) and boiling. Because the recovered starches show some signs of damage (rugulose surfaces after damaging by pressure) and because they are partially clustered, the registering of definite features known on starches of economic species, such as the typical distal linear fissure or the sometimes wavy arrangement of amylose/amylopectin layers, could not be observed clearly.

A single starch on the same artifact was identified as one produced by the genus *Phaseolus* (Figure 5.10g–i). Its maximum size, together with its oval and partially lenticular shape after rotation, the characteristics of its wavy Maltese cross and lamellae, and the projection of an open longitudinal fissure, place this starch within the mentioned genus. Because some of the other Fabaceae starches documented here could have some of these traits if they are rotated, it is possible that all of them could be from the same starchy source as the one identified as *Phaseolus*.

Maize

A cluster consisting of about 100 oval, polygonal and truncated (bell-shaped) starches was recovered in artifact No. 1 (Tables 5.6 and 5.7; Figure 5.13a–c). Due to the nature of this cluster, small starches with less characteristic traits of diagnostic maize starch (*Z. mays*) are common. This same situation also occurs in clusters of maize starches observed in modern comparative collections in which smaller starch grains are usually more abundant than bigger and diagnostic ones. In this case, together with some diagnostic maize starches there are high amounts of plain smaller starches—that is, starches that do not have all the diagnostic traits that are expected in maize starches. Because all the starches within the cluster are heavily mixed together, it was not possible to verify in a detailed way all the morphometric characteristics that would allow us to propose a final and definite identification. Because some of the diagnostic maize starches are surrounded by many "nondiagnostic" starches (which could also have been produced by maize, according to our reference data), it is reasonable to propose a tentative identification for this group of starches that must have a common origin. Based on its shapes and size ranges, this kind of starch is typical of indigenous maize landraces such as the lowland South American *Cateto Cristalino*, which is a variety with hard and vitreous endosperm that usually requires the grinding of the caryopsis for producing flour. Artifact No. 2 yielded a single maize starch that has all the diagnostic elements expected for starches produced in some maize landraces: size (11.58×9.14 μm), oval and wavy-oval shape (after rotation), eccentric Maltese cross with wavy arms, and a double border that is considered as a definite diagnostic feature in this kind of starches (Figure 5.13d-e).

Chili pepper

A single starch tentatively identified as chili pepper (to the genus level) was registered on artifact No. 1 (Tables 5.6 and 5.7; Figure 5.14). Based on its shape (in centric and eccentric views), its smooth or blurry Maltese cross, and its fissure after rotation, together with its maximum length (20.16 × 19.0 μm), it is more related to the starches produced in the fruits of *Capsicum chinense* or *C. baccatum baccatum*, which are chili landraces that probably originated in the northern lowlands of South America and lowland Bolivia (which includes the Bolivian Amazon) (Pagán-Jiménez et al. 2015; Perry et al. 2007).

5.3.3   STEP Goyave

Four samples have been studied from this site (Nos. 1–4; see Table 5.5). It should be noted that the samples registered extremely low amounts of starches. This can be related to the conditions of the artifacts once they were recovered and processed during and after the archaeological excavations (but they were not washed). Only artifacts Nos. 1 and 4 yielded ancient starch grains, and in both cases the quantity of them was minimal (Table 5.8): one starch ascribed to chili pepper on artifact No. 1, and three starches, one ascribed to Fabaceae and two others identified as maize, on artifact No. 4. The other two artifacts (Nos. 2 and 3), as we mentioned earlier, did not reveal any ancient starch.

   Table 5.8 and Figures 5.15–5.17 synthesize the results obtained by this study. It should be noted that in Table 5.8, ubiquity (expressed in %) combines approximate (or "cf.") and secure identifications and refers to the occurrence of the identified taxa between the sample spectra. Species richness also combines both approximate and secure identifications per sample.

Chili pepper

A single starch identified as chili pepper (to the genus level) was registered on artifact No. 1 (Table 5.8; Figure 5.15). Based on its shape (oval in centric view and lenticular in eccentric

Table 5.8 Starch grain distribution, ubiquity of taxa, and species richness of the samples from STEP Goyave.

	Artifact #3, used face	Artifact #4, used face	Artifact #5, used face	Artifact #6, used face	Total Starches	Ubiquity (%)
	(IN-04)	(IN-05)	(IN-06)	(IN-07)		
	Passive grinding stone	Passive grinding stone	Passive grinding stone	Passive grinding stone		
Seeds/Grains/Fruits						
Bean (Fabaceae)				1	1	25
Maize (*Zea mays*)				2	2	25
Chili pepper (*Capsicum* spp.)	1				1	25
Not identified						
Total starches	1	0	0	3	4	—
Species richness	1	0	0	2	—	—

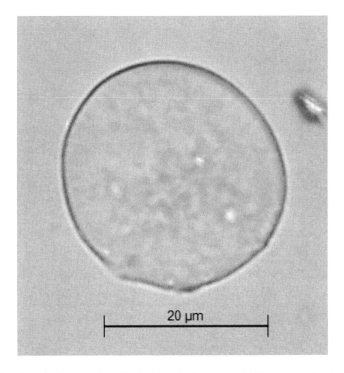

Figure 5.15 Starch grain from artifact No. 1, identified as one of chili pepper (*Capsicum* sp.). Partial edge-cracking can be noted as perpendicular striations beginning at the border.

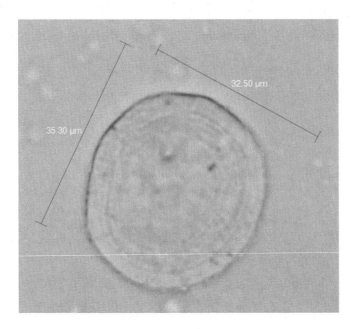

Figure 5.16 Recovered ancient starch ascribed to bean Fabaceae.

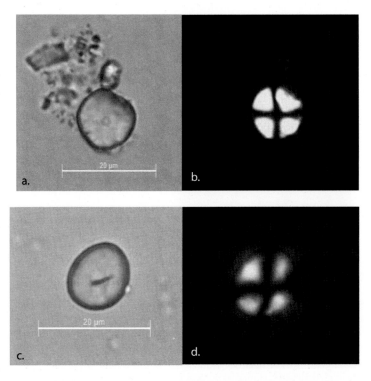

Figure 5.17 Ancient starches (a, c), diagnostic of maize. Images in (b) and (d) are different aspects (dark field and polarization) of the starches shown in images (a) and (c).

view), its smooth or blurry Maltese cross, and its linear fissure after rotation, together with its maximum length (28.04 × 26.43 µm), this starch is more related to the ones produced in the fruits of *Capsicum chinense* and *C. annuum annuum*, which are chili landraces that probably originated in northern lowland South America and northern Central America, respectively (see Perry et al. 2007, supporting material). We were not able to reach a higher taxonomic level, because this starch shows signs of alteration due to pressure (light edge cracking and a huge central depression) that does not allow capture of all the features that are needed to propose a final identification.

Bean (Fabaceae)

A single starch identified to the family level as Fabaceae on artifact No. 4 shows morpho-metrical characteristics that are typical of many domestic and wild species of this family (Table 5.8; Figure 5.16). However, the noted maximum length (35.30 µm) is more common in useful Fabaceae specimens of the genera *Phaseolus* (from which domestic beans derives) and *Canavalia*. Both plant genera produce seeds that are edible after submitting them to various ways of processing such as grinding (to make flour) and boiling. Because the recovered starch shows some signs of damage produced by heat in a partially dry environment (e.g., surface particulate and vitreous appearance), the registering of definite features known on starches of economic or domestic species, such as the typical longitu-dinal and linear fissure in centric or eccentric view, and the characteristic kidney shape commonly registered in the starches of useful beans, could not be observed clearly. How-ever, it should be noted that the source of this starch (the seed) was heated previous to its grinding with the lithic artifact.

Maize

Two individual starch grains that are diagnostic of maize (*Z. mays*) were registered in artifact No. 4, together with a Fabaceae specimen described earlier (Table 5.8; Figure 5.17). These starches share traits that are diagnostic of the mentioned species, such as a double border surrounding each grain, the general registered shapes (oval and lightly pentagonal, respec-tively), and the projection of the Maltese crosses, which in both cases are lightly eccentric crosses with wavy arms. Moreover, these starches have dimensions of 12.8 × 12.4 µm and 12.26 × 10.64 µm that place them close to the mean size of the starches of many modern indigenous landraces (see Pagán-Jiménez 2007, Appendix B; Pagán-Jiménez 2015). These types of maize starch are produced by both major kinds of endosperm: crystalline/vitreous (hard endosperm) and floury (soft endosperm).

5.3.4 Parking de Roseau

Two lithic grinding artifacts have been studied from this site (Nos. 1 and 2; Table 5.5; Fig-ure 5.18). These grinders, with evident central concavities in each side, were possibly used for the processing of plant materials (see contribution by Sebastiaan Knippenberg in this volume). Our analysis reveals that both artifacts were probably used for grinding materials different from starchy organs. In only one case, a single starch from a tuber (ascribed to the genus Dioscorea or yam), with light signs of damaging by dry heat was recovered in artifact No. 2.

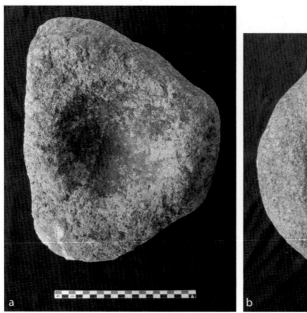

Figure 5.18 Sampled artifacts: (a) artifact No. 1 (unwashed) and (b) artifact No. 2 (unwashed). Note the pronounced concavities in both grinding tools. Scale bar in image (a) is 20 cm, and in image (b) is 10 cm.

Photo by S. Knippenberg.

Yam *(*Dioscorea *sp.)*

A single starch grain with signs of damage by heat in a dry environment (without water) was recovered from artifact No. 2 (Figure 5.19; Table 5.9). It has a generally oval shape and a maximum length of 38.52 μm. The distal end of this starch is slightly concave, which is a characteristic previously documented in starches of various *Dioscorea* specimens (Pagán-Jiménez 2015). Also, the layering pattern (lamellae) consists of a combination of concentric rings in the proximal area and partial rings (or lines) toward the distal end, which is also common in *Dioscorea* sp. starches. A single transversal fissure over the hilum is common in starches of some *Dioscorea* species, although in this case this feature could have been altered by the fold and depression registered in this same area. Damage signs consist in the accumulation of small particles in different areas on the surface or edges of the starch, and in a smooth and depressed fold around the hilum. Both signs are consistent with the toasting or parching of the organ source (partially dry) before grinding.

5.3.5   Final remarks

Regarding the association between human actions and plant use, as well as starch grain occurrence and preservation on archaeological artifacts, it must be said that among all the microbotanical remains that have been studied, such as pollen grains and phytoliths, starch grains appear to be the only ones that can be directly correlated to human plant processing

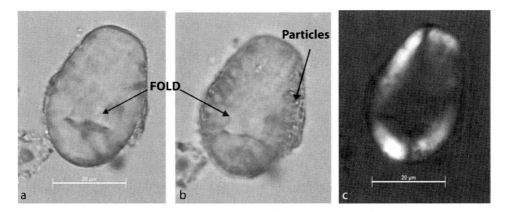

Figure 5.19 Starch grain identified as *Dioscorea* sp. (yam). To the left, the starch showing layering and fissure patterns consistent with those produced by previously studied *Dioscorea* starches (see Pagán-Jiménez 2015). Center, the same starch with a different focus showing particles and a fold, both associated to damage produced by the action of heat in a dry environment (cooking dry masses or dough). To the right, the same starch under cross-polarized light showing a partial Maltese cross and the clear depressed area in the hilum.

Table 5.9 Tuber starches found on two artifacts.

	Artifact #7, used face	Artifact #8, used face	Total Starches	Ubiquity (%)
	(IN-08)	*(IN-09)*		
	Grinding mortar, used concavity	Grinding mortar, used concavity		
Tubers				
Dioscoreaceae (Yam)		1	1	100
Not identified				
Total starches	0	1	1	—
Species richness	0	1	—	—

and use (Holst et al. 2007; Pagán-Jiménez 2009; Pagán-Jiménez et al. 2005; Pearsall et al. 2004; Perry 2004). Starch residues are not "free" in nature such as pollen and phytoliths, although they can be accidentally transported by humans because of contamination with modern industrial or food derivatives usually employed in our daily lives. Thus, pedological and taphonomical processes ascribed to other plant structures such as pollen and phytoliths (e.g., "pollen rain" and phytolith formation and natural dispersion after plant decay) do not apply to starch grains by any circumstance (see Beck and Torrence 2006; Pagán-Jiménez 2007). However, in order to avoid contamination of ancient samples with modern starches that could be accidentally transported by us to the field or to the laboratory, a set of procedures have been established for measuring this potential problem. Used protocols have been designed for avoiding contamination while constant testing of laboratory consumables and reagents have been implemented for measuring potential interference of modern starch grains in ancient artifact samples and residues. For the past 15 years our laboratory has constantly proven to be free of contamination with modern residues, including modern starches.

The limited number of studied samples (N=9) is sufficient to place the identified plants in the chronological and geographical contexts of the artifacts, but not to infer the economic or cultural importance of one plant over others at the intra- or intersite level. For doing so at different contextual, chronological and geographical scales, the study of many other artifacts (such as stone pounding tools, scrapers, etc.) is necessary, or at least the availability of a larger number of samples per site. The low number of starch grains recovered in this study should be related to the previous handling of the artifacts, notably concerning CHU Belle-Plaine. These artifacts were previously washed and this may have potentially removed ancient starches associated with the function of the grinding tools. However, two other possibilities could account for the low number of recovered starches: (a) the sampled sections did not have pores, cracks, or irregular surfaces for allowing the incrustation of ancient starches, or (b) the artifacts were not used primarily for grinding starchy organs. The artifacts studied here are interpreted as grinding tools based on their starch content, though it was not possible to determine their intensity use rate. Food and condiment preparation is inferred as the primary function of the identified taxa within the cultural systems briefly approached here. However, a more accurate contextual interpretation of the possible foodstuffs confectioned on the artifacts could not be allowed this time.

5.4   Ceramic petrography

Gilles Fronteau and Martijn M. van den Bel

The ceramic studies of pre-Columbian series have progressively developed for various areas of the Antilles, allowing a better understanding of the indigenous productions and exchanges in the Caribbean area before the arrival of Europeans (Hofman 1993; Hofman et al. 2007; Venter et al. 2012). The technical links between the various chronocultural entities are always discussed. But ceramic assemblages also seem to be one of the best tools to identify the complex organization and succession of human communities in the Caribbean archipelago.

Petrographic characterizations of pre-Columbian ceramics in the Caribbean and of the surrounding continental areas are now quite common (see Donahue et al. 1990; Fuess 1995; Fuess et al. 1991; O'Conner and Smith 2003; Catlin et al. 2005; Fitzpatrick et al. 2008; Pavia et al. 2013; Shearn 2014). When combined with stylistic analysis, they allow definition of not only the relative chronology of the various ceramic complexes but also their movements and links over time and space. Each new study helps to fill the numerous gaps that still exist (Ting et al. 2016, 2018).

Geochemical analyses of ceramics provide important results in areas dominated by volcanic geology and demonstrate that material supplies were systematically carried out in the immediate vicinity of the place of residence (Walter 1991). Here, we identify variability in temper through petrographic analyses to characterize the materials used in ceramic production and determine the presence or absence of grog temper. We then evaluate whether or not grog can be considered as a probable cultural marker, which may indicate changes between Saladoid and Troumassoid cultures (see Donahue et al. 1990).

Grog is crushed pottery, added to clay matrix as a temper, mainly to limit shrinkage during firing (Rye 1981:116–117; Rice 1987:75). Indeed, because grog is not revealed when using geochemical analyses and is frequently confused with ferruginous fragments or pisoliths under stereomicroscopic, optical petrography remains the best method to highlight the presence of this temper (Whitbread 1986).

Ceramic studies in the French Lesser Antilles, mainly performed with the naked eye, rarely mention the presence of grog temper. Microscopical analysis in this part of the Caribbean generally focuses on the composition of the clay by identifying and quantifying the different mineralogical elements, as done on Martinique for Saladoid ceramics (Gautier 1974; Belhache et al. 1991; Walter 1991, 1992). On Guadeloupe, grog as a temper in pre-Columbian ceramic series has been macroscopically attested for only a few sites, such as Capesterre-Belle-Eau, Basse-Terre (Toledo i Mur et al. 2004:32), Toulourous, or Marie-Galante (Colas et al. 2002:23–24). Despite this apparent absence in the French West Indies, grog has been identified on southern Lesser Antilles islands, such as Grenada (Goodwin 1979:309–312), Cariacou (Fitzpatrick et al. 2008:63), Trinidad (Harris 1972:6–7; Venter et al. 2012), and Barbados (P. Drewett and Harris 1991:182). Concerning the Northern Lesser Antilles, grog has been identified in pre-Columbian ceramic assemblages by Hoffman (1979:38) for the Mill Reef site on Antigua, a finding that was confirmed a decade later by Donahue et al. (1990) for the islands of Barbuda, Montserrat, Anguilla, and St. Martin. A decade later, under the impulse of James Petersen, grog was identified for Troumassoid ceramics from the Muddy Bay site at Antigua, which featured grog and sand (Murphy 1999:234–235), and many post-Saladoid ceramics (N=294) from Anguilla of which the Late Ceramic Age site of Sandy Hill was the most abundant in grog (Crock 2000:228–229, Table 42). However, another series of analysis by Crock does not mention the presence of grog at Anguilla and Salt River (Crock et al. 2008). Macroscopic analysis on 65 sherds from Golden Rock (St. Eustatius) also evidenced grog as a temper (Versteeg and Schinkel 1992, Appendix 1:236). However, these observations have been challenged by Corinne Hofman (1993:195), who proposed that the red particles may not be grog but rather could be pisoliths or small lateritic nodules. In short, this debate can be avoided when microscopical analysis is applied, as recently done by Stienaers et al. (2020). Following this method, we initiate the study of three new ceramic assemblages from the Guadeloupe archipelago.

Donahue et al. (1990:252) proposed two hypotheses concerning the presence of grog when considering Saladoid and post-Saladoid ceramics: (a) grog either represents a local (Troumassoid) innovation or (b) it represents the introduction of a novel technique of pottery manufacturing having Barrancoid influences coming from the South American mainland during the second half of the first millennium CE. The latter hypothesis was elaborated by Petersen et al.:

> More specifically, the earlier Modeled-Incised ceramics can be likely divided into at least two subsets. The first of these is labeled here tentatively as complex IA, much like the distinction between "Barrrancas" Barrancoid and "Los Barrancos" Barrancoid in the Orinoco region (Boomert 2000; Rouse and Cruxent 1963; Sanoja and Vargas 1983). Complex IA generally includes thin, relatively hard, painted/slipped ceramics, which were largely open bowls with flanged rims and thicker, softer, unpainted/slipped typical jars and bowls, with and without flanged rims. Although mostly cauixi tempered, this complex also includes lesser amounts of crushed up rock and "grog" (sherd) temper constituents and the texture of the ceramic paste is almost gritty in some cases. Vessel forms typically include bell-shaped and other bowl and jar forms.
>
> (Petersen et al. 2001:251)

The apparent dichotomy between the Saladoid and post-Saladoid pottery assemblages found some confirmation by additional microscopic analysis executed by Petersen, published in the dissertations of John Crock (2000) and Reginald Murphy (1999), and at the Tutu site (Lundberg et al. 2002, Fig. 6.2). Other LCA sites, such as Salt River (O'Conner and Smith 2001) and, to a lesser extent, Peter Bay (O'Conner and Smith 2003:388), on the Virgin Islands, and Baie Orientale 2, on St. Martin, also feature grog (Bonnissent 2008:157). However, recent petrographic analysis on the Troumassoid site of BK 77 at St. Martin did not reveal grog in the ceramic assemblage as did the analysis performed on LCA ceramics from the island of Nevis (Fronteau in Sellier-Ségard et al. 2020:169–174; Lawrence et al. 2021).

Nonetheless, the interesting proposition made by Donahue et al. is explored here by means of the three LCA sites excavated on Guadeloupe, focusing on the possibility of another wave of immigration from the mainland into the (Lesser) Antilles that ended the long Saladoid ceramic tradition and introduced the Troumassoid, which is, among others, materialized by the presence of grog as a temper material. This hypothesis is in contrast with the actual perception of this turning point in Caribbean archaeology, according to which the Troumassoid series represents a regional and fluid development out of the Late Cedrosan Saladoid subseries under Barrancoid influence (Hofman et al. 2007:252) at least in the southern Lesser Antilles. During the second half of the first millennium CE, important social modifications must have taken place that were materialized by diversification in the ceramic register as well as an increase of archaeological (Troumassoid) sites in the Lesser Antilles (Bright 2011:163; Hofman 2013). Through the analysis of ceramic paste, our perspective is less fluid and actually rather chaotic with respect to the arrival of distinct groups from the mainland into the Lesser Antilles.[2]

5.4.1   *Geological setting*

The Guadeloupe archipelago is located in the northern part of the volcanic arc of the Lesser Antilles, where magmatic products are related to the subduction of the North American plate below the Caribbean plate (Bouysse et al. 1990). The Guadeloupe archipelago is rather unique in the Lesser Antilles because the island shows both the recent active volcanic arc (Basse-Terre) and the old extinct arc (Grande-Terre) (Mattinson et al. 1980; Corsini et al. 2011), separated by a narrow strait or Salt River (see Figures 1.2 and 1.3). Grande-Terre features a long Pliocene-Pleistocene shallow-water carbonate platform with four sedimentary sequences separated by erosional unconformities linked to tectonic events (Munch et al. 2013). The limestone is mainly coralline or rhodolithic, with various ages according to the sedimentary unit concerned. A large part of the western area of Grande-Terre is covered by clay fill-in and vertisols (see Figure 2.3b). Basse-Terre is part of the active volcanic arc of the Lesser Antilles, with six interlocked volcanic complexes. Its bedrock is entirely volcanic, whereas clay-filled and littoral sandy or clayey sediments may be found near the coast (Figure 2.3a, c-d). The Leeward or Capesterre volcanic part of Basse-Terre is part of the Southern Axial Chain with imbricated composite volcanics dating from 1.02–0.435 Ma (Lahitte et al. 2012). More specifically, the local volcanic rocks mainly comprise andesitic lavas and tephras (Dumon et al. 2009).

5.4.2   *Material and methods*

The focus of this study is the recognition of the temper to highlight the main features of the various ceramic fabrics, a first step before the reconstruction of the stage of *chaîne opératoire*, or identification of provenance areas in the Lesser Antilles islands, as described by Ting et al. (2016, 2018). For the methods and description of the modal series of the ceramic assemblages, see Chapter 4.

Petrography is one of the best and quickest tools to identify the main components of ceramic temper (Quinn 2009, 2013; Smith and Herbert 2010). It provides geological background as well as textural characterization to reveal the presence and the variety of specific tempers such as grog, bones, or plant inclusions that are sometimes impossible to identify with other geochemical techniques (Peacock 1970; Whitbread 1986).

As a preliminary study aimed to confirm and discuss the content or the lack of volcanic sand in certain ceramic sherds from Guadeloupe, 24 thin sections were prepared from samples collected from three different sites, in order to characterize the main paste observed during the ceramic analysis. The samples were prepared according to the standard procedures, largely described in Quinn (2013), but without slip-covering them, in order to allow further observations in SEM, cathodoluminescence, or fluorescence microscopy. The observations were realized with optical polarized light microscopes Olympus BX-61, link to a QICAM Fast 1394 Digital Camera, from QImaging, and image analysis softwares Saisam and Areas from Microvision Instruments.

5.4.3 Petrographic analysis

In total, 24 samples have been taken from three ceramic assemblages presented in this book, to wit CHU Belle-Plaine, STEP Goyave, and Parking de Roseau (Table 5.10). All sites are considered LCA habitation sites, more or less intensively, as demonstrated by the density of the postholes and pits per excavated surface (see Chapter 3).

CHU Belle-Plaine (BP)[3]

Five sherds analyzed formed a unique group (Group 1) for which grog is the main temper (Table 5.11). One sample, however (BP-49), shows more vegetal elements and less grog temper, but the other petrographic features of this sample are very close to the others, leading us to consider that these differences may vary within the same group. Only a larger sample will show that a separation for this group is needed.

The clay matrix is very poor in loam and seems quite pure. The detrital inclusions are very scarce (less than 1%) and limited to two types of elements: very small grains (very fine sand and coarse silt) and middle to coarse grains. These elements are mainly angular quartz grains, but a few amphiboles and volcanic rock fragments are present too, only in very low amounts (1:3 per sample). Grog temper, from 50 µm to 2000 µm, is very abundant (more than 20 elements per sample) and the grog itself has frequently a different composition than the including sherd, having sometimes more small opaque material and/or sometimes more silt. Organic inclusions sometimes show preserved vegetal microstructures (plant remains), but numerous grains are made only of opaque black matter featuring microcracks and are hollow in the middle (carbonaceous residues). A few amber to brown elements are probably phosphoric remains; they are mainly observed in the sherds containing less grog and more vegetal inclusions. Some ferruginous elements are present, but without typical pedological morphologies or discriminating features. They probably are pedological mixed clay/iron oxide elements. Interestingly, microcracks never showed up in the grog temper, but were thwarted by grog, whereas the vegetal and carbonaceous inclusions are frequently cracked. Macroporosity is quite abundant, represented

Table 5.10 Samples for petrographic analysis per site.

CHU Belle-Plaine (BP)					*Naked eye*
EC	Feature	Type	SM	Firing	Paste
46	186	Pit	2a	R	Sand + mica
47	186	Pit	6f	R	Végétal + pisoliths
48	186	Pit	8	R	Sand
49	186	Pit	8	R	Végétal + pisoliths
60	200	Pit	iia	R	Grog + some sand
STEP Goyave (SG)					
4	13	Pit	iiia	R	Grog + some sand
15	**55**	Pit	iib	R	Grog + some sand
27	186	Pit	ivb	R	Grog + some sand
51	**62**	Pit	iiic	R	Grog + some sand
79	**5.1**	Post hole	ib	O/R	Sand + feldspaths
Parking de Roseau (PDR)					
5	S5s	Beach	5c	R	Sand + mica
16	S6	Beach	7b	O/R	Sand + pisoliths
17	S6	Beach	1b	O	sand
23	S7s	Beach	1c	R	Végétal + pisoliths
38	S1n	Beach	10b	R	Grog + some sand
62	S5n	Beach	2c	R	Végétal + pisoliths
81	35	Pit	7b	R	Grog + some sand
104	220	Pit	3b	R	Grog + some sand
131	**412**	Pit	2a	O/R	Sand + feldspaths
132	**412**	Pit	2d	R	Sand + feldspaths
148	**156**	Pit	2a	R	Grog + some sand
174	**178**	Pit	3c	O/R	Sand + pisoliths
203	**178**	Pit	7e	R	Grog + some sand
380	**365**	Pit	8a	R	Grog + some sand

Feature numbers in bold have been dated.

by shrinkage cracks but also by small or larger rounded vacuoles, and is probably the result of totally altered organic elements.

STEP Goyave (SG)

Five sherds were petrographically analyzed (Table 5.11). The samples form two groups (Group 1 and 2). In the main one (Group 1, with four samples), grog is the main temper and in the last sherd (SG-79, attributed to Group 2) grog is absent, but numerous inclusions of sand and volcanic rock fragments are present (Figure 5.20).

In Group 1, as in CHU Belle-Plaine site, a clear variability is observed, and sherds are not exactly equals, but altogether they form a quite homogeneous group. The clay matrix is slightly loamy and contains 2–3% to 5–7% of detrital inclusions, corresponding to a matrix of unsorted elements from dominant silt/loam (less than 63 μm) to few sand grains (max.

Table 5.11 Results of the petrographic analysis per site.

CHU Belle-Plaine (BP)

EC	Grog	Sand	Lithoclasts	Lithoclasts	Plant fragments + residues	Iron oxides elements
		(Qz + other min.)	(volcanic lavas)	(volcanic cinders)		
46	+++	+ (incl. 2 Amph)	+ (2 fragments)	0	++	++
47	+++	+	0	0	++	++
48	+++	+ (incl. 1 Amph)	+ (1 fragment)	0	++	++
49	++	+	0	0	+++	+
60	+++	+ (incl. 1 Amph)	0	0	+	+
STEP Goyave (SG)						
4	++	+ (incl. Fk)	0	0	+	+
15	+++	++ (incl. Fk+Pl)	0	0	+	++
27	++	+ (incl. Fk)	0	0	+	+++ (incl. pisol)
51	+	+	0	0	+++	+
79	0	+++ (incl. Fk, Pl, Amph, Px)	++	+	0	+
Parking de Roseau (PDR)						
5	0	+++ (incl. F+Px)	+ (1 fragment)	0	+	+
16	+	+	0	0	+	++
17	0	+	+	+++	0	+
23	0	+	+	+++	0	+
38	+	++	+	0	+	++
62	+++	+	0	0	++	+++ (incl. pisol)
81	0	+++	++	0	0	+
104	+	+	0	0	+	+
131	+	+ (incl. Fk+Px)	+	+	+	+
132	0	+	+	+++	0	+
148	+++	+	+ (1 fragment)	0	++	++
174	++	+	+ (1 fragment)	0	+	++
203	0	+++	+	0	0	+
380	0	+++	++	+	+	++

around 1000 μm in length). The latter elements are mainly angular quartz grains, but two samples show pristine feldspars. Grog temper is very abundant (more than 20 elements per sample), having clear angles varying from 75 μm to 1000 (or, rarely, 2000) μm in dimensions. The fabric of the grog fragments is sometimes made of only one or two types, but sometimes it seems more diversified. Organic inclusions are not abundant; elements showing preserved vegetal microstructures are scarce, except for one sherd where ten elements were observed. We prefer not to consider a specific subgroup for this sample (SG-51) that is rich in organic inclusions, because all other petrographic features are identical to the main group of STEP Goyave grog-tempered sherds. It may be necessary, however, to recognize here a subgroup if further study is carried out showing more samples with abundant plant residues. Ferruginous

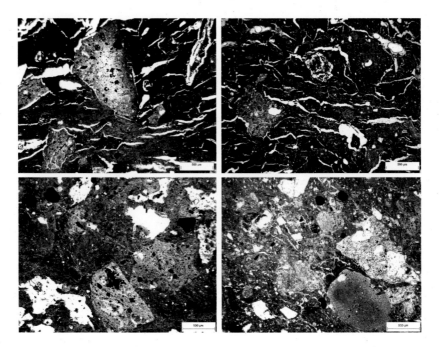

Figure 5.20 Microphotographs of thin sections taken from STEP Goyave (plane-polarized light—PPL); (a–c) grog-tempered sherds, and (d) sandy matrix mainly with volcanic lithoclasts and isolated volcanic minerals.

Photo: G. Fronteau.

elements are present, and small, rounded iron oxidized grains are quite numerous. In one sherd, where these elements are more numerous, three laminated ferruginous pisoliths (length greater than 2000 μm) are observed. The abundance of microcracks varies from one sherd to another, perhaps linked to burial processes. Rounded vacuoles seem to be rare to absent.

The sample SG-79 (which forms Group 2), did not show any grog inclusions and is very different from the main group, with a clear sandy matrix from 20 to 30% of the observed areas, containing no grog or plant inclusions. The sand elements include monomineral crystals (quartz, feldspar, amphiboles, pyroxenes) and rounded volcanic lithoclasts. Two kinds of lithoclasts are observed: volcanic lava fragments, with feldspar microliths and rare phenocrystals, and volcanic cinder fragments, composed of only a fine, crystallized mesostase and amorphous volcanic glass. These silico-detrital inclusions measure mainly around 125–250 μm (fine sand), but a few elements of 500 μm are observed too.

Parking de Roseau (PDR)

Fourteen potsherds were petrographically analyzed from the Parking de Roseau site (Table 5.11). According to the types and amount of nonplastic elements, we divided the samples into four groups: (1) ceramics with abundant grog temper, (2) ceramics with some to rare grog temper, (3) ceramics with volcanic cinders (without any grog) and (4) ceramics with volcanic sands (without any grog). The 14 samples are equally distributed among these four groups. However, Groups 1 and 3 are quite homogeneous, whereas Groups 2 and 4 are more heterogeneous and may include various subgroups of ceramic fabrics (Figure 5.21).

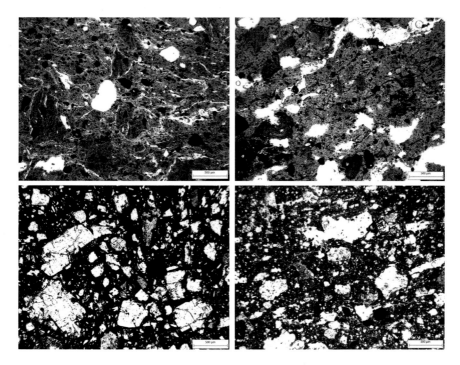

Figure 5.21 Microphotographs of thin sections taken from Parking de Roseau (plane-polarized light—PPL); (a) grog-tempered sherd, (b) matrix-rich sherd with very little temper (sparse grog fragments and volcanic material), (c) sandy matrix with abundant volcanic cinders, and (d) sandy matrix with numerous volcanic lithoclasts and isolated volcanic minerals.

Photo: G. Fronteau.

In Group 1 (three samples), grog is the main temper. The unsorted clay matrix contains very few silt and detrital inclusions, from silt to medium sand, representing less than 5% of the observed areas. The detrital grains are mainly angular quartz grains, but a few heavily altered feldspar and pyroxenes were observed too. Grog temper is dominant (or very abundant), with more than 20 elements per sample, sometimes with straight edges varying in size from 75 μm to 1000 (or, rarely, 2000) μm. The fabric of the grog fragments is made of only one or two paste types, with a fine clay matrix, few inclusions, or only a few quartz grains and grog. Interestingly, grog fragments themselves also include grog. Sometimes it seems more diversified, because amounts of loam and sand vary from one grog fragment to another. It must be noted here that we never observed grog made of ceramics fragments linked to Groups 3 and 4. Organic inclusions are rare and correspond to carbonaceous elements without microstructural features; some of them are only partly preserved or are preserved as vacuolar porosities. Ferruginous elements are present, showing themselves as small, rounded iron oxidized grains or laminated pisoliths.

In Group 2 (four samples), grog is also present but in lesser quantities. There are only about five grog fragments by thin section and no grog temper longer than 500 μm. In Group 2, one sample (PDR-38) shows some differences from the other grog sherds: the grog is very dark, with a lot of fragments less than 250 μm and no fragments longer than 500 μm. In Group 2, other aplastic inclusions are not well represented, however; less than 5% of the observed areas were seen under the microscope. These rare inclusions are clearly unsorted particles corresponding to isolated, weathered volcanic minerals such as quartz, few pla-gioclases, and k-feldspar, very few altered pyroxenes, and volcanic lithoclasts, plants, or ferruginous elements. In these sherds, cracks are abundant to very abundant.

In Group 3 (four samples), grog is totally absent, and the clay is mixed with unsorted vol-canic fragments made of isolated sub- to automorphous small feldspar crystals 100–200 µm long (euhedral grains) and subrounded silicate rock fragments (anhedral grains) with very small feldspar crystals in a few to noncrystallized mesostase. These inclusions, measuring from 50 µm to 2000 µm, are interpreted as volcanic cinders. They represent 5–15% of the observed surfaces and sometimes even 25–30% in a few limited areas. Others fragments of volcanic lavas—lithoclasts with phenocrystals or isolated minerals other than feldspars—are very rare or absent in Group 3. Ferruginous elements and plant remains are also rare to absent.

In Group 4 (three samples), too, grog is totally absent and the volcanic sandy elements represent the main aplastic component (25–30% of the observed surfaces). Unlike the previous group, the inclusions do not correspond to cinders but to automorphic crystals. For two of the three samples, inclusions seem quite well sorted; length varies from 250 to 500 µm (medium-grained sand), with very few fine sands and loam/silt grains. In the last sherd, however, sand inclusions seem to be less sorted, and contain more weathered minerals. The proportion of the various microlithic and porphiric volcanic rocks varies a little from one sample to another, but because of the rather small number of studied sherds, we choose to put them all in a same group. The mineralogy of lavas observed is coherent with the petrography of the Madeleine Soufrière volcano described by others (Lefevre and Cocusse 1985), with feldspar (mainly plagioclases, few k-feldspar), olivine (largely altered in iddingsite) and pyroxene (probably augite). Feldspars are more abun-dant minerals, followed by pyroxenes. Plant fragments and ferruginous elements are rare.

5.4.4   *Comparison of the three sites*

The results of the thin sections show that ceramics from these sites include various fabrics. The studied sherds reveal various quantities of grog (Group 1 and 2) as well as sherds with-out grog of which the main aplastic inclusions are volcanic cinders (Group 3), but mainly with volcanic sands (Group 4). Plant inclusions are rare and most often observed at the same time as soil elements (ferruginous pisoliths) (Table 5.12). This ferruginous nodules and plant remains are believed to be extracted together with the raw clay, as well as the smallest quartz grains from the loam granulometry. Thus, the latter inclusions belong to the clay source and are not voluntarily added by the potter. The fact that these elements were still part of the fired vessel is merely due to a quick cleaning of the raw clay material without an intensive process of purification. However, when comparing the three sites, some identified elements may also reflect different clay and temper sources or supply strategies. The plant remains and pedological features seem to be linked to a fine matrix and to sourcing in or near coastal marshes, whereas volcanic sands could be associated with the addition of lithic fragments form the regolith.

When comparing the ceramic repertoire and the presence of the three main aplastics inclu-sions (Figure 5.22), two-thirds of the forms are tempered with grog, whereas the last third did not contain grog at all. All slipped-wares (N=6) are grog-tempered, they correspond to small-to-medium open straight-walled (tronconic-shaped) bowls (N=4) and one bell-shaped vessel with pierced notches on the careen. The non-grog-tempered series reveal only mod-eled appendices materialized by an effigy vessel with small, decorated handles, and another small bowl with handles.

In order to define potential links between the compositions of ceramics and cultural transitions or exchanges, it is important to identify the most significant vessel forms (see chapters 2 and 4). A typical but important vessel is the red-slipped bell-shaped vessel (SG-27) found at STEP Goyave, which shows clear Saladoid attributes. It suggests an earlier occupation at this site, which is confirmed by the oldest radiocarbon date, found in a round pit (F 112) located a few meters to the north of pit F 186 in which this vessel was found. Numerous outward thickened rims of SG-27, generally attributed to the Saladoid series (SG-SM IVc), were found in various pits of which F 174 was dated slightly prior to cal 1000 CE. This date can be considered as the limit of the (Late) Saladoid series on Guadeloupe and the northern Lesser Antilles. It is noteworthy that this particular form has no outward thickened rim, common for (Late) Saladoid bell-shaped vessels, which might suggest a local or early Troumassoid adaptation to this vessel type, as observed at the Anse à la Gourde site (Pater and Teekens 2004, Fig. 6.4). The fact this stylistically earlier vessel has a grog temper is indeed of first importance, because it establishes a link between the older Saladoid and later Troumassoid ceramics in the use of grog temper.

Another highly diagnostic element for the Mamoran Troumassoid subseries is grooved incisions, or *cannelures*, either wide linear parallel or complex curvilinear designs, and, in the case for the studied sites, often in combination with red slip and, more importantly, with folded lips towards the interior (BP-SM 3a; SC-SM IVa; PDR-SM 10b: see Figure 4.4). The vessel PDR-38 represents such design as clearly identified in two dated pits (F 178 and F 222) at Parking de Roseau, both with a similar calibrated date of about cal 1200 CE. The petrographic analysis of this sample places it in Group 2 of the ceramics of this site, revealing small quantities of grog mixed with a loamy clay. The vessel BP-47, a small bowl with convex profile, may also be indicative because it features grooved linear incisions on the outside and red slipping on the inside, and clearly evokes Mamoran Troumassoid characteristics. The petrographic analysis of this sample revealed a heavy charge of grog in its paste.

The very common larger bowls (BP-SM 6f and 8; SC-SM IIIa; PDR-SM 4a and SM 9a) are represented by convex or straight rims with thinned lips, often featuring some scratching, predominantly applied on the outside (BP-48, PDR-131, and PDR 148). At Parking de Roseau, ten specimens were found in dated pit F 178, one in dated pit F 174, and one in dated pit F 222, suggesting a calibrated date around cal 1200 CE, which falls within the range of the CHU Belle-Plaine from where the analyzed fragment was taken. In southeastern Martinique, these recipients were observed at the Troumassoid sites of À-Tout-Risque, Paquemar, and notably Macabou (Allaire 1977, Figs. 38–43), dated between cal 1000–1300 CE (ibid.: 319; Grouard et al. 2016).

Another interesting category is represented by small to medium-sized bowls (SG-4, SG-15, and SG-51; PDR-104 and PDR 174) and large platters (PDR-62) with rectilinear profiles. These vessels have rectilinear incisions applied to the interior to mark the (reflecting) rim or applied upon the thickened rim. Half of the samples have red slipping on the inside. Although not sampled for CHU Belle-Plaine, these vessels are certainly present at this site, as represented by BP-SM 3 (N=11) of which one element can be attributed to the previously mentioned folded lip vessels. Small to medium-sized bowls are very popular at Parking de Roseau (PDR-SM 2b-c and 3b-c), but far less popular at STEP Goyave, which is probably due to the total ceramic sample size. Without doubt, they can be attributed to the Mamoran Troumassoid subseries (Rouse and Morse 1999:39–43). The petrographic analysis shows that these recipients are predominantly grog-tempered, except for SG-79, which is tempered with an abundant quantity of volcanic sand.

Table 5.12 Combination of Tables 5.10 and 5.11. Feature numbers in bold have been radiocarbon dated.

EC	Feature	Type	SM	Firing	Naked eye Paste	Groups	Group intr.	Grog	Sand (Qz + other min.)	Lithoclasts (volcanic lavas)	Lithoclasts (volcanic cinders)	Plant fragments + residues	Iron oxides
CHU Belle-Plaine (BP)													
46	186	Pit	2a	R	Sand + mica	1a	1	+++	+ (incl. 2 Amph)	+ (2 fragments)	0	++	++
47	186	Pit	6f	R	Végétal + pisoliths	1a	1	+++	+	0	0	++	++
48	186	Pit	8	R	sand	1a	1	+++	+ (incl. 1 Amph)	+ (1 fragment)	0	++	++
49	186	Pit	8	R	Végétal + pisoliths	1a	1	++	+	0	0	+++	+
60	200	Pit	iia	R	Grog + some sand	1	1	+++	+ (incl. 1 Amph)	0	0	+	+
STEP Goyave (SG)													
4	13	Pit	iiia	R	Grog + some sand	1	1	++	+ (incl. Fk)	0	0	+	+
15	**55**	Pit	iib	R	Grog + some sand	1b	1	+++	++ (incl. Fk+Pl)	0	0	+	++
27	186	Pit	ivb	R	Grog + some sand	1c	1	++	+ (incl. Fk)	0	0	+	+++ (incl. pisol)
51	**62**	Pit	iiic	R	Grog + some sand	1a	1	+	+	0	0	+++	+
79	**5.1**	Post	ib	O/R	Sand + feldspaths	2	2	0	+++ (incl. Fk, Pl, Amph, Px)	++	+	0	+

Parking de Roseau (PDR)

5	S5s	Beach	5c	R	Sand + mica	2	4	0	+++ (incl. F+Px)	+ (1 fragment)	0	+	+
16	S6	Beach	7b	O/R	Sand + pisoliths	1	2	+	+	0	0	+	++
17	S6	Beach	1b	O	sand	3	3	0	+	+	+++	0	+
23	S7s	Beach	1c	R	Végétal + pisoliths	3	3	0	+	+	+++	0	+
38	S1n	Beach	10b	R	Grog + some sand	1b	2	+	++	+	0	+	++
62	S5n	Beach	2c	R	Végétal + pisoliths	1c	1	+++	+	0	0	++	+++ (incl. pisol)
81	35	Pit	7b	R	Grog + some sand	2	2	0	+++	++	0	0	+
104	220	Pit	3b	R	Grog + some sand	1	3	+	+	0	0	+	+
131	**412**	Pit	2a	O/R	Sand + feldspaths	1	2	+	+ (incl. Fk+Px)	+	+	+	+
132	**412**	Pit	2d	R	Sand + feldspaths	3	3	0	+	+	+++	0	+
148	**156**	Pit	2a	R	Grog + some sand	1a	1	+++	+	+ (1 fragment)	0	++	++
174	**178**	Pit	3c	O/R	Sand + pisoliths	1	1	++	+	+ (1 fragment)	0	+	++
203	**178**	Pit	7e	R	Grog + some sand	2	4	0	+++	+	0	0	+
380	**365**	Pit	8a	R	Grog + some sand	2	4	0	+++	++	+	+	++

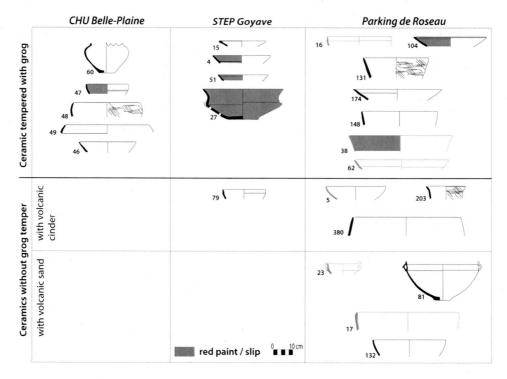

Figure 5.22 Subdivisions of vessels according to paste types.

Photo: G. Fronteau.

Small bowls with "banded" or flexed rims are rather popular at all sites (BP-SM 6c-e; SC-SM IIc and IIIb; PR-SM 1c and 2c-d) but our analyzed specimens (SG-79 and PDR-23), although slightly different regarding their size, do not contain grog at all. These specimens were found at the beach zone of Roseau and may be attributed to later series such as Cayo. Interestingly, similar bowls (PDR-5 and 132) with beveled lips do not contain grog; of these, one was found at the beach and the other in the deeper feel of dated pit F 412.

Finally, there are restricted (large) vessels, which are rather rare for these Troumassoid series (BP-SM 7a, 8; SC-SM V and VIa; PDR-SM 8 and 9). In our petrographic analysis, they are represented by one grog-rich sample (BP-49) and one with volcanic sand temper (PDR-380).

Despite the fact that these vessels are not very common, they are clearly part of the Troumassoid output, considering other specimens found in dated pits.

5.4.5   *Discussion*

Donahue et al. (1990:252) proposed two hypotheses concerning the presence of grog when considering Saladoid and post-Saladoid ceramic series: (a) grog either represents a local (Troumassoid) innovation or (b) it represents the influence of Barrancoid practices, coming from the South American mainland, mainly during the midst of the first millennium CE. The latter hypothesis (b) was elaborated by Petersen et al. (2001:251), who observed that the earlier Modeled-Incised Barrancoid ceramics were largely open bowls with flanged rims and thicker, softer, unpainted slipped typical jars and bowls, with and without flanged rims. These vessel forms are mostly caraipé (burnt tree bark of the *Licania* sp.) tempered but also include lesser amounts of crushed up rock and grog (sherd) temper.

The apparent dichotomy between the Saladoid and post-Saladoid series found some confirmation through additional microscopic analysis executed by Petersen, which has been published in the dissertations by Crock (2000) and Murphy (1999). Other LCA sites, such as Salt River (O'Conner and Smith 2001) and, to a lesser extent, Peter Bay (O'Conner and Smith 2003:388), on the Virgin Islands, as well as the Baie Orientale 2 site, on St. Martin, feature grog (Bonnissent 2008:157).

The interesting proposition made by Donahue et al. (1990) needs further exploration by means of the three LCA sites excavated on Guadeloupe, focusing on the possibility of another wave of immigration from the mainland into the (Lesser) Antilles that ended the long Saladoid ceramic tradition and introduced the Troumassoid, which is, among others, materialized by the presence of grog as a temper. This hypothesis is in contrast with other interpretations of this turning point in Caribbean archaeology in which the Troumassoid series represents a regional and fluid development out of the late Cedrosan Saladoid series under Barrancoid influences (Hofman et al. 2007:252) or, at least, for the southern Lesser Antilles. During the second half of the first millennium CE, important social modifications must have taken place that are materialized by diversification in the ceramic register as well as an increase in population evidenced by an increase of Troumassoid archaeological sites in the Lesser Antilles (Bright 2011:163; Hofman 2013). Through the analysis of paste, our perspective is less fluid and rather suggests a more chaotic period of development by means of the arrival of distinct groups from the mainland into the Lesser Antilles.

Our analysis of 24 samples, taken from three different contemporary sites, shows that grog temper is present at all sites. Prior to this work, grog as a temper was hardly known and/ or not well identified for pre-Columbian ceramic assemblages on Guadeloupe. Our petrographic analysis also showed that all samples contained a small amount of quartz grains, and sometimes volcanic sands or cinders, pedological iron oxide particles in various quantities. Plant residues are also frequent, but never in dominant quantities. Therefore, it is difficult to tell whether this matter was intentionally added to the raw clay or if it was already present in the natural clay. However, the high quantities of organic matter in the CHU Belle-Plaine samples may suggest it was added to the clay by potters at this site.

The near absence of lithoclasts for the samples from STEP Goyave and CHU Belle-Plaine is interesting, since both sites are located on volcanic soils, suggesting that clay was taken elsewhere, perhaps in coastal marshes or areas covered with thick clayey soils. In the case of CHU Belle-Plaine, the clay source should reveal amphiboles.

Grog as a temper is recorded as one temper mode, probably used, according to various *chaînes opératoires*, alongside other practices that preferred either fine clays with little amount of aplastic inclusions or clays enriched with volcanic sands or cinders. Widely accepted among ceramic specialists, the grog presence is principally related to the fact that it resists thermal shocks better (Rye 1981:116–117; Rice 1987:75). At CHU Belle-Plaine, despite the fact that the majority was taken from one pit, it has been observed in various vessel shapes. The samples from STEP Goyave were taken from different pits providing different vessel shapes and showing an assemblage dominated by grog as a temper. Parking de Roseau, pertaining to a larger sample, shows more variety in paste fabrics where grog and sand represent both halves of the analyzed collection.

Considering the different vessel shapes, decoration modes, and temper, as presented in Figure 5.22, in combination with the radiocarbon dates and cultural affiliation of this collection—the bell-shaped vessel (SG-27) must be attributed to the Late Saladoid series and not, like all the others, to the Troumassoid series. We observe that all red slipped elements are tempered with grog. Indeed, STEP Goyave is a multicomponent site, and its earlier Saladoid occupation is attested for by many other Saladoid ceramic traits, notwithstanding that the majority of the ceramic assemblage as well as the radiocarbon dates adhere to the Troumassoid series.

The presence of grog in the "Barrancoid-influenced" Cedrosan Saladoid subseries in the midst of the first millennium CE needs further attention here as it draws upon *Terra firma* influences. Despite the fact that Petersen et al. (2001) pointed towards small amounts of grog for these series, Boomert (2000:119, 204) does not agree with this statement for the Barrancoid series for Venezuela. However, he does attribute grog to other assemblages, such as the ones found at Los Cedros and Palo Seco on Trinidad (ibid.:132, 155). In fact, grog as a temper appears indeed to be rare in pre-Columbian Venezuelan sites as it only occurs at LCA sites in the Llanos and in two Ronquinan groups of the Middle Orinoco as defined by Howard in the 1940s (Gassón 2002:257, 274; Roosevelt 1980). But next to the mouth of the Orinoco River, grog is abundant among nearly all LCA ceramic complexes (cal 900–1500 CE) along the coast of the Guianas from Guyana in the west to Marajó Island (Brazil) in the east (Evans and Meggers 1960; Boomert 1980; Rostain 1995; van den Bel 2015; Saldanha 2016; Roosevelt 1991; Schaan 2004; Meggers and Evans 1957). The presence of grog has been attested for only by the naked eye and confirmed by microscopic analysis only for Cayenne Island (van den Bel et al. 2014). Nevertheless, we think that the Guianas represent an important hearth for the origins of grog in the Lesser Antilles, passing through the mouth of the Orinoco or going directly to the islands, as did the Kalinago in the 16th century (see Boomert 1986).

If grog temper is considered an innovation coming from the mainland, then, by consequence, previous ceramic series, such as the Cedrosan Saladoid subseries, are without grog. Since we have not personally analyzed such earlier assemblages (this should be future research) we can only rely on the literature, mainly represented by observations taken by the naked eye. Donahue et al. (1990:242, Table IV) showed that samples taken from Saladoid sites, such as Trants, on Montserrat, or Sufferer's, on Barbuda, were indeed devoid of grog. It is said about Cedrosan Saladoid ceramics found on the inner arc of the Lesser Antilles that on the basis of a low magnification microscope, temper constituents generally include "volcanic tuff, quartz, magnetite, feldspar, and hornblende/tourmaline, among others" (Petersen and Watters 1995:134). For Guadeloupe, recent macroscopic data on Cedrosan and Barrancoid-influenced Saladoid pastes has been provided by a small number of archaeological excavations at Bisdary (Gourbeyre, Basse-Terre) (Hildebrand in Romon et al. 2006: 80; but relying on Chancerel in Etrich et al. 2003:73–108) and at Grand Carbet (Capesterre-Belle-Eau, Basse-Terre) (Chancerel in Toledo i Mur 2004:32) for which grog was not attested.

5.4.6 Conclusion

The Guadeloupean test case, explored in this study, showed the abundance of grog-tempered ceramics for the Troumassoid series, and notably the Mamoran subseries. And even if we underline that future microscopical analysis is needed for both Saladoid and Troumassoid sites on various islands in order to pinpoint the inception data and place of arrival of grog-tempered ceramics in the Lesser Antillean arch, we can already confirm part of the Donahue et al. (1990) hypothesis about the importance of grog as a marker for important changes in pre-Columbian ceramic production in the Lesser Antilles.

The STEP Goyave site showed that Late Saladoid bell-shaped vessels also contained grog, suggesting a possible pre-Troumassoid inception at Guadeloupe or perhaps an innovation signaling the end of the Saladoid era, just before cal 900 CE. It is still difficult to specify if it is related to a true Troumassoid migration from the mainland around this date, or to a lingering Barrancoid influence among the Late Saladoid population of the Windward Islands. However, it appears once more evident that grog marks cultural changes in the first millennium CE; hence, now we may also add Guadeloupe to the list of Caribbean islands affected by this change.

Notes

1   Also note the starch samples analyzed by Ruth Dickau in the previous chapter.
2   This contribution benefited from useful remarks made by John Crock for which we would like to thank him. It is also a slightly extended version of a paper called *Anthropogenic Temper* by the same authors and published in the BSGF – Earth Sciences Bulletin (2021).
3   In order to separate the EC numbers per site, the site initials have replaced them. These initials have also been added to the modal series for this chapter.

6 Synthesis

The Troumassoid Turning Point: local development or introduction of new houses, subsistence patterns, and ceramics?

Martijn M. van den Bel, Sebastiaan Knippenberg, Sandrine Grouard, Thomas Romon, Noémie Tomadini, and Nathalie Serrand

This synthetic chapter tries to redefine the transition from Late Saladoid to Troumassoid on Guadeloupe at the end of the first millennium CE—what we have called in our subtitle *The Troumassoid Turning Point*. In other words, what differences and similarities between the Late Saladoid and Troumassoid ceramic series on Guadeloupe can point out what happened on this island around cal 900–1000 CE that generally makes up for the division between the Early and the Late Ceramic Age? We certainly do not want to attempt a theoretical analysis of labels and boxes, but we want to focus on the data we have produced in order to compare the data sets. Our results for the Troumassoid sites can be reduced to three topics or themes for comparison, namely: (1) habitation (house plans, pits, and burials); (2) material culture (ceramic and lithic material), and (3) subsistence (environmental conditions and food consumption). However, not all data on these topics or elements are available for the preceding Late Saladoid sites on Guadeloupe, which will certainly hamper this analysis. If necessary, we shall find comparable data on other islands than Guadeloupe and, in this manner, stretch our comparison or questionnaire to a larger area and review the cultural chronology at the end.

The sites presented here have many contemporaneous sites. Only a few have been excavated extensively, but these are also considered multicomponent sites, such as the most recent occupations of Bisdary, Anse à la Gourde, Stade José Bade, and Morel (see Table 1.4). Except for Bisdary and CHU Belle-Plaine, all sites are on the coast and have access to water, whether rivers, lagoons, or the beach, providing access to terrestrial and marine resources.

6.1 Habitation: house plans, pits, and burials

The sites are generally characterized by rather flat pieces of land on which the houses and gardens were constructed and planted. Common ground or (central) plazas have not been detected, probably because of the small excavated surfaces or due to their absence. However, spaces between house locations (HL) are clearly visible at the sites discussed, delimiting a first apprehension of village organization and burials. The empty spaces between the HLs at La Pointe de Grande Anse and STEP Goyave are evident examples. The area with stake alignments in between the northern and southern zones at CHU Belle-Plaine also reveals a boundary, perhaps one represented by a garden or—further research is needed here—rice rat

DOI: 10.4324/9781003181651-6

or agouti pens (further discussion follows). The houses at Parking de Roseau are also clearly separated and might have functioned simultaneously.

We observe two types of house construction. Type 1 is based on a firm central construction with deep postholes, as witnessed at La Pointe de Grande Anse and STEP Goyave, and Type 2 is based on much smaller postholes for the entire construction, as found at CHU Belle-Plaine and Parking de Roseau. Presumably this means a lighter construction for the latter case, but the surfaces appear similar in size. Furthermore, we do not know with certainty whether these two types are contemporaneous, although the results of our radiocarbon measurements suggest that the Type 1 constructions with large postholes can be attributed to the (Late) Saladoid habitations and the buildings with smaller postholes to the later Troumassoid occupations. However, it must be born in mind that the Type 1 buildings may represent communal structures and might be found among contemporaneous Type 2 buildings. Suppositions like these can be tested only by opening up larger excavation areas.

La Pointe de Grande Anse represents a particular case, as pointed out already in a paper by van den Bel and Romon (2010). There is a discrepancy of about 400 years between the radiocarbon dates taken from the postholes and those from the burials in the same house. To put it in other words: the burials found in House Location 1 (HL 1) have been dated to the 11th century CE, whereas the posts of the building in which the burials were found are dated to the late seventh century CE; and for HL 2 the burials were dated to the 14th century and the posts to the tenth century (see Figure 3.4; Table 1.3). The so-called old-wood effect may explain these differences if the builders used aged trees and our samples came from the interior of a trunk—which is something we do not know. So, our question is: What circumstance would permit us to suggest that the postholes are dated much older than the burials? Such a question may somehow be rather awkward because the house plans clearly suggest contemporaneity between them and the burials: the burials are neatly located in a section of the house. It is furthermore also common knowledge that there is a customary relationship between burials and house plans that is largely attested for in the Lesser Antilles (see Curet and Oliver 1998), and on Guadeloupe too, notably the site of Anse à la Gourde. Anse à la Gourde also yielded much older dates for postholes than burials (Bright 2003:31; Delpuech et al. 2001b; Hofman and Hoogland 2004:51; Morsink 2006:49).

This problem has partly been solved by Christophe Tardy's identification of the tree species that was used for the charred wooden post F 935 in House Location 2, which was radiocarbon dated 1245 ± 30 BP (KIA-36677). According to Tardy, the charcoal sample (100 microns) was incompletely burned, revealing a vitrified aspect. The sample also showed many isolated or accolated veins, one parenchyma circumvascular and one parenchyma with large, irregular sinuous bands. Furthermore, the punctuations represented ornamentations that resemble a legume. All of these anatomical characteristics suggest that the samples can be attributed to the *Cynometra/Hymenea* genus, formerly assumed to belong to the Caesalpinideae but at present to the Fabaceae family. This tentative identification corresponds to the vernacular name of the West Indian locust tree, or courbaril, on Guadeloupe. Different varieties are grouped under this generic name in the Antilles, representing a large tree unmistakably suitable for construction (see Longwood 1971:24), but actually better known for its gums, or *copal*.

A few criteria must now be taken into account: a) the oldest courbaril trees may reach just over 300 years (see Locosselli 2017) and it is therefore possible that a very old courbaril tree has been used as a post in both house locations, knowing that the sample had to be taken from the inside of the tree; b) a locust trunk is very thick and certainly needs to be worked into suitable posts for house construction and, finally, c) what age of trees did pre-Columbian

Guadeloupeans prefer? The answer to the third question is unknown, but chopping down very old trees, perhaps with deteriorated qualities, may seem rather unlikely. However, to obtain a notion of how such a choice is made, one must refer to ethnographic examples. For instance, aged round wood more than 20 cm in diameter is not cut down by the modern Palikur of the eastern Guianas for use as building material in permanent constructions (Ogeron et al. 2018:18). Although the choice of round wood is probably related to the environment and cultural tradition, the fact that the discrepancy is present at both house locations is highly remarkable.

It may seem that this fact is rather extraordinary, but this appears not to be the case. The site of Anse à la Gourde, on Grande-Terre, showed similar discrepancies as its burials were radiocarbon dated between 1025 and 1515 CE, whereas the postholes surrounding these burials were radiocarbon dated between cal 600 and 800 CE (Delpuech et al. 2001b:65; Bright 2003:34). Although Late Saladoid ceramics were also present at Anse à la Gourde—as is the case at La Pointe de Grande Anse—the myriad of features did not render a clear correlation between the burials and a house plan: the radiocarbon dates of the postholes are clearly older than those of the burials. Although further sites have not shown this difference, it should be kept in mind that extensive excavations with house plans and burials remain exceptional on Guadeloupe and in the Lesser Antilles in general.

Nonetheless, this apparent discrepancy at both sites led us to think that each of the abandoned or former houses at these prehistoric villages represented a burial house, or a "House of the Dead," as this phenomenon was called by Hofman and Hoogland (2013). These grouped burials are in contrast with those from Saladoid times, which occur more isolated or dispersed, sometimes inside and outside a house location as well as in midden areas, and may also reveal skeletons in stretched position, such as have been found at St. Eustatius (Golden Rock), St. Martin (Hope Estate) and Barbados (Port St. Charles and Goddards). For this reason, we may suggest that the burial modes changed from Saladoid to Troumassoid times from scattered burials across the habitation site towards concentrated burials or perhaps cemeteries in (abandoned) villages, creating a place of rendez-vous and possibly ancestor worship. However, further research is needed to confirm this hypothesis.

This picture cannot be deduced for CHU Belle-Plaine despite its contemporaneity. It reveals diversity as it shows only two burials, suggesting a much smaller and perhaps different type of (habitation) site when compared to the other coastal sites. However, within the framework of the previously sketched idea, this twin burial may be considered as the couple that once occupied the house locations at CHU Belle-Plaine.

STEP Goyave is rather problematic, as this site did not yield any bone material at all due to the local nature of the volcanic subsoil, but the presence of shallow oval pits reveals the presence of burials. This is probably also the case at Parking de Roseau, but the latter site yielded small rectangular pits and not ovoid or round ones as is usually the case. One such pit, at Parking de Roseau, revealed a beautiful complete vessel placed upside-down, possibly covering a bundle of bones if it were in fact a burial pit. In addition, the buried vessel is a unique specimen at the site and may represent an object of exchange with populations from the mainland. When considering its shape and decoration modes, it may be affiliated with the Cayo ceramics as well as the notched bowls, and it evokes a later, perhaps historic, occupation of the Roseau site covering the first encounters with the Europeans in the 16th and 17th centuries, as confirmed by the imported wares and glass beads.

Compared to sites such as Anse à la Gourde, Capesterre, or even Golden Rock, the La Pointe de Grande Anse and STEP Goyave buildings resemble their house plans according to posthole types and dimensions, but differ from the smaller (about 30–40 m²), round, and heavily stacked Late Ceramic Age (LCA) houses in the Virgin Islands (Righter 2002b) or the Dominican

Republic (Samson 2010, 2013). Indeed, the LCA buildings from CHU Belle-Plaine and Parking de Roseau do not resemble them either (i.e., no post stacking, oblong, and somewhat larger surfaces). Consequently, it is highly probable that this reflects a cultural difference between the Lesser Antilles and the Greater Antilles, although it should be noted that the smaller stacked posts delimiting the house walls may have disappeared in the plowing zone during colonial times. Finally, we must not forget that houses on stilts remain a true possibility for pre-Columbian housing. One of the rare mentions of house construction in the Lesser Antilles supports this idea and is given for a Kalinago village, despite a rather ambiguous description:

> It is necessary to know that all their huts are supported by stilts taller than the size of a man which they call *ouaccabou*, on which ends they rest sticks spanning across the house, placed closely to each other, and there they put their furniture such as reed boxes, bows, arrows and other stuff, and to get up there they do not use any stairs but the force of their arms and legs, clinging on to the stilts in the same manner as a monkey does, and they are rather agile in doing so, males and females.[1]

Other important features at the sites discussed are the large circular pits, which were found in small concentrations of three to five. The majority of these pit concentrations were paired or functioned with a house location, suggesting a direct link between the building and the pits and thus reflecting a daily activity. It is presumed that these pits had a specific function, but a few among them ended up as waste pits (also containing some faunal remains and shells), providing layers with contemporaneous vessel shapes and reliable radiocarbon dates. They were rather deep pits, most often with straight walls and flat or slightly convex bottoms yielding a cylindrical shape. Many of these pits featured only two layers and contained hardly any artifacts, and sometimes a few large boulders at the bottom. Steroid analysis by Jago Birk shows that they were not used as latrines. The micromorphological research by Cammas and Brancier reveals that they were left open and filled up quickly with colluvial material and sediment from the village surface. The phytoliths identified in this colluvial material did not yield any cultigens but remind us that the site of Roseau was surrounded by bamboo and grasses, whereas Belle-Plaine, by contrast, was amid trees and high bushes. Unfortunately, the primary function of the circular pits remains unclear, but it can be suggested that they may have been used to stock various foodstuffs in worked or unworked state, such as maize cobs and tubers, but also for fermenting nuts and/or tubers.

6.2 Material culture: ceramics and lithics

The most abundant material finds certainly encompass artifacts made of stone and ceramics. The majority of these artifacts were found in features such as pits, burials, or postholes as no surface collecting was executed except for the few beach trenches at Parking de Roseau. The pottery study presented here shows a first register of vessel shapes for the Troumassoid ceramic series of the Guadeloupean archipelago. The lithic study shows the predominance of food-processing tools and that the availability of ceremonial objects was more uneven in the Troumassoid period.

Ceramics

The bulk of the ceramics presented can be attributed to the Troumassoid series of the northern Lesser Antilles. The ceramic study furnishes a number of vessel shapes such as platters, large and small bowls, trays, cups, and legged griddles, which are all contemporaneous vessel shapes and roughly dated to the first quarter of the second millennium, cal 1000–1300 CE. Red slip is the major decoration mode, followed by some incision, grooving, and scratching. Highly recognizable vessels are the red-slipped (grooved) necked pots with a lip bent towards the interior, which can be found on St. Martin too (see van den Bel in Sellier-Ségard et al. 2020). Next to these marvelous pots we also refer to simple convex and tronconical bowls some with, but mostly without, red paint on the interior. Their much larger counterparts can be found as very large tronconical pots or very large bowls or platters, sometimes with carinations. Crudely or quickly finished large bowls with similarly large bases are also characteristic. Legged griddles, probably an introduced feature deriving from the southern Lesser Antilles, were new elements but do not represent the dominant type on Guadeloupe.

Interestingly, the paste of this Troumassoid ceramic repertoire includes volcanic sand, but it has also been enriched with fine, probably sieved, grog. This feature is difficult to ascertain without a microscope and has not been recognized hitherto in Troumassoid series from the Lesser Antilles except for the mere presence of grog by Donahue et al. (1990) in the Leeward Islands. It is considered here that the presence of grog may represent a cultural marker for the LCA on Guadeloupe and, consequently, the northern Lesser Antilles and notably the Troumassoid series of Guadeloupe and perhaps the Troumassoid series in general. The origin of this particular temper mode remains unknown, but it may be an innovation coming from *Terra firma* and possibly from as far as the mouth of the Amazon River where grog temper is common from the beginnings of the first millennium CE onwards (Schaan 2004).

Apart from a few Saladoid sherds, notably at STEP Goyave, we also discovered more recent material showing Ostionoid or Taíno influences from the north and possible Suazoid tendencies from the south. CHU Belle-Plaine and Parking de Roseau yielded pottery with some Ostionoid influences, which can also be translated as Suazoid vessel shapes. Apparently, both appeared on Guadeloupe within this timeframe, but this subject certainly needs further investigation.

Parking de Roseau also presents some evidence of Cayo ware and perhaps long-distance trade with the mainland when considering the vessel showing coffee bean eyes deposited into a rectangular (funerary) pit. Both CHU Belle-Plaine and Parking de Roseau are considered entirely Troumassoid and perhaps already Suazoid by the end of the occupation, but further comparative material is needed to draw more secure conclusions (for Roseau, see also Bochaton et al. 2021). Thus, all these assumptions suggest influences upon the Troumassoid ceramic register of Guadeloupe, which can be situated towards the end of the prime time span of cal 900 to 1300 CE.

In addition to these influences we also wish to point out the differences between the Guadeloupean Troumassoid and Late Saladoid assemblages (cal 600–900 CE). For this matter, we first need to describe the (Late) Saladoid series of Guadeloupe. We note that sites of this series persist nearly to the end of the first millennium CE on Guadeloupe, including Morel III (Clerc 1968, 1970), Anse à la Gourde (Delpuech et al. 2001b), Tourlourous (Colas et al. 2002; Serrand et al. 2016), Rivière-Grand-Carbet (Toledo i Mur et al. 2004), the most recent occupation of Allée Dumanoir (Etrich et al. 2003), Petite Rivière à la Désirade (de Waal 2006), Bisdary (Romon et al. 2006), Yuiketi (Bonnissent 2011), and Parking Roches gravées (Romon et al. 2019). These sites are contemporaneous with other published sites in the northern Lesser Antilles on islands such as Antigua, St. Eustatius, St. Martin, Saba, Anguilla, and St. Thomas (see Rouse and Faber Morse 1999; Murphy 1999, 2004; Versteeg and Schinkel 1992; Bonnissent 2008; Hofman 1993; Crock 2000; Righter 2002a). The available ceramic Late Saladoid registers for Guadeloupe, as mentioned, reveal mainly open, carinated, hemispherical, and oval bowls (small and large), and some low bowls or platters occasionally decorated with red paint and, to a lesser extent, incisions. Griddles are not legged and have triangular lips. Red-painted ware dominates and is sometimes accompanied with white, black, or orange painted designs on both vessel interiors and exteriors. Incisions form contouring parallel lines or complex spiraling motifs, sometimes accompanied by plastic modeling such as handles, nubbins, and adornos.

The Late Saladoid ceramic repertoire differs clearly from that of Early Saladoid times (cal 0–500 CE) by the quasi-absence of zone-incised crosshatched incisions (ZIC), white-on-red painting (WOR), and white-and-red (WAR) painting as well as typically thin-walled, oval incised bowls (see Delpuech et al. 2002; Etrich 2003; Bonnissent and Romon 2004; Hildebrand in Romon et al. 2006). New vessel shapes were introduced beginning in cal 400 CE due to Barrancoid influences (e.g., eared handles and pedestalled boat-shaped vessels, incense burners, flaring rim bowls and rim flanges), developing into a Late Cedrosan Saladoid subseries. By the end of the first millennium, the Troumassoid series appeared on Guadeloupe, replacing the former. The origins of the northern post-Saladoid series are usually attributed to further local development out of the Late Cedrosan Saladoid subseries (Rouse and Faber Morse 1999; Rouse 1992; Petersen et al. 2004; Hofman et al. 2007; Hofman 2013). However, the Guadeloupean series presented here show little continuum or development out of the previous series around cal 1000 CE, when comparing vessel shapes and, to a lesser extent, decoration modes. Furthermore, the introduction of legged griddles from the Windward Islands and the appearance of grog as a temper mode, perhaps originating from the mainland, suggest important movements or influences coming from the south as previously witnessed by the Barrancoid influences half a millennium before, which might also be considered to represent a turning point. It is felt that the Saladoid elements did not slowly fade away or simply "fusion" into the subsequent Troumassoid series, but were surpassed by the latter as if another regime had been installed. Flaring and outward-thickened rims as well as median bell-shaped vessels disappeared completely; red paint started to dominate (black, white, and orange are now absent) and complex incisions in cartouches fully disappeared as well.

Lithics

The lithics found at the four sites represent an assemblage characteristic of a settlement context, as most rocks found can be associated with food processing or other household related activities. The many querns and actively used grinding stones attest to the first aspect, whereas the expedient flint, jasper and chalcedony tools as well as the hammer and polishing stones served a diversity of tasks related to the second aspect. The presence of ground stone axes shows the significance of woodworking at the sites, most likely related to the construction of houses and manufacture of canoes.

The local geological setting determining the degree of proper rock material availability had a significant effect on the variation in abundance regarding certain tool types. On the southern volcanic island of Basse-Terre, particularly the communities of Parking de Roseau, La Pointe de Grande Anse and, to a smaller degree, STEP Goyave benefited from easy access to coarse, hard, and tough igneous rock varieties, exemplified by the large number of use-modified tools such as hammers, grinders and querns. The inhabitants of CHU Belle-Plaine on northern Grande-Terre, however, were deprived of such rocks in their direct environment and as a result the number of these types of stone tools is much smaller.

That the studied communities did not live in isolation is shown by the presence of exotic raw materials and artifacts, originating from nearby, but also more distant islands. All sites yielded Long Island flint that may have been acquired through intercommunity exchange. The larger assemblages of Parking de Roseau and La Pointe de Grande Anse also included a number of other exotics that came from more distant islands. Tuffaceaous grey-green mudstone axes derived from St. Martin, whereas the jadeitite fragment found at La Pointe de Grande Anse points to the existence of an exchange network that even encompassed a larger region, minimally extending to Hispaniola and perhaps even farther. To what degree the relative richness of exotics within the assemblages from Parking de Roseau and La Pointe de Grande Anse actually reflect a higher status of both communities when compared to STEP Goyave and CHU Belle-Plaine is hard to evaluate, as both former sites produced larger lithic assemblages than the two latter ones, biasing the results. This especially applies to comparing Parking de Roseau and La Pointe de Grande Anse on the one hand with the small assemblage from CHU Belle-Plaine on the other hand. The assemblage of STEP Goyave is more or less equal in size to the one from La Pointe de Grande Anse and the difference in the number of exotics between both sites may be significant. This suggests that the community of STEP Goyave did not participate in the exchange network of these valuables, which may be a reflection of lower status.

Another striking characteristic is the poverty of artifacts associated with ritual and cosmology. None of the four sites discussed in this work yielded *cemí* three-pointer stones, and surprisingly the smallest assemblage of all four included a sculptured stone head that may be regarded as another form of *cemí*. As with the exotic axes, this poverty in ritual and cosmological valuables may reflect a lower status of these sites when compared to, for example, Anse à la Gourde (Knippenberg 2006:193–214). It may, however, also be an indication that Anse à la Gourde played a different ritual or cosmological role when compared to the sites in this study. Apart from being a settlement, Anse à la Gourde was an extensive burial site, where more than 80 individuals were interred (Delpuech et al. 2001b; Hoogland et al. 2001, 2010). It may be precisely this aspect that resulted in the discard of a relatively high number of *cemí* three-pointer stones, when we take into account that these objects were associated with ancestor worship (Oliver 2009).

The lithic assemblages from all four sites share characteristics that firmly place them in the Ceramic Age. The use of an expedient flake technology is a recurrent feature among, not only Ceramic Age communities in the Lesser Antilles (Crock and Bartone 1998; DeMille 1996; Knippenberg 2006; Walker 1980), but also other Ceramic Age societies in the world, as (for example) research on Bronze Age flint-working in northwestern Europe has shown (see van Gijn and Niekus 2001). In addition, the basic use of ground stone petaloid axes and adzes used for woodworking is a typical feature introduced by Ceramic Age communities into the region (Knippenberg 2006). This accounts as well for the more frequent use of large and flat stone slabs and hand-held tools in food-grinding activities.

Despite this Ceramic Age "signature," changes can be discerned when comparing the different phases of this period. These changes relate to a combination of shifting social relationships, associated networks, and socioeconomic complexity, as well as alterations in values and beliefs. Most visible, and therefore most striking, is the disappearance in the fifth century CE of the rich and diverse lapidary industry, so characteristic of the earliest Ceramic Age communities. It involved a whole array of differently colored rocks and semiprecious stones, with provenances not only in the Antilles but also on the South American mainland (Cody 1991; Hofman et al. 2007; Knippenberg 2006; Queffelec et al. 2008). The lithic assemblages from the four sites discussed in this work can be truly designated as poor in this respect, clearly showing that they date from the period after the collapse of this network. Lapidary work is represented by only a single bead made of quartz, found at La Pointe de

Grande Anse. Not only this very low abundance, but also the presumably more local provenance of the quartz rock is very typical of the later phases of the Ceramic Age (Knippenberg 2006:157–220). This not only attests to the collapse of a long-distance exchange network in which settlements in the Lesser Antilles, on Puerto Rico and the South American mainland were tied, but it also shows a change towards the appreciation of specific local materials because now quartz, calcite, and diorite became more prominent, whereas carnelian, a local material as well, disappeared (Knippenberg 2006:157–220). This collapse of an exchange network in which certain highly valued lapidary artifacts were frequently bartered among various settlement sites in the Lesser Antilles and Puerto Rico was associated with changes in the distribution of Long Island flint. This was less widespread, and its abundance at sites on the islands surrounding Antigua dropped markedly (Knippenberg 2006:223–263). This is also witnessed on Guadeloupe, when the assemblages from Early Ceramic Age sites of Morel and Gare Maritime (Knippenberg 2006, 2012a; Queffelec et al. 2018) are compared to those from the younger sites in this study. To what degree this drop had already started during the Late Saladoid phase of the Early Ceramic Age (cal 400–850 CE) is to some degree blurred by limited and contrasting data. The Saladoid occupation at Anse à l'Eau (c. cal 500–850 CE) shows a drop in use, whereas the small sample for the contemporaneous occupation at Anse à la Gourde (cal 500–850 CE) produced a high reliance on Long Island flint similar to that of the Morel and Gare Maritime sites (Knippenberg 2006:174–177).

As noted earlier, interisland exchange between the different Late Ceramic Age communities inhabiting the Antilles remained to play a significant role, as exemplified by the continuing exchange of St. Martin greenstone axes throughout an extensive part of the region. Alongside the exchange of this valued axe material, new stone materials appeared for the first time, among which jadeitite is the most significant and widespread example (Harlow et al. 2019; García-Casco et al. 2013; Schertl et al. 2018). The introduction of this highly valued semiprecious stone material coincides with the first appearance of Ceramic Age communities in the Greater Antilles (Harlow et al. 2019; García-Casco et al. 2013; Schertl et al. 2018; for a different viewpoint, see Rodríguez Ramos 2010, 2011). From this period onwards we see other metamorphic rock materials with a possibly Greater Antillean origin entering the Lesser Antilles as well (Breukel 2019; Knippenberg 2006).

Cemi three-pointer stones also became a more important item of exchange. Being almost absent in the earliest phase of the Early Ceramic Age (cal 400 BCE to 400 CE), they became more recurrent in the later phase (400–850 CE), and they were a prominent artifact especially during the Late Ceramic Age (Knippenberg 2006). It is interesting to note that some of the assemblages rich in *cemi* three-pointers, such as Anse à la Gourde, demonstrate the use of specimens made from both local limestone and a variety of exotic rock materials (Knippenberg 2006:203–209), suggesting that local rock availability was not the sole determining factor; rather, the origin of the stone, and therefore the origin of the *cemi*, formed an intrinsic part of its use and value.

These data seem to support a notion that on the one hand, regular intercommunity contact became more regional (less widespread and lower abundance of Long Island flint), but on the other hand, long-distance distribution of valuables still occurred (St. Martin greenstone, jadeitite, and other metamorphic rock axes), perhaps at a lower frequency. Compared to the Early Ceramic Age, long-distance exchange of lapidary artifacts, the network in which these later valuables spread also exhibits a geographical shift towards the west, more firmly incorporating the Greater Antilles and losing a significant influx from the South American mainland. Archaeological evidence on the latest phase of the Late Ceramic Age (1250–1492 CE) occupation suggests that in the northern Lesser Antilles sociocultural changes occurred just prior to the arrival of Columbus. Not only the abundance of sites dropped (see, for example, de Waal 2006; Wilson 1990), but the region also witnessed the appearance of small sites that were culturally affiliated outside the region, as work at Kelbey's Ridge, on Saba, and at Morne Cybèle and Morne Souffleur, on La Désirade (Guadeloupe), has shown (de Waal 2006; Hofman and Hoogland 2004; Hofman et al. 2004). The disappearance of *cemí* three-pointer stones made from St. Martin calci-rudite is associated with this transition as well (Knippenberg 2006:254–261).

The limited data from the previously mentioned La Désirade sites as well as from the latest occupation contexts at Parking de Roseau show an absence of Long Island flint, a characteristic unique to the Guadeloupean archipelago during the Ceramic Age (Knippenberg 2006:157–220). It demonstrates that during this phase, access to Long Island flint had ceased, despite the relatively close location of these sites to this highly valued flint source. Although to some degree blurred by the low number of Guadeloupean sites and the small size of the assemblages, these few cases, in which we receive a glimpse of the communities just prior to the arrival of Columbus, suggest that significant sociopolitical changes occurred in the archipelago, in which microregional networks collapsed and were redefined.

6.3   Subsistence: environment and food consumption

Apart from migration and cultural differences, Amerindian settlement and the environmental exploitation of Guadeloupe were coupled to the Caribbean climate and in particular to the movements of the Intertropical Convergence Zone (ITCZ). It is widely accepted now that an extended dry period swept the region during roughly the late first millennium CE with a severe drought towards the end of this time frame, which was followed by relatively moist conditions (Hodell et al. 1991; Higuera-Gundy et al. 1999; Haug et al. 2001, 2003; Lane et al. 2009, 2011, 2014; Caffrey et al. 2015).

This drought is generally related to the collapse of the Maya realm in Mexico and Guatemala, but it also coincides with the end of the Saladoid in the northern Lesser Antilles by the end of the first millennium CE. This larger climatic picture has also been identified in the French Lesser Antilles (Bertran et al. 2004; Beets et al. 2006; Malaizé et al. 2011; Siegel et al. 2015; Hofman et al. 2021). As demonstrated by Jorda, the site of Roseau revealed coastal transformation and beach formation before the end of the first millennium CE (Phase C), similar to Anse à la Gourde, where the lagoon disappeared. Although little paleoclimatic research has been conducted on Guadeloupe, Beets et al. (2006:279) suggest that the site of Anse à la Gourde was abandoned by its Late Cedrosan Saladoid inhabitants because of this particular drought, after which it was inhabited again by a Troumassoid population from about cal 1000 CE onwards.

A similar scenario may also have occurred on a much larger scale on Guadeloupe when adding the data presented here (see Appendix 1). Troumassoid inception can be pinned to the very end of the first millennium CE, whereas Late Saladoid radiocarbon dates at sites such as La Pointe de Grande Anse, STEP Goyave, Bisdary, La Ramée, and Stade de José Bade finish just after cal 900 CE, leaving a maximum 100-year overlap with the succeeding Troumassoid occupation with, for example, Roseau, which began after 1200 BP (see Figure 6.1). In this manner an abandonment of Guadeloupe by the Late Saladoid population, perhaps instigated by the drought, may serve as an alternative hypothesis versus the actual idea of the origins of the Troumassoid population being a slow process of transformation out of the Saladoid.

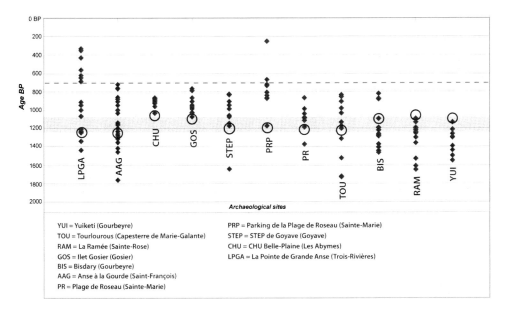

Figure 6.1 Chronology of excavated Saladoid and Troumassoid sites on Guadeloupe showing the overlap between Late Saladoid and Mamoran Troumassoid sites. See Appendix 1 for related radiocarbon dates.

Photo: M. van den Bel.

The large circular pits encountered at these sites contained phytoliths related to the environment of the site when abandoned. Phytoliths related to crops were not found in these pits, but the analysis by Dickau and Watling rather showed the background vegetation of the site in question. The pits contained phytoliths indicating both arboreal (forested) and open (grassy) spaces. Two hypotheses have been forwarded: the first suggests clearing within a forested area (disturbance), and the second proposes the decomposition of vegetal material brought onsite. The second is favored here. The presence of bamboo and palms is attested for, but they appear to be rare, although it is also stated that the environment of the site changed remarkably during its occupation.

The Amerindians of STEP Goyave, CHU Belle-Plaine, and Roseau processed plants in mortars, on grinding stones, and in pottery, as witnessed by the starch analysis of Pagán-Jiménez and Dickau. Although further starch analysis is needed, the Amerindians consumed maize, beans, chili pepper, cocoyam, and Indian yams as well as unidentified other taxa. These starch residues clearly indicate that cultivated food, and therefore horticulture, was part of the LCA subsistence economy on Guadeloupe and falls within the larger framework of cultivated plants during the LCA in the Lesser Antilles (see Pagán-Jiménez 2013). The edible plants were tended and cultivated in their gardens, perhaps around or in proximity of their villages, but there is no evidence for such a hypothesis except for the stake concentration at CHU Belle-Plaine, which may be considered to represent a garden, at least for beans, which are typically grown on stakes (see Figure 3.6).

Shell remains

Of the four sites presented in the book, only three yielded assemblages of invertebrate remains (none were found at La Pointe de Grande Anse). However, the part associated with Amerindian contexts remains small, with less than 50 remains at each site. This is unfortunately a common observation for Amerindian sites located on the island of Basse-Terre in Guadeloupe, and on other volcanic islands. This fact is mainly due to the poor preservation conditions in the acidic laterites and clays produced by the pedological alteration of the volcanic and volcano-detrital substratum.

The three altered assemblages are thus little representative and cannot represent correctly the role of invertebrates as an alimentary resource or as a raw material at these sites, and even less for the Troumassoid period in Basse-Terre, on Guadeloupe, or elsewhere. Fortunately, we can turn to a larger corpus of more than 30 invertebrate assemblages from different sites in Guadeloupe and other Lesser Antillean islands (see Appendix 2). It provides hints of information on the Amerindian ways of exploiting molluscan and crustacean resources between cal 600 and 1500 CE. Nevertheless, this corpus remains unsatisfactory given the unequal levels of excavating methods, importance, and accuracy (including sieved materials) of the assemblages, state of understanding of the site's spatial layout and function, and accuracy of the radiocarbon dates. Thus, at this stage, only coarse and simplified trends emerge along the time range from the Late Saladoid to the end of the Troumassoid period in terms of exploitation strategies for invertebrates (Serrand 2007a-b, 2008; Serrand and Bonnissent 2018).

The first visible pattern is the stronger convergence of the exploitation modes on Saladoid sites compared to later Troumassoid contexts. Even if the small number of studied sites (eight Saladoid *vs* 26 Troumassoid) may be a limiting bias, observations are very continuous on Saladoid settlements, showing:

- An emphasis on land invertebrates, land crabs, and/or freshwater snails such as *Neritina virginea* and *N. punctulata* (> 15% MNI or even 25% MNI of the total shells and crabs individuals);
- An exploitation of marine gastropods mostly collected on the rocky shores and in the sandy seagrass areas with the most productive species, to wit *Cittarium pica* and *Lobatus gigas*, which are not systematically targeted in search of high-efficiency returns;—a very low representation of bivalves (< 5% MNI);
- A well-developed and diversified shell industry with artifacts related to tool and ornamental products for which the second one includes rather standardized productions from one site to another, such as abundant discoid millimetric beads, discs and quadrangular pieces of ornaments, mother-of-pearl inlays, etc.

Later Troumassoid sites are characterized by less standardized patterns of exploitation, a fact that may echo what is classically considered the result of a regionalization process with a growing complexity and variety in site locations, spatial, economic, and sociopolitical organizations, and craft styles and productions. In this period, exploitation strategies may have depended more on the functional organization of the site within a broader landscape. However, a few points clearly differ from earlier Saladoid contexts:

- High percentages of land invertebrates (crabs and freshwater snails) are less systematic: freshwater snails are often absent while land crabs are only sometimes represented in abundance, such as at BK 76 and BK 77, on St. Martin, and Est de Mouton de Bas, on Guadeloupe;

- Exploited marine molluscs are more diverse, although *Cittarium pica* and *Lobatus gigas* remain the major gastropods. They are complemented with bivalves, whose numbers are often high and whose variety is also growing;
- More distant and varied environments are exploited, including mangrove and lagoon contexts;
- The shell industry, still developed and diversified, producing now more varied and less standardized ornamental artifacts.

These rough sketches suggest that Saladoid communities gathered select but mostly easily accessible invertebrate resources from a limited range of terrestrial, freshwater, and marine settings, with no evident preference for high-energetic return species, with the possible exception of land crabs (Serrand 2007a-b). Nonetheless, things need to be refined, as it appears that the earliest sites of the shell register have very low land crab numbers. On the other hand, it seems that Troumassoid communities gathered more diversified invertebrate resources in a larger range of marine settings, within less standardized patterns from one site to the other (Serrand 2007a-b). In consequence, it has to be explored in the future how specific socioeconomic contexts, such as specialized and/or satellite sites, may be translated into specific exploitation strategies of invertebrates. In addition, other contextual parameters are likely at stake, such as the evolving paleoclimatic and paleoenvironmental conditions, as opined earlier, and their correlation with the availability and abundance of resources (Serrand 2007a), some of which, moreover, may be, in later Troumassoid times, in a depleted state due to earlier exploitation pressures. A first attempt at aligning paleoclimatic and archaeofaunal data was presented by Nathalie Serrand and Dominique Bonnissent in 2016 for the St. Martin contexts. It suggests possible connections between paleoenvironmental parameters such as dry conditions, and the changing of relative contributions of some resources, for example the comeback of bivalves (a resource that was highly exploited during Pre-Ceramic times and rather neglected during Saladoid times), an interesting fact for key targeted resources and possible cultural markers of specific periods. However, this first attempt will have to be fine-tuned in the future, utilizing additional data and critically examining radiometric dates, site contexts, and functions alongside accurate paleoclimatic data.

Faunal remains

Unlike the Saladoid period, during which subsistence economies were particularly open and diversified and all environments, even those farthest from the sites, were exploited, the Troumassoid period is generally characterized by an increasingly intensive exploitation of the ecosystems closest to the sites, but also by a subsistence economy that tended to specialize in a few species (Grouard 2007). Indeed, specialized sites are common in the Guadeloupean archipelago during this period: Pointe du Helleux for marine crabs (Grouard 2001), Grande Anse de Terre-de-Bas (Les Saintes) and Caille à Bélasse (Petite-Terres) for marine turtles, and the l'Embouchure de la Rivière de Baillif site for tunas (Grouard 2010b). In Martinique, at the sites of Les Salines, Anse Trabaud, Paquemar, and Macabou, the number of taxa as well as the index of richness and diversity differ considerably among sites (Grouard 2013). However, this difference is probably due to the accuracy of the sieving process employed at the sites. Indeed, the spectrum is rich and diversified at Macabou due to fine-mesh sieving of the sediment, while at Salines and Anse Trabaud, where manual collecting was carried out during the fieldwork, most certainly the largest skeletal parts were favored. Thus, the Trou-massoid occupation of Macabou is characterized by a broad-spectrum subsistence economy, including land crabs, sea urchins, tunas, surgeonfish, rice rats, parrot fish, and iguanas, all caught in the direct environment of the site. On St. Martin (Baie aux Prunes and Pointe du Canonnier; see Bonnissent and Stouvenot 2005; Grouard 2005), hunting and fishing were focused on rice rats and specific fish species: groupers, snappers, and cardinals, also present in large quantities near the sites.

The subsistence economies of the CHU Belle-Plaine and La Pointe de Grande Anse sites are in accordance with the data obtained for the other Troumassoid sites studied in the French West Indies. We observe rich subsistence economies with a specialization on fish at La Pointe de Grande Anse and on rice rats and agoutis at CHU Belle-Plaine. Furthermore, we notice a higher exploitation of species deriving from ecosystems near the sites such as coral/rock bottoms and deep-water channels at La Pointe de Grande Anse and forested areas at CHU Belle-Plaine. However, it should be noted that the data obtained at the latter site are exceptional in the Guadeloupean archipelago. Indeed, most pre-Columbian sites generally yield 80–90% fish bone remains, with mammals being a minor component. When present in large quantities, the hunting fauna appears to be more similar to that found in ancient Sala-doid levels than to that in Troumassoid ones.

Apparently, CHU Belle-Plaine was a site specialized on hunting rice rats and agoutis, two beautiful rodents that probably flourished on the Lesser Antillean islands during the Troumassoid period. Du Tertre (1654) and Rochefort (1658) described them for Marti-nique. At the very end of the 19th century, Martinican rice rats (*Megalomys desmarestii*: Fischer 1829) were still observed in large numbers near the city of Saint-Pierre, accord-ing to the statement of Dr. G. Kingsley Noble to Glover M. Allen in the first quarter of the 20th century. Indeed, a certain M. Delphin Duchamp, a Martinican farmer, report-edly told Noble during a trip to Guadeloupe in 1914 that "about five years before the eruption of Mount Pelée they used to exist in great numbers among the cocoanut planta-tions along the Rivière Blanche" (Allen 1942) in northwestern Martinique. Therefore, like agoutis, they were naturally attracted to cultivated fields. This commensalism made hunting easy. However, it is also possible that these animals were "tamed" and kept in open "pens." Some small islands in the Grand Cul-de-Sac-Marin could even have been used as natural enclosures. This is not domestication but rather stock-keeping, which is a reasoned stage of predation and allows livestock management, without, however, acting on the fertility and reproduction of kept individuals (unlike domestication). This would explain the joint presence of very young and very old individuals in the same assemblage.

Indeed, the present Amerindians of Amazonia do not domesticate animals because they do not appropriate the animal (notion of reciprocity), but they bring certain small animals into the domestic sphere to raise and feed: pets that they tame (Erikson 1987). This taming, as opposed to hunting, which is based on a unilateral taking of game, makes it possible to sym-bolically counterbalance the destructive role of hunting by feeding certain young animals in the village: they are pampered, fed, cared for, but not consumed. The combined presence of these two forms of relations with the animal world makes it possible to rediscover the Amazonian ideology based on the notion of reciprocity (Erikson 1987). Finally, the CHU Belle-Plaine site could therefore testify to a hunting activity of pilori rats and agoutis, based on the notion of livestock kept in semiliberty, where the capture of young animals and older adults is made possible.

6.4   Chronology

As mentioned, the change from the Early to the Late Ceramic Age or from the (Late) Sala-doid to the Suazoid ceramic series is generally seen as an internal development or indigenous process (S. Fitzpatrick 2015:318; Bérard 2019:61). For this matter, the Troumassoid series is seen as transitional or as an in-between series by archaeologists (Allaire 2013b). As stated in Chapter 1, Troumassoid ceramics find their origins in the southern Lesser Antilles where they appeared at about cal 600–700 CE, and apparently they remained there before going farther north by the end of the first millennium, merging with the existing but waning Saladoid popu-lation and subsequently evolving into a regional Troumassoid called Mamoran Troumassoid (Petersen et al. 2004). In this perspective, the movement towards the northern Lesser Antilles is represented by the Troumassan Troumassoid, and the Late Saladoid population can be iden-tified as that of the Mill Reef complex, corresponding to the radiocarbon dates of the Indian Creek site of Antigua (Rouse and Faber Morse 1999:46, Table 1). Mamoran Troumassoid has also been found on St. Martin (Bonnissent 2008), Saba (Hofman 1993), and Anguilla (Crock 2000), but has not been recognized as such in the Virgin Islands, which show a gap in the chronology around cal 1000 CE, as witnessed, for example, on St. Thomas, where the Saladoid series had already disappeared about 200 years earlier (Lundberg 2002:167, Fig. 5.1).

In the Lesser Antilles, the Troumassoid series stands for divergence and regional diversity (Rouse 1992), but "the most striking feature of this transition is the break with the rela-tive homogeneity that characterized the previous period" (Bérard 2019:61). The transition between the Early and Late Ceramic Age is marked by a number of important changes on cultural, sociopolitical, economic, and demographic grounds (Hofman et al. 2007, 2008; Hofman 2013). The number of sites on the Antilles increased, suggesting population growth, territoriality, and regionalization, as is shown for Guadeloupe (de Waal 2006; Hofman and Hoogland 2004), St. Martin (Bonnissent 2008), and Martinique (Grouard 2008, 2010a).

These changes have similarities or reflect a similar development in the eastern Greater Antilles or northern Caribbean. Here an LCA expansion is observed when the people pro-ducing the Ostionoid ceramic series colonized Jamaica, the Bahamas, and Cuba, carrying a thin, mostly undecorated red-ware pottery that is believed to have evolved out of the earlier Saladoid ceramic series (S. Fitzpatrick 2015:315). Just like Troumassoid in the Lesser Antil-les, the Ostionoid ceramic series has many manifestations or styles in the Greater Antilles. Several Ostionoid subseries have been recognized, such as Ostionan, Chican, Meillacan, and Palmettan. Parallel to this local development in the Greater Antilles, the Late Cedrosan Saladoid ceramic series persisted in the Leeward Islands, with Guadeloupe being the south-ern frontier (Keegan 2000; Versteeg and Schinkel 1992; Crock 2000; Murphy 1999, 2004; Bonnissent 2008; Delpuech et al. 2001b).

According to Rouse (1992), the Troumassoid was replaced in the southern Lesser Antilles by migrants from *Terra firma* producing the so-called Suazoid ceramics around cal 1000 CE. This LCA image has been put in perspective by Rouse et al. (1995), who propose the Trou-massan Troumassoid subseries as the early phase and the Suazan Troumassoid subseries as a later phase (see also Petersen et al. 2004). Considering Guadeloupe, the Troumassan Trou-massoid of the Windward Islands appears to be absent because the Late Cedrosan Saladoid ceramics continue here until about cal 900 CE. Hence, the Guadeloupean Troumassoid series started just before cal 1000 CE, as did the Suazan Troumassoid series in the Windward Islands. For this matter, the Mamora Bay complex of Antigua, as defined by Rouse and Faber Morse (1999), now refers to the Mamoran Troumassoid ceramic subseries for the Leeward Islands between St. Martin and Guadeloupe. According to Rouse and Faber Morse (1999:39–43), this Mamora Bay complex features Saladoid remnants such as black, red, and white slips, rectilinear and curvilinear incisions, and all kinds of adornos, including anthropomorphic ones and so-called body stamps. Indeed, their Mamora Bay sample features classic Saladoid traits, and we believe it may be an admixture of the previous Mill Reef complex, knowing that the Mamora Bay complex radiocarbon dates are not considered older than about cal 900 CE, which appears to be the youngest date for Mamoran Troumassoid in Guadeloupe.

The Mamoran subseries was followed by the Suazan Troumassoid subseries around cal 1300 CE. More generally, the Suazan Troumassoid subseries—sometimes called the Suazoid series—show even fewer colored slips and wall incisions but feature finger- or finger-nail impressions along the rims of vessels as well as scratched surfaces and human-faced adornos (Petersen et al. 2004). At least in the Leeward Islands, the Suazan subseries features some influences from the Greater Antilles, which have been attributed to the Chican Ostionoid subseries (see Hofman 1993). Prior to the European encounter the Taíno of the Greater Antilles were at the center of a large network exchanging ideas, people, and sacred objects like *cémis* and vomiting spatulas (Hofman et al. 2007).

The descendants of the Suazoid are believed to have met the first Europeans by the end of the 15th century. They were called the "infamous caribes" by the Spanish (Allaire 2013a). However, whether this population was the same as the Kalinago encountered by the French on Guadeloupe in 1635 is doubtful, as Spanish control, disease, and slave raiding in the Lesser Antilles and on the mainland extensively influenced the indigenous demography, warfare, and sociopolitical organization, leaving the area astray and open to migration for other Amerindians and Europeans. These newly arrived Amerindians from the mainland called themselves Kalinago, according to French sources, and inhabited the majority of the Lesser Antilles. Their ceramics have been attributed to the so-called Cayo complex and resemble the historic ceramic series from the Guianas such as found in French Guiana. The latter was recently dubbed the Malmanoury complex; it developed out of the pre-Columbian Koriabo complex in historic times (van den Bel et al. 2015; van den Bel 2020). Both complexes can be dated largely to the 16th and 17th centuries and also feature European objects such as iron tools, imported European ceramics, and glass beads.

6.5   Final remarks

The transition from the Early to the Late Ceramic Age does not appear as smooth as was stated previously (Boomert 2004:244–245). Whether it concerned one and the same people is even more difficult to say, although future DNA research may point out any variation. However, as generally acknowledged, important cultural differences have been observed because of this transition, such as a change in funerary modes on Guadeloupe and elsewhere in the Lesser Antilles (Hofman and Hoogland 2013). It is believed, however, that other important developments, in addition to the climate change, must be added here in order to better define the LCA transition.

In fact, the results discussed and the comparative analysis with contemporaneous and earlier sites in the Guadeloupean archipelago and beyond have inspired the title of this work, as stated in the Foreword. Important changes or innovations took place by the end of the first millennium CE instead of local divergence, which has been covered up by a lack of data and archaeological theory to dismantle obsolete ideas about Caribs and Arawaks, and perhaps bored with concepts such as migration and diffusion. Obviously, the historic terminology had to be discarded by a modernizing discipline, but how this transition was realized or conceived of has been left blank, confronting us today with even more boxes and labels than before.

Nonetheless, the Guadeloupean sites presented here are considered fully post-Saladoid sites based on their ceramic register, ignoring the Saladoid occupations of STEP Goyave and La Pointe de Grande Anse. We believe that the general results discussed reveal many changes and no evident continuity with the previous Saladoid sites. The most important elements of change are: (1) the switch from roundhouses with deep central posts to round-houses without central posts; (2) the switch from "randomly" positioned graves in the village (plaza, midden, house) to grouped burials within houses, suggesting ancestor veneration; (3) these burials are accompanied by more evident/increasing manipulation of the human remains as well as secondary burials and fewer grave goods; (4) a clearly different ceramic register revealing little continuity accompanied by the innovation of grog as a temper; (5) a short period of about 100 years of cohabitation with the previous Saladoid occupation based on the radiocarbon dates for Troumassoid and Late (Terminal) Saladoid on Guadeloupe.

We consider these changes to have taken place in the tenth century CE—that is, during a rather short period for such profound changes—suggesting more than the subtle waning of a Saladoid culture or cultural influences coming from the exterior. Hence, we suggest this century to have been a turning point, pivoting around the previously mentioned elements, but, to another degree, also corresponding to climate change that caused continuous drought in the Caribbean at the end of the first millennium ce. The latter event may have helped to terminate the (Late) Saladoid in the northern Lesser Antilles, creating altogether a void for other populations such as the (Troumassan) Troumassoid in the southern Lesser Antilles to move towards the north.

Note

1   "*Il faut scavoir que toutes leurs Cabannes sont appuyées sur des pilliers au bout desquels plus hauts qu'un grand homme que ils nomment Ouaccabou, au bout desquels il y apuis apres des bastons qui sont tous en travers de la maison assez proches les uns des autres, et la dessus ils y mettent tous leurs meubles comme coffres de rozeau, arcz, flesches et autres choses, et pour y monter ils n'ont ny eschelles ny degrez*" (Iguimbertine Library at Carpentras, France, Ms 590, f. 55r). One may read here "human-tall posts upon which a wooden floor is constructed" or "posts upon which the roof is constructed and where objects are stowed away." The absence of stairs and the monkey-like ascent for both women and men is remarkable.

7 Epilogue

From Saladoid to Troumassoid: a ceramic analysis

Arie Boomert

The second half of the first millennium CE was one of exceptional dynamism in the coastal zone of the South American mainland as well as the Caribbean archipelago. Major cultural, sociopolitical, ethnic, and ritual reformulations took place in both areas during this episode, which in the Lesser Antilles is known as the transitional phase between the Saladoid and Troumassoid ceramic series. As in-depth research on this alteration has been scarce, that of the present volume, focusing on Guadeloupean sites that date from this period and can be expected to shed light on the Troumassoid Turning Point, thus represents a timely and much needed exercise. This investigation is all the more interesting because the Guadeloupean archipelago is situated at the margin of both regional Troumassoid centers: the Windward Islands in the south and the Leeward Islands in the northwest, and although it can be considered to have formed part of the latter interaction sphere, it appears to have been influenced from the Windward Islands as well.

With respect to the time frame in question, it is well to keep in mind that this period was one of intense climatic alteration, which may have triggered important cultural and societal changes or at least seriously aggravated them. Following a relatively wet episode, by cal 750 CE an interval of intense droughts and frequent hurricane landfalls commenced in the West Indies, lasting until about cal 1000/1050 CE. This stage corresponds to the Terminal Classic Drought in Mesoamerica, which had such detrimental effects on Maya civilization. Without assuming a direct analogy, clearly, the possibility that the period of extremely dry years in the West Indies had similarly serious cultural, technological, and social consequences cannot be neglected (Florès Blancaneaux 2009). In the Lesser Antilles the episode of repeated severe droughts must have had repercussions for the availability of fresh water, especially in the low-lying Limestone Caribbean. Rivers obviously carried much less rainwater, springs would have run dry, and several streams would have become dry ghauts, with severe consequences for the freshwater fish and invertebrate fauna.

Surely, the prolonged droughts had an impact on food procurement, although the actual effects are difficult to gauge. Horticulture may have been damaged in general, but the cultivation of water-demanding cultivars such as maize and various fruit trees especially would have been impinged upon negatively. In contrast, the growing of root crops, for instance cassava, tannia, and sweet potatoes, is not likely to have been affected seriously. Changing foodways due to a tendency towards more intensive exploitation of marine resources such as reefs and mangroves and a lessening dependence on the inland tropical forest have been hypothesized for this period. Perhaps the no doubt much increased dry-season burning of the forest played a major role in this respect. Indeed, on various islands, notably Martinique, such an intra-insular movement towards coastal areas with abundant possibilities for fishing, hunting sea mammals, and collecting invertebrates has been established for the transitional

DOI: 10.4324/9781003181651-7

episode between Saladoid and Troumassoid (Bright 2011). Clearly, it was the favorable environmental situation of the Saladoid to Troumassoid communities in the Lesser Antilles that allowed satisfying adaptation to the altered climatic situation in the archipelago and prevented full disfunctioning of Amerindian society.

Apart from taking place in an environmentally alterating setting, the Saladoid to Troumassoid transition occurred in a highly dynamic social realm. Distinct cultural traditions matured in the episode between about cal750 and 900 CE due to indigenous development and population movement or a combination of both. On the mainland, the Dabajuroid series spread along the Venezuelan coast to the east specifically in this period, establishing itself in the Cumaná area and the Margarita archipelago. Further east, in the Orinoco Valley and the easternmost portion of the mainland coastal zone, the Barrancoid series was replaced by the Arauquinoid tradition, which expanded towards Trinidad, here supplanting the strongly Barrancoid-influenced Saladoid communities, which had founded a major interaction network with Tobago and the southern Windward Islands. While the latter remained structured as aggregates of kin-based tribal societies, at the other end of the Antillean archipelago, in Puerto Rico and Hispaniola simultaneously the Saladoid series evolved into the Elenan and Ostionan Ostionoid subseries, ultimately giving rise to the development of multivillage chiefdom polities. In how far the Saladoid-Troumassoid transition was affected or even initiated by one or more of these social, cultural, demographic, political, and possibly ethnic developments on the mainland and the Greater Antilles is still poorly understood.

A matter to be addressed at this stage of the discussion is the necessity of establishing clearly which local ceramic complexes in the Lesser Antilles can be assigned to the Troumassoid series. In other words, how do we define the Troumassoid series and its substituent subseries? When Rouse first conceived of the Troumassoid series, he saw it essentially as a transitional pottery assemblage restricted to the Windward Islands, chronologically to be placed between the Saladoid and what he then called the Suazoid series. The contemporary developments in the Leeward Islands, including Guadeloupe, were classified within the Elenoid series because of their surmised close affinities with the ceramic evolution in Puerto Rico and the Virgin Islands (see Rouse and Allaire 1978). Subsequently, following Rouse's revision of the Antillean cultural chronology due to his introduction of the subseries concept, the post-Saladoid pottery complexes of the Leewards were assigned to the Elenan Ostionoid subseries while the Troumassoid series of the Windward Islands was divided into two subsequent subseries, Troumassan and Suazan, of which the latter replaced the notion of a Suazoid series. Moreover, Rouse's extensive fieldwork in Antigua allowed him to distinguish a number of subsequent ceramic complexes at the Indian Creek site, of which he designated the Mill Reef complex to Late Saladoid times and the two subsequent pottery assemblages of the island, Mamora Bay and Freeman's Bay, to a Mamoran Troumassoid subseries, considered to be largely contemporaneous with the Troumassan and Suazan Troumassoid subseries of the Windward Islands (see Rouse 1992). Finally, realizing that the Mill Reef complex can better be understood as the first of the Mamoran development, he assigned this assemblage to this subseries rather than to the Saladoid series (Rouse et al. 1995). The post-Cedrosan cultural chronology involving the concept of the Troumassoid series as outlined previously has been generally accepted throughout the Lesser Antilles (e.g., Boomert 2014; Hofman 2013; Petersen et al. 2004).

The post-Saladoid pottery complexes recognized on Antigua can be assumed to represent the type sites of two subsequent chronological phases of the Mamoran subseries in the Leeward Islands (and Guadeloupe): (1) Early Mamoran, characterized by the Mill Reef complex, which can be presumed largely contemporaneous with the first part of the Troumassan subseries of the Windwards (about cal 750–900 CE), and (2) Late Mamoran, typified by the Mamora Bay and Freeman's Bay complexes, concurrent with the last part of the Troumassan subseries and the entire Suazan subseries in the Windwards (about cal900–1350/1400 CE). According to pottery characteristics and radiocarbon dates, Early to Late Mamoran settlement sites have been identified on most of the Leeward Islands, but especially pottery related to the Mill Reef complex and dating from Early Mamoran times is less clearly definable in the Guadeloupean archipelago. This may be due, at least partially, to the transitional position of these islands between the Leewards and the Windwards. Indeed, in the Late Mamoran epoch, various settlement sites in the Guadeloupean islands show influence from the Suazan subseries of the Windwards or can be identified as belonging to this characteristic pottery assemblage.

The Saladoid legacy is obvious in the various Early Mamoran local pottery complexes of the Leeward Islands. However, the clearly Saladoid ceramic features shown by Mill Reef and the other Early Mamoran assemblages do not reflect a directly Lesser Antillean Cedrosan heritage, but one closely affiliated with the Cuevas and Longford complexes of Puerto Rico and the Virgin Islands, respectively. Formerly assumed to have ended about cal600 CE, the available radiocarbon measurements suggest that Cuevas and Longford continued locally until at least cal 800 CE or even later (Rodríguez Ramos 2010; Rodríguez Ramos et al. 2015). Altogether, the Early Mamoran ceramic production seems to have become geared to utilitarian activities: vessels appear to have been expedient and functional, growing into being heavy, soft, and predominantly rather crude in form and technology. From now onwards, many vessel surfaces were scratched with a fine multiple-toothed comb or scored with a blunt tool. Temper consists of chunks of large grit, volcanic sand, crushed shell, grog (chamotte), or coral fragments. Grog temper was predominant on Guadeloupe, notably on Basse-Terre. Open vessel shapes, predominantly plates and bowls, were dominant in Early Mamoran times as opposed to restricted forms. Rims are simple and vertical, or triangular or rounded in cross section, showing flat lips, while some are interiorly thickened and "folded over." Bases are flat, concave, or, rarely, footed or convex.

A minority of the vessels is decorated. Painting is frequent. Many vessels are partially or wholly covered with a monochrome red or red-orange wash or slip. Polychrome, white-and-red painted (positive) motifs, closely resembling those of the Cuevas and Longford complexes, are typical of especially the northern Leewards: towards the south, they become scarce. Designs are rectilinear, broad, and somewhat sloppy, including white chevrons, crosses, or straight diagonal striping on red-painted surfaces and thin white lines bordering red zones. Incision is the most common Mamoran decorative technique. It includes broad and shallow parallel horizontal lines (below vessel rims) and bold curvilinear designs such as spirals, ovals, and circles. Occasionally white-filled, fine-line incised ovoid patterns enclosing red or black painted designs are rare. Modeling is infrequent. Rims are often decorated with tabular lugs or dimples, vessel walls with pierced side lugs. Complex modeling includes bird-shaped adornos (especially pelicans), horned lugs, occasionally showing a central perforation or depression, perhaps representing bats, and anthropomorphic face designs on vessel walls. The Early Mamoran pottery artifacts comprise predominantly griddles, incense burners, pottery stands, body stamps, and spindle whorls. The griddles are flat or legged (tripod) and sometimes red-painted. The Guadeloupean sites discussed in this volume that at least partially reflect the Early Mamoran pottery features noted include La Pointe de Grande Anse and STEP Goyave.

The Troumassan Troumassoid subseries of the Windward Islands, Barbados, and Tobago shows similarities to as well as differences from its Mamoran Troumassoid counterpart of the Leewards. Partially, this may be due to its geographical situation: some of the outstanding

Troumassan pottery modes may have been transmitted from the mainland and Trinidad through Tobago to the Windward Islands. Generally speaking, the transition from Cedrosan to Troumassan is characterized by an episode in which the typically Saladoid pottery repertoire was rapidly replaced by less elaborately decorated ceramics and, moreover, a growing dichotomy developed between a high-quality, decorated ceremonial ware and a low-quality, predominantly plain domestic ware. It would fully crystallize in the next episode, that of Suazan Troumassoid times, and reflects clearly distinct pottery functions and different occupational and gender associations. From the outset Troumassan pottery is fairly thick, relatively soft, and tempered abundantly with (often volcanic) sand or grit, minor amounts of grog, or crushed shell particles. High-quality ware surfaces are sometimes irregular, pitted, and often burnished, while the low-quality ware is generally scraped or scratched. Scraping marks are thin and light, deriving from temper dragged across the vessel surface. Scratching is occasioned primarily by smoothing the vessel surface with a bundle of grass or small twigs.

Vessels include relatively large and sturdy, predominantly open (unrestricted) and hemispherical bowls or trays next to inturned (restricted) bowls and jars. Altogether, they closely resemble the Mamoran vessel repertoire. Rims are often inward or outward thickened, rounded, flanged, and triangular in cross section, beveled or flattened, while bases are typically concave, tripod footed, annular, or provided with high pedestals. Late Cedrosan pottery ornamentation such as vestigial white-on-red painting and zoned bichrome designs in red and black, often separated by incision, reflect some form of Saladoid continuity. The same applies to several pottery classes decorated with characteristically Barrancoid motifs. From the outset, monochrome red painting covering entire vessel surfaces and red-painted rims are common, as are blackened interiors. (In the last case, the substance used is often thought to be asphalt.) The distinction between the fine and coarse ware becomes most apparent with the Late Troumassan introduction of the highly decorated Caliviny ceremonial pottery category, showing the application of an often creamy clay wash and highly burnished or polished, sheeny, yellow, or yellowish-grey surfaces. Motives include predominantly black-painted linear ornaments, including scrolls, geometric shapes, crosshatches, and parallels, on glossy buff or red surfaces. Most likely, Caliviny painting represents an indigenous Troumassoid development in the Windward Islands and Barbados. Incision is less common. It includes predominantly large and deep (grooved) curvilinear designs such as wavy lines, volutes, arcs, spirals, circles, and parentheses. Modeled-incised biomorphic head lugs are rare, embellishing only a few Early Troumassan ovoid animal effigy vessels showing dimpled rims and crude turtle- or bird-shaped head lugs. The majority of Troumassan rim appendages typically include simple, triangular, or rounded rim points, scalloped and flat tabular (trapezoidal) and (double) horned lugs. The latter, occasionally showing a central perforation or depression, may represent bat adornos. They have been likened to the Elenan Ostionoid pottery lugs of the Virgin Islands and eastern Puerto Rico. Indeed, the iconography of these lugs is strikingly parallel to that of many Chican Ostionoid (Taíno) vessel adornos from Hispaniola and Puerto Rico, but close parallels are known from Trinidad's Bontour complex and various Arauquinoid assemblages of the mainland. The Troumassan pottery artifacts, finally, include spindle whorls, small round discs possibly used as covers or vessel lids, pottery stamps, "sherd scrapers" made of worn potsherds, pottery stands, support rings, incense burners, female figurines, and flat or footed (tripod) cassava/maize griddles.

Obviously, the ceramic elements first appearing in Mill Reef and related complexes that can be identified as diagnostically Mamoran Troumassoid as opposed to Late Cedrosan Saladoid include scratched surfaces, monochrome red painting, broad and shallow curvilinear incision, as well as footed griddles. All of these diagnostically Early Mamoran pottery features duplicate the Troumassan Troumassoid modes that distinguish this subseries from the Late Cedrosan earthenware and, consequently, justify considering Early Mamoran and Troumassan to represent two geographically distinct Troumassoid interaction spheres. This is shown as well by the close affinities between the Troumassan and Early Mamoran vessel repertoires. The individual character of both interaction spheres is shown by the presence of Caliviny linear painting on the ceremonial pottery of the Windwards and Barbados as opposed to the Cuevas/Longford-like polychrome-painted ceramics in the Early Mamoran of the Leeward Islands. While the former can be taken to have developed indigenously, not reflecting any mainland influence, the Mill Reef type of polychrome designs are apparently due to interaction with Puerto Rico and the Virgin Islands. As such, they are not the result of the continuation of local Saladoid painted motifs in the Leewards. That not all southern influence in the Troumassan pottery can be rejected is shown by the presence of the horned lugs, which may signify bats. The latter are typical of the Arauquinoid series on the mainland and in Trinidad, and due to their presence in the Greater Antilles in fact represent a pan-Caribbean motif.

Of course, this relatively fine-tuned analysis describes the features of the ceramic development from Saladoid to Troumassoid, but does not touch at all the question of why it took place. A more elaborate framework is needed to attempt to understand this cultural transformation, involving all relevant environmental, economic, social, political, demographic, and religious ramifications. For the moment only a few lines of thinking can be put forward that may be relevant for comprehending this process to some extent. As we have seen, the episode in which the Saladoid-Troumassoid transition occurred is one of severe climatic alteration and multiple cultural mutations, also involving population movement, in the coastal zone of the South American mainland and Trinidad. Clearly, the rapid Arauquinoid expansion towards the north led to the disintegration of the Saladoid/Barrancoid interaction sphere, and the extant cultural relationships, political alliances, and social networks connecting the Amerindian communities of Trinidad and Tobago with the southern Windwards were reformulated essentially. No doubt, this transition was associated with at least partial population change, especially in Trinidad. As shown in this volume, the social impacts of the Saladoid-Troumassoid alteration are reflected by major changes in settlement patterns and forms of house construction as well as mortuary practices, suggesting increasing manipulation of human remains as forms of expression of ancestor veneration.

Profound spiritual and societal change is indicated also by the simultaneous reduction of zoomorphic head lugs and the gradually growing anthropomorphic imagery shown on vessels. Major religious dissatisfaction in the transitional Saladoid-Troumassoid period is suggested by the apparently deliberate destruction of many small stone specimens of Saladoid three-pointers (*trigonolitos*), ubiquitous as shamanistic paraphernalia and most likely serving as objects for magically induced vegetative propagation, a form of iconoclasm which presumably took place at least in the Guadeloupean archipelago (Clerc 1973). It has been hypothesized that the mutilation of these three-pointers reflects a loss of confidence in their spiritual power caused by the prolonged dry and stormy climatic conditions of this episode. Moreover, Petitjean Roget (2010) has suggested that the petroglyphs of the Lesser Antilles were principally made in this particular time period as a form of response to the droughts experienced. Being principally situated near water sources, these rock drawings, which he assumes were intended to magically regulate mythic or actual extremes, would have functioned as forces or guardians protecting humanity from both floods and droughts. Finally, the changed climatic conditions would have prompted a tendency towards greater reverence for existing and persisting spring wells. Altogether, it is quite apparent that the Saladoid to Troumassoid development represents one of the most profound cultural, social, and spiritual alterations in the pre-Columbian era of the Lesser Antilles.

Résumé

En France, l'archéologie préventive a débuté officiellement en 2002 avec la création de l'Inrap et s'applique également aux départements d'Outre-Mer, tel que l'archipel de la Guadeloupe. Cette archéologie, guidée par la loi et partiellement par l'importance des prescriptions de fouilles du Ministère de la Culture, produit bon nombre de rapports de fouilles administratifs et scientifiques, qui, sous embargo pendant quatre ans, ont souvent été oubliés dans les bibliothèques des Services de l'Archéologie. Rares sont les travaux qui aboutissent à une publication scientifique. Cette situation a rendu peu favorable la diffusion de l'archéologie préventive française, notamment dans la Caraïbe. En outre, son accès y est limité, en raison de la barrière des langues, la communauté archéologique étant principalement hispanophone et anglophone. Ainsi, le travail des archéologues des îles françaises demeure quasiment inconnu au sein de la communauté scientifique de la Caraïbe. Ce manuscrit tente de pallier à ce problème épineux.

Ce travail présente les résultats de quatre fouilles préventives qui partagent plus ou moins la même fourchette chronologique, celle de l'Âge Céramique tardif, ou *Late Ceramic Age,* Néoindien récent, ce qui se traduit également par les Cultures du Troumassoïde (AD 900–1500). Les quatre sites (La Pointe de Grande Anse, CHU Belle-Plaine, STEP Goyave et Parking de Roseau) ont fait l'objet de fouilles préventives suite à l'implantation inévitable de projets de construction.

Les résultats sont scindés selon les études spécifiques et présentés par les archéologues et spécialistes ayant participé aux rapports de fouilles: datations radiocarbones, géomorphologie et environnements, habitats et villages, sépultures humaines, fosses profondes, matériels céramiques et lithiques précolombiens, porcelaines et verres européens, faune invertébrée et vertébrée, restes botaniques de phytolithes et amidons, stéroïdes fécaux, microanalyses des sédiments et des céramiques.

Le Troumassoïde étant une période précolombienne non homogène mais unique, les auteurs ont pu rassembler leurs données et proposer une analyse à l'échelle multiscalaire: inter-sites, la Guadeloupe et les Petites Antilles. Nos données interrogent également la question des origines de cette période céramique tardive précédant l'arrivée des premiers Européens. L'état des connaissances actuelles suggère que les dits troumassoïdes seraient le résultat d'une paisible évolution culturelle à partir de la période précédente dite saladoïde, s'éclatant finalement en un patchwork de styles différents. Finalement, nous proposons l'idée que cette évolution soit beaucoup moins fluide qu'on ne le pensait jusqu'à présent et potentiellement plus incisive avec l'arrivée de peuples différents venus du continent au cours de la phase finale du Saladoïde.

Nous souhaitons que cet effort collectif permettra de révéler la qualité de l'archéologie préventive et l'investissement des archéologues travaillant aux Antilles françaises malgré les barrières de l'insularité de la Caraïbe, des langues et des techniques de fouilles.

Bibliography

Ahlbrinck, W. 1931. *Encyclopaedie der Karaïben. Behelzend Taal, Zeden en Gewoonten Dezer Indianen*. Geïllustreerd door E. La Rose, Teekenaar bij den Opnemingsdienst te Paramaribo, Verhandelingen der Koninklijke Akademie van Wetenschappen te Amsterdam, Afdeeling Letterkunde, Nieuwe Reeks 27(1). Koninklijke Akademie van Wetenschappen, Amsterdam

Allaire, L. 1977. *Later Prehistory in Martinique and the Island Caribs: Problems in Ethnic Identification*, Unpublished Ph.D. Yale University, ms

Allaire, L. 1984. A reconstruction of early historical Island Carib pottery, *Southeastern Archaeology* 3 (2): 121–133

Allaire, L. 1990a. *Prehistoric Taino Interaction with the Lesser Antilles: The View from Martinique, F.W.I.*, Paper presented at the 55th Annual Meeting of the Society for American Archaeology, Las Vegas, Nevada, April 18–22, 1990, ms

Allaire, L. 1990b. Understanding Suazey, *Proceedings of the Eleventh Congress of the International Association for Caribbean Archaeology held San Juan de Puerto Rico July and August 1985*, A.G. Pantel Tekakis, I. Vargas Arenas and M. Sanoja Obediente (eds), 715–728. La Fundacion arqueologia, antropologica e hsitorica de Puerto Rico, La Universidad de Puerto Rico, Recinto de Rio Piedras, United States Department of Agriculture, Forest Service, San Juan

Allaire, L. 1997. Anse Trabaud: rapport 1997, *Le néolithique de la Martinique dans son contexte antillais.*, J.P. Giraud (ed), Projet collectif de recherche, SRA Martinique, ms

Allaire, L. 2013a. Ethnohistory of the Caribs, *The Oxford Handbook of Caribbean Archaeology*, W.F. Keegan, C.L. Hofman & R. Rodrigues Ramos (eds), 97–108. Oxford University Press, Oxford

Allaire, L. 2013b. Pensées et arrière-pensées sur la chronologie post-saladoïde de la Martinique, *Martinique, Terre amérindienne: Une approche multidisciplinaire*, B. Bérard (ed), 77–83. Sidestone Press, Leiden

Allaire, L. and D.T. Duval. 1995. St. Vincent revisited, *Proceedings of the XV International Congress for Caribbean Archaeology, Puerto Rico 1993*, R.E. Alegría and M. Rodríguez (eds), 255–262. Centro de Estudios Avanzados de Puerto Rico y el Caribe, Fundación Puertorriqueña de la Humanidades, Universidad del Turabo, San Juan de Puerto Rico

Allen, G.M. 1942. *Extinct and Vanishing Mammals of the Western Hemisphere*, American Committee for International Wildlife Protection 11—Special publication of the American Committee for International Wild Life Protection. The Intelligence Printing Co., Lancaster

Amouric, H., G. Guionova and L. Vallauri. 2012. Céramiques aux îles d'Amérique. La part de la Méditerranée (XVIIe-XIXe s.), *Actes du X congrès international de la céramique médiéval de Méditerranée à Silves, octobre 2012*, M.-J. Gonçalves and S. Gomez-Martinez (eds), 440–454. Camara Municpal, Silves

Anderson, J.-B., K. Milliken, D. Wallace, A. Rodriguez and A. Simms. 2010. Coastal impactunderestimated from rapid sea level rise underestimated, *EOS Transactions American Geophysical Union* 91 (23): 205–206

Anderson, J.-B., D. Wallace, A. Simms, A. Rodriguez and K. Milliken. 2014. Variable response of coastal environments of the northern Gulf of Mexico to sea-level rise and climate change: implications for future change, *Marine Geology* 352: 348–366

Atchison, J. and R. Fullagar. 1998. Starch residues on pounding implements from Jinmium rock-shelter. A closer look, *Recent Australian Studies of Stone Tools*, R. Fullagar (ed), 109–126, Sydney University Archaeological Methods Series 6, Sydney

Avery, G. 1993. *A Chronological Framework for Middle Style Olive Jar Rims*, Paper presented at the Annual Meeting of the Florida Anthropological Society, ms

Avery, G. 1997. *Pots as Packaging: The Spanish Olive Jar and Andalusian Transatlantic Commercial Activity, 16th–18th Centuries*, Unpublished Ph.D. University of Florida, ms

Badillo, J., Sued. 1995. The Island Caribs. New approaches to the question of ethnicity in the early colonial Caribbean, *Wolves from the Sea: Readings in the Anthropology of the Native Caribbean*, N.L. Whitehead (ed), 61–89, Caribbean Series 14. KITLV Press, Leiden

Balfet, H., M.-F. Fauvet-Berthelot and S. Monzon. 1989. *Lexique et typologie des poteries*. Presse du CNRS, Paris

Ball, T., K. Chandler-Ezell, R. Dickau, N. Duncan, T.C. Hart, J. Iriarte, C. Lentfer, A. Logan, H. Lu, M. Madella, D.M. Pearsall, D.R. Piperno, A.M. Rosen, L. Vrydaghs, A. Weisskopf and J. Zhang. 2016. Phytoliths as a tool for investigations of agricultural origins and dispersals around the world, *Journal of Archaeological Science* 68: 32–45

Banks, W. and C. Greenwood. 1975. *Starch and Its Components*. Edinburgh University Press, Edinburgh

Barbotin, M. 1970. Les sites archéologiques de Marie-Galante (Guadeloupe), *Compte-rendu des communications du Troisième Congrès International d'Etudes des Civilisations Précolombiennes des Petites Antilles*, R.P. Bullen (ed), 27–43. Grenada National Museum, Grenada

Barfleur, J.-L. 2002. *Espace Littoral et Milieux Humides: Belle Plaine (Abymes)*. Agence Warichi

Barton, H. and P.J. Matthews. 2006. Taphonomy, *Ancient Starch Research*, R. Torrence and H. Barton (eds), 75–94. Left Coast Press, Walnut Creek

Barton, H., R. Torrence and R. Fullagar. 1998. Clues to stone tool function re-examined: comparing starch grain frequencies on used and unused Obsidian artefacts, *Journal of Archaeological Science* 25: 1231–1238

Bates, R.L. and J.A. Jackson (eds). 1984. *Dictionary of Geological Terms*, 3rd edition. Anchor Press & Doubleday, New York

Beck, H.C. 1981. *Classification and Nomenclature of Beads and Pendants*. George Shumway Publisher, York, Pennsylvania [Reprint of 1928 original in Archaeologia 77, Society of Antiquaries of London]

Beck, W. and R. Torrence. 2006. Starch pathways, *Ancient Starch Research*, R. Torrence and H. Barton (eds), 53–74. Left Coast Press, Walnut Creek

Beets, C.J., S.R. Troelstra, P.M. Grootes, M.-J. Nadeau, K. van der Borg, A.F.M. de Jong, C.L. Hofman and M.P.L. Hoogland. 2006. Climate and Pre-Columbian settlement at Anse à la Gourde, Guadeloupe, Northeastern Caribbean, *Geoarchaeology* 21: 271–280

Belhache, P., M. Hubau, N. Platel, C. Ney, R. Chapoulie and M. Schvoerer. 1991. Le dégraissant des céramiques précolombiennes de la Martinique: Méthodologie, *Proceedings of the XIV Congress of the International Association for Caribbean Archaeology held in Barbados 1991*, A. Cummins and P. King (eds), 1–10. Barbados Museum and Historical Society

Bérard, B. 2004. *Les premières occupations agricoles de l'arc antillais, migration et insularité. Le cas de l'occupation saladoïde ancienne de la Martinique*, Ph.D. University Paris 1 (2003), BAR International Series 1299, Paris Monographs in American Archaeology 15. Archaeopress, Paris & London

Bérard, B. 2008. Lithic technology. A way to more complex diversity in Caribbean Archaeology, *Crossing the Borders: New Methods and Techniques in the Study of Archaeology Materials of the Caribbean*, C.L. Hofman, M.P.L. Hoogland and A.L. van Gijn (eds), 90–100. University of Alabama Press, Tuscaloosa

Bérard, B. (ed). 2013a. *Martinique, Terre amérindienne. Une approche multidsiciplinaire*. Sidestone Press, Leiden

Bérard, B. 2013b. Introduction. *Martinique, Terre amérindienne: Une approche multidisciplinaire*, B. Bérard (ed), 33–34. Sidestone Press, Leiden

Bérard, B. 2019. About boxes and labels: a periodization of the Amerindian occupation of the West Indies, *Journal of Caribbean Archaeology* 19: 51–67

Bérard, B. and G. Lafleur. 2013. Français et Indiens dans les Caraïbes au XVIIe siècle, *Français et Indiens d'Amérique: histoire d'une relation singulière, XVIe XXIe s.*, M. Augeron and G. Havard (eds), 53–64. Rivages du Xantons, Paris

Bérard, B. and G. Vernet. 1997. *La Savane des Pétrifications, Sainte-Anne. Opération de fouille programmée*. Document final de syntèse AFAN, SRA Guadeloupe, ms

Bercht, F., E. Brodsky, J.A. Farmer, and D. Taylor (eds). 1997. *Taíno. Pre-Columbian art and Culture from the Caribbean*. The Monacelli Press, New York

Berman, M.J. and D.M. Pearsall. 2008. At the crossroads: starch grain and phytolith analyses in Lucayan prehistory, *Latin American Antiquity* 19: 181–203

Bertran, P., D. Bonnissent, D. Imbert, P. Lozouet, N. Serrand and C. Stouvenot. 2004. Paleoclimat des Petites Antilles depuis 4000 ans BP: l'enregistrement de la lagune de Grand-Case à Saint-Martin, *Comptes rendus Géoscience* 336 (16): 1501–1510

Blair, H. Elliot, L.S.A. Pendleton and P. Francis Jr (eds). 2009. The beads of St. Catherines Island, *American Museum of Natural History Anthropological Papers* 89: 1–312

Blanshard, J.M.V. 1987. Starch granule structure and function, *Starch: Properties and Potential*, T. Galliard (ed), 16–54. John Wiley, New York

Blum, M., A. Sivers, T. Zayac and R. Goble. 2003. Middle Holocene Sea-Level and evolution of the Gulf of Mexico Coast, *Gulf Coast Association of Geological Societies Transactions* 53: 64–77

Bobrowski, P.T. and Ball, B.F. 1989. The theory and mechanics of ecological diversity in archaeology, *Quantifying Diversity in Archaeology*, R.D. Leonard and G.T. Jones (eds), 4–12. Cambridge University Press, Cambridge

Bochaton, C., B. Ephrem, B. Bérard, D. Cochard, B. Ephrem, M. Gala, K. Korzow Richter, A. Le Lay, S. Renou and A. Lenoble. 2021. The pre-Columbian site of Roseau (Guadeloupe, F.W.I.): intra-site chronological variability of the subsitence strategies in a Late Ceramic archaeological vertebrate assemblage, *Archaeological and Anthropological Sciences* 13: 16. https://doi.org/10.1007/s12520-020-01246-4

Bodinier, J.-L. 1992. *Les Anneaux de la Mémoire*. Exposition, Château des Ducs de Bretagne, CIM Corderie Royale

Bodu, P. 1984. *Rapport d'activités du 21 janvier 1984–30 janvier 1984*. Musées de la Guadeloupe, ms

Bonnissent, D. 2006. La Basse-Terre précolombienne, *Basse-Terre, patrimoine d'une ville antillaise*, M.E. Desmoulins (dir), 14–33. Editions Jasor, Pointe-à-Pitre

Bonnissent, D. 2008. *Archéologie précolombienne de l'Ile de Saint-Martin, Petites Antilles (3300 BC–1600 AD)*, 2 Vols., Ph.D. Université d'Aix-Marseille I, ms [published in 2010 by Éditions universitaires européennes, Paris]

Bonnissent, D. 2011. *Le village néoindien de Yuiketi: habitat et pratiques agricoles, Guadeloupe, Gourbeyre, Bisdary*, Rapport final d'opération fouille archéologique Inrap, ms

Bonnissent, D. 2012. Saint-Martin, Pointe du Canonnier, *Bilan Scientifique Régional* 2012: 110–114

Bonnissent, D. (ed). 2013. *Les gisements précolombiens de la Baie Orientale: campements du Mésoindiens et du Néoindien sur l'île de Saint-Martin (Petites Antilles)*, Documents d'archéologie française 107. Éditions de la Maison des sciences de l'homme, Paris

Bonnissent, D. and C. Hénocq. 1999. Saint-Martin, Hope Estate, *Bilan Scientifique* 1998: 40–41

Bonnissent, D., C. Hénocq and C. Stouvenot. 2002. Le Site Amérindien de Hope Estate (Saint-Martin, Petites Antilles): Extension et Chronologie, *Archéologie Précolombienne et Coloniale des Caraïbes, Actes du 123e Congrès National des Sociétés Historiques et Scientifiques, Antilles/Guyane 1998*, A. Delpuech, J.P. Giraud and A. Hesse (eds), 177–194. Éditions du CTHS, Paris

Bonnissent, D. and T. Romon (eds). 2004. *Occupations précolombiennes et coloniales des Petites Antilles. Fouilles de la Cathédrale de Basse-Terre*. Document final d'opération Inrap, ms

Bonnissent, D. and C. Stouvenot. 2005. Un site d'habitat Post- Saladoïde dans les Terres-Basses: Baie Aux Prunes (Plum Bay) Saint-Martin, Petites Antilles, *XX Congress for Caribbean Archaeology, June 2003*, 2 Vols., C. Tavarez Maria and M.A. Garcia Arévalo (eds), 31–40. Museo del Hombre, Fundacion Garcia Arévalo, Santo-Domingo

Boomert, A. 1980. Hertenrits: an Arauquinoid complex in North West Surinam, *Journal of Archaeology and Anthropology* 3 (1): 68–104

Boomert, A. 1986. The Cayo complex of Saint Vincent: ethnohistorical and archaeological aspects of the Island Carib problem, *Antropológica* 66: 3–68

Boomert, A. 2000. *Trinidad, Tobago and the Lower Orinoco Interaction Sphere, An Archaeological/ Ethnohistorical Study*, Ph.D. University of Leiden. Cairi Publications, Alkmaar

Boomert, A. 2004. Koriabo and the polychrome tradition: the late- prehistoric era between the Orinoco and Amazon Mouths, *Late Ceramic Age Societies in the Eastern Caribbean*, A. Delpuech and C.L. Hofman (eds), 251–266, Paris Monographs in American Archaeology 14, BAR IS 1273. Archaeopress, Oxford

Boomert, A. 2010. *Anse du Coq and Plage de Roseau. Notes on the ceramics of two late-prehistoric sites in the Guadeloupean archipelago*, ms

Boomert, A. 2011. Searching for Cayo in Dominica, *Proceedings of the 23rd Congress for the International Association of Caribbean Archaeology, Antigua 2009*, S. Rebovich (ed), 655–677. Dockyard museum, English Harbour

Boomert, A. 2013. Gateway to the mainland, Trinidad and Tobago, *The Oxford Handbook of Caribbean Archaeology*, W.F. Keegan, C.L. Hofman and R. Rodriguez Ramos (eds), 141–154. Oxford University Press, Oxford

Boomert, A. 2014. The Caribbean islands, *The Cambridge World Prehistory, Vol 2: East Asia and the Americas*, C. Renfrew and P.G. Bahn, (eds), 1217–1234. University of Cambridge Press, Cambridge

Bouchon, C., Y. Bouchon-Navaro and M. Louis. 2002. Les écosystèmes marins côtiers des Antilles, *La pêche aux Antilles (Martinique et Guadeloupe)*, G. Blanchet, B. Gobert and J.-A. Guerdrat (eds), 21–43. IRD éditions, Marseille

Bouchon, C., P. Portillo, M. Louis, F. Mazéas and Y. Bouchon-Navaro. 2008. Evolution récente des récifs coralliensdes îles de la Guadeloupe et de Saint-Barthélemy, *Revue d'écologie (Terre & Vie)* 63: 45–65

Bouysse, P., R. Schmidt-Effing and D. Westercamp. 1983. La Desirade Island (Lesser Antilles) revisited: lower Cretaceous radiolarian cherts and arguments against an ophiolitic origin for the basalt complex, *Geology* 11: 244–247

Bouysse, P., D. Westercamp and P. Andreieff. 1990. The Lesser Antilles island arc, *Proceedings of ODP Sci. Results* 110: 29–44. https://doi.org/10.2973/odp.proc.sr.110.166.1990

Bozarth, S.R. 1992. Classification of opal phytoliths formed in selected dicotyledons native to the Great Plains, *Phytolith Systematics: Emerging Issues: Advances in Archaeological and Museum Sciences*, G. Rapp Jr. and S.C. Mulholland (eds), 193–214. Plenum Press, New York

Brace, S., S.T. Turvey, M. Weksler, M.L.P. Hoogland and I. Barnes. 2015. Unexpected evolutionary diversity in a recently extinct Caribbean mammal radiation, *Proceedings of the Royal Society B* 282: 20142371

Bradley, J.W. 2014. Glass beads from Champlain's habitation on Saint Croix Island, Maine, 1604–1613, *Beads: Journal of the Society of Bead Researchers* 26: 47–63

Brancier, J. 2016. *Géoarchéologie Des Occupations Précolombiennes de Guyane Française: Étude Des Marqueurs Pédo-Sédimentaires de L'anthropisation*, Unpublished Ph.D. University of Paris I Panthéon–Sorbonne, ms

Brancier, J., C. Cammas, D. Todisco et E. Fouache. 2014. A micromorphological assessment of anthropogenic features in pre-Columbian French Guiana Dark Soils (FGDS): first results, *Zeitschrift Für Geomorphologie, Supplementary Issues* 58 (2): 109–39

Brancier, J., C. Cammas, D. Todisco, A. Jégouzo, T. Romon and M.M. van den Bel. 2018. Origine, characterisation et modes d'occupation des anthroposols précolombiens: approche micromorphologique compare de deux sites en Martinique et Guyane française, *Géomorphologie, paléoenvironnements et géoarchéologie des mondes tropicaux* 24 (3): 301–319

Breton, R. 1665. *Dictionnaire Caraïbe François, meslé de quantité de remarques historiques pour l'esclaircissement de la langue*. Gilles Bouquet, Auxerre

Breton, R. 1978. *Relations de l'île de la Guadeloupe faites par les missionnaires dominicains à leur général en 1647*. Société d'Histoire de la Guadeloupe, Basse-Terre [re-edition 1647]

Breukel, T.W. 2019. *Tracing Interactions in the Indigenous Caribbean through a Biographical Approach. Microwear and Material Culture across the Historical Divide (AD 1200–1600)*, Ph.D. Leiden University, ms

Briand, J., 2012. *Belle-plaine, Les Abymes, Guadeloupe (DOM),* Rapport final d'opération diagnostic archéologique Inrap, ms

Briand, J. 2013. *STEP de Sainte-Claire, Goyave, Guadeloupe,* Rapport final d'opération diagnostic archéologique Inrap, ms

Bright, A. 2003. *Spatial Dynamics and Social Development in the Northern Lesser Antilles. A Pilot Study based on Settlement Structure at the Site of Anse à la Gourde, Guadeloupe,* Master Thesis University of Leiden, ms

Bright, A. 2011. *Blood is Thicker than Water: Amerindian Occupation and the Intra- and Inter-insular Relationships in the Windward Islands*, Ph.D. University of Leiden. Sidestone Press, Leiden (first edition)

Brill, R.H., I.L. Barnes, S.S.C. Tong, E.C. Joel and M.J. Murtaugh. 1991. Laboratory studies of some European artifacts excavated on San Salvador Island, *Proceedings of the First San Salvador Conference: Columbus and his World*, D.C. Gerace (ed), 247–292. College of the Finger Lakes, Bahamian Field Station, Fort Lauderdale

Bronk Ramsey, C. 2005. *OxCal Program Version 3.10. Radiocarbon Accelerator Unit*, University of Oxford

Bullock, P., N. Fedorrof, A. Jongerius, G. Stoops and T. Tursina. 1985. *Handbook for Soil Thin Section Description*. Waine Research Publications, Wolverhampton

Burac, M. (ed). 2000. *Guadeloupe, Martinique et Guyane dans le monde américain: Réalités d'hier, mutations d'aujourd'hui, perspectives 2000*. Karthala/GEODE Caraïbe, Paris & Schoelcher

Burney, D.A. and L. Pigott-Burney. 1994. Holocene charcoal stratigraphy from Laguna Tortuguero, Puerto Rico, and the timing of human arrival on the island, *Journal of Archaeological Science* 21: 273–281

Caffrey, M.A., S.P. Horn, K.H. Orvis and K.A. Haberyan. 2015. Holocene environmental change at Laguna Saladilla, coastal north Hispaniola, *Palaeography, Palaeoclimatology, Paleoecology* 436: 9–22

Cammas, C. 2013. *Rapport d'analyse micromorphologique sur le site de le Cité de la Connaissance, Baillif, Basse-Terre, Guadeloupe*, ms

Cammas, C., J. Blanchard and P. Broutin. 2012. Fossés « collecteurs » et mares sur plateau, apport de l'analyse micromorphologique sur les modes d'occupation des sols: le cas du site de Bussy Saint-Georges (Seine-et-Marne, époque romaine—haut Moyen Age), *Actes du Colloque "Le sol face aux changements globaux" Journées d'Etude des Sols, 19–23 mars 2012 à Versailles*, 150–151. AFES, INRA, AgroParisTech, Paris

Cammas, C. and J. Wattez. 2009. L'approche micromorphologique: méthode et application aux stratigraphies archéologiques, *La géologie, les sciences de la terre appliquées à l'archéologie*, A. Ferdière (ed), 181–216. Éditions Errance, Paris

Carter, J. 1982. Spanish olive jars from Fermeuse Harbour, Newfoundland, *Revue de la culture matérielle* 16: 99–108

Casagrande, F., P. Bertran, J.-J. Faillot, C. Fouilloud, S. Grouard, M. Hildebrand, S. Kayamaré, T. Romon and N. Serrand. 2016. *La Ramée, Sainte-Rose, Guadeloupe,* Rapport d'opération fouille archéologique Inrap, ms

Catlin, B., M. Smith and J.B. Petersen. 2005. Mineralogical and petrological investigation of prehistoric ceramic sherds from the island of Anguilla in the Northern Lesser Antilles island chain of the Caribbean, *Geological Society of America National Meeting* 37 (7): 276

Chalumeau, F. 2009. Christophe Colomb et la découverte de la Guadeloupe, *Généalogie et Histoire de la Caraïbe*, Numéro spécial novembre 2009: 1–27

Chandler-Ezell, K., D.M. Pearsall and J.A Zeidler. 2006. Root and Tuber Phytoliths and Starch Grains Document Manioc (Manihot esculenta), Arrowroot (Maranta arundinacea), and Llerén (Calathea allouia) at the Real Alto Site, Ecuador, *Economic Botany* 60: 103–120

Chanlatte Baik, L.A. 1984. *Arqueología de Vieques. Centro de investigationes arqueologicas.* Universidad de Puerto Rico Recinto de Rio Piedras

Chaplin, R.E. 1971. *The Study of Animal Bones from Archaeological Sites.* Seminar Press, London/ New York

Christman, R.A. 1953. Geology of St. Bartholomew, St. Maarten and Anguilla, *Bulletin of the Geological Society of America* 64: 65–96

Clerc, E. 1968. Sites précolombiens de la cote nord-est de al Grande-Terre de Guadeloupe, *Proceedings of the Second International Congress for the Study of pre-Columbian Cultures in the Lesser Antilles held in Barbados 1967*, R.P. Bullen (ed), 47–60. The Barbados Museum and Historical Society, Barbados

Clerc, E. 1970. Recherches archéologiques en Guadeloupe, *Paralèlles* 36–37: 69–88

Clerc, E. 1973. Les Trois-Pointes des Sites Précolombiens de la Côte Nord-Est de la Grande-Terre de la Guadeloupe, *Proceedings of the Fourth International Congress of pre-Columbian Cultures held in St. Lucia 1971*, R.P. Bullen (ed), 73–81. St Lucia Archaeological and Historical Society, Castries

Cody, A.K. 1991. *Prehistoric Patterns of Exchange in the Lesser Antilles: Materials, Models, Preliminary Observations*, Master Thesis Diego University, ms

Colas, C., P. Bertran, G. Chancerel, A. Chancerel and J-M. Richard. 2002. *Le Tourlourous, Marie Galante, Guadeloupe, 97108005 AH.* Document final de synthèse DRAC, Inrap, ms

Cooper, J., A.V.M. Samson, M.A. Nieves, M.J. Lace, J. Caamano-Dones, C. Cartwright, P.N. Kambesis and L. del Olmo Frese. 2016. The Mona Chronicle': the archaeology of early religious encounter in the new world, *Antiquity* 90 (352): 1054–1071

Corsini, M., J.M. Lardeaux, C. Verati, E. Voitus and M. Balagne. 2011. Discovery of Lower Cretaceous synmetamorphic thrust tectonics in French Lesser Antilles (La Désirade Island, Guadeloupe): implications for Caribbean geodynamics, *Tectonics* 30: TC4005. https://doi.org/10.1029/2011TC002875

Courtaud, P. 1996. "Anthropologie de sauvetage": vers une optimisation des méthodes d'enregistrement, *Bulletin et Mémoire de la Société d'Anthropologie de Paris* 3–4: 157–167

Courty, M.-A., P. Goldberg and R.-I. Macphail. 1989. *Soil Micromorphology in Archaeology.* Cambridge University Press, Cambridge

Crock, J.G. 2000. *Interisland Interaction and the Development of Chiefdoms in the Eastern Caribbean,* Unpublished Ph.D. University of Pittsburgh, ms

Crock, J.G. and R.N. Bartone. 1998. Archaeology of Trants, Montserrat. Part 4. Flaked stone and stone bead industries, *Annals of Carnegie Museum* 67: 197–224

Crock, J.G., B.F. Morse, J.B. Petersen, C. Descantes and M.D. Glascock. 2008. Preliminary interpretations of ceramic compositional analysis from Late Ceramic Age sites in Anguilla and the Salt River Site in St. Croix, *Journal of Caribbean Archaeology*, C. Descantes, R.J. Speakman, M.D. Glascock and M.T. Boulanger (éds.), 45–56, Special Publication 2: An Exploratory Study into the Chemical Characterization of Caribbean Ceramics

Crock, J.G. and J.B. Petersen. 1999. *A Long and Rich Cultural Heritage: The Anguilla Archaeology Project 1992–1998. A Report Prepared for the Anguilla Archaeological and Historical Society, The Valley, Anguilla, British West Indies*, ms

Crowther, A., M. Haslam, N. Oakden, D. Walde and J. Mercader. 2014. Documenting contamination in ancient starch laboraties, *Journal Archaeological Science* 49: 90–104

Curet, L.A. and J. Oliver. 1998. Mortuary practices, social development, and ideology in Precolumbian Puerto Rico, *Latin American Antiquity* 9 (3): 217–239

Deagan, K. 1987. *Artifacts of the Spanish Colonies of Florida and the Caribbean, 1500–1800. Vol. I: Ceramics, Glassware, and Beads.* Smithsonian Institution Press, Washington

Debet, B. and M. Py. 1975. Classification de la céramique non tournée protohistorique du Languedoc Méditerranéen, *Revue archéologique de Narbonnaise*, Supplément 4. CNRS/Secrétariat à la culture/ Université de Montpellier III, Paris

Delpuech, A. 1998. *Le Patrimoine des Communes de la Guadeloupe.* Edition Flohic, Charenton-le-Pont

Delpuech, A. 2001. *Guadeloupe amérindienne, Guides archéologiques de la France.* Éditions du patrimoine, Paris

Delpuech, A. 2007. Archéologie amérindienne en Guadeloupe, *Les nouvelles de l'archéologie* 108–109: 10–19

Delpuech, A. 2016. Mangiando nemici o eroi. La complessa storia culturale e il cannibalismo nelle popolazioni delle Piccole Antille, *Ligabue Magazine* 68: 54–89

Delpuech, A. and C. Hofman (eds). 2004. *Late Ceramic Societies in the Eastern Caribean. Environmental and Social Context*, British Archaeological Reports, International Series 1273, Paris Monographs in American Archaeology 14. Archaeopress, Oxford

Delpuech, A., C.L. Hofman and M.L.P. Hoogland. 1994. *Rapport de sondages archéologiques: Anse Duquerry, Chemin de la Coulisse, Vallée d'Or, Pointe de Grande Anse. Trois-Rivières, Guadeloupe,* Rapport SRA, ms

Delpuech, A., C.L. Hofman and M.L.P. Hoogland. 1995. *Rapport de fouille programmée. Grande Anse, Terre-de- Bas Guadeloupe (n° de site 97130003),* Rapport SRA, ms

Delpuech, A., C.L. Hofman and M.L.P. Hoogland. 2001a. Excavations at the site of Anse à la Gourde, Guadeloupe. Organisation, history, and environmental setting, *Proceedings of the XVIII International Congress for Caribbean Archaeology held in Grenada*, 156–162. Association International d'Archéologie de la Caraïbe, Région Guadeloupe, Basse-Terre

Delpuech, A., C.L. Hofman and M.L.P. Hoogland. 2001b. *Fouille programmée pluriannuelle 1995–2000, Rapport de Synthèse.* Conseil Régional de la Guadeloupe/Municipalité de Saint-François/DRAC/RUL, ms

Delpuech, A., C.L. Hofman and M.L.P. Hoogland. 2002. Premiers horticulteurs amérindiens dans l'archipel guadeloupéen: Morel I (Le Moule) et la question huecan/cedrosan saladoïdes, *Archéologie précolombienne et coloniale des Caraïbes*, A. Delpuech, J.-P. Giraud & A. Hesse (eds), 127–149, Actes des congrès nationaux des sociétés historiques et scientifiques, 123e Antilles-Guyane, 1998. Editions CTHS, Paris

DeMille, C.N. 1996. *Analysis of the Post Saladoid Lithic Assemblage, Muddy Bay (PH-14), Antigua, 1994, Archaeological Investigations at Muddy Bay (PH-14), Antigua, West Indies: A Post-Saladoid Settlement*, A.R. Murphy (ed), 155–190, ms

DeMille, C.N. 2005. *A Tale of Chert with a Side of Shell. The Preceramic Occupation of Antigua, West Indies,* Unpublished Ph.D. University of Calgary, ms

Dickau, R., M.C. Bruno, J. Iriarte, H. Prümers, C.J. Betancourt, I. Holst and F.E. Mayle. 2012. Diversity of cultivars and other plant resources used at habitation sites in the Llanos de Mojos, Beni, Bolivia: evidence from macrobotanical remains, starch grains, and phytolithes, *Journal of Archaeological Science* 39: 357–370

Dickau, R., J. Iriarte, F.E. Mayle and B.S. Whitney. 2013. Differentiation of Neotropical Ecosystems by Modern Soil Phytolith Assemblages and its Implications for Paleoenvironmental and Archaeological Reconstruction, *Revue of Palaeobotany and Palynology* 193: 15–37

Dodson, P. and D. Wexlar. 1979. Taphonomic investigations of owl pellets, *Paleobiology* 5: 275–284

Donahue, J., D.R. Watters and S. Millspaugh. 1990. Thin petrography of Northern Lesser Antilles ceramics, *Geoarchaeology* 5 (3): 229–254

Drewett, P.L. 2000. *Prehistoric Settlements in the Caribbean. Fieldwork in Barbados, Tortola and the Cayman Islands,* Archetype Publications of the Barbados Museum and Historical Society, Saint Michael

Drewett, P.L. and S.M. Fitzpatrick. 2000. Barbados ceramics: scientific analysis, *Prehistoric Settlements in the Caribbean, Fieldwork in Barbados, Tortola and the Cayman Islands*, P.L. Drewett (ed), 141–146. Archetype Publications of the Barbados Museum and Historical Society, Saint Michael

Drewett, P.L. and M. Hill Harris. 1991. The Archaeological Survey of Barbados: 1985–87, *Proceedings of the XII Congress of International Association for Caribbean Archaeology held in Cayenne 1987*, L. Sickler Robinson (éd.), 175–202. AIAC, Martinique

Dubelaar, C. 1984. *A Study on South American and Antillean Petroglyphs*, Unpublished Ph. D, Leiden University, ms

Dubelaar, C. 1995. *The Petroglyphs of the Lesser Antilles, the Virgin Islands and Trinidad,* Publications of the Foundation for Scientific Research in the Caribbean 35, Amsterdam

Ducos, P. 1975. Analyse statistique des collections d'ossements d'animaux, *Archaeozoological Studies,* A.T. Clason (ed), 35–44. North-Holland Publ. Co. and American Elsevier, Amsterdam, Oxford, New York

Duday, H. 2005 L'archéothanatologie ou archéologie de la mort, *Objets et méthodes en paléoanthropologie,* O. Dutour, J.-J. Hublin and B. Vandermeersch (eds), 153–215. Éditions CTHS, Paris

Duday, H., P. Courtaud, E. Crubezy, P. Sellier and A-M. Tillier. 1990. L'anthropologie de terrain: reconnaissance et interprétation des gestes funéraires, *Bulletins et Mémoires de la Société d'Anthropologie de Paris* NS 2 (3–4): 29–50

Duday, H. and P. Sellier. 1990. L'archéologie des gestes funéraires et la taphonomie, *Les nouvelles de l'Archéologie* 40: 12–14

Dumon, A., E. Bourdon, B. Lachassagne and B. Ladouche. 2009. *Caractérisation hydrogéologique du basin versant de la Rivière Pérou à Capesterre-Belle-Eau—Guadeloupe.* BRGM, Public report RP-56766-FR

Durocher, M. 2021. *Histoire biologique et culturelle de deux rongeurs emblématiques des Petites Antilles: approches bioarchéologiques,* Unpublished Ph.D. Muséum national d'Histoire naturelle, ms

Durocher, M., V. Nicolas, S. Perdikaris, D. Bonnissent, G. Robert, K. Debue, A. Evin and S. Grouard. 2020. Archaeobiogeography of extinct rice rats (Oryzomyini) in the Lesser Antilles during the Ceramic Age (500 BCE to 1500 CE), *The Holocene* 31 (10): 433–455

Du Tertre, J.B. 1654. *Histoire générale des isles de St Christophe, de la Guadeloupe, de la Martinique et autres dans l'Amérique.* Chez Th. Jolly, Paris

Du Tertre, J.B. 1667–71. *Histoire générale des Antilles habitée par les français.* 4 Tomes. Chez Th. Jolly, Paris

Erikson, Ph. 1987. De l'apprivoisement à l'approvisionnement: chasse, alliance et familiarisation en Amazonie indigène, *Techniques et Culture* 9: 105–140

Etrich, C. 2002. *Déviation de la RN 1. Capesterre-Belle-Eau (Guadeloupe). Source Pérou, Marquisat, Allée du Manoir, Rivière de Grand Carbet. Basse-Terre.* Document final de syntèse Inrap, ms

Etrich, C. 2003. *"24 rue Schoelcher" (97 Guadeloupe), Basse-Terre,* Rapport de diagnostic Inrap, ms

Etrich, C., P. Bertran, G. Chancerel, P. Fouéré, F. Honoré and C. Stouvenot. 2003. *Le Site de 'L'Allée Dumanoir', Déviation de la RN 1 Capesterre Belle-Eau (Guadeloupe 97).* Inrap /Conseil Régional de la Guadeloupe/DRAC Guadeloupe, ms

Etrich, C., L. Bruxelles, F. Casagrande, L. Cummings, N. Sellier-Ségard, N. Serrand, C. Stouvenot and C. Yost. 2013. *De l'ichali au chemin de fer, Moulin à eau à Capesterre Belle-Eau, Guadeloupe (971),* Rapport de fouille archéologique Inrap, ms

Evans, C. and B.J. Meggers. 1960. *Archaeological Investigations in British Guiana,* Bulletin Bureau of American Ethnology 177. United States Government Printing Office, Washington DC

Falci, C.G., A.C.S Knaf, A. Van Gijn, G.R. Davies and C.L. Hofman. 2020. Lapidary production in the eastern Caribbean: a typo-technological and microwear study of ornaments from the site of Pearls, Grenada, *Archaeological and Antropologickal Sciences* 12 (53): 1–16

Feller, C., M. Fournier, D. Imbert, C. Caratini and L. Martin. 1992. Datations ^{14}C et palynologie d'un sédiment tourbeux continu (0-7 m) dans la mangrove de Guadeloupe (F.W.I.): résultats préliminaires, *Evolution des littoraux de Guyane et de la zone caraïbe méridionale pendant le quaternaire,* M.-T. Prost (éd), 193–202. ORSTOM, Paris

Feuillet, N., I. Manighetti and P. Tapponnier. 2002. Arc parallel extension and localization of volcanic complexes in Guadeloupe, Lesser Antilles, *Journal Geophysical Research* 107 (B12): 2331. https://doi.org/10.1029/2001JB000308

Fischer, J.B. 1829. *Synopsis Mammalium.* J.G. Cottae, Stuttgardtiae

Fitzpatrick, E.A. 1993. *Soil Microscopy and Micromorphology.* Wiley, New York

Fitzpatrick, S.M. 2013. The Southern Route Hypothesis, *The Oxford Handbook of Caribbean Archaeology,* W.F. Keegan, C.L. Hofman and R. Rodrígues Ramos (eds), 198–204. Oxford University Press, Oxford

Fitzpatrick, S.M. 2015. The pre-Columbian Caribbean: colonization, population dispersal, and island adaptations, *Paleoamerica* 1 (4): 305–331

Fitzpatrick, S.M., J.A. Carstensen, K.M. Marsaglia, C. Descantes, M.D. Glascock, Q. Kaye and M. Kappers. 2008. Preliminary petrographic and chemical analyses of prehistoric ceramics from Caria-cou, West Indies, *Journal of Caribbean Archaeology*, C. Descantes, R.J. Speakman, M.D. Glascock & M.T. Boulanger (eds), 59–83, Special Publication 2: An Exploratory Study into the Chemical Characterization of Caribbean Ceramics

Florès Blancaneaux, A. 2009. *Contribution à l'étude de la disparition de la culture saladoïde aux Petites Antilles: correlation préhistorique possible entre climat et culture*, Unpublished Ph.D. Université des Antilles, ms

Forsyth, C.I., Major. 1901. The musk-rat of Santa Lucia (Antilles), *Annals and Magazine of Natural History Series* 7 (7): 204–206

Fouéré, P. 2003. Les objets lithiques. Étude techno-archéologique, *Rivière du Grand Carbet, Capes-terre-Belle- Eau (97). Un habitat amérindien multiphasé*, A. Toledo i Mur (ed), 60–71, Rapport de fouille Inrap, ms

Fouéré, P. 2006. Le matériel lithique, *Fouille préventive de la Gare Maritime de Basse Terre (Guade-loupe)*, T. Romon (dir), 82–101, Rapport de fouille Inrap, ms

Fouéré, P., S. Bailon, D. Bonnissent, A. Chancerel, P. Courtaud, M.F. Deguilloux, S. Grouard, A. Lenoble, P. Mora, J. Monney, K. Pinçon, A. Queffelec and C. Stouvenout. 2015. *La grotte de Morne Rita, Capesterre de Marie-Galante (Guadeloupe): Nouvelles données*, Paper Presented at the XXVI Congress of the International Association for Caribbean Archaeology, Sint Maarten, ms

Fronteau, G. and M.M. van den Bel. 2021. Anthropogenic temper versus geological and pedological inclusions: grog temper as a possible chrono-cultural marker for the Late Ceramic Age in the pre-Columbian Lesser Antilles, Special Issue Gearcheology J. Curie, S. Vandevelde, A. Quiquerez and C. Petit, *BSGF – Earth Sciences Bulletin* 192: 17, https://doi.org/10.1051/bsgf/2021009

Fuess, M.T. 1995. Preliminary archaeological research of prehistoric Amerindian sites on Antigua, Northern Lesser Antilles, *Proceedings of the XV International Congress of Caribbean Archaeology held in Puerto Rico 1993*, R.E. Alegria and M. Rodriguez (eds), 173–180. Centro de Estudios Avan-zados de Puerto Rico y el Caribe, Fundacion Puertorriqueña de la Humanidades y la Universidad del Turabo, San Juan

Fuess, M.T., J. Donahue, D.R. Watters and D. Nicholson. 1991. A report on thin section petrography of the ceramics from Antigua, Northern Lesser Antilles: method and theory, *Proceedings of the XIV Congress of the International Association for Caribbean Archaeology held in Barbados 1991*, A. Cummins and P. King (eds), 25–39, Barbados Museum and Historical Society

Fullagar, R. 2006. Starch on artifacts, *Ancient Starch Research*, R. Torrence and H. Barton (eds), 177–204. Left Coast Press, Walnut Creek

Gagnepain, J., C. Luzi, N. Serrand and C. Stouvenot. 2007. *Première approche du site de Caille à Bélasse*, Rapport de fouille programmée, campagne 2006–2007, ms

García-Casco, A., S. Knippenberg, R. Rodríguez Ramos, G.E. Harlow, C.L. Hofman, J. Pomo and I.F. Blanco-Quintero. 2013. Pre-Columbian jadeite artifacts from the Golden Rock Site, St. Eustatius, Lesser Antilles, with special reference to jadeite artifacts from Elliot's, Antigua: implications for potential source regions and long-distance exchange networks in the Greater Caribbean, *Journal of Archaeological Science* 40: 3153–3169

García-Casco, A., A. Rodriguez-Vega, J. Cárdenas Párraga, M.A. Iturralde-Vinent, C. Lázaro, I. Blanco Quintero, Y. Rojas Agramonte, A. Kröner, K. Núñez Cambra, G. Millán, R.L. Torres-Roldán and S. Carrasquilla. 2009. A new jadeitite jade locality (Sierra del Convento, Cuba): first report and some petrological and archeological implications, *Contributions to Mineralogy and Petrology* 158: 1–16

Garrabé, F. and P. Andreieff. 1988. *Grande Terre: notice explicative, Carte géologique à 1/50 000, Département de la Guadeloupe*, avec la collaboration de Ph. Bouysse et J. Rodet. Ministère de l'Industrie, des P. et T. et du Tourisme, BRGM, Service Géologique National, Orléans

Garrad, C. 2001. *Glass Trade Beads and the Petun*. www.wyandot.org/petun/RB%2031%20to%2036/PRI32.pdf, accessed 14 Dec. 2013.

Gassón, R.A. 2002. Orinoquia: the archaeology of the Orinoco River Basin, *Journal of World Prehistory* 16 (3): 237–311

Gautier, J. 1974. Étude des pâtes céramiques de la Martinique pré-colombienne, *Proceedings of the Fifth International Congress for the Study of Pre-Columbian Cultures of the Lesser Antilles held in Antigua July 22–28 1973*, R.R. Bullen (ed), 133–139. The Antigua Archaeological Society

Gilbert, A. 1990. Les pétroglyphes de la Martinique et de la Guadeloupe, *Congrès du Cinquantenaire de la Sociedad Espeleofica de Cuba, La Havane, 15–19 janvier 1990*, ms

Goggin, J.M. 1960. *The Spanish Olive Jar: An Introductory Study*, Yale University Publications in Anthropology 62. Yale University Press, New Haven

Goggin, J.M. 1968. *Spanish Majolica in the New World*, Yale University Publications in Anthropology 72. Yale University Press, New Haven

Goldberg, P. and R.-I. Macphail. 2006. *Practical and Theoretical Geo-Archaeology*. Blackwell Scientific, Oxford

Goodwin, C. 1979. *The Prehistoric Cultural Ecology of St. Kitts, West Indies: A Case Study in Island Archaeology,* Unpublished Ph.D. Arizona State University, ms

Gott, B., H. Barton, S. Delwen and R. Torrence. 2006. Biology of starch, *Ancient Starch Research*, R. Torrence and H. Barton (eds), 35–46. Left Coast Press, Walnut Creek

Grayson, D.K. 1984. *Quantitative Zooarchaeology: Topics in the Analysis of Archaeological Faunas.* Academic Press, Orlando

Grouard, S. 2001. *Subsistance, systèmes techniques et gestion territoriale en milieu insulaire antillais précolombien—Exploitation des Vertébrés et des Crustacés aux époques Saladoïdes et Troumassoïdes de Guadeloupe (400 av. J.-C. à 1500 ap. J.-C.),* Unpublished Ph.D. Université de Nanterre-Paris X, ms

Grouard, S. 2005. Une Population De Pêcheurs-Piégeurs- Collecteurs À Baie Aux Prunes / PlumBay, Saint-Martin, Petites Antilles, *Proceedings of the XX Congress for Caribbean Archaeology, June 2003*, 307–316. Santo-Domingo

Grouard, S. 2007. Modes de vie des Précolombiens des Antilles françaises. Synthèse des données archéozoologiques, *Les Nouvelles de l'Archéologie* 108–109: 91–101

Grouard, S. 2008. *Rapport de fouille programmée pluriannuelle du site amérindien de Macabou (Commune du Vauclin, Martinique, 97232001), Campagne 2008.* Service Régional de l'Archéologie de Martinique, Muséum national d'Histoire naturelle, Association Ouacabou, ms

Grouard, S. 2010a. *Rapport de fouille programmée pluriannuelle du site amérindien de Macabou (Commune du Vauclin, Martinique, 97232001), Campagne 2009 (04 au 30 avril 2009),* Rapport préliminaire en vue de la préparation du Document Final de Synthèse, Ministère de la Culture, Direction du Patrimoine, Sous-Dir. de l'Archéologie de Martinique, ms

Grouard, S. 2010b. Caribbean Archaeozoology, *Estado actual de la Arqueozoología Latinoamericana /Current Advances in Latin-American Archaeozoology*, G. Mengoni Goñalons, J. Arroyo-Cabrales, O.J. Polaco and F.J. Aguilar (eds), 89–109. Instituto Nacional de Antropología e Historia y Consejo Nacional para la Ciencia y la Tecnología, México

Grouard, S. 2013. Chasses, Pêches et Captures des faunes vertébrées et crustacées des occupations côtières céramiques récentes du sud de la Martinique (Saladoïde récent, Vè siècle ap. J.-C.–Suazoïde récent, XVe ap. J. C., *Martinique Terre Amérindienne: Une approche pluridisciplinaire*, B. Bérard (ed), 115–162. SidestonePress, Leiden

Grouard, S. 2016. Analyse faune vertébrée et invertébrée, *Guadeloupe, Les Abymes CHU Belle-Plaine. Un site précolombien à l'intérieur des terres*, M. van den Bel (dir.), 127–139, Rapport d'opération archéologique Inrap, ms

Grouard, S., M. Ballinger, B. Bérard, K. Debue, Y. Franel. 2016. Opération 2009 de fouille programmée sur le site Précolombien de Macabou (site n°97231001 AP), *Bilan Scientifique Martinique* 2009: 56–60

Grouard, S. and M. Durocher. 2019. *MIGGRANT (MorphométrIe Géométrique et Génétique sur les Rongeurs des Petites ANTilles), Dynamiques archéobiogéographiques insulaire de deux rongeurs précolombiens des Petites Antilles: changements biologiques, migrations et translocations, PEPS*

ECOMOB Ecologie des mobilités: espèces invasives, dispersion, migration, recomposition dans des mondes en mutation, INEE CNRS, ms

Grouard, S. and E. Pellé. 2009. La faune de la fosse 3, *Le site de La Pointe de Grande Anse. Une occupation amérindienne et coloniale dans le sud de Basse-Terre, Commune de Trois-Rivières, Guadeloupe*, M.M. van den Bel (dir.), 71–79, Rapport d'opération archéologique Inrap, ms

Grouard, S. and S. Perdikaris. 2019. *From Frog to Bat: The Extraordinary Bestiary of the Pre-Columbians from the Caribbean*, Paper presented at SAA 84th Annual Meeting at Albuquerque, NM, Session ID: 4320, The Intangible Dimensions of Food in the Caribbean Ancient and Recent Past, ms

Grouard, S. and N. Serrand. 2005. *Rapport de fouille programmée du site Amérindien de Macabou*, Rapport d'opération de fouille archéologique programmée, ms

Guilloré, P. 1985. *Méthode de fabrication mécanique et en série des lames minces*. 2e Édition. Doc. Ronéot. IAPG, Département des sols, Paris

Hamilton, W.R., A.R. Woolley and A.C. Bishop. 1992. *Minerals, Rocks and Fossils*. Hamlyn Guide, Reed International Books Limited, Hong Kong

Hardy, M., 2008. *Saladoid Economy and Complexity on the Arawakan Frontier*, Unpublished Ph.D. Florida State University, ms

Harlow, G.E. 1993. Jadeitites, albitites and related rocks from the Motagua Fault Zone, Guatemala, *Journal of Metamorphic Geology* 12: 49–68

Harlow, G.E., M.J. Berman, J. Cárdenas-Párraga, A. Hertwig, A. Garcia-Casco and P.L. Gnivecki. 2019. Pre-Columbian jadeitite artifacts from San Salvador Island, Bahamas and comparison with jades of the eastern Caribbean and jadeitites of the greater Caribbean region. *Journal of Archaeological Science: Reports 26*, Article 101830. https://doi.org/10.1016/j.jasrep.2019.04.019.

Harlow, G.E., A.R. Murphy, D.J. Hozjan, C.N. DeMille and A.A. Levinson. 2006. Pre-Columbian jadeite axes from Antigua, West Indies. Description and possible sources, *Canadian Mineralogist* 44: 305–321

Harlow, G.E., V.B. Sisson and S.S. Sorensen. 2011. Jadeitite from Guatemala: new observations and distinctions among multiple occurrences, *Geologica Acta* 9 (3): 363–387

Harris, E., M. Brown, G. Brown. 1993. *Practices of Archaeological Stratigraphy*. Academic Press, London

Harris, P.B., O'. 1972. *Notes on Trinidad Archaeology*. Trinidad and Tobago Historical Society (South Section). Trinidad and Tobago Historical Society, Pointe-à-Pierre

Harris, P.B., O'. 1983. Antillean axes/adzes: persistence of an Archaic tradition, *Proceedings of the Ninth International Congress for the Study of the pre-Columbian Cultures of the Lesser Antilles, Santo Domingo 1981*, L. Allaire and F.-M. Mayer (eds), 257–290. Centre des Recherches Caraïbes, Université de Montréal

Haslam, M. 2004. The decomposition of starch grains in soils: implications for archaeological residue analyses, *Journal of Archaeological Science* 31 (12): 1715–1734

Haug, G.H., D. Günther, L.C. Peterson, D.M. Sigman, K.A. Hughen and B. Aeschlimann. 2003. Climate and the collapse of the Maya civilization, *Science* 299: 1731–1735

Haug, G.H., K.A. Hughen, D.M. Sigman, L. Peterson, L. and U. Rohl. 2001. Southward migration of the Intertropical Convergence Zone through the Holocene, *Science* 293: 1304–1308

Haviser, J.B. 1987. *An Archaeological Excavation at the Cupecoy Bay Site (SM-001), St. Maarten, Netherlands Antilles*, Report of the Archaeological and Anthropological Institute of the Netherlands Antilles 6, ms

Haviser, J.B. 1999. Hope Estate: Lithics, *Archaeological Investigations on St. Martin (Lesser Antilles). The Sites of Norman Estate, Anse des Pères, and Hope Estate. With a contribution to the 'La Hueca problem'*, C.L. Hofman and M.L.P. Hoogland (eds), 189–202, Archaeological Studies Leiden University 4. Leiden University Press, Leiden

Henry, A.G., H.F. Hudson and D.R. Piperno. 2009. Changes in starch grain morphology from cooking, *Journal of Archaeological Science* 36: 915–922

Henry, A.G. and D.R. Piperno. 2008. Using plant microfossils from dental calculus to recover human diet: a case study from Tell al-Raqā'i, Syria, *Journal of Archaeological Science* 35: 1943–1950

Higuera-Gundy, A., M. Brenner, D.A. Hodell, J.H. Curtis, B.W. Leyden and M.W. Binford. 1999. A 10,300 14C yr record of climate and vegetation change from Haiti, *Quaternary Research* 52: 159–170

Hodell, D.A., J.H. Curtis, G.A. Jones, A. Higuera-Gundy, M. Brenner, M.E. Binford and K.T. Dorsey. 1991. Reconstruction of Caribbean climate change over the past 10,500 years, *Nature* 352: 790–793

Hoffman, Ch. A. 1979. The ceramic typology of the Mill Reef site, Antigua, Leeward Islands, *Journal of the Virgin Islands Archaeological Society* 7: 35–51

Hoffman, Ch. A. 1991. Archaeological Investigations at the Long Bay Site, San Salvador, Bahamas, *Proceedings of the First San Salvador Conference: Columbus and his World*, D.T. Gerace (ed), 237–245. College Center of the Finger Lakes, Bahamian Field Station, Fort Lauderdale

Hofman, C.L. 1999. Three Late Prehistoric Sites in the Periphery of Guadeloupe: Grande Anse, Les Saintes and Morne Cybèle 1 and 2, La Désirade, *Proceedings of the XVI International Congress for Caribbean Archaeology*, Guadeloupe 1995, Vol. 2, 156–167. CRG, Basse-Terre

Hofman, C.L. 1993. *In Search of the Native Population of Pre-Columbian Saba, Part 1. Pottery Styles and Their Interpretations,* Unpublished Ph.D. University of Leiden, ms

Hofman, C.L. 2001. Saint-François, Anse à la Gourde, *Bilan Scientifique de la Région Guadeloupe* 2000: 32–36

Hofman, C.L. 2013. The post-Saladoid in the Lesser Antilles (A.D. 600/800-1492), *The Oxford Handbook of Caribbean Archaeology*, W.F. Keegan, C.L. Hofman and R. Rodrigues Ramos (eds), 205–220. Oxford University Press, Oxford

Hofman, C.L. and M.L.P. Hoogland. 2003. Plum Piece, evidence for Archaic seasonal occupation on Saba, northern Lesser Antilles around 3300 BP, *Journal of Caribbean Archaeology* 4: 12–27

Hofman, C.L. and M.L.P. Hoogland. 2004. Social dynamics and change in the Northern Lesser Antilles, *Late Ceramic Age Societies in the Eastern Caribbean*, A. Delpech and C.L. Hofman (eds), 47–58, BAR International Series 1273, Paris Monographs in American Archaeology 14. Oxford University Press, Oxford

Hofman, C.L. and M.L.P. Hoogland. 2012. Caribbean encounters: rescue excavations at the early colonial Island Carib site of Argyle, St. Vincent, *Analecta Praehistorica Leidensia* 43–44: 63–76

Hofman, C.L. and M.L.P. Hoogland. 2013. From corpse taphonomy to mortuary behavior in the Caribbean: a case study from the Lesser Antilles, *The Oxford Handbook of Caribbean Archaeology*, W.F. Keegan, C.L. Hofman and R. Rodríguez Ramos (eds), 452–469. Oxford University Press, Oxford

Hofman, C.L., M.L.P. Hoogland and A. Delpuech. 1999. New perspectives on a Huecan Saladoid assemblage on Guadeloupe: the case of Morel I, *Archaeological investigations on St. Martin (Lesser Antilles). The Site of Norman Estate, Anse des Pères and Hope Estate with a contribution to the 'La Hueca problem'*, C.L. Hofman and M.L.P. Hoogland (eds), 303–312, Archaeological Studies Leiden University 4. Leiden University Press, Leiden

Hofman, C.L., J.R. Pagán-Jiménez, M.H. Field, H. Hooghiemstra, J.A.M. Vermeer, P. Jorissen, S. Knippenberg, B. Bérard and M.L.P. Hoogland. 2021. Mangrove archives: Unravelling human-environment interactionsfrom deeply buried deposits at the site Anse Trabaud, Martinique, Lesser Antilles (1290–780 calBP), *Environmental Archaeology,* https://doi.org/10.1080/14614103.2021.1921676

Hofman, C.L., A.J. Bright, M.L.P. Hoogland and W.F. Keegan. 2008 Attractive ideas, desirable goods: Examining the Late Ceramic Age relationships between Greater and Lesser Antillean societies, *Journal of Island and Coastal Archaeology* 3 (1): 17–34

Hofman, C.L., A.J. Bright, A. Boomert and S. Knippenberg. 2007. Island rhythms: the web of social relationships and interaction networks in the Lesser Antillean Archipelago between 400 and 1492, *Latin American Antiquity* 18 (3): 243–268

Hofman, C.L., A.D. Delpuech, M.L.P. Hoogland and M.S. de Waal. 2004. Late Ceramic Age Survey or the northeastern Islands of the Guadelpoupen Archipelago: Grande Terre, La Désirade and Petite-Terre, *Late Ceramic Societies in the Eastern Caribbean*, A. Delpuech and C.L. Hofman (eds), 159–182, British Archaeological Reports International Series 1273, Paris Monographs in American Archaeology 14. Oxford University Press, Oxford

Holst, I., J. Moreno and D. Piperno. 2007. Identification of teosinte, maize, and Tripsacum in Meso-america by using pollen, starch grains, and phytoliths, *Proceedings of the National Academy of Sciences* 104 (45): 17608–17613

Honeychurch, L. 1995. *The Dominica Story: A History of the Island*. Macmillan, Basingstoke

Honoré, S. 2014. Evaluation du potential archéologique du site de l'Anse du Coq, Marie-Galante, Gua-deloupe, *Archéologie caraïbe*, B. Bérard and C. Losier (eds), 19–36, Taboui 2. Sidestone Press, Leiden

Hoogland, M.L.P., C.L. Hofman and R.G.A.M. Panhuysen. 2010. Interisland dynamics: evidence for human mobility at the site of Anse à la Gourde, Guadeloupe, *Island Shores, Distant Pasts: Archaeo-logical and Biological Approaches to the Pre-Columbian Settlement of the Caribbean*, S.M. Fitzpatrick and A.H. Ross (eds), 148–162. University Press of Florida, Gainesville

Hoogland, M.L.P., T. Romon and P. Brasselet. 2001. Excavations at the site of Anse à la Gourde, Gua-deloupe. Troumassoid burial practices, *Proceedings of the XVIII International Congress for Carib-bean Archaeology held in Grenada*, Vol. 2, 173–178. Association International d'Archéologie de la Caraïbe, Région Guadeloupe, Basse-Terre

Hopwood, A.T. 1926. A fossil rice-rat from the Pleistocene of Barbuda, *Annals and Magazine of Natu-ral History* 9 (17): 328–330

Iriarte, J. 2003. Assessing the feasibility of identifying maize through the analysis of cross-shaped size and three-dimensional morphology of phytoliths in the grasslands of southeastern South America, *Journal of Archaeological Science* 9: 1085–1094

Iriarte, J., B. Glaser, J. Watling, A. Wainwright, J.J. Birk, D. Renard, S. Rostain and D. Mckey. 2010. Late Holocene Neotropical agricultural landscapes: phytolith and stable carbon isotope analysis of raised fields from French Guianan coastal Savannahs, *Journal of Archaeological Science* 37: 2984–2994

Iriarte, J. and E. Paz. 2009. Phytolith analysis of selected native plants and modern soils from south-eastern Uruguay and its implications for paleoenvironmental and archeological reconstruction, *Qua-ternary International* 193 (1–2): 99–123

Jean-Joseph, S. 2014. *Caractérisation chrono-culturelle du site précolombien Grande Anse des Salines, Sainte-Anne, Martinique,* Unpublished Master Thesis Université Toulouse Le Mirail & Ecole des hautes Etudes en Sciences sociales, ms

Jegouzo, A., L. Baray, C. Martin, F. Ravoire, T. Romon et M.M. van den Bel. 2018. *Cimetière Du Fort—Rue Hurtaud,* Rapport d'opération fouille archéologique Inrap, ms

Jesse, C. 1963. The Spanish Cedula of December 23, 1511, on the subject of the Caribs, *Caribbean Quarterly* 9 (3): 22–32

Jesse, C. 1966. St. Lucia: the romance of its place names, *Saint Lucia Miscellany* 1. St. Lucia Archaeo-logical and Historical Society, Castries

Juggins, S. 2010. *C2 Software, Version 1.6.*

Karklins, K. 2012. Guide to the description and classification of glass beads found in the Americas, *Beads: Journal of the Society of Bead Researchers* 24: 62–90

Karklins, K. and A. Bonneau. 2019. Evidence of Early 17th-Century glass beadmaking in and around Rouen, France, *Beads: Journal of the Society of Bead Researchers* 31: 3–8

Keegan, W.F. 2000. West Indian archaeology. Part 3. Ceramic age, *Journal of Archaeological Research* 8 (2): 135–167

Keegan, W.F. 2006. Caribbean area, *Handbook of Latin American Studies: No. 61—Social Sciences*, T. North, K.D. MaCann and L. Boudon (eds), 29–36. University of Texas Press, Austin

Keegan, W.-F., C.L. Hofman and R. Rodriguez Ramos (eds). 2013. *The Oxford Handbook of Caribbean Archeology*. Oxford University Press, Oxford

Kemp, A.-C., B.-C. Horton, J.-P. Donnelly, M.-E. Mann, M. Vermeer and S. Rahmstorf. 2011. Climate related sea-level variations over the past two millennia, *PNAS* 108 (27): 11017–11022

Kidd, K.E. and M.A. Kidd. 2012. A classification system for Glass Beads for the use of field archaeolo-gists, *Beads: Journal of the Society of Bead Researchers* 24: 39–61

Kingsley, S., E. Gerth and M. Hughe. 2012. Ceramics from the Tortugas shipwreck: a Spanish-operated Navio of the 1622 Tierra Firme Fleet, *Ceramics in America*, R. Hunter (ed), 76–97. University Press New England, Hanover

Klosowska, B.B., S.R. Troelstra, J.E. van Hinte, D. Beets, K. van der Borg and A.F.M. de Jong. 2004. Late Holocene environmental reconstruction of St. Michiel saline lagoon, Curacao (Dutch Antilles), *Radiocarbon* 46 (2): 765–774

Knippenberg, S. 1999a. Anse des Pères. Lithics, *Archaeological Investigations on St. Martin (Lesser Antilles). The Sites of Norman Estate, Anse des Pères, and Hope Estate with a contribution to the 'La Hueca problem'*, C.L. Hofman and M.L.P. Hoogland (eds), 87–104. Archaeological Studies Leiden University 4. Leiden University Press, Leiden

Knippenberg, S. 1999b. Norman Estate. Lithics, *Archaeological Investigations on St. Martin (Lesser Antilles). The Sites of Norman Estate, Anse des Pères, and Hope Estate with a contribution to the 'La Hueca problem'*, C.L. Hofman and M.L.P. Hoogland (eds), 35–46, Archaeological Studies Leiden University 4. Leiden University Press, Leiden

Knippenberg, S. 2004. Distribution and exchange of lithic materials: three-pointers and axes from St. Martin, *Late Ceramic Societies in the Eastern Caribbean*, A. Delpuech and C.L. Hofman (eds), 121–138, BAR International Series 1273, Paris Monographs in American Archaeology 14. Oxford University Press, Oxford

Knippenberg, S. 2006. *Stone Artefact Production and Exchange among the Lesser Antilles*, Ph.D. University of Leiden, Archaeological Studies Leiden University 13. Leiden University Press, Leiden

Knippenberg, S. 2009a. *Lithics from Lavoutte, St. Lucia. A Report on the Analysis of the 2009 Field-season Material*, Unpublished report Leiden University, ms

Knippenberg, S. 2009b. Le mobilier lithique amérindien, *Le site de La Pointe de Grande Anse. Une occupation amérindienne et coloniale dans le sud de Basse-Terre, Commune de Trois-Rivières, Guadeloupe*, M.M. van den Bel (dir), 61–71, Rapport de fouille archéologique Inrap, ms

Knippenberg, S. 2011a. Much to choose from. The use and distribution of siliceous Stone in the Lesser Antilles, *Communities in Contact. Essays in Archaeology, Ethnohistory & Ethnography of the Amerindian circum Caribbean*, C.L. Hofman and A. van Duijvenbode (eds), 171–185. Sidestone Press, Leiden

Knippenberg, S. 2011b. *Lithic Procurement and Stone Tool Manufacture on St. John, US Virgin Islands*, Paper presented at the Twentieth fourth Congress of the International Association for Caribbean Archaeology, Fort-de-France, Martinique, ms

Knippenberg, S. 2012a. Examen de la matière première lithique du site de la Gare Maritime à Basse Terre, *Bilan Scientifique de la Région Guadeloupe* 2009: 52–53

Knippenberg, S. 2012b. *Jadeitite Axe Manufacture in Hispaniola. A Preliminary Report on the Lithics from the Playa Grande Site, Northern Dominican Republic*, Unpublished report Leiden University, ms

Knippenberg, S. in prep. Back to basics. Raw material availability, rock acquisition, and stone tool manufacture and exchange among the Lesser Antilles

Knippenberg, S., R. Rodríguez Ramos, H.P. Schertl, W.V. Maresch, A. Hertwig, A. García-Casco, G.E. Harlow, A. López and C.L. Hofman. 2012. *The Manufacture and Exchange of Jadeitite Celts in the Caribbean*, Paper presented at the European Mineralogical Conference 2012, 2–6 September, Frankfurt, Germany. http://meetingorganizer.copernicus.org/ EMC2012/EMC2012-400.pdf

Knippenberg, S., and A. Verbaas. 2012. Steen, *Opgraven langs de Rijksweg A2 te Stein Heidekampweg, Stein-Steinerbos en Geleen-Chemelot*, I.M. van Wijk, L. Meurkens & A. Porreij-Hylkema (eds), 113–125. Archol Rapport 150, Leiden

Korth, W.W. 1979. Taphonomy of micro vertebrate fossil assemblages, *Annals of Carnegie Museum* 48: 235–285

Lafleur, G. 1993. *Sainte-Claude, Histoire d'une commune de Guadeloupe*. Karthala, Paris

Lahitte, P., A. Samper and X. Quidelleur. 2012. DEM-based reconstruction of southern Basse Terre volcanoes (Guadeloupe Archipelago, FWI): contribution to the Lesser Antilles Arc rates and magma production, *Geomorphology* 136: 148–164

Lammers-Keijsers, Y.M.J. 2008. *Tracing Traces from Present to Past. A Functional Analysis of Pre-Columbian Artefacts from Anse à la Gourde and Morel, Guadeloupe, FWI*, Ph.D. Leiden Univesity, Archaeological Studies Leiden University 15. Leiden University Press, Leiden

Lane, C.S., S.P. Horn and M.T. Kerr. 2014. Beyond the Mayan lowlands: impacts of the Terminal Classic drought in the Caribbean Antilles, *Quaternary Science Reviews* 86: 89–98

Lane, C.S., S.P. Horn, C.I. Mora and K.H. Orvis. 2009. Late-Holocene paleoenvironmental change at mid-elevation on the Caribbean slope of the Cordillera Central, Dominican Republic: amulti-site, multi-proxy analysis, *Quaternary Science Reviews* 28: 2239–2260

Lane, C.S., S.P. Horn, K.H. Orvis and J.M. Thomason. 2011. Oxygen isotope evidence of Little Ice Age aridity on the Caribbean slope of the Cordillera Central, Dominican Republic, *Quaternary Research* 75: 461–470

Lasserre, G. 1978. *La Guadeloupe*, 3 Vols. Editions Kolodziej, Paris

Lawrence, J., S.M. Fitzpatrick and C.M. Giovas. 2021. Petrographic analysis of Pre-Columbian pottery from Nevis, Eastern Caribbean, *Journal of Archaeological Science: Reports* 35. https://doi.org/10.1016/j.jasrep.2020.102741

Lefevre, C. and P. Cocusse. 1985. Etude pétrographique et minéralogique des laves du Massif volcanique Madeleine-Soufrière de Guadeloupe (Petites Antilles). Implications magmatologiques, *Bull. Minéral.* 108: 189–208

Le Lay, A. 2013. *Étude du mobilier céramique du site de l'arrière-plage de Roseau. Vers une caractérisation culturelle de l'occupation post-Saladoïdes en Basse Terre de Guadeloupe (1000–1500 apr. J.-C.),* Unpublished Master 2, Université de Paris I-Panthéon Sorbonne, ms

Le Moyne de Morgues, J. and T. de Bry. 1591. *Brevis narratioeorum quae in Florida mericae provincia Gallisacciderunt, secunda in illamnavigatione duce Renato de Landonniere Classis praefecto anno M. D. LXIIII. Quae estsecunda pars Americae [. . .].* J. Wechel, Frankfurt

Leonard, R.D. and G.T. Jones. 1989. *Quantifying Diversity in Archaeology.* Cambridge University Press, Cambridge

Leudtke, B.E. 1992. *An Archaeologist's Guide to Chert and Flint.* Archaeological Research Tools 7. University of California, Los Angeles

Locosselli, G., S. Krottenhaler, P. Pitsch and G. Ceccantini. 2017. Age and growth rate of congeneric tree species (Hymenaea spp.—Leguminosae) inhabiting different tropical biomes, *Erdkunde* 71 (1): 45–57

Longwood, F.R. 1971. *Present and Potential Commercial Timbers of the Caribbean: With Special Reference to the West Indies, the Guianas and Brititsh Honduras.* U.S. Department of Agriculture, Forest Service

Loy, T.H. 1994. Methods in the analysis of starch residues on prehistoric stone tools, *Tropical Archaeobotany: Applications and New Developments*, J.G. Hather (ed), 86–114. Routledge, London

Loy, T.H., M. Spriggs and S. Wickler. 1992. Direct evidence for human use of plants 28,000 years ago: starch residues on stone artefacts from the Northern Solomon Islands, *Antiquity* 66: 898–912

Lundberg, E.R. 2002. Tutu pottery and ceramic chronology, *The Tutu Archaeological Village Site, A Mutidisciplinary Case Study in Human Adaptation*, E. Righter (ed), 167–198, Interpreting the remains of the past 2. Routlegde, London

Lundberg, E.R., J.H. Burton and W.C. Lynn. 2002. Investigation of ceramic variability at the Tutu site through acid-extraction elemental analysis, *The Tutu Archaeological Village Site, A Mutidisciplinary Case Study in Human Adaptation*, E. Righter (ed), 199–208, Interpreting the Remains of the Past 2. Routlegde, London

Lyman, L.R. 1994. Quantitative units and terminology in zooarchaeology, *American Antiquity* 59 (1): 36–71

MacKenzie, W.S., A.E. Adams and K.H. Brodie. 2017. *Rocks and Minerals in Thin Section: A Colour Atlas*, 2nd edition. CRC Press, Boca Raton

Malaizé, B., P. Bertran, P. Carbonel, D. Bonnissent, K. Charlier, D. Galop, D. Imbert, N. Serrand, C. Stouvenot and C. Pujol. 2011. Hurricanes and climate in the Caribbean during the past 3700 years BP, *The Holocene* 21 (6): 911–924

Mans, J. 2012. *Amotopoan Trails: A recent archaeology of Trio movements*, Ph.D. Leiden University, Mededelingen van het Rijksmuseum voor Volkenkunde 41. Sidestone Press, Leiden

Martias, R. 2008. *Terre de Haut "ZAC Marigot" (Guadeloupe)*, Rapport de diagnostic Inrap, ms

Martin, C.J.M. 1979. Spanish Armada pottery, *International Journal of Nautical Archaeology* 8: 279–302

Mattinson, J.M., L.K. Fink and C.A. Hopson. 1980. Geochronologic and isotopic study of the La Désirade island basement complex: jurassic oceanic crust in the Lesser Antilles?, *Contributions to Mineralogy and Petrology* 71: 237–245

McKey, D., S. Rostain, J. Iriarte, B. Glaser, J. Birk and I. Holst. 2010. Pre-Columbian agricultural landscapes, ecosystem engineers, and self-organized patchiness in Amazonia. *Proceedings of the National Academy of Science of the United States of America* 107 (17): 7823–7828

McKusick, M.B. 1960. *Distribution of Ceramic Styles in the Lesser Antilles, West Indies,* Unpublished Ph.D. Yale University, ms

Meggers, B.J. and C. Evans. 1957. *Archaeological Investigations at the Mouth of the Amazon*, Bulletin of the Bureau of American Ethnology, 167. United States Government Printing Office, Washington DC

Mestre, M., F. de Berton, C. Fouilloud and C. Grancha. 2001. *Site de Moulin à Eau. Déviation RN1, Capesterre-Belle Eau (Guadeloupe),* Rapport de fouille AFAN/Conseil Régional de la Guadeloupe, ms

Mickleburgh, H.L. and J.R. Pagán-Jiménez. 2012. New insights into the consumption of maize and other food plants in the pre-Columbian Caribbean from starch grains trapped in human dental calculus, *Journal of Archaeological Science* 39: 2468–2478

Milliken, K., J.B. Anderson and A.B. Rodriguez. 2008. A new composite Holocene sea-level curve for the northern Gulf of Mexico, *Response of Gulf Coast Estuaries to Sea-Level Rise and Climate Change*, Anderson, J.B. and A.B. Rodriguez (eds), 1–11. Geological Society of America, Special Paper 443

Mims, S.L. 1912. *Colbert's West India Policy*, Yale Historical Studies 1. Yale University Press, New Haven

Mol, A.A.A. 2007. *Costly Giving, Giving Guaízas: Towards an Organic Model of Exchange of Social Valuables in the Late Ceramic Age Caribbean*, Master Thesis University of Leiden. Sidestone Press, Leiden

Moreau, J.P. 1992. *Les Petites Antilles, de Christophe Colomb à Richelieu.* Éditions Karthala, Paris

Moretti, J. (2003) *Les plantes tinctoriales de Guyane française et leurs utilisastions traditionnelles,* Unpublished Ph.D. University of Reims-Champagne-Ardenne, ms

Morsink, J. 2006. (Re-) *Constructing Constructions. Quotidian life and social practice at Anse à la Gourde,* Unpublished Master Thesis University Leiden, ms

Mouer, L., D.C. Mclearen, R. Taft Kiser, C.P. Egghart, B. Binns and D. Magoon. 1992. *Jordan's Journey: A Preliminary Report on Archaeology at Site 44PG302, Prince George County, Virginia, 1990–1991*, Report prepared for the Virginia Department of Historic Resources, Richmond, ms

Munch, P., J.F. Lebrun, J.J. Cornee, I. Thinon and P. Guennoc. 2013. Pliocene to Pleistocene carbonate systems of the Guadeloupe archipelago, French Lesser Antilles: a land and sea study (the KaShallow project), *Bulletin Société Géologique de France* 184: 99–110

Munsell Soil Color Charts. 1990. *Munsell Soil Color Charts.* Macbeth Division of Kollmorgen Instruments Corporation, Baltimore (Revised Edition)

Murphy, A.R. 1999. *The Prehistory of Antigua, Ceramic Age: Subsistence, Settlement, Culture and Adaptation within an Insular Environment,* Unpublished Ph.D. University of Calgary, ms

Murphy, A.R. 2004. Life in an insular environment: the case of Antigua, *Late Ceramic Age Societies in the Eastern Caribbean*, A. Delpuech and C.L. Hofman (eds), 205–213, BAR International Series 1273, Paris Monographs in American Archaeology 14. Oxford University Press, Oxford

Murphy, A.R., A.J. Hozjan, C.N. deMille and A.A. Levinson. 2000. Pre-Columbian gems and ornamental materials from Antigua, West Indies, *Gems & Gemology* 36 (2): 234–245

Navarrete, M., Fernandez de. 1922. *Viajes de Cristóbal Colón.* Calpe, Madrid

Newsom, L.A. and E.S. Wing. 2004. *On Land and Sea: Native American uses of biological resources in the West Indies.* University of Alabama Press, Tuscaloosa

O'Conner, B.C. and M.S. Smith. 2001. Comparative ceramic petrography of pottery from St. Croix, United States Virgin Islands: Aklis, Salt River, Prosperity and Northside sites, *Proceedings of the XIX International Congress for Caribbean Archaeology held in Aruba 2001*, 2 Vols, Publications of the Museo Arqueologico Aruba 9, L. Alofs and R. Dijkhoff (eds), 29–42. Archaeological Museum Aruba, Aruba

O'Conner, B.C. and M.S. Smith. 2003. Petrographic analysis of ceramic sherds from the prehistoric sites of Peter Bay and Trunk Bay, St. John, United States Virgin Islands, *Proceedings of the XX International Congress for Caribbean Archaeology held in Santo Domingo 2003*, 2 Vols. C. Tavárez María and M.A. García Arévalo (eds), 385–390. Museo del Hombre Dominicano y Fundación García Arévalo, Santo Domingo

Ogeron, C., G. Odonne, A. Cristinoi, J. Engel, P. Grenand, J. Beauchêne, B. Clair and D. Davy, 2018. Palikur traditional roundwood construction in eastern French Guiana: ethnobotanical and cultural perspectives, *Journal of Ethnobiology and Ethnomedicine* 14: 28; https://doi.org/10.1186/s13002-018-0226-7

Oliver, J.R. 1995. A prehistoric longhouse structure (FAL-7), in Maticora Valley, Western Venezuela, *Proceedings of the XVI Congress of the International Association for Caribbean Archaeology held in Basse-Terre 1995*, R.E. Alegria and M. Rodríguez (eds), 143–157. Conseil Régional de Guadeloupe, Basse-Terre

Oliver, J.R. 2009. *Caciques and Cemí Idols. The Web Spun by the Taíno Rulers between Hispaniola and Puerto Rico*. University of Alabama Press, Tuscaloosa

Pagán-Jiménez, J.R. 2005. *Estudio interpretativo de la cultura botánica de dos comunidades precolombinas antillanas. La Hueca y Punta Candelero, Puerto Rico*, Ph.D. Instituto de Investigaciones Antropológicas, Universidad Nacional Autónoma de México, México D.F.

Pagán-Jiménez, J.R. 2007. *De antiguos pueblos y culturas botánicas en el Puerto Rico indígena. El archipiélago borincano y la llegada de los primeros pobladores agroceramistas*, Paris Monographs in American Archaeology 18, BAR International Series. Archaeopress, Oxford

Pagán-Jiménez, J.R. 2009. Nuevas Perspectivas Sobre Las Culturas Botánicas Precolombinas de Puerto Rico: Implicaciones Del Estudio de Almidones En Herramientas Líticas, Cerámicas y de Concha, *Cuba Arqueológica* II (2): 7–23

Pagán-Jiménez, J.R. 2011. Early phytocultural processes in the pre-colonial Antilles: a pan-Caribbean Survey for an ongoing starch grain research, *Communities in Contact: Essays in Archaeology, Ethnohistory, and Ethnography of the Amerindian circum-Caribbean*, C.L. Hofman and A. van Duijvenbode (eds), 87–116. Sidestone Press, Leiden

Pagán-Jiménez, J.R. 2012. Early use of maize and other food crops among Early Ceramic and later Neoindian traditions in northeastern Amazonia revealed by ancient starch grains from ceramic and lithic artefacts of the Chemin Saint-Louis archaeological site, French Guiana, *Archaeology and Anthropology* 17 (2): 78–107

Pagán-Jiménez, J.R. 2013. Human-plant dynamics in the precolonial Antilles, a synthetic update, *The Oxford Handbook of Caribbean Archaeology*, W. Keegan, C.L. Hofman and R. Rodríguez Ramos (eds), 391–406. Oxford University Press, Oxford

Pagán-Jiménez, J.R. 2015. *Almidones. Guía de material comparativo moderno del Ecuador para los estudios paleoentobotánicos en el neotrópico*. Aspha Ediciones, Buenos Aires

Pagán-Jiménez, J.R. and L. Carlson. 2014. Recent archaeobotanical findings of the hallucinogenic snuff cojoba (Anadenanthera peregrina (L.) Speg.) in precolonial Puerto Rico, *Latin American Antiquity* 25: 101–116

Pagán-Jiménez, J.R., M.A. Rodríguez López, L.A. Chanlatte Baik and Y. Narganes Storde. 2005. La temprana introducción y uso de algunas plantas domésticas, silvestres y cultivos en Las Antillas precolombinas. Una primera revaloración desde la perspectiva del "Arcaico" de Vieques y Puerto Rico, *Diálogo Antropológico* 3 (10): 7–33

Pagán-Jiménez, J.R., R. Rodríguez-Ramos and C.L. Hofman. 2019. On the way to the islands: the role of domestic plants in the initial peopling of the Antilles, *Early Settlers of the Insular Caribbean. Dearchaizing the Archaic*, C.L. Hofman and A. Antczak (eds), 89–106. Sidestone Press, Leiden

Pagán-Jiménez, J.R., R. Rodríguez-Ramos, B. Reid, M.M. van den Bel and C.L. Hofman. 2015. Early dispersals of maize and other food plants into the Southern Caribbean and Northeastern South America, *Quaternary Science Reviews* 123: 231–246

Pané, R. 1999. *An Account of the Antiquities of the Indians*. A new edition, with an introductory study, notes, and appendixes by José Juan Arrom. Translated by Susan C. Criswold. Duke Univerisity Press, Durham & London

Pater, E.M. and P.C. Teekens. 2004. *Anse à la Gourde: The Pottery Assemblage. A Stylistic, Morphological, and Chronological Study of the Early and Late Ceramic Age Pottery from the Excavation Units, Shovels and Mechanical Units on Anse à la Gourde, Guadeloupe FWI,* Unpublished Master Thesis University of Leiden, 2 Vols., ms

Pavia, J.A., K.M. Marsaglia, S.M. Fitzpatrick. 2013. Petrography and provenance of sand temper within ceramic sherds from Carriacou, Southern Grenadines, West Indies, *Geoarchaeology* 28: 450–477

Peacock, D.P.S. 1970. The scientific analysis of ancient ceramics: a review, *World Archaeology* 1: 375–389

Pearsall, D.M. 1982. Phytolith analysis: applications of a new paleoethnobotanical technique in archaeology, *American Anthropology* 84: 862–871

Pearsall, D.M. 2000. *Paleoethnobotany: A Handbook of Procedures*, 2nd edition. Academic Press, New York

Pearsall, D.M., K. Chandler-Ezell and J.A. Zeidler. 2004. Maize in ancient Ecuador: results of residue analysis of stone tools from the real Alto site, *Journal of Archaeological Science* 31 (4): 423–442

Pearsall, D.M. and D.R. Piperno. 1990. Antiquity of maize cultivation in Ecuador: summary and reevaluation of the evidence, *American Antiquity* 55: 324–337

Perry, L. 2001. *Prehispanic Subsistence in the Middle Orinoco Basin: Starch Analysis Yield New Evidence,* Unpublished Ph.D. Department of Anthropology, Southern Illinois University, ms

Perry, L. 2002a. Starch analyses reveal multiple functions of quartz "Manioc" grater flakes from the Orinoco Basin, Venezuela, *Interciencia* 27 (11): 635–639

Perry, L. 2002b. Starch granule size and the domestication of manioc (Manihot esculenta) and sweet potato (Ipomoea batatas), *Economic Botany* 56 (4): 335–349

Perry, L. 2004. Starch analyses reveal the relationship between tool type and function: an example from the Orinoco Valley of Venezuela, *Journal of Archaeological Science* 31 (8): 1069–1081

Perry, L. 2005. Reassessing the traditional interpretation of 'manioc' artifacts in the Orinoco Valley of Venezuela, *Latin American Antiquity* 16 (4): 409–426

Perry, L., R. Dickau, S. Zarrillo, I. Holst, D.M. Pearsall, D.R. Piperno, M.J. Berman, R.G. Cooke, K. Rademaker, A.J. Ranere, J. Scott Raymond, D.H. Sandweiss, F. Scaramelli, K. Tarble and J.A. Zeidler. 2007. Starch fossils and the domestication and dispersal of chili peppers (Capsicum spp.) in the Americas, *Science* 315: 986–988

Petersen, J.B. 1996. Archaeology of Trants, Montserrat. Part 3. Chronological and settlement data, *Annals of Carnegie Museum* 65 (4): 323–361

Petersen, J.B., M.J. Heckenberger and E. Góes Neves. 2001. A prehistoric ceramic sequence from the central Amazon and its relationship to the Caribbean, *Proceedings of the XIX International Congress for Caribbean Archaeology held in Aruba 2001,* 2 Vols, Publications of the Museo Arqueologico Aruba 9, L. Alofs and R. Dijkhoff (eds), 250–259. Archaeological Museum Aruba, Aruba

Petersen, J.B., C.L. Hofman and A.L. Curet. 2004. Time and culture: chronology and taxonomy in the Eastern Caribbean and the Guianas, *Late Ceramic Societies in the Eastern Caribbean*, A. Delpech and C.L. Hofman (eds), 17–32, BAR International Series 1273, Paris Monographs in American Archaeology 14. Oxford University Press, Oxford

Petersen, J.B. and D.R. Watters. 1995. A preliminary analysis of Amerindian ceramics from the Trants Site, Montserrat, *Proceedings of the XVI Congress of the International Association for Caribbean Archaeology held in Basse-Terre 1995*, R.E. Alegria and M. Rodríguez (eds), 131–140. Conseil Régional de Guadeloupe, Basse-Terre

Petitjean Roget, H. 2010. L'implantation et la symbolique des pétroglyphes des Antilles: Un modèle amazonien? *Proceedings of the Twenty-second Congress of Caribbean Archaeology held in Jamaica 2007*, 566–577

Petitjean Roget, H. 2011. Contribution à l'étude de l'art rupestre des Antilles. Vers une tentative d'identification des représentations gravées, *Proceedings of the XXIII Congress of The International*

Association for Caribbean Archaeology held in Antigua 2009, S.A. Rebovich (ed), 474–490. Dockyard Museum, English Harbour, Antigua

Petitjean Roget, H. 2015. *Les Tainos, les Callinas des Antilles*, 2 Vols. IACA, Basse-Terre

Pinchon, R. 1967. *Quelques aspects de la nature aux Antilles*. Ozanne, Fort-de France

Pinçon, K. 2013. *Caractérisation chrono-culturelle du site amérindien de Macabou. Etude des restes céramiques*, Unpublished Master Thesis University of Paris I–Panthéon Sorbonne, ms

Piperno, D.R. 1989. The occurrence of phytoliths in the reproductive structures of selected tropical angiosperms and their significance in tropical paleoecology, paleoethnobotany and systematics, *Review of Palaeobotany and Palynology* 61 (1–2): 147–173

Piperno, D.R. 2006. *Phytoliths: A Comprehensive Guide for Archaeologists and Paleoecologists*. Altimira Press, Oxford

Piperno, D.R. and T.D. Dillehay. 2008. Starch grains on human teeth reveal early broad crop diet in northern Peru, *Publications of the National Academy of Science* 105: 19622–19627

Piperno, D.R. and I. Holst. 1998a. The presence of starch grain on prehistoric stone tools from the Humid Neotropics: indications of early tuber use and agriculture in Panama, *Journal of Archaeological Science* 25: 765–776

Piperno, D.R. and I. Holst. 1998b. *The Silica Bodies of Tropical American Grasses: Morphology, Taxonomy, and Implications for Grass Systematics and Fossil Phytolith Identifications*, Smithsonian Contributions in Botany 85. Smithsonian Institution Press, Washington, DC

Piperno, D.R. and D.M. Pearsall. 1998a. *The Origins of Agriculture in the Lowland Neotropics*. Academic Press, San Diego

Piperno, D.R. and D.M. Pearsall. 1998b. *The Silica Bodies of Tropical American Grasses: Morphology, Taxonomy, and Implications for Grass Systematics and Fossil Phytolith Identification*, Smithsonian Contributions to Botany. Smithsonian Institution Press, Washington, DC

Piperno, D.R., A.J. Ranere, I. Holst and P. Hansell. 2000. Starch grains reveal early root crop horticulture in the Panamanian Tropical Forest, *Nature* 407: 894–897

Pointier, J.-P. and D. Lamy. 1998. *Guide des Coquillages des Antilles*, Collection 'Découvre la Mer'. PLB Éditions, Paris

Poplin, F. 1976a. A propos du Nombre de Restes et du Nombre d'Individus dans les échantillons d'ossements, *Cahier du Centre de Recherche Préhistorique de l'Université de Paris* I (5): 61–74

Poplin, F. 1976b. Essai d'ostéologie quantitative sur l'estimation du Nombre d'Individus, *Kölner Jahrbuch für Ur- und Frühgeschichte*, F.H. Schwabedissen (ed), 153–164. Mann, Berlin

Poplin, F. 1977. Problèmes d'ostéologie quantitative relatifs à l'étude de l'écologie des hommes fossils, *Approche écologique de l'Homme fossile* 47: 63–68

Pregill, G.K., D.W. Steadman and D.R. Watters. 1994. Late quaternary vertebrate faunas of the Lesser Antilles: historical components of Caribbean biogeography, *Bulletin of the Carnegie Museum of Natural History* 30: 1–51

Queffelec, A., P. Fouéré, C. Paris, C. Stouvenot and L. Bellot-Gurlet. 2018. Local production and long-distance procurement of beads and pendants withhigh mineralogical diversity in an early Saladoid settlement of Guadeloupe (French West Indies), *Journal of Archaeological Science: Reports* 21: 275–288

Quinn, P.S. 2009. *Interpreting Silent Artefacts: Petrographic Approaches to Archaeological Ceramics*. Archaeopress, Oxford

Quinn, P.S. 2013. *Ceramic Petrography: The Interpretation of Archaeological Pottery and Related Artefacts in Thin Section*. Archaeopress, Oxford

Reichert, E.T. 1913. *The Differentiation and Specificity of Starches in Relation to Genera, Species, Etc.* Carnegie Institution of Washington, Washington

Reid, B. (ed) 2018. *The Archaeology of Caribbean and Circum-Caribbean Farmers (6000 BC–AD 1500)*. Routledge, London

Reimer, P.J., M.G.L. Baillie, E. Bard, A. Bayliss, J.W. Beck, C.J.H. Bertrand, P.G. Blackwell, C.E. Buck, G.S. Burr, K.B. Cutler, P.E. Damon, R.L. Edwards, R.G. Fairbanks, M. Friedrich, T.P.Guilderson, A.G. Hogg, K.A. Hughen, B. Kromer, G. McCormac, S. Manning, C. Bronk Ramsey,

R.W. Reimer, S. Remmele, J.R. Southon, M. Stuiver, S. Talamo, F.W. Taylor, J. van der Plicht and C.E. Weyhenmeyer. 2004. INTCAL04 terrestrial radiocarbon age calibration, 0–26 CAL KYR BP, *Radiocarbon* 46 (3): 1029–1058

Reimer, P.J., M.G.L. Baillie, E. Bard, A. Bayliss, J.W. Beck, P.G. Blackwell, C. Bronk Ramsey, C.E. Buck, G.S. Burr, R.L. Edwards, M. Friedrich, P.M. Grootes, T.P. Guilderson, I. Hajdas, T.J. Heaton, A.G. Hogg, K.A. Hughen, K.F. Kaiser, B. Kromer, F.G. McCormac, S.W. Manning, R.W. Reimer, D.A. Richards, J.R. Southon, S. Talamo, C.S.M. Turney, J. van der Plicht, C.E. Weyhenmeyer. 2009. IntCal09 and Marine09 radiocarbon age calibration curves, 0–50,000 years cal BP, *Radiocarbon* 51: 1111–1150

Reynal de Saint-Michel, A. 1966. *Notice explicative des Feuilles de Basse-Terre et des Saintes, Carte Géologique détaillée de la France*, Département de la Guadeloupe. Ministère de l'Industrie, Paris

Rice, P.M. 1987. *Pottery Analysis. A Sourcebook*. University of Chicago Press, Washington

Richard, G. 1994. Premier indice d'une occupation précéramique en Guadeloupe continentale. *Journal de la Société des Américanistes* 80: 241–242

Richard, G. 2004. *Site de l'arrière plage de Roseau, Commune de Capesterre Belle-Eau, Section Saint Marie, Guadeloupe. Opération de sondages numéro de site 971 0734 AP: Opération réalisée au cours du second semestre 2001 et premier trimestre 2002*. SRA, CRG, ms

Richard, G. 2005. Le site archéologique de la plage de Roseau, à Capesterre-Belle-Eau, révélateur d'une occupation Caraïbe insulaire en Guadeloupe, *Comptes rendus du XXe Congrès International d'Études des Civilisations Amérindiennes des Petites Antilles*, G. Tavarez and M.A. Garcia Arévalo (eds), Vol. 1, 15–22. Museo del Hombre Dominicano and Fundacion Garcia Arévalo, Santo Domingo

Righter, E. (ed) 2002a. *The Tutu Archaeological Village Site, A Mutidisciplinary Case Study in Human Adaptation*. Routlegde, London

Righter, E. 2002b. Post hole patterns: structures, chronology and spatial distribution at the Tutu site, *The Tutu Archaeological Village Site, A Mutidisciplinary Case Study in Human Adaptation*, E. Righter (ed), 284–341, Interpreting the Remains of the Past 2. Routlegde, London

Rochefort, C., de. 1658. *Histoire naturelle et morale des Antilles de l'Amérique*. Arnould Leers, Rotterdam

Rodríguez Ramos, R. 2001. *Lithic Reduction Trajectories at La Hueca and Punta Candelero Sites, Puerto Rico*, Unpublished Master Thesis University of Texas A&M, ms

Rodríguez Ramos, R. 2005. The function of edge-ground cobble put to the test: an initial assessment, *Journal of Caribbean Archaeology* 5: 1–22

Rodríguez Ramos, R. 2010. *Rethinking Puerto Rican Precolonial History*. University of Alabama Press, Tuscaloosa

Rodríguez Ramos, R. 2011. The circulation of jadeitite across the Caribbeanscape, *Communities in Contact: Essays in Archaeology, Ethnohistory & Ethnography of the Amerindian Circum-Caribbean*, C.L. Hofman and A. van Duijvenbode (eds), 117–136. Sidestone Press, Leiden

Rodríguez Suárez, R. and J.R. Pagán-Jiménez. 2008. The burén in precolonial Cuban archaeology: new information regarding the use of plants and ceramic griddles during the Late Ceramic age of eastern Cuba gathered through starch analysis, *Crossing the Borders: New Methods and Techniques in the Study of Archaeological Materials from the Caribbean*, C.L. Hofman, M.P.L. Hoogland and A-L.van Gijn (eds), 159–172. University of Alabama Press, Tuscaloosa

Rodríguez Ramos, R., J.M. Torres, W.J. Pestle, J. Oliver and M. Rodríguez López. 2015. Hacia una periodización histórica para el Puerto Rico precolonial, *Proceedings of the XXVth International Congress for Caribbean Archaeology*, L. del Olmo (ed), 495–520. ICP/CEAPRC/UPR, San Juan

Romon, T. 2010. *Dothémare—Morne L'Epingle, Les Abymes, Guadeloupe*, Rapport de diagnostic archéologique Inrap, ms

Romon, T., P. Bertran, P. Fouéré and M. Hildebrand. 2006. *Gourbeyre, Bisdary (Guadeloupe). Un site amérindien de piedmont*, Rapport final de fouille Inrap, ms

Romon, T., P. Bertran, P. Fouéré, M. Hildebrand and N. Serrand. 2013. Le site de la Gare maritime de Basse-Terre (Guadeloupe), *Martinique, Terre amérindienne. Une approche multidsiciplinaire*, B. Bérard (ed), 223–234. Sidestone Press, Leiden

Romon, T., P. Bertran, P. Foueré, M. Hildebrand, N. Serrand and C. Vallet. 2006. *Fouille préventive de la Gare Maritime, Basse-Terre (Guadeloupe)*, Rapport final de fouille Inrap, ms

Romon, T. and D. Bonnissent (eds). 2004. *Occupations précolombiennes et coloniales des Petites Antilles. Fouilles de la Cathédrale de Basse-Terre*. Document final d'opération Inrap, ms

Romon, T., N. Bourgarel, F. Casagrande, C. Jorda, G. Lafleur, N. Sellier-Ségar and M.M. van den Bel. 2019. *Fouilles archéologiques preventives au Parc archéologique des roches gravées à Trois-Rivières "Entrée du Parc"*, Rapport de fouille archéologique Inrap, ms

Romon, T. and G. Chancerel. 2002. *Ilet Gosier, rapport de sauvetage urgent*, Rapport AFAN, ms

Romon, T., X. Rousseau and G. Chancerel. 2003. *Ilet du Gosier (Gosier, Guadeloupe)*, Rapport de sauvetage urgent SRA Guadeloupe, ms

Roosevelt, A.C. 1980. *Parmana: Prehistoric Maize and Manioc Subsistence along the Amazon and Orinoco*, Studies in Archaeology. Academic Press, New York

Roosevelt, A.C. 1991. *Moundbuilders of the Amazon: Geophysical Archaeology on Marajó Island, Brazil*, Studies in Archaeology. Academic Press, San Diego

Rostain, S. 1995. *L'occupation amérindienne ancienne du littoral de Guyane*, Ph.D. Université de Paris I-Panthéon-Sorbonne, 2 Vols., 1994, Travaux et Documents Microfiches 129. Éditions de l'ORSTOM, Paris

Roulet, E. 2016, La famille. L'habitation sucrière de la Compagnie des îles de l'Amérique à la Guadeloupe (1642–1649), *Revue d'histoire de l'Amérique française* 69 (3): 35–57

Rouse, I.B. 1939. *Prehistory in Haiti: A Study in Method*, Ph.D. Yale University, Yale University Publications in Anthropology 21. Yale University Press, New Haven

Rouse, I.B. 1951. Areas and periods of culture in the Greater Antilles, *Southwestern Journal of Anthropology* 3 (4): 248–265

Rouse, I.B. 1960. The classification of artefacts in archaeology, *American Antiquity* 25 (3): 313–323

Rouse, I.B. 1961. Archaeology in lowland South America and the Caribbean 1935–60, *American Antiquity* 27 (1): 56–62

Rouse, I.B. 1965. Caribbean ceramics: a study of method and theory, *Ceramics and Man*, F.R. Matson (ed), 88–103, Viking Fund Publications in Anthropology 41. Wenner-Gren Foundation for anthropological research, New York

Rouse, I.B. 1974. The Indian creek excavations, *Proceedings of the Fifth International Congress for the Study of Pre-Columbian Cultures of the Lesser Antilles, Antigua, July 22–28, 1973*, R.P. Bullen (ed), 166–176. The Antigua Archaeological Society

Rouse, I.B. 1976. The Saladoid sequence on Antigua and its aftermath, *Proceedings of the Sixth International Congress for the Study of Pre-Columbian Cultures of the Lesser Antilles, Pointe à Pitre, Guadeloupe, July 6–12, 1975*, R.P. Bullen (ed), 35–41. Département d'Histoire et d'Archéologie, Pointe-à-Pitre

Rouse, I.B. 1983. Diffusion and interaction in the Orinoco Valley and on the Coast, *Proceedings of the Ninth International Congress for the Study of the pre-Columbian Cultures of the Lesser Antilles, Santo Domingo 1981*, L. Allaire and F.M. Mayer (eds), 3–13. Centre des Recherches Caraïbes, Université de Montréal

Rouse, I.B. 1986. *Migrations in Prehistory. Inferring Population Movement from Cultural Remains*. Yale University Press, New Haven

Rouse, I.B. 1992. *The Tainos. Rise and Decline of the People Who Greeted Columbus*. Yale University Press, New Haven

Rouse, I.B. 1995. *Ceramic Chronology of the Leeward Islands*, Paper to be presented to the XVI International Congress for Caribbean Archaeology on Guadeloupe, July 1995, ms

Rouse, I.B. and L. Allaire. 1978. Caribbean, *Chronologies in New World Archaeology*, R.E. Taylor and C.W. Meighan (eds), 432–482. Academic Press, New York

Rouse, I.B. and J.M. Cruxent. 1963. *Venezuelan Archaeology*. Yale University Press, New York

Rouse, I.B. and B. Faber Morse. 1999. *Excavations at the Indian Creek Site, Antigua, West Indies*, Yale University Publications in Anthropology 82. Yale University Press, New Haven

Rouse, I.B., B. Faber Morse and D. Nicholson. 1995. Excavations at Freeman's Bay, Antigua, *Proceedings of the XV International Congress for Caribbean Archaeology*, R.E. Alegria and M. Rodriguez (eds), 445–458. Centro de Estudios Avanzados de Puerto Rico y el Caribe, Fundación Puertorriqueña de la Humanidades, Universidad del Turabo, San Juan de Puerto Rico

Rousseau, X. 2004. Les premiers établissements européens de Guadeloupe: Opération de synthèse de prospection archéologique pluri-annuelle 1994–1997, *Bulletin de la Société d'Histoire de la Guadeloupe* 137

Ruig, M. 2001. *Les pétroglyphes amérindiens de la Basse-Terre, Guadeloupe. Prospection thématique et relevée d'art rupestre*, Rapport de prospection DRAC/RUL, ms

Rumrill, D.A. 1991. The Mohawk glass trade bead chronology: ca. 1560–1785, *Beads: Journal of the Society of Bead Researchers* 3: 5–45

Rye, O.S. 1981. *Pottery Technology: Principles and Reconstruction*. Taraxacum, Washington, DC

Saldanha, J., Darcy de Moura. 2016. *Poços, Potes e Pedras: Uma Longa História Indígena na Costa da Guayana*. Unpublished Ph.D. University of São Paulo, ms

Samper, A., X. Quidelleur, P. Lahitte and D. Mollex. 2007. Timing of effusive volcanism and collapse events within an oceanic arc island: Basse-Terre, Guadeloupe archipelago (Lesser Antilles Arc), *Earth and Planetary Science Letters* 258: 175–191

Samson, A.V.M. 2010. *Renewing the house: Trajectories of social life in the yucayeque (community) of El Cabo, Higüey, Dominican Republic, AD 800 to 1504*, Ph.D. Universtiy of Leiden. Sidestone Press, Leiden

Samson, A.V.M. 2013. Household archaeology in the pre-Columbian Caribbean, *The Oxford Handbook of Caribbean Archaeology*, W. Keegan, C.L. Hofman and R. Rodríguez Ramos (eds), 363–377. Oxford University Press, Oxford

Samuelian, C., D. Bonnissent, S. Grouard, C. Jorda, N. Sellier- Segard and N. Serrand. 2016. COM, *Saint-Martin, Grand-Case, Rue des Flamboyants*, Rapport d'opération de fouille archéologique préventive Inrap, ms

Sangster, A., M. Hodson and H. Tubb. 2001. Silicon deposition in higher plants, *Studies in Plant Science* 8: 85–113

Sanoja, M. Obediente and I. Vargas Arenas. 1983. *New Light on the Prehistory of Eastern Venezuela*, F. Wendorf and A. Close (eds), 205–244, Advances in World Archaeology 2. Academic Press, New York

Schaan, D.P. 2004. *The Camutins Chiefdom: Rise and Development of Social Complexity on Marajo Island, Brazilian Amazon*, Unpublished Ph.D. University of Pittsburgh, Pittsburgh, ms

Schertl, H.-P., W.V. Maresch, S. Knippenberg, A. Hertwig, A. López Belando, R. Rodríguez Ramos, L. Speich and C.L. Hofman. 2018. Petrography, mineralogy and geochemistry of jadeite-rich artefacts from the Playa Grande excavation site, northern Hispaniola: evaluation of local provenance from the Río San Juan Complex, *HP-UHP Metamorphism and Tectonic Evolution of Orogenic Belts*, L. Zhang, Z. Zhang, H.-P. Schertl and C. Wei (eds), 474. Geological Society, London

Schertl, H.P., W.V. Maresch, K.P. Stanek, A. Hertwig, M. Krebs, R. Baese and S.S. Sergeev. 2012. New occurrences of jadeitite, jadeite quartzite and jadeite-lawsonite quartzite in the Dominican Republic, Hispaniola: petrological and geochronological overview, *European Journal of Mineralogy* 24: 199–216

Schinkel, K. 1992. The Golden Rock Features, *The Archaeology of St. Eustatius. The Golden Rock Site*, A. Versteeg and K. Schinkel (eds), 143–212, Publication of the St. Eustatius Historical Foundation 2, Publication of the Foundation of Scientific Research in the Caribbean Region 131

Schumann, W., 2001. *Gemstones of the World*, revised and expanded edition. Sterling Publishing Co. Inc., New York

Sellier-Ségard, N. 2013. *Pont à Popo—Domaine Taonaba, Les Abymes, Guadeloupe,* Rapport d'opération diagnostic archéologique Inrap, ms

Sellier-Ségard, N., P. Bertholet, F. Casagrande, A. Coulaud, P.-Y. Devillers, B. Farago-Szekeres, G. Fronteau, V. Geneviève, C. Jorda, S. Grouard, P.-F. Mille, C. Samuelian, N. Serrand, N. Tomadini and M.M. van den Bel. 2020. *Un village de bord de mer du Néoindien recent et une installation de la fin du XVIIe siècle: un atelier de production de chaux, Parcelle BK 77, rue de l'Espérance, Grande-Case, Saint-Martin*, 2. Vols, Rapport final d'opération de fouille Inrap, ms

Sellier-Ségard, N. and C. Samuelian. 2017. *Un Village de Bord de Mer du Néoindien Récent à Grand-Case (Saint-Martin, Petites Antilles),* Paper presented at the 26th Congress of the International Association for Caribbean Archaeology, Saint-Martin, French Lesser Antilles, July 19–24, ms

Serrand, N. 2002. *Exploitation des invertébrés marins et terrestres par les populations Saladoïdes et post-Saladoïdes du Nord des Petites Antilles (env. 500 B.C.—1200 A.D.),* Unpublished Ph.D. Paris I–Panthéon Sorbonne, ms

Serrand, N. 2004. Les Restes de Mollusques et de Crustacés de l'Occupation Amérindienne de la Cathédrale de Basse-terre, *Le site de la Cathédrale de Basse-Terre, Guadeloupe,* D. Bonnissent (ed), 45–60, Rapport d'opération de fouille archéologique préventive Inrap, ms

Serrand, N. 2005. Les Restes de Mollusques du Site saladoïde Moyen-Tardif du Diamant à Dizac, Martinique (450–700 apr. J.-C.): Une Exploitation entre Mer et Mangrove. Résultats préliminaires, *Proceedings of the 20th International Congress of the Association for Caribbean Archaeology, Dominican Republic 2003*, G. Tavárez María and M.A. García Arévalo (eds), 159–168. International Association for Caribbean Archaeology, Museo del Hombre Dominicano, Fundación GarcíaArévalo, Santo Domingo

Serrand, N. 2006. La Malacofaune, *Le site de la Gare Maritime de Basse-Terre, Guadeloupe,* T. Romon (ed), 126–184, Rapport d'opération de fouille archéologique préventive Inrap, ms

Serrand, N. 2007a. L'économie des sociétés précolombiennes des Petites Antilles. Contribution des données sur l'exploitation des invertébrés marins et terrestres, *Les Nouvelles de l'Archéologie* 108–109: 78–90

Serrand, N. 2007b. Exploitation des invertébrés par les sociétés précolombiennes des Petites Antilles, *Journal de la Société des Américanistes* 93 (1): 7–47

Serrand, N. 2007c. L'Exploitation des Invertébrés durant l'Occupation Céramique tardive du Sud de la Martinique: Aperçu Diachronique au travers des Sites de Dizac, Salines, Trabaud et Macabou, *Proceedings of the 21st International Congress of the Association for Caribbean Archaeology, Trinidad 2005*, B. Reid, H. Petitjean Roget and A. Curet (eds), 421–428. International Association for Caribbean Archaeology, University of the West Indies, School of Continuing Studies, Saint Augustine

Serrand, N. 2008. The use of molluscs in the Precolumbian Amerindian Lesser Antilles: human, animal, and environmental parameters (with an emphasis on metrics), *Molluscs and other Marine Resources*, K. Szabó and I. Quitmyer (eds), 21–34, Archaeofauna 17. Archaeopress, Oxford

Serrand, N. 2011. *ZAC de Dothémare tranche A2, Les Abymes, Guadeloupe*, Rapport d'opération de diagnostic archéologique Inrap, ms

Serrand, N. 2013. Les Restes d'Invertébrés Marins des Dépôts post-Saladoïdes, *Les gisements précolombiens de la Baie Orientale: campements du Mésoindien et du Néoindien sur l'île de Saint-Martin (Petites Antilles)*, D. Bonnissent (ed), 212–218, Documents d'archéologie française 107. Éditions de la Maison des sciences de l'homme, Paris

Serrand, N. 2016. L'Etude des Restes d'Invertébrés Marins, *COM, Saint-Martin, Grand-Case, Rue des Flamboyants*, C. Samuelian (ed), 127–149, Rapport d'opération de Fouille archéologique préventive Inrap, ms

Serrand, N. 2018a. *Guadeloupe, Le Moule Montal, Rue des Falaises*, Rapport de diagnostic Inrap, ms

Serrand, N. 2018b. *Guadeloupe, Les Abymes, Petit-Pérou, Lotissement MAEWA*, Rapport de diagnostic Inrap, ms

Serrand, N., L. Bernard, F. Casagrande, P.-Y. Devillers, J.-G. Ferrié, V. Merle, N. Sellier-Ségard and M. van den Bel. 2019. *DROM, Guadeloupe, La Désirade, Est de Mouton de Bas, Terre-de-Bas de Petite-Terre Rapport de sondages.* SRA Guadeloupe / Inrap NAOM, ms

Serrand, N. and D. Bonnissent. 2018. *Interacting Pre-Columbian Amerindian Societies and Environments: Insights from Five Millennia of Archaeological Invertebrate Record on the Saint-Martin Island (French Lesser Antilles)*, Paper presented at the the 81st SAA Annual Meeting, Orlando, Florida, April 6–10, 2016, ms

Serrand, N., D. Bonnissent, P. Bertran, F. Casagrande, A. Dietrich, S. Grouard, S. Orsini, E. Ribechini, T. Romon and N. Sellier-Ségard. 2016. *Stade Jose Bade: Les occupations cedrosan-saladoïde et troumassan troumassoïde de Tourlourous, Capesterre-de- Marie-Galante, Guadeloupe,* Rapport d'opération de fouille archéologique Inrap, 2. Vols, ms

Serrand, N., F. Casagrande and C. Jorda. 2014. *Plage de Roseau, Sainte-Maire, Capesterre-Belle-Eau, Guadeloupe,* Rapport d'opération diagnostic archéologique Inrap, ms

Serrand, N., S. Orsini, E. Ribechini and F. Casagrande. 2018. Bitumen residue on a Late Ceramic Age three-pointer from Marie-Galante, Guadeloupe: chemical characterization and ligature evidence, *Journal of Archaeological Science: Reports* 21: 243–258

Shearn, I. 2014. *Pre-Columbian Regional Community Integration in Dominica, West Indies,* Unpublished Ph.D. University of Florida, ms

Shepard, A. 1956. *Ceramics for the Archaeologist.* Carnegie Institution of Washington 609, Washington, DC

Siegel, P.E. 1996. An interview with Irving Rouse, *Current Anthropology* 37 (4): 671–689

Siegel, P.E. 1997. Ancestor worship and cosmology among the Taino, *Taíno. Pre-Columbian Art and Culture from the Caribbean,* F. Bercht, E. Brodsky, J.A. Farmer and D. Taylor (eds), 106–111. The Monacelli Press, New York

Siegel, P.E., J. Jones, D. Pearsall, N. Dunning, P. Farrell, N. Duncan, J. Curtis and S. Singh. 2015. Paleoenvironmental evidence for first human colonization of the eastern Caribbean, *Quaternary Science Reviews* 129 (1): 275–295

Smith, M. and J. Herbert. 2010. Identifying Grog in archaeological pottery, *First Annual Reconstructive/ Experimental Archaeology Conference (RE-ARC),* Gastonia

Stienaers A, B. Neyt, C. Hofman and P. Degryse. 2020. A petrographic and chemical analysis of Trinidad pre-colonial ceramics, *STAR: Science & Technology of Archaeological Research* 6: 72–86

Stoops, G., V. Marcelino and F. Mees (eds). 2010. *Interpretation of Micromorphological Features of Soils and Regoliths.* Elsevier, Amsterdam

Stouvenot, C. 2001. *Diagnostic archéologique Déviation RN 1, Capesterre-Belle Eau (Guadeloupe),* Rapport de diagnostic AFAN/DRAC/CRG, ms

Stouvenot, C. 2003. Les objets lithiques. Matières premières lithiques, *Rivière du Grand Carbet, Capesterre-Belle-Eau (97). Un habitat amérindien multiphasé,* A. Toledo i Mur (ed), 54–59, Rapport Inrap, ms

Stouvenot, C. 2010. *Le dépotoir précolombien du site de Belle-Plaine, une occupation troumassan troumassoïde, Les Abymes, Guadeloupe. Service régional de l'archéologie,* DRAC Guadeloupe, ms

Stouvenot, C. 2013. *Compte rendu de sondages archéologiques. Projet d'aménagement de la plage de Roseau,* ms

Stouvenot, C., J. Beauchene, D. Bonnissent and C. Obelin. 2015. Datations radiocarbone et « effet vieux bois » dans l'arc antillais: état de la question, *Proceedings of the 25th International Congress for Caribbean Archaeology,* L. del Olmo (ed), 459–494. ICP/ CEAPRC/UPR, Rio Piedras

Stouvenot, C. and F. Casagrande. 2015. *Recherche des occupations précolumbiennes dans les hauteurs de Capesterre-Belle-Eau (Guadeloupe): resultats préliminaires,* Paper Presented at the XXVI Congress of the International Association for Caribbean Archaeology, Sint Maarten, ms

Stuiver, M., P.J. Reimer, E. Bard, J. Warren Beck, G.S. Burr, K.A. Hughen, B. Kromer, G. McCormac, J. van der Plicht and M. Spurk. 1998. INTCAL98 Radiocarbon age calibration, 24,000–0 Cal BP, *Radiocarbon* 40 (3): 1041–1083

Ting, C., B. Neyt, J. Ulloa Hung, C.L. Hofman and P. Degryse. 2016. The production of pre-Colonial ceramics in northwestern Hispaniola: a technological study of Meillacoid and Chicoid ceramics from La Luperona and El Flaco, Dominican Republic, *Journal of Archaeological Science: Reports* 6: 376–385

Ting, C., J. Ulloa Hung, C.L. Hofman and P. Degryse. 2018. Indigenous technologies and the production of early colonial ceramics in Dominican Republic, *Journal of Archaeological Science: Reports* 17: 47–57

Todisco, D. and C. Cammas. 2011. *Approche géoarchéologique et micromorphologique d'un cimetière colonial: conditions de milieu et préservation des os humains en contexte tropical humide à Baillif (Guadeloupe),* ms

Toledo i Mur, A., P. Bertrand, G. Chancerel, P. Fouéré, C. Fouilloud, H. Maheux, C. Stouvenot and C. Vallet. 2004. *Rivière du Grand Carbet, Capesterre-Belle-Eau (97). Un habitat amérindien multiphasé.* Document final de synthèse Inrap/SRA/CRG, ms

Toledo i Mur, A., G. Chancerel, P. Fouéré, C. Fouilloud, R. Martias and C. Stouvenot. 2003. *Fromager, Capesterre-Belle-Eau (97). Un habitat de plaine amérindien (700–1150 AD).* Document final de synthèse Inrap/CRG, ms

Tomadini, N. 2018. *Hommes et animaux dans les colonies françaises des Petites Antilles du XVIIe à la fin du XIXe siècle: changements, résiliences et adaptations mutuelles,* Unpublished Ph.D. Museum national d'Histoire naturelle, 2 Vols, ms

Tomadini, N. and S. Grouard. 2018. La faune, *Parking de Roseau (Capesterre-Belle-Eau, Guadeloupe). Sainte-Marie avant l'arrivée de Christophe Colomb*, M. van den Bel (dir.), 182–184, Rapport d'opération archéologique Inrap, ms

Tomblin, J.F., 1975, The Lesser Antilles and Aves Ridge, *The Ocean Basins and Margins, Vol. 3: The Gulf of Mexico and the Caribbean*, A.E.M. Nairn and F.G. Stehli (eds), 467–499. Plenum, New York

Torrence, R. 1986. *Production and Exchange of Stone Tools.* Cambridge University Press, Cambridge

Torrence, R. and H. Barton (eds). 2006. *Ancient Starch Research.* Left Coast Press, Walnut Creek

Trouessart, E.L. 1885. Note sur le rat Mosque des Antilles, type du sous-genre Megalomys et sur la place de se sous genre dans le groupe des rats Americains ou Hesperomyidae, *Annales des Sciences Naturelles, Zoologie* 19 (5): 1–18

Ugent, D., S. Pozorski and T. Pozorski. 1986. Archaeological Manioc (Manihot) from coastal Peru, *Economic Botany* 40 (1): 78–102

Vacher, S., S. Jérémie and J. Briand. 1998. *Amérindiens du Sinnamary (Guyane): archéologie en forêt équatoriale*, Document d'Archéologie française 70. Éditions de la Maison des sciences de l'Homme, Paris

van den Bel, M.M. 2007. *Grande Anse, Parcelle AT 972, Commune de Trois-Rivières Guadeloupe*, Rapport de diagnostic Inrap, ms

van den Bel, M.M. 2012. *Mamiel RN 5, Les Abymes, Guadeloupe*, Rapport final d'opération diagnostic archéologique Inrap, ms

van den Bel, M.M. 2015. *Archaeological Investigations between Cayenne Island and the Maroni River: A Cultural Sequence of Western Coastal French Guiana from 5000 BP to Present.* Ph.D. University of Leiden. Sidestone Press, Leiden

van den Bel, M.M. 2017. *Mysterious LCA Pits in the Hinterland of Grande-Terre- Guadeloupe*, Paper presented at the 26th IACA Congress Session 2—Pre-Columbian Archaeology, held on Sint-Maarten 19 July 2015, ms

van den Bel, M.M. 2020. Les Caribes de Colomb et Callinago de Breton. Rencontres historiques et archéologiques avec les Caraïbes de la Guadeloupe, *Bulletin de la Société d'Histoire de la Guadeloupe* 187: 7–66

van den Bel, M.M., M. Belarbi, F. Casagrande, R. Dickau, G. Fronteau, S. Grouard, C. Jorda, K. Karklins, S. Knippenberg, T. Leblanc, J.R. Pagán-Jiménez, N. Serrand, N. Tomadini and S. Troelstra. 2018a. *Parking de Roseau, Saint-Marie avant l'arrivée de Christophe Colomb, Capesterre-Belle-Eau, Guadeloupe*, Rapport d'opération de fouille archéologique Inrap, ms

van den Bel, M.M., J. Birk, J. Brancier, G. Fronteau, S. Grouard, S. Knippenberg and J. Watling. 2016. *'Un site à l'intérieur des terres' CHU Belle- Plaine, Les Abymes, Guadeloupe*, Rapport d'opération de fouille archéologique Inrap, ms

van den Bel, M.M., N. Biwer, H. Civarelli, M. Belarbi, G. Lafleur, F. Casagrande, S. Knippenberg, G. Fronteau, J.R. Pagán-Jiménez, J. Beauchêne and A. Coulaud. 2017. *'STEP Sainte-Claire' Un morne rouge à la capesterre de la Basse-Terre à double occupation, Goyave, Guadeloupe*, Rapport final d'opération archéologique Inrap, ms

van den Bel, M.M., N. Biwer, H. Civarelli, A. Jégouzo and X. Peixoto. 2018b. Les structures d'exploitation et de production du sucre, La fouille du moulin à eau de Sainte-Claire (Guadeloupe), les entrepôts de l'Habitation la Caravelle (Martinique) et l'usine sucrerie d'Ouangani (Mayotte), *Les Nouvelles de l'Archéologie* 150: 46–41 van den Bel, M.M., F. Casagrande, T. Romon, S. Knippenberg, C. Tardy, S. Grouard and E. Pellé. 2009. *Le site de la Pointe Grande Anse: Une occupation amérindienne et coloniale dans le sud de Basse-Terre, Commune de Trois-Rivières, Guadeloupe*, Rapport de fouille Inrap, ms

van den Bel, M.M., J.R. Pagán- Jiménez and G. Fronteau. 2014. Le Rorota revisité: résultats des fouilles préventives à PK 11, Route des Plages, Île de Cayenne (Guyane française), *Archéologie caraïbe*, B. Bérard and C. Losier (eds), 37–76, Taboui 2. Sidestone Press, Leiden

van den Bel, M.M. and T. Romon. 2010. A Troumassoid site at Trois-Rivières, Guadeloupe FWI: funerary practices and house patterns at La Pointe de Grande Anse, *Journal of Caribbean Archaeology* 9 (1): 1–17

van Gijn, A.-L. 1996. Flint exploitation on Long Island, Antigua, West Indies, *Analecta Praehistorica Leidensia* 26: 183–197

van Gijn, A.-L. and M.J.L.Th. Niekus. 2001. Bronze Age Settlement Flint from the Netherlands. *The Cinderella of Lithic Research, Patina. Essays presented to Jay Jordan Butler on the Occasion of his 80th Birthday*, W.H. Metz, B.L. van Beek and H. Steegstra (eds), 305–320. Groningen, Amsterdam

Vauchelet, E. 1892. La découverte de Guadeloupe, *Annales de Géographie* 5 (2): 92–96

Venter, M.L., J.R. Ferguson and M.D Glascock. 2012. *Ceramic Production and Caribbean Interaction: A View from Trinidad's Northern Range*, Poster presented at the 77th Annual Meeting of the Society for American Archaeology in Memphis

Verbaas, A. and A.-L. van Gijn. 2007. Querns and other hard stone tools from Geleen- Janskamperveld, Excavations at Geleen-Janskamperveld 1990–1991, P. van der Velde (ed), *Analecta Praehistorica Leidensia* 39: 191–204

Versteeg, A. 1989. The internal organization of a pioneer settlement in the Lesser Antilles: the Saladoid Golden Rock Site on St. Eustatius, Netherlands Antilles, *Early Cerramic Populations Lifeways and Adaptive Strategies in the Caribbean*, P.E. Siegel (ed), 171–192, BAR International series 506. Archaeopress, Oxford

Versteeg, A. and K. Schinkel (eds). 1992. *The Archaeology of St. Eustatius. The Golden Rock Site*, Publication of the St. Eustatius Historical Foundation 2, Publication of the Foundation of Scientific Research in the Caribbean Region 131

Vidal, N. 1999. Le Site Précolombien de la Plage Dizac au Diamant, Martinique, *Proceedings of the XVI International Congress of the Association for Caribbean Archaeology, Guadeloupe*, Vol. 2, 7–16. CRG, Basse-Terre

Waal, M., de. 2006. *Pre-Columbian Social Organisation and Interaction Interpreted through the Study of Settlement Patterns. An Archaeological Case-study of the Pointe des Châteaux, La Désirade and Les Îles de la Petite Terre micro- region, Guadeloupe, FWI*, Ph.D. University of Leiden, ms

Wadge, G., 1994. The Lesser Antilles, *Caribbean Geology: An Introduction*, S.K. Donovan and T.A. Jackson (eds), 167–178. U.W.I. Publishers' Association, Kingston

Wagner, G.E. 2008. What seasonal diet at a fort ancient community reveals about coping mechanisms. *Case Studies in Environmental Archaeology*, 2nd edition, E. Reitz, C. M. Scarry, S. J. Scudder (eds), 277–296, Interdisciplinary Contributions to Archaeology. Springer, New York

Walker, J.B. 1980. *Analysis and Replication of the Lithic Artifacts from the Sugar Factory Pier Site, St. Kitts, West Indies*, Master Thesis State University of Washington, ms

Walker, J.B. 1997. Taíno stone collars, elbow stones, and three-pointers, *Taíno. Pre-Columbian Art and Culture from the Caribbean*, F. Bercht, E. Brodsky, J.A. Farmer and D. Taylor (eds), 80–91. The Monacelli Press, New York

Walter, V. 1991. Analyses pétrographiques et minéralogiques de céramiques précolombiennes de Martinique, *Caribena, Cahiers d'études américanistes de la Caraibe* 1: 13–54

Walter, V. 1992. Etude physico- chimiques de céramiques précolombiennes de la Martinique, *Caribena, Cahiers d'études américanistes de la Caraibe* 2: 159–179

Warmke, G.L. and R.T. Abbott. 1961. *Caribbean Seashells. A Guide to the Marine Mollusks of Porto Rico and other West Indian Islands, Bermuda and the Lower Florida Keys*. Livingston Publishing Compagny, Narberth

Watling, J., and J. Iriarte. 2013. Phytoliths from the coastal savannas of French Guiana, *Quaternary International* 287: 162–180

Watters, D.R. 1980. *Transect Surveying and Prehistoric Site Locations on Barbuda and Montserrat, Leeward Islands, West Indies*, Unpublished Ph.D. University of Pittsburgh, Ann Arbor

Watters, D.R. 1994. Archaeology of Trants, Montserrat, Part I. Field methods artefact density distributions, *Annals of the Carnegie Museum* 63: 265–295

Watters, D.R. and J.B. Petersen. 1993. Preliminary report on the archaeology of the Rendezvous Bay Site, Anguilla, *Proceedings of the 14th International Congress for Caribbean Archaeology, Barbados 1991*, A. Cummins and P. King (eds), 25–33. Barbados Museum and Historical Society, St. Ann's Garrison

Watters, D.R. and J.B. Petersen. 1999. Trants, Montserrat: The 1995 field season, *Proceedings of the 16th International Congress for Caribbean Archaeology*. Basse-Terre, Guadeloupe 1995, 27–29. CRG, Basse-Terre

Watters, D.R. and R. Scaglion. 1994. Beads and pendants from Trants, Montserrat: implications for the prehistoric lapidary industry of the Caribbean, *Annals of the Carnegie Museum* 63: 215–237

Westercamp, D. and H. Tazieff. 1980. *Martinique. Guadeloupe. Saint-Martin. La Désirade. Guides géologiques régionaux*. Masson, Paris

Whitbread, I.K. 1986. The characterisation of argillaceous inclusions in ceramic thin sections, *Archaeometry* 28: 79–88

Wilson, S.M. 1990. The prehistoric settlement pattern of Nevis, West Indies, *Journal of Field Archaeology* 16: 427–440

Wilson, S., E. Wing, L. Kozuch, L. Newsom and J.D. Rogers. 2006. *The Prehistory of Nevis, a Small Island in the Lesser Antilles*, Yale University Publications in Anthropology 87. Department of Anthropology, Yale University & Peabody Museum of Natural History, New Haven

Wing, E.S. 2001. The sustainability of resources used by Native Americans on four Caribbean Islands, *International Journal of Osteoarchaeology* 11 (1): 112–126

Winter, J.D. 2005. *An Introduction to Igneous and Metamorphic Petrology*. Prentice Hall, New York

Yacou, A. and J. Adélaïde-Merlande (eds). 1993. *La découverte et la conquête de la Guadeloupe. Contributions du Centre d'études et de recherches caribéennes*. Karthala, Paris

Appendix 1

List of radiocarbon dates of large-scale excavated sites on Guadeloupe

Site	N° Lab.	Age Conv	Deviation	δ13C	Deviation	Reference	Material other than charcoal
La Pointe de Grande Anse	KIA-36671	1230	30	−25.97	0.36	van den Bel et al. 2009	
La Pointe de Grande Anse	KIA-36672	1340	25	−23.97	0.34	van den Bel et al. 2009	unreliable
La Pointe de Grande Anse	KIA-36673	945	35	−25.95	0.24	van den Bel et al. 2009	
La Pointe de Grande Anse	KIA-36674	945	30	−25.59	0.32	van den Bel et al. 2009	
La Pointe de Grande Anse	KIA-36675	915	50	−24.17	0.25	van den Bel et al. 2009	bone; unreliable
La Pointe de Grande Anse	KIA-36676	565	25	−17.74	0.28	van den Bel et al. 2009	bone; unreliable
La Pointe de Grande Anse	KIA-36676	*348*	39	−13.8	0.16	van den Bel et al. 2009	bone; unreliable
La Pointe de Grande Anse	KIA-36676	*431*	22	−12.53	0.15	van den Bel et al. 2009	bone; unreliable
La Pointe de Grande Anse	KIA-36677	1245	30	−24.14	0.23	van den Bel et al. 2009	
La Pointe de Grande Anse	KIA-36678	1065	30	−25.81	0.43	van den Bel et al. 2009	
La Pointe de Grande Anse	KIA-36679	625	30	−26.36	0.28	van den Bel et al. 2009	
La Pointe de Grande Anse	KIA-36681	x	x	x	x	van den Bel et al. 2009	bone; unreliable
La Pointe de Grande Anse	KIA-36681	*620*	25	−9.8	0.16	van den Bel et al. 2009	bone; unreliable
La Pointe de Grande Anse	KIA-36681	*625*	25	−12.18	0.3	van den Bel et al. 2009	bone; unreliable
La Pointe de Grande Anse	KIA-36680	690	30	−24.5	0.3	van den Bel et al. 2009	
La Pointe de Grande Anse	KIA-36682	650	140	−28.18		van den Bel et al. 2009	bone; unreliable
La Pointe de Grande Anse	KIA-36683	330	25	−26.54	0.31	van den Bel et al. 2009	

(*Continued*)

(Continued)

Site	N° Lab.	Age Conv	Deviation	δ13C	Deviation	Reference	Material other than charcoal
La Pointe de Grande Anse	KIA-36684	1000	30	−27.6	0.27	van den Bel et al. 2009	
La Pointe de Grande Anse	KIA-36685	x	x	x	x	van den Bel et al. 2009	bone; unreliable
La Pointe de Grande Anse	KIA-36685	*1435*	20	−11.04	0.13	van den Bel et al. 2009	bone; unreliable
La Pointe de Grande Anse	KIA-36685	*1340*	20	−12.12	0.24	van den Bel et al. 2009	bone; unreliable
La Pointe de Grande Anse	KIA-31187	1210	20	−26.12	0.28	van den Bel et al. 2009	
CHU Belle-Plaine	POZ-63014	960	40	−27.3	0.6	van den Bel et al. 2016	
CHU Belle-Plaine	POZ-63015	900	30	−25.3	0.8	van den Bel et al. 2016	
CHU Belle-Plaine	POZ-63016	870	30	−25.1	1.7	van den Bel et al. 2016	
CHU Belle-Plaine	POZ-63017	885	30	−29.9	1.7	van den Bel et al. 2016	
CHU Belle-Plaine	POZ-63018	915	30	−27.4	0.7	van den Bel et al. 2016	
CHU Belle-Plaine	POZ-63019	875	30	−30.6	1.5	van den Bel et al. 2016	
CHU Belle-Plaine	POZ-63020	930	30	−27	1.1	van den Bel et al. 2016	
CHU Belle-Plaine	POZ-63021	1030	35	−29.2	1.6	van den Bel et al. 2016	
CHU Belle-Plaine	POZ-63022	890	30	−27.3	1.7	van den Bel et al. 2016	
CHU Belle-Plaine	POZ-63024	960	30	−24.7	1.8	van den Bel et al. 2016	
STEP Goyave	POZ-75039	835	30	−27.9	1.3	van den Bel et al. 2017	
STEP Goyave	POZ-75040	1145	35	−28.8	2.8	van den Bel et al. 2017	
STEP Goyave	POZ-75041	905	35	−28.4	0.7	van den Bel et al. 2017	
STEP Goyave	POZ-75042	950	30	−29.2	1.9	van den Bel et al. 2017	
STEP Goyave	POZ-75043	825	30	−30.1	0.9	van den Bel et al. 2017	
STEP Goyave	POZ-75044	1060	30	−28	2.4	van den Bel et al. 2017	
STEP Goyave	POZ-75045	1640	35	−26.3	0.5	van den Bel et al. 2017	
STEP Goyave	POZ-75046	1170	30	−28.1	1.6	van den Bel et al. 2017	
STEP Goyave	POZ-75047	985	30	−35.1	1.2	van den Bel et al. 2017	
STEP Goyave	POZ-75049	1070	30	−24.1	1.5	van den Bel et al. 2017	

Site	N° Lab.	Age Conv	Deviation	δ13C	Deviation	Reference	Material other than charcoal
Parking de Roseau	POZ-84383	720	30	−28.2	0.4	van den Bel et al. 2018a	
Parking de Roseau	POZ-84384	1170	30	−23.5	0.5	van den Bel et al. 2018a	
Parking de Roseau	POZ-84387	870	30	−30.9	0.4	van den Bel et al. 2018a	
Parking de Roseau	POZ-84388	805	30	−32.4	0.2	van den Bel et al. 2018a	
Parking de Roseau	POZ-84389	875	30	−30.7	0.4	van den Bel et al. 2018a	
Parking de Roseau	POZ-84390	735	30	−28.5	0.3	van den Bel et al. 2018a	
Parking de Roseau	POZ-84391	670	30	−30.3	0.5	van den Bel et al. 2018a	
Parking de Roseau	POZ-84393	805	30	−33.7	0.5	van den Bel et al. 2018a	
Parking de Roseau	UBA-25514	840	40	AMS corrected		Serrand et al. 2014	
Parking de Roseau	UBA-25187	255	25	AMS corrected		Serrand et al. 2014	bone
Plage de Roseau	LY-12005	865	30	unknown		www. banadora,org	shell
Plage de Roseau	LY-12006	1085	30	unknown		www. banadora,org	shell
Plage de Roseau	LY-12007	1185	30	unknown		www. banadora,org	shell
Plage de Roseau	LY-12008	1040	30	unknown		www. banadora,org	shell
Plage de Roseau	LY-12009	1115	35	unknown		www. banadora,org	carbonates
Plage de Roseau	LY-12010	0	0	unknown		www. banadora,org	
Plage de Roseau	LY-12011	1370	30	unknown		www. banadora,org	shell
Plage de Roseau	LY-12012	1080	30	unknown		www. banadora,org	shell
Plage de Roseau	*LY-2217*	985	35	unknown		www. banadora,org	bone
Anse à la Gourde	GrN-26152	720	40	unknown		Morsink 2006	
Anse à la Gourde	GrN-26155	760	40	unknown		Morsink 2006	
Anse à la Gourde	GrN-26151	770	45	unknown		Morsink 2006	
Anse à la Gourde	GrN-22725	860	25	unknown		Bright 2003	
Anse à la Gourde	GrN-26154	880	40	unknown		Morsink 2006	
Anse à la Gourde	GrN-22798	910	25	unknown		Morsink 2006	

(*Continued*)

(Continued)

Site	N° Lab.	Age Conv	Deviation	δ13C	Deviation	Reference	Material other than charcoal
Anse à la Gourde	GrN-26153	910	40	unknown		Morsink 2006	
Anse à la Gourde	GrN-22797	950	50	unknown		Morsink 2006	
Anse à la Gourde	GrN-22796	1000	25	unknown		Morsink 2006	
Anse à la Gourde	GrN-22795	1030	40	unknown		Morsink 2006	
Anse à la Gourde	GrN-26160	1140	40	unknown		Delpuech et al. 2001b	
Anse à la Gourde	GrN-22726	1160	40	unknown		Bright 2003	
Anse à la Gourde	GrN-25530	1200	25	unknown		Delpuech et al. 2001b	
Anse à la Gourde	GrN-25533	1235	25	unknown		Delpuech et al. 2001b	
Anse à la Gourde	GrN-25531	1255	25	unknown		Delpuech et al. 2001b	
Anse à la Gourde	GrN-25529	1260	25	unknown		Delpuech et al. 2001b	
Anse à la Gourde	GrN-25528	1275	25	unknown		Delpuech et al. 2001b	
Anse à la Gourde	GrN-25532	1275	25	unknown		Delpuech et al. 2001b	
Anse à la Gourde	GrN-26157	1310	30	unknown		Delpuech et al. 2001b	
Anse à la Gourde	GrN-26156	1350	50	unknown		Delpuech et al. 2001b	
Anse à la Gourde	GrN-26161	1420	30	unknown		Delpuech et al. 2001b	
Anse à la Gourde	GrN-26158	1460	40	unknown		Delpuech et al. 2001b	
Anse à la Gourde	GrN-26159	1460	40	unknown		Delpuech et al. 2001b	
Anse à la Gourde	GrN-25534	1760	25	unknown		Delpuech et al. 2001b	
Bisdary	KIA-28187	825	25	−28.5	0.15	Romon et al. 2006	
Bisdary	KIA-28189	875	25	−24.85	0.05	Romon et al. 2006	
Bisdary	KIA-28188	880	20	−27.87	0.05	Romon et al. 2006	
Bisdary	KIA-28190	1095	25	−25.21	0.09	Romon et al. 2006	
Bisdary	KIA-28186	1190	20	−27.04	0.06	Romon et al. 2006	
Bisdary	KIA-28198	1215	25	−26.55	0.08	Romon et al. 2006	
Bisdary	KIA-28196	1235	30	−27.74	0.08	Romon et al. 2006	humic acids

Site	N° Lab.	Age Conv	Deviation	δ13C	Deviation	Reference	Material other than charcoal
Bisdary	KIA-28196	1260	25	−28.4	0.13	Romon et al. 2006	alkali residu
Bisdary	KIA-28197	1270	20	−27.96	0.06	Romon et al. 2006	
Bisdary	KIA-28185	1275	25	−25.99	0.08	Romon et al. 2006	
Bisdary	KIA-28193	1285	30	−26.46	0.2	Romon et al. 2006	alkali residu
Bisdary	KIA-28193	1355	25	−25.63	0.09	Romon et al. 2006	humic acids
Bisdary	KIA-28194	1370	20	−27.18	0.12	Romon et al. 2006	
Bisdary	KIA-28192	1405	25	−28.07	0.19	Romon et al. 2006	
Bisdary	KIA-28195	1445	25	−28.01	0.11	Romon et al. 2006	
Bisdary	KIA-28184	1465	20	−24.79	0.06	Romon et al. 2006	
Bisdary	KIA-28191	3300	30	−25.27	0.12	Romon et al. 2006	alkali residu
Bisdary	KIA-28191	3315	25	−27.1	0.09	Romon et al. 2006	humic acids
Ilet du Gosier	Lyon-8396	770	30	unknown		Banadora	
Ilet du Gosier	Lyon-8398	785	30	unknown		Banadora	
Ilet du Gosier	Lyon-8395	865	30	unknown		Banadora	
Ilet du Gosier	Lyon-8397	910	30	unknown		Banadora	
Ilet du Gosier	Lyon-8392	945	30	unknown		Banadora	
Ilet du Gosier	Lyon-8390	970	30	unknown		Banadora	
Ilet du Gosier	Lyon-8473	990	30	unknown		Banadora	
Ilet du Gosier	Lyon-8394	1025	30	unknown		Banadora	
Ilet du Gosier	Lyon-8391	1035	30	unknown		Banadora	
Ilet du Gosier	Lyon-8393	1070	30	unknown		Banadora	
La Ramée	Beta-244985	1130	40	−26.3		Casagrande et al. 2016	
La Ramée	Beta-244986	1220	40	−25.5		Casagrande et al. 2016	
La Ramée	Beta-244987	1200	40	−26.5		Casagrande et al. 2016	
La Ramée	Beta-244988	1300	40	x		Casagrande et al. 2016	

(*Continued*)

(Continued)

Site	N° Lab.	Age Conv	Deviation	δ13C	Deviation	Reference	Material other than charcoal
La Ramée	Beta-244989	1530	40	−24.5		Casagrande et al. 2016	
La Ramée	Beta-244990	1240	40	−27.7		Casagrande et al. 2016	
La Ramée	Beta-244991	1250	40	−27.3		Casagrande et al. 2016	
La Ramée	Beta-244992	1190	40	−24.7		Casagrande et al. 2016	
La Ramée	Beta-244993	1650	40	−26		Casagrande et al. 2016	
La Ramée	Beta-244994	1360	40	−26.6		Casagrande et al. 2016	
La Ramée	Beta-244995	1090	40	−26.4		Casagrande et al. 2016	
La Ramée	Beta-244996	1090	40	−27		Casagrande et al. 2016	
La Ramée	Beta-244997	1610	40	−27.7		Casagrande et al. 2016	
Toulourous (Stade José Bade)	UBA-22204	835	30	−32.4		Serrand et al. 2016	
Toulourous (Stade José Bade)	UBA-22859	855	30	AMS corrected		Serrand et al. 2016	
Toulourous (Stade José Bade)	UBA-22198	910	40	−21.1		Serrand et al. 2016	
Toulourous (Stade José Bade)	UBA-22861	980	25	AMS corrected		Serrand et al. 2016	
Toulourous (Stade José Bade)	UBA-22199	1030	30	−25.5		Serrand et al. 2016	
Toulourous (Stade José Bade)	UBA-22862	1130	30	AMS corrected		Serrand et al. 2016	
Toulourous (Stade José Bade)	UBA-22203	1170	30	−28.4		Serrand et al. 2016	
Toulourous (Stade José Bade)	UBA-22858	1200	30	AMS corrected		Serrand et al. 2016	
Toulourous	x	1310	40	unknown		Serrand et al. 2016	
Toulourous (Stade José Bade)	UBA-22860	1520	30	AMS corrected		Serrand et al. 2016	
Toulourous	x	1520	40	unknown		Serrand et al. 2016	
Toulourous	x	1720	40	unknown		Serrand et al. 2016	

Site	N° Lab.	Age Conv	Deviation	δ13C	Deviation	Reference	Material other than charcoal
Toulourous (Stade José Bade)	UBA-22196	1730	50	−37.2		Serrand et al. 2016	
Yuiketi	KIA-30791	1135	30	−28.4	0.14	Bonnissent 2011	alkali residu
Yuiketi	KIA-30791	1210	35	−25.79	0.25	Bonnissent. 2011	humic acids
Yuiketi	Beta-263858	1210	40	−26.6		Bonnissent 2011	
Yuiketi	KIA-30792	1215	35	−30.09	0.05	Bonnissent. 2011	
Yuiketi	Beta-244104	1260	40	−25		Bonnissent 2011	
Yuiketi	Beta-244110	1290	40	−25.3		Bonnissent 2011	
Yuiketi	Beta-244109	1300	40	−23		Bonnissent 2011	
Yuiketi	Beta-271114	1390	40	−25.2		Bonnissent 2011	
Yuiketi	Beta-244103	1400	40	−24.9		Bonnissent 2011	
Yuiketi	Beta-244105	1500	40	−25		Bonnissent 2011	
Yuiketi	KIA-30793	1550	25	−28.84	0.13	Bonnissent 2011	
Yuiketi	Beta-244108	2830	40	−26		Bonnissent 2011	
Yuiketi	Beta-263859	3810	40	−24.8		Bonnissent 2011	

* *Remarks by Tomasz Goslar (pers. comm 2020) considering Poznan δ13C values, note that the δ13C values we determine, cannot be used for palaeoecological reconstructions. The reason is that we measure them in the GRAPHITE prepared from the samples, and the graphitisation process introduces significant isotopic fractionation. The second point is that the AMS spectrometer (unlike normal mass spectrometer) introduces fractionation too. Therefore our δ13C values reflect the original isotopic composition in the sample only very roughly.*

Nevertheless, our δ13C measurement is fully suitable for fractionation correction of 14C/12C ratios—and we always do so.

** *Remarks by Christian Hamann from Kiel (pers. comm. 2020): Some of the measurements on bone were performed using the mineral (apatite) fraction. This is still state of the art for creamted bones, but inhumated bones are much more susceptible to contamination. From what I know only one lab is still applying the method to non-cremated bones and all other labs (including the Leibniz-Lab) refrained from it.*

The collagen content of all bones where collagen was used for dating is very low (<1% by weight). It is consensus in the radiocarbon community, that bones exhibiting less than 1% collagen can not be dated reliably.

δ13C values reported were measured by the AMS, therefore far less reliable than proper IRMS measurements and should only be published with reservations. Also d13C of collagen cannot be compared to d13C from apatite directly.

The charcoal samples KIA-36672 didn't go through the proper ABA pretreatment (it dissolved alkali treatment) and only the humic acids were dated. This has to be regarded an unreliable date as well.

In summary, I would consider all of the measurements on bone as well as KIA-36672 to be unreliable, at least from today's point of view.

Appendix 2
List of sites studied by N. Serrand

Island	Site	Excavation	References
Anguilla*	RENDEZ-VOUS BAY 1	test pits	Watters and Petersen 1993
Anguilla*	RENDEZ-VOUS BAY 2	test pits	Watters and Petersen 1993
Barbuda*	SUFFERERS 1	test pits	Watters 1980
Barbuda*	SUFFERERS 2	test pits	Watters 1980
Barbuda*	HIGHLAND ROAD	test pits	Watters 1980
Barbuda*	OVERVIEW CAVE	test pits	Watters 1980
Barbuda*	INDIAN TOWN TRAIL	test pits	Watters 1980
Guadeloupe	GARE MARITIME BT	excavation	Romon et al. 2006, 2013; Serrand 2006
Guadeloupe	CATHEDRALE BASSE TERRE	excavation	Romon and Bonnissent 2004; Serrand 2004
Guadeloupe	STE ROSE LA RAMEE 1	excavation	Casagrande et al. 2016
Guadeloupe	STE ROSE LA RAMEE 2	excavation	Casagrande et al. 2016
Guadeloupe	CAILLE A BELASSE	excavation	Gagnepain et al. 2007
Guadeloupe	PETITE-TERRE, EST DE MOUTON DE BAS	test pits	Serrand et al. 2019
Guadeloupe	MOULE MONTAL	diagnostic	Serrand 2018a
Marie-Galante	STADE J. BADE saladoïde	excavation	Serrand et al. 2016
Marie-Galante	STADE J. BADE troumassoïde	excavation	Serrand et al. 2016
Marie-Galante	BAS DE LA SOURCE	excavation	x
Martinique	LE DIAMANT	excavation	Vidal 1999; Serrand 2005
Martinique	SALINES 1	test pits	Serrand 2007c
Martinique	TRABAUD	test pits	Allaire 1997; Serrand 2007c
Martinique	SALINES 2	test pits	Jean-Joseph 2014; Serrand 2007c
Martinique	MACABOU	excavation	Grouard and Serrand 2005
Montserrat*	RADIO ANTILLES	test pits	Watters 1980
Montserrat*	TRANTS	excavation	Petersen 1996; Watters and Petersen 1999
Montserrat*	WINDWARD BLUFF	test pits	Watters 1980
Nevis*	HICHMAN'S	test pits	Wilson et al. 2006
Nevis*	INDIAN CASTLE	test pits	Wilson et al. 2006
Nevis*	SULPHUR GHAUT	test pits	Wilson et al. 2006
Saint-Martin	POINTE DU CANONNIER	excavation	Bonnissent 2012
Saint-Martin	BAIE ORIENTALE post-Saladoid	excavation	Bonnissent 2013; Serrand 2013

Island	Site	Excavation	References
Saint-Martin	BK76	excavation	Samuelian et al. 2016; Serrand 2016
Saint-Martin	BK77	excavation	Sellier-Ségard and Samuelian 2017
Saint-Martin	BK78	excavation	Sellier-Ségard et al. 2020
Saint-Martin*	HOPE ESTATE	excavation	Bonnissent and Hénocq 1999; Bonnissent et al. 2002

*See Serrand 2002

Index